I0827930

My Life and Career as a Biblical Scholar

My Life and Career as a Biblical Scholar

JOHN VAN SETERS

CASCADE *Books* • Eugene, Oregon

MY LIFE AND CAREER AS A BIBLICAL SCHOLAR

Cascade Books
An Imprint of Wipf and Stock Publishers
199 W. 8th Ave., Suite 3
Eugene, OR 97401

www.wipfandstock.com

PAPERBACK ISBN: 978-1-4982-9955-8
HARDCOVER ISBN: 978-1-4982-9956-5
EBOOK ISBN: 978-1-4982-9957-2

Cataloging-in-Publication data:

Names: Van Seters, John, author.

Title: My life and career as a biblical scholar / John Van Seters

Description: Eugene, OR: Cascade Books, 2018. | Includes bibliographical references.

Identifiers: ISBN: 978-1-4982-9955-8 (paperback). | ISBN: 978-1-4982-9956-5 (hardcover). | ISBN: 978-1-4982-9957-2 (ebook).

Subjects: LCSH: Van Seters, John. | Bible. Old Testament—Criticism, interpretation, etc.

Classification: BS1161 V35 2018 (print). | BS1161 (epub).

10/19/18

To Peter Erb

Contents

Preface

This book, which attempts to tell the story of my life as a scholar of the ancient Near Eastern world and of the Hebrew Bible within that context, is based primarily upon extensive documentation of the rise and development of my career from early in my academic life down to the present time and not just from memory alone. This means that I have tried to recover as best I could the way that I felt and thought about both religious and academic maters at various stages during my upbringing in a very religious family and my subsequent attempts to deal with that way of thinking once I encountered the academic world of the University of Toronto and my doctoral studies at Yale. This experience of coming to terms with one's religious past within the quite different academic environment has happened to a lot of scholars but few say anything about it in their later academic life. Yet there are many young students and scholars, especially in biblical studies, who need to understand that many of their professors have gone down this same path in their own careers.

The other point that I try to make in this reconstruction of my academic life is that I did not belong to a "school" of biblical study and interpretation. Unlike the "Albright school," which was so prominent in America and had so many followers of Albright and his "offspring," there was nothing equivalent at the University of Toronto or Yale, and I had complete freedom to develop my own approach and move forward in my own direction without accepting a particular basic school of thought. This meant that from the very beginning of my career, with the academic tools that I had been given, I had to work out my own understanding of the Near Eastern or biblical material, and to build on that new approach step by step, which so often put me at odds with positions held by various schools of thought. Needless to say, it took a long time to master such an approach, first as it applied to Genesis and then to the Pentateuch as a whole, as well as to the historical books from Joshua to 2 Kings, and particularly to the story of David. This program of research put me at odds with the various "schools" of biblical studies, whether in American or European, although I was certainly not the only such maverick. The story of my life, which follows, relates the interaction of this experience throughout the course of my career.

As I look back on the story of my life I am constantly amazed at the wonderful career that unfolded, with the making of so many friends in so many different places, all of which was beyond my wildest dreams. Even though I have listed a large number of mentors and friends in this book, there were many more that could not be included. This means that I encountered and had close relationships with scholars reflecting many different approaches to the discipline of biblical studies from so many different countries and academic institutions. With these I was in constant dialogue in my books and articles. My primary interest was in the historical period during which the biblical narratives were written, and within the context of the wider ancient Near Eastern world. This approach led me to become acquainted with the wider culture of Mesopotamia, Egypt and the whole of Syria-Palestine, as well as the archaeology and history of these regions. In addition, my academic studies in the classics led me to understand the relevance of the culture of ancient Greece, which had a long historical association with the ancient Levant, and which in turn had a close and prolonged relationship with Israel and Judah. Consequently, throughout my career I always maintained in close contact with my classical colleagues.

For the last few years while writing up this memoir I have no longer had much academic contact with biblical scholars or been engaged with them in biblical studies, and my travels away from Waterloo, Ontario, where I live have been very limited. This has not been a matter of choice but for reasons beyond my ability to alter. However, during this time, and for a long time previous, my good friend Peter Erb and I have enjoyed each other's company once a week over coffee. He has read through the manuscript of this book and suggested some changes, although he is not responsible for the final result. To him I dedicate this book for his longstanding support and friendship.

Introduction

In this story of my life I have written an account of my development as a scholar from my youth up to the present. While the narrative has focused primarily on my academic career, this cannot be properly understood without knowing something about my background from my youth onwards, the religious environment in which I grew up, and my education from earliest grade school to my post graduate studies. This also applies to an account of my family life throughout my career, which I have tried to keep to a minimum, but I have included enough to explain much that went into the particular form of the background in which my academic life took shape. In reading scholarly works from the past I have often wanted to know more about a particular scholar's past, his or her training and the academic environment of the time that produced their training. Indeed, I have often encountered scholars making guesses about my past and background that have been misleading and inaccurate. Furthermore, it is fair to say that my education history has been quite unusual and helps to explain the way in which I developed as a scholar quite distinct from any particular "school."

As indicated below, I was born in the middle of the depression (1935), the fourth child in a family of six children. My parents were Dutch immigrants who had a farm in Bronte, Ontario, but soon lost it in those hard times and so the family moved to Toronto to find employment there. They were very hard times but we survived. My father was a strict Calvinist whose creed included hard work, and I was thoroughly indoctrinated in this viewpoint and way of life and I practiced it with zeal and enthusiasm well into my college years. Along with my brother Arthur I was set on pursuing a life in the Presbyterian ministry and selected my college program of study accordingly. Certain circumstances, however, lead me into post graduate studies at Yale and that changed my whole outlook on life and scholarship. That will all be laid out in what follows. The point that I try to make in this life of scholarship is that one must learn to ask the right questions and then search with an open mind for the right answers. Sometimes those answers only come slowly and over a long period of time and the result of frequent reexamination.

The book is divided into a number of chapters which constitute various stages in the growth and development of my career and especially the contributions, as I see it, that I have made to the discipline of Ancient Near Eastern and biblical scholarship. In many cases these contributions and radical changes have been disputed and rejected, most often with little discussion, but wherever there was serious debate I have always been ready and eager to respond. In this presentation I include a number of cases in which subsequent to the publication of my studies I have been vindicated by archaeological discoveries and other forms of evidence. What is perhaps even more important is that this history of my career exhibits in my work both a consistency and a steady growth which confirms the course that I took and any particular article or book must be seen in the light of this larger perspective and not merely as a debate over one particular article. This book attempts to provide an overview of just such a process.

Alongside of the publication of books and articles is the presentation of numerous papers at academic meetings and conferences over a very wide range of institutions in North America, Europe, Great Britain, Israel and South Africa. These, of course, were followed by responses, which had to be addressed immediately and in any subsequent publication. This process also enabled me to become personally acquainted with a large number of scholars from many different countries and institutions. Each of the different countries and regions tended to reflect quite different perspectives, methods and "schools" of thought, which was a challenge if one was to communicate and make a case for one's particular understanding of a biblical text or the reconstruction of a historical period of the ancient past. My approach was not to join any particular school but to engage with a broad number of them as a constant challenge to my own research.

The primary function of a scholar in any academic institution, and for which he is paid, is teaching and this I did in four different institutions, the longest stint being the twenty-three years at the University of North Carolina in Chapel Hill. In addition to the classroom lectures and all that goes with it there were many administrative tasks involved to keep the departmental programs and responsibilities running smoothly, especial, if you are a department chair, which I was at Chapel Hill for ten years. Consequently, a substantial portion of my memoir is taken up with my involvement in these responsibilities. In addition to these employment obligations, I was also a family man and all the responsibilities and challenges that come with this status are very much a part of my life. I did not live in an ivory tower and so I have included a number of examples of how I met those obligations. Yet the main focus throughout remains on my life as a scholar.

Over the years from a very early age I have compiled a large number of letters and documents and a selection of these have been the main sources of my presentation. During the email age I made paper copies of important documents but a few computer disasters have created some holes in the history. Nevertheless, the accumulation of important papers has allowed me to quote from correspondence and publications when such confirmation was deemed necessary. Of course there is a bias, as there is with every autobiography, but I hope that the reader finds enough substance to get a useful portrait of biblical and Near Eastern scholarship of the past and of my role in it. There have been many changes in the last fifty years in which I have been directly involved. Early in life when times were hard and horizons seemed limited, I could never have imagined that I would have such an outcome as this. For all of that and for all those who helped make it possible I am truly grateful.

1

Youth, Family Background, and Early Education

Let me begin by making some remarks about my youth and family background. I was born in Hamilton, Ontario, on May 2, 1935, as one of six children, the son of Dutch immigrants who, at the time of my birth, farmed a tract of land in Bronte, Ontario, between Hamilton and Toronto. My father was originally from a farming community in South Holland (Stellendam), while my mother was from Amsterdam. They emigrated from the Netherlands to western Canada in the 1920s, my mother with other members of her family while my father came to Canada alone. They met in Alberta and were married there. After a couple of years living in British Columbia (where the eldest two children, my sister Philippina and my oldest brother Hugo, were born), they moved to Ontario in the depression years to try to make a living at farming. My brother Arthur and I were born while the family lived on the farm. However, my parents could not make a go of the farm in the depression years of the mid-30s, and so the family moved to Toronto to try to find work there. The youngest two children, Richard and Fred, were born in Toronto. I grew up in Toronto and received all of my education there from primary and secondary schools to a university degree at the University of Toronto. I was a Toronto boy in every respect, with my grade school days spent in the heart of the city, the "Annex," and high school and college days living in the suburb of Willowdale, in North York, just north of Toronto.

During my childhood years we lived in a number of different rentals on the west side of Toronto. While I was still in kindergarten we moved to Howland Avenue. This was in 1940, the early war years. I attended Huron Street School for the rest of my elementary education. In addition to being a farmer by upbringing my father had picked up some skills as a mechanic and had a job as a mechanic at City Dairy, later Borden's Dairy, on Spadina Circle. (Many years later, when I was in college and looking for summer employment, I got a job in the same dairy. There were still people at the dairy who remembered my father and it may have been that fact that was part of the reason why they offered me the job.) While working at the dairy, my father went to Central Tech in the evenings to learn the skill of welding and to take up a war-time job of working as a welder on the minesweepers that were being built in the Toronto harbor during the war. As kids we sometimes went down to watch them launch one of these big ships, which for us was quite an event.

Those war years were hard times for a big family of eight, plus a grandmother who lived with us. I remember those years well. Everyone who was old enough, as young as 10 yrs old, got odd jobs or part-time work to add to the common family kitty, whether shoveling snow, cutting lawns, selling Christmas cards door to door, delivering newspapers, or working in grocery stores; you name it, we did it. Sometimes we got second hand clothes from some families in the church. Buying day-old bread was common. After the war when the shipyards closed down, it took a while before my father could find a good job. He went back to night-school and took a course in blueprint reading that allowed him to become a welding inspector on the assembly line for Massey-Harris (Ferguson), where he worked for the next twenty-five years. Even this job experienced seasonal lay-offs and strikes, during which he tried to find fill-in jobs. It is not surprising that my father was a strong supporter of socialism as reflected in the CCF (NDP).

The only other family that we had living close by were two of my mother's brothers and their wives: Uncle Ren (Hubert) and Aunt Hattie, and Uncle Bill (Hubert) and Aunt Margaret. They never had any children while I was young, although Uncle Bill and Aunt Margaret finally had two daughters when I was a teenager. So the two uncles and aunts were at our place for every major occasion such as Christmas and Easter and for many other times as well, and they were very good to us kids as much as those hard times would allow. During the war, Uncle Ren and Aunt Hattie both worked at a war munitions factory building aircraft. My Uncle Bill joined the air-force and finally got his wings, as bombardier, but never actually made it overseas before the end of the war. In addition, there were lots of Dutch friends that visited us so that there was a lot of Dutch spoken and we learned to speak and understand it, even though English was the language commonly spoken at home. During the war years of 1940–45 there was a lot of activity at both the public school and the boy-scouts movement to do projects for the war effort. When Victory Europe Day came, ending the war in Europe, there was a massive celebration for that great event. We also began to receive news from relatives in the Netherlands for the first time since the war's beginning and sent parcels of food and used clothes to them, because things were pretty desperate for them by the end of the war.

Early Education

I had a good primary education at Huron Street School, in spite of the fact that the main building was already very old when I was there and has long since been removed and replace. The school also had a newer annex which I believe still stands. But the school's outdoor play area had no playing fields, only a large area covered with concrete, so there was little development of any sports program. There was no gym or other facilities indoors for sports. Among all the teachers that I had at that school one stands out as one of the finest that I have ever encountered: Mr. Gilbert. He was my teacher in grade 6 and again in grade 8. He came to the school after the end of the war where he had been an officer in the army. I first remember him as visiting the school with a bandage rapped around his head from a wartime injury. His first year back in teaching in September of 1945 was the year that I was in his sixth-grade class. He was not a rigid disciplinarian as one might have expected, although outside the classroom he always had the appearance of a gentleman with a cane or umbrella as he walked. He did not speak often of the war experience, but I remember that first remembrance-day service after the war ended. It took place in the school kindergarten room, the largest room in the school and it was standing room only. Afterwards Mr. Gilbert told a deeply moving story of how he was assigned as a major in the army to lead a special mission and had to ask for volunteers. So many stepped forward that he had to choose which would go and which stay behind. Then he told us that less than half returned from that mission. His own voice trembled as he recalled the episode, but it had a great impact on me, and I am sure many others in the class. Even though he was naturally reserved, he gave us a glimpse into his own soul and into the meaning of the day for him that I have never forgotten.

Mr. Gilbert was "old school" and did not entirely approve of the new textbooks and approaches to the various parts of the curriculum, so he made use of some older textbooks. Where he got them, I do not know and how he got by with using his approach puzzles me, but he did. He had a way of approaching every subject, whether math or English grammar or art or literature that made it so interesting that you wanted to get your mind involved. For the first time I flourished in school. I can still remember some of those lessons to this day. He did not just have us memorizing poetry. We had to compete with each other in reciting the poems from memory with feeling and interpretation. In art the rage at that time was self-expression, plaster anything you like on a piece of paper. But Mr. Gilbert was an artist, especially with his landscapes in watercolors, and he taught us how to make a simple picture that we could enjoy. He had a whole set of basic examples and I still remember them. He taught us perspective in art, how to do a multi-colored wash, especially for sunsets. I had him as teacher again in grade 8 and he prepared me for high school so that in some subjects I was already ahead of the level in my first year. No teacher in my early years instilled in me the love of learning more than he did and I am sure that I was not alone.

One other thing must be said about Huron Street School. It was a school with a very diverse student body, even back then when Toronto as a whole was still very British. There was a large Jewish community in that part of Toronto and a significant number attended Huron Street School so that on Jewish holy days their absence from school was quite noticeable. We had Jewish neighbors, the Fishbanes, and Jerry Fishbane was a classmate of mine, so we often walked to school together and our families got along very well. Jerry even taught me the odd word in Yiddish. There were also some Chinese in the school, and one in my class, children of the Chinese grocers on Bloor Street. Also in that part of Toronto was an old Black community that dated back to the days of the underground railway, and some of these were students at our school. (This was before the influx of Caribbean immigrants.) And there were offspring of immigrants like us to counterbalance the predominantly British population. This diversity was a great asset because it was not at all common in many other parts of the city, and not at all the case where I went to High School in North York.

I received my secondary education at Earl Haig Collegiate in the five-year college prep program (1949–54). This was the only secondary school in North York at the time I entered secondary school, but during my third year another one was built, and others added quickly in the years that followed. The region on the northern boundary of what was then the City of Toronto was experiencing very rapid growth and we had been part of that growth, moving into a new home, the first that we actually owned. My youngest two brothers went to a brand new elementary school just across the street from where we lived, which even had a large playing field. We were also very close to Hog's Hollow, the large ravine of the upper Don River, a great place for kids to explore. Earl Haig was a good school that produced lots of good students for university, particularly the University of Toronto, although some brave souls went further afield, to Western or Queens. My brother Art and I were there together in high-school and shared many of the same classes. My oldest brother and my sister were no longer in school. Art and I were active in a number of groups and in sports, particularly basketball because we were tall, but Art was a much better player than I was. We sang in the school's Gilbert and Sullivan operettas and in the Glee club, and we were also involved in a religious student group, the Inter-School Christian Fellowship.

In secondary school education one had to begin making elective choices at least by the second year based upon certain perceived interests which could change in a subsequent year. Art was convinced by his second year that he was going into the ministry and picked Latin as an option. I had other ideas, so I picked art, probably because of what I had learned from Mr. Gilbert. But I soon tired of it and by third year I too wanted to take Latin, but that would mean I was a year behind. I talked to the Latin teacher Ms. Verra Vanderlip, and she said that if I was willing to work hard, I could make it up on my own. She would tutor me on the side until I caught up with the rest. This was completely voluntary on her part. She also taught my brother Greek as an extra. There is a sequel to this story. When I was in graduate school at Yale I again ran into Verra Vanderlip. She had decided to go into graduate studies and get her doctorate in order to teach at the college level and she was enrolled at Yale in the classics department. We ended up graduating in the same year, and since our names were so close in the alphabet we marched together in the graduation procession. Verra and others like her reflected the quality of education that I received at Earl Haig.

Religious Background

Before going on to discuss my college education and graduate studies, I want to reflect on my religious life and indoctrination during my childhood and youth. I was brought up in a conservative Calvinist Christian home and environment. While I happily identified myself as evangelical and was strongly in favor of those who were not Christians being persuaded to become believers, I was not so comfortable with the label of "fundamentalist" because it reflected so often a more non-reflective brand of Christianity in which theological discussion was minimal, apart from a few dogmas—the fundamentals—which were merely accepted without question. Although my father was brought up in what in North America is called the Christian Reformed Church, he made a decision early on to change to that other Calvinist church in Canada, the Presbyterian Church, and we were brought up within this Scottish tradition. For the whole time that we lived in the Annex we attended Knox Presbyterian Church on Spadina Ave., and were very active in church life. By father was an elder in the church (probably the only blue collar worker to attain that position, since the congregation members were otherwise well to do). We were active in many phases of church life and trained to know the Bible; I memorized large portions of it, always in the King James Version, along with the Westminster catechism. Every Sunday after church at dinner time my father regularly analyzed the sermon, usually for its orthodoxy, its exegesis and its evangelical appeal. We were also trained at home in the Heidelberg catechism, which my father preferred. We read a lot of Christian literature; one of my father's favorites was Gresham Machen of Westminster Theological Seminary (of whom we had a photo portrait on the wall in our house); another was Abraham Kuyper, a noted Dutch theologian and politician. My grandfather, a mayor of a small town in Holland, had been a member of Kuyper's party. Above all, we were imbued with Calvin, his *Institutes* and his commentaries. The various ministers of the churches where my father served as elder soon became aware of his expertise in Calvinism and the *Institutes*. It is fair to say that I was thoroughly indoctrinated at an early age and a very large part of my youth was taken up with church life and religious activity beyond the confines of the church. I attended meetings of evangelical churches other than my own, including that of Charles Templeton, and revival crusades of Billy Graham and others. I even worked a couple of summers at Canadian Keswick, a resort in Muskoka, Ontario, for mostly well-heeled Christians who wanted to spend their evenings listening to "leading" Christian speakers, e.g. faculty members from Wheaton College and Moody

Bible Institute, or major preachers. I sat in on many of these and honed my skills at critical evaluation of their talks. I loved to engage in "Bible study," as it was called, and in theological debate. Of the six children in our family, those who were most inclined in this direction were my sister Phil, my brother Art and myself. This was the situation throughout my youth before Art and I went on to college. Whether at church and through its broader activities or at school or within the family circle, most of our friends were Christians.

It is not surprising, therefore, that both Art and I aspired to religious careers and felt "called" to the Christian ministry. We often served as leaders of youth groups and were frequently called upon to speak at Christian gatherings or in church on "Youth Sunday" and had a fairly broad recognition within such circles for leadership. Our parents, of course, strongly supported such aspirations, and while they could not do much in the way of financial assistance, they were most willing to help in any way they could. When it came to deciding just what course of study to follow within the wide range of possibilities which the University of Toronto offered, Art and I went to visit Dr. Stanley Glen, the Principle of Knox College, the Presbyterian Seminary in Toronto. (Art would himself become the principle of Knox College in later years.) Dr. Glen, himself a New Testament scholar, would advise up to go to University College and take an honors program of study in the Department of Oriental Languages and Literature (Near Eastern Studies) as it was then called, with a special concentration in Hebrew and Greek. And that is what we did. There never seemed to be the slightest doubt that this was the wisest and best choice.

My brother Art and I entered University College in the fall of 1954. I had a small scholarship that went towards fees for the first year. Most of my expenses were covered by a combination of money saved from my previous earnings, especially summer jobs, supplemented by a Government of Ontario bursary, based on a means test. This allowed me to concentrate all of my time during the school year on my studies, without my family having to put out any money for fees, which they could not afford to do. Only in the summer did I work to earn money for the coming school year. The first two years I commuted from home to the university but in the last two years of college I lived in residence, and by the time I graduated I was completely debt free. It was a wonderful college experience and I thrived on it. I had seven different professors of Hebrew language over a four-year period, covering grammar and syntax and readings in Pentateuch and historical books, prophets, Psalms, Qoheleth and even the Mishna. I had four years of Near Eastern history from ancient Sumer to the present, including of course ancient Israel and early Christianity and the history of Islam, as well as the modern Near East. In classics I had four years of Greek, three years of Classical history of Greece and Rome, Greek philosophy, and Greek art and archaeology. In addition to my required courses I had a few other courses outside my honors concentration. I also did a senior thesis paper on the Dead Sea Scrolls. Many would regard my education as very narrow because it did not include mathematics, physical and life sciences, or social sciences, but the concentrated focus was wonderful and all of it was related to my goals and interests.

During the time that I was in university, I continued to be very active in evangelical Christian groups, along with my brother Art, especially in Inter-Varsity Christian Fellowship, organizing meetings, attending conferences, and morning prayer-meetings. We even served on the executive committee that organized an evangelizing mission with John Stott, a British clergyman, conducted throughout the university. While living on campus, I was also active again in Knox Presbyterian Church on Spadina Ave. By this time I was beginning to confront, through my studies and the university environment, a more critical approach to understanding the Bible and read a lot of theologically conservative literature that attempted to address these issues. The whole process left me uneasy, with many questions. Yet, I was so embedded within a very supportive religious and family community of belief and world-view that I was reluctant to venture too far from those bounds. Nevertheless, I did begin to read books by those outside the bounds of strict orthodoxy, such as George Ernest Wright, and to meet such individuals who still viewed themselves as evangelical Christians, but emphasized intellectual honesty. Too often I felt that the defenders of the faith were being dismissive and dishonest about real issues.

In addition to my involvement in IVCF, the department also had a student Near East club, heavily promoted by the faculty but run by the students. In my senior year I was the president. One of the meetings we had centered on the book of Daniel. One of the members of the faculty, Professor McCullough, would present arguments for the view that the book was of Hellenistic/Maccabean date. Representing the traditional view we had asked Dr. Fitch of Knox Church, and he had agreed. But before the time of the meeting he indicated that he could not come and so the position was presented by a conservative graduate student. He did his best, using a range of works by conservative scholars, but it was fairly clear through the presentations and the discussion that followed, that the conservative position was untenable. This was for me a serious blow to conservative views of biblical prophecy.

In my own studies for my senior research paper dealing with the Dead Sea Scrolls —a "safe" area of study—I tried to understand the religious thought of the Essenes within the wider context of the Judaism of the day, including Christianity, but especially rabbinic Judaism. This represented my first attempts at a comparative religions approach. Methodologically, it was hardly sophisticated because I had no real training in this area. Nevertheless, it was for me a quite new way of looking at the religious traditions within Judaism and Christianity, and of trying to understand the great gap between the Old Testament and the New Testament. The orthodox notion that the age of the Old Testament revelation of promise ended at some vague point in time and then centuries later a new Christian era of fulfillment began, with this great black hole between, made no sense. I could see that a lot had happened between the two that was decisive for understanding the various traditions of the later period.

Religiously, I was still an evangelical Christian, but intellectually I was beginning to move away from the narrow confines of orthodoxy to accept more critical positions of biblical interpretation.

Yale and Princeton Years

During my senior year in college I was nominated by my department for a Woodrow Wilson Fellowship for graduate studies and subsequently won this very prestigious award and applied to Yale Graduate School's Department of Near Eastern Civilizations. I was accepted and this meant postponing my plans to enter a theological seminary on graduation. I spent the summer doing foreign language preparation in anticipation of these requirements when I got to Yale. My brother Arthur and his newly-wedded wife Rowena were also headed south of the border to Philadelphia where he would enter the quite conservative Westminster Theological Seminary to begin his theological training. We had intended to travel together by car but those plans there disrupted at the U.S. border and I had to proceed on my own by buss to New Haven. It was my first experience in which I was entirely alone to make all the arrangements for my lodgings in the Graduate School residence with a roommate whom I had never met before, and registration in my program with all my choices on my own. I did not know another person at Yale or in the city of New Haven. Yale Grad School, however, was a wonderfully receptive and welcoming place and my roommate from the deep-south was very friendly and helpful. He was in Philosophy and from time to time he took me as a guest to the Yale Grad Philosophy Club, which was most interesting.

The program of study in Near Eastern Civilizations was rather informally constructed out of the possible offerings of the various faculty members in the department, under the direction of the chairman, Professor Albrecht Goetze. The basic course for all students entering the ancient Near East side of the program was Goetze's comprehensive review of the history of the civilizations of the Near East from the fourth millennium BCE down to the time of Alexander, with Professor W. Kelly Simpson covering Egypt. It was a very impressive course, with Goetze supplying bibliographies, including the most up-to-date publications, for every lecture. He also finished off each presentation with slides of relevant archaeological data and artifacts. Kelly Simpson followed the same routine. With Professor Marvin Pope I did some work on the Dead Sea Scrolls, reading the newly published Isaiah scroll and the Habakkuk Commentary. I also took Aramaic and Ugaritic with him. Pope was a very generous and humorous person. As an extra I did a one semester course in Hebrew Bible on Exodus with Professor Brevard Childs. This was his first year at Yale Divinity School and there were only two of us in the course, which was conducted in his office. It was a very solid and thorough course on critical scholarship with good secondary reading. There were lots of German texts including my first encounter with works by Gerhard von Rad. Childs was also sympathetic to someone like me who was struggling to come to terms with critical scholarship from a conservative Christian background, and he invited me to his home to talk with me about it. He was very kind and generous with his time.

One of the most stimulating and influential courses that first year at Yale was a seminar by Professor Erwin Goodenough, on Hellenism and Hellenistic Judaism in the Greco-Roman period. There were about six of us from both Near Eastern Studies and Religious Studies, and from both OT and NT studies. The course consisted of reading a vast quantity of literature, beginning with classical literature in translation from Homer, the Greek tragedies, comedies, and philosophers as background to Philo Judaeus and Josephus, which we also read. Philo was one of Goodenough's specialties and we read a number of his books on the subject. Along side of this reading of sources, we read various notable works on the study of religion in general and classical religion in particular. He did this because he wanted us to ask good questions. That was what the whole seminar was all about. Your preparation for the seminar was to come to class with those questions. When someone threatened to side-track the seminar with a bad question or comment, he would ignore it and suddenly turn to someone else: "Van Seters, you had a question!" and you had better be prepared to have one or two handy.

Goodenough was then working on his *Jewish Symbols of the Greco-Roman Period* and 8 volumes were completed by that time (1958–59). We were also introduced to his work on the Dura Europos Synagogue, which came out in the later volumes. There was a lot of discussion about method in the study of religion and how to read Jewish symbols, and the degree to which Christianity was influenced by Hellenism in the NT and in the later church fathers. My Toronto undergrad program in both classics and Near Eastern studies was a great help to me in this course. Later when I went to Princeton Seminary, I was disappointed by my class on New Testament Introduction and other such courses that related to the Hellenistic world. They seemed so shallow by comparison. All my future work in this area was touched in one way or another by this experience with Goodenough, especially the massive reading he required as background to the field.

While at Yale I attended the Evangelical Free Church in New Haven. I was caught between two worlds, that of my devout conservative Christian past that I was reluctant to give up, and the development of new scholarly critical skills and a whole new way of looking at my religious tradition and the biblical text. My friendships had been so completely dominated by my church life, by evangelical Christian youth groups in high school and college, and by family life and family friends. In college I had been inclined to regard my professors with some suspicion, when it came to matters of faith. But with Childs and Pope they seemed to know where I was coming from and were very kind and patient. While attending the Free Church, I met the pastor's daughter, Elizabeth Malmberg, and was also drawn into the life of the church, as well. This tension between two worlds would be a dominant aspect of my life for several years, and it was always a question of how to negotiate between these two conflicting loyalties.

During the second semester of my first year at Yale I had to decide between whether I would stay at Yale or go to a theological seminary to get my B.D., before proceeding further with my studies. My plan at that point was to prepare for a career of teaching in a theological seminary, for which I needed some theological training. I could have stayed at Yale, taking my degree at the divinity school on "holy hill" as Goetze called it. But as a Presbyterian I chose to go to Princeton Theological Seminary in New Jersey. Goetze and Goodenough tried to talk me out of it with offers of scholarship aid. Goodenough even took me to lunch in his college and when he saw that I had made up my mind to go to Princeton, he said that any time I wanted to return to Yale, there would be adequate financial support waiting for me. Princeton Seminary had no such financial support for mere B.D. students so during the summer I had to work on a construction job in Woodbridge, Connecticut, for a building contractor (the Lohn brothers who were connected with the Free Church). While at Princeton I also did various weekend jobs: in a seminary choir, as a pastor's assistant, running a youth group in Trenton, New Jersey. By the end of my first Yale year, Elizabeth and I were very serious about each other and carried on a steady correspondence between Princeton and New Haven. We were engaged at Christmas time and married the following June. Our son Peter was born during the second semester of my second Princeton year.

With only a few exceptions, there is little to say about my course work at Princeton. A lot of time was spent on courses of a practical nature that related to running a church, but that were not relevant to my future career. Given my background at Toronto and Yale, I was relieved from introductory language courses in Hebrew and Greek, and did not have to attend lectures in OT history and introduction, but just wrote a couple of papers instead. In place of these I was allowed to do some graduate courses. I did a little Syriac and some colloquial Palestinian Arabic (at Princeton University), and a graduate course with R. B. Y. Scott on OT Theology. Scott was at Princeton University, but helped out the seminary because of a vacancy in Old Testament. However, the one redeeming feature of my time at Princeton was the presence of Gerhard von Rad during the second year when he was invited to Princeton as a visiting professor and I was able to take some advanced courses with him. He had just produced his remarkable *Old Testament Theology*, two volumes in German. The second volume on the theology of the prophetic tradition had just appeared in 1960 and he was giving lectures on an English translation of this volume. (I have his signature in my copy of the German edition.) There were only a small number of students in this class, perhaps because his English was not so good and he had a heavy German accent. But one adjusted to it very quickly. For me at that stage of my career this approach to the Bible was fascinating and I was completely won over to German biblical scholarship. In addition to this course I also did an advanced graduate course with him on form criticism.

A further word must be said about von Rad's time at Princeton. What I found very disturbing about Princeton seminary was the very poor reception that von Rad was given by the faculty, especially in the biblical department. In one class I had with a New Testament Professor (Otto Piper), he went out of his way to denigrate the biblical theology of von Rad. Von Rad was never invited to give a public lecture at PTS, whereas he was invited to both Harvard and Yale divinity schools to give public lectures there and enjoyed the experiences at both places very much. He especially commented on the very warm reception that he had received from G. Ernest Wright at Harvard. In later years I would have my own very pleasant acquaintance with Ernest Wright. Both Wright and von Rad were deeply committed to the theology of *Heilsgeschichte*, as was Brevard Childs at Yale. At Princeton, however, von Rad was lonely and he made it a habit on Wednesday afternoon's to invite a group of grad students (I was included) to have tea in his apartment, served by his wife (who spoke better English than he did and helped him with it when he needed it). This was a chance to informally discuss other scholars in the field of biblical studies, especially Germany, and also his relationship with Karl Barth. They were good friends and that is what made the situation so confusing because the following year Karl Barth visited Princeton and was treated with the highest honors and gave a lecture in the university chapel (a cathedral in size) because there was nothing grand enough at the seminary. The difference in the respect accorded to the two was incomprehensible. So a few of us at Princeton had von Rad all to ourselves, which would never have happened had we gone to Heidelberg.

There was an attitude in America in the Albright School that was highly suspicious of German scholarship and declared such works as that of Martin Noth as *nihilistic* (see John Bright) and this colored the whole outlook of American scholarship to so much of German biblical studies. From my personal experience of von Rad's work and teaching I saw how completely unjust such judgments were and I was quite won over to this more critical perspective. Princeton had now become much too conservative for me. My third year was largely a case of putting in time to get my degree. I did take the time to do a special lengthy research paper on a set topic "The Doctrine of Creation in the Old Testament." This was supposed to be in competition for a graduate scholarship ($1,000), but I was the only one who submitted a paper. Needless to say, I won the prize and received honors for the paper. The whole thing was so badly handled that the day on which I was to be notified, nothing happened. When I asked the dean about it, he had heard nothing from the biblical department. Apparently, Charles Fritch, the Old Testament professor, had forgotten about it and had not let his new colleague James Barr see the paper. They rushed the whole matter through and I received notification of the award a little late. When I received the paper back there were no comments and no indication that anyone had seriously looked at it. For me, what was important is that I had taken up von Rad's discussion about the place of the creation theme in Second Isaiah and arrived at a somewhat different perspective from his. Notwithstanding my deep respect for von Rad, with my critical Yale training I found that I could think through some of these issues from my own perspective. On this particular issue my view was vindicated by other scholarship in later years.

When I finally received my divinity degree from PTS, we packed up our belongings and together with Elizabeth and our son Peter we headed back to New Haven. I was given the J. J. Obermann fellowship at Yale, and with Elizabeth working as a visiting nurse in New Haven, we made out fine. I also persuaded Princeton to allow me to use my fellowship from PTS for summer research and study, instead of doing construction work. Soon after I arrived back at Yale I submitted my Princeton research paper to Brevard Childs for his appraisal, because I had to map out my study program for the coming year if I was going to do a doctoral dissertation with him. As indicated earlier, I never did receive a proper evaluation of my research project at Princeton. Childs took some time to respond, writing copious notes and then returned it. He was quite unhappy with it and told me rather bluntly that it would probably be best if I worked on something else for my doctorate with another faculty member. What upset him so much is that I had tried to apply insights that I had learned in my work with Goodenough on the study of religion to the notions of creation in the OT. This went strongly against his Barthian *Heilsgeschichte* theology. We remained on friendly terms, but it was clear that I could not get a degree in biblical studies at Yale. So I had to switch fields. Since North American scholarship in the 1960s considered all study of Near Eastern civilization of the second and first millennium BCE as within the range of biblical studies anyway, the shift to another topic in this area was not as drastic as it might appear.

My program at Yale picked up where it had left off three years earlier. With Albrecht Goetze I studied Old Babylonian Akkadian, reading Mari, Nuzi and Alalakh texts, which were frequently referred to by scholars in their studies of the book of Genesis. I also did a course on comparative Semitic linguistics with Goetze, another of his specialties. Jim Muhley and an Israeli student were also in these classes, and we spent a lot of time together. Some others at Yale at that time in Religious Studies specializing in Hebrew Bible were George Coats, Roy Mellugin, Malcolm Clark, Bruce Birch, Gene Tucker, and Erhard Gerstenberger (on a post-doctorate from Heidelberg). I would have a lot of contact with them in the years to come. With Marvin Pope I worked on Ugaritic. During this term I met Professor Harald Ingholt for the first time. His field was archaeology of the Levant and he had been on sabbatical leave during my first year at Yale. I took a course in Syrian archaeology, in which he had done his own work while at the American University in Beirut, directing the Danish excavations at Hama and tomb excavations at Palmyra. He was an authority in both Near Eastern and classical archaeology. He also offered a course in Palestinian archaeology. Given this kind of training, I decided to do a project in second millennium BCE Near Eastern history and archaeology, which would equip me with the expertise that was needed for Old Testament studies of the 60s.

There was a particular episode in Ingholt's Palestinian archaeology course that I regard as quite important for understanding the development of my thinking in biblical studies. Ingholt reported that an article written by W. F. Albright, "Abraham the Hebrew," had recently appeared and he assigned to me the task of reporting on this piece of history writing. It was full of references to archaeological evidence and my task was to look at all of this evidence and do a critical evaluation of it: "Be sure to check all of the footnotes." In carrying out this assignment what I was amazed to find was the thesis Albright constructed about Abraham as a donkey caravaneer was based upon very flimsy and often quite erroneous evidence. The head of this great American school of biblical studies could not be trusted as an authority on archaeological matters, and this implicated so many of the other members of the "Albright School." With my critique of this article Ingholt was in entire agreement. This was in 1963. It would be several years later that I would produce a more thorough examination of the work of the Albright School as it had to do with the pre-history of "ancient Israel."

After my comprehensive exams in mid-1963, I submitted my proposal to work on the problem of the Hyksos, and this was accepted. I would do this under Harald Ingholt. At the time Kelly Simpson was on sabbatical leave, and when he returned he was concerned that I did not have any Egyptian for such a project. So while I was doing research for my dissertation I studied Egyptian at the same time. I was never proficient at Egyptian, but I learned enough so that I was able to handle the Egyptian evidence I needed with Simpson making sure that I did not make any egregious errors. One important piece of evidence that attracted my attention was an Egyptian text, the "Admonitions of Ipuwer," which had been dated to the First Intermediate Period and used as a description of conditions in the First Intermediate Period. However, to me it seemed that the "Admonitions" reflected rather the conditions in the Eastern Delta region during the Second Intermediate Period, prior to the establishment of Asian control in that region, and I wrote up an article making my case for this new dating. Kelly Simpson supported my views and urged me to submit it to the prestigious *Journal of Egyptian Archaeology*, published by the British Museum in London. They accepted it and it appeared as "A Date for the 'Admonitions' in the Second Intermediate Period," later that year in 1964.

Year of Research and Study in the Near East

I completed my dissertation by the summer of 1964, and Inghold and Kelly Simpson submitted it to Yale press, and even before the oral exam it was accepted for publication. So there was no doubt about the results of my oral exam. I also had an offer of a position at Waterloo Lutheran University in Waterloo Ontario, Canada, beginning in the fall of 1965. In the interim, members of the faculty felt that it would be a good thing for me if I spent the coming year in the Near East at the American School of Oriental Research (later called The Albright Institute) in East Jerusalem. Inghold was able to get a research fellowship from the Dean of the Graduate School (Augusta-Hazard Fellowship 1964–65) to cover my expenses ($4,000), and Simpson was able to get me a small grant for a short trip to Egypt while in Jerusalem. Pope, who had a strong connection with ASOR in Jerusalem, made the necessary connections there. The help and support from the whole faculty was very gratifying. The plan was to go by freighter from New York to Beirut. (Pope said it was "the only way to go.") Inghold supplied me with some personal connections with his friends in Beirut. From there we would go by way of Damascus and Amman to East Jerusalem (at that time under Jordan). What all of these faculty members knew from experience, and what I would confirm, was that there was no substitute for living and traveling in the Near East for several months, which would be so important to one's future career of teaching.

After checking the shipping schedules in the New York Times, I booked passage for myself, Elizabeth, and three-year-old Peter, on a freighter of the Holland American Line, which sailed from New York in mid-October. There were a couple dozen passengers on board, mostly families from Lebanon, Syria, and Egypt, returning home from America. While spending two weeks at sea, from New York to Beirut (with only a brief stop in Malta harbor for a crew change), we had a chance to become good friends with some of the families, especially those from Egypt. When we told them that we intended to make a trip to Egypt they gave us their addresses and phone numbers so we could look them up. The Atlantic crossing was rather rough but once in the Mediterranean, the weather was beautiful. The food and accommodations were very good and the children tended to be spoiled by the ship's crew.

Once we had landed in Beirut, I booked a room in the small hotel in Ras Beirut, that had been recommended, and we made contact with some of Inghold's old friends. I also got in touch with William Ward at the American University of Beirut, whose work I had used in my dissertation. As a student of Inghold I also received the royal treatment at the Beirut museum with a fine tour of the antiquities rooms. After a few days in Beirut we were anxious to get on to our final destination. So we booked an overland taxi and left at 8 a.m. from Beirut to Damascus, in another taxi from there to Amman, and finally a third taxi to Jerusalem, arriving in the early evening at ASOR. We had a late supper and checked into our rooms there, a small apartment on the basement level of the director's residence. Paul Lapp was the resident director at ASOR at the time, but he was on leave doing some work for a US aid program, so Nancy Lapp took charge of the housekeeping matters and Edward (Ted) Campbell of McCormick Theological Seminary (Chicago) was acting director. Prescott Williams of Austin Texas was visiting professor. Bruce Dalberg and family were also visiting at the school for the year. These families included several children so that there were four of them (including our Peter) who were three to four years old and could play together, with the mothers taking turns supervising them.

One of the major organized activities at the school was that of conducting field trips to various archaeological sites, using vehicles either owned by the school or those belonging to people connected with the school. We could also rent a taxi for the day at reasonable rate. At that time there was complete freedom of movement throughout the whole of the West Bank area, as well as the whole of Jordan. We made a number of trips to the north, including Gibeon, Mizpah, Shechem (Ted Campbell and Prescott Williams were part of the Harvard–McCormick excavations there), Samaria, Tirzah, and many others. We traveled down to Qumran near the north-west shore of the Dear Sea and explored the ruins and the caves on the slopes above the site. We had the whole place to ourselves with not a tourist in sight. (It was a completely different tourist site with a gift shop and guides when I visited it again in 2002). We visited Jericho more than once and the Roman city of Jerash in Trans-Jordan. We explored various sites on the east side of the Jordan valley as far as Pella and made another trip to the highlands of Moab, to Madaba and other sites. Some trips were made by just the three of us, Elizabeth, Peter and me, one to Hebron and another to Jericho using the local buses. It was easy and cheap to travel by bus to many places. Towards the end of our stay, Elizabeth and I with another couple made an overnight trip to Petra, by means of a rented Volkswagen. Peter stayed with the Williams family while we were gone. This was a wonderful trip in early May, with the whole of Petra to ourselves. There were no big fancy hotels then. We stayed in a small guest house in the centre of Petra. There were no vendors with souvenirs, only the odd Bedouin boy trying to sell something he had found on the site, coins, statues, etc. We also visited the Crusader fortress at Kerak on the way back. These many trips and the pictures taken were invaluable aids for teaching the history, geography and archaeology of this region later in my teaching career.

Alongside of those fascinating and instructive field trips, there was, of course, the less glamorous, but equally necessary task of working on revisions to my book in the libraries of ASOR and the other institutions in East Jerusalem. I wanted to check as much as possible the archaeological material, especially the pottery and artifacts to which I made reference in my study. One much discussed problem at that time was the so-called Middle Bronze I period. ASOR itself had a small collection of MB I potsherds that I wanted to examine, as well as those on display in the Palestinian Museum, and the relevant archaeological publications in the ASOR library. I learned that Paul Lapp, the director of ASOR, was also working on MB I and was currently excavating some newly discovered MB I period tombs. So shortly after I arrived I arranged to have a conversation with him about this issue. I began my telling him that from my careful scrutiny of W. F. Albright's article on "Abram the Hebrew" I found myself in complete disagreement with him both on his dating and his interpretation of MB I and its origins. I also wanted to study the little collection of MB I pottery sherds at the School. His response to my remarks completely shocked me. He told me that what I said about Albright's errors was nothing new. He and others within the "Albright school" were aware of them. So I asked him where I could find some publication of these criticisms, and he replied that they would not appear until the old man was dead! I told him that I rejected such an approach and would publish my dissertation very soon. He also proceeded to instruct me that I was not to use the potsherd study collection, which Nancy Lapp, his wife, had specifically pointed out to me when I first arrived, without his supervision. I soon discovered that all of the publications in the ASOR library that had anything with MB I had been removed and were in the director's quarters. I was not going to beg him for my use of these. Instead, I discovered the riches of the library at the École biblique et archéologique française de Jérusalem, which Marvin Pope had told me about, and I was more than welcome to make use of those facilities. This institute was only a short distance from ASOR and I spent a lot of time there. I rarely used the ASOR library for anything. While I was rewriting each chapter of my dissertation, Elizabeth was retyping on our portable typewriter the revised manuscript to be submitted to Yale Press. It was finally sent to the press before we left Jerusalem in May.

It was common practice for those who were staying at ASOR to become involved in an archaeological expedition during their stay, one that was conducted by the director of ASOR. Paul Lapp was planning to dig at the EB IV-MB I cemetery site of Bab ed-Dhra in Jordan on the south eastern side of the Dead Sea. However, he was careful to say nothing about it to me. Instead he urged Ted Campbell to persuade me to join J. B. Pritchard's dig in February at Tell es-Saidiyeh in the Jordan valley. I was unaware, of course, that Lapp was quite contemptuous of Pritchard's archaeological work and there was no love lost between them. Even Campbell did not have any high regard for it, but he knew that Lapp and I would never get along and Lapp certainly did not want anyone who might conceivably compete with his interest in MB I. When necessary he feigned politeness, but otherwise he was not in the least bit helpful. Ted Campbell, on the other hand, was generally quite supportive and we became good friends, even though we were always in disagreement on issues related to the views of the Albright school, since he himself was a Johns Hopkins graduate and a very close friend of G. Ernest Wright.

The Trip to Egypt

In the month of January, which was wet and cold in Jerusalem, we decided that this was a good time to make a trip to Egypt, where it was quite sunny and pleasant during the day. We booked a very inexpensive flight with the aid of a travel agent near ASOR and flew from the airport in north Jerusalem with Jordanian Airlines (a DC 3), flying on the east side of Dead Sea. This route was necessary because a direct flight over the heartland of Israel was forbidden. We then flew across the Sinai Peninsula to Cairo. During the flight I visited the cockpit with my son Peter and we had a great view of the Sinai from there. We stayed in the Garden City Hotel in central Cairo midway between the Nile Hilton and the Sheppard's Hotel. Our hotel was small and inexpensive, and therefore often used by academics. It was also quite close to the Cairo

Museum, which we visited, and not far from the American Research Center in Egypt, whose personnel were most helpful in giving advice and assistance for what I needed to do on my project. For a few days I did a little sightseeing with my family, including the Cairo zoo, which was a favorite with Peter. The three of us visited the pyramids of Giza and Sakkara, including a trip into one of the finely decorated tombs, and also visited a number of other notable sites around the city of Cairo. After this I set about making arrangements for my trip north to the Delta. From the antiquities officials at the Cairo Museum I received the necessary papers for the trip, and using the Egyptian funds that I was given by Kelly Simpson, I set out for Zagazig (ancient Bubastis), where the regional office of the Antiquities Department was located. I was put up in a very rudimentary hotel. My plan was to spend each day doing field trips in the region, usually by taxi, which was fairly cheap, and then return to Zagazig at the end of the day. While I was in Zagazig I had a problem about getting anything to eat. Apart from buying some fruit in a market there was nowhere to get any prepared meal, because it was Ramadan. So I called up a doctor who lived in Zagazig and whom I had met on board ship, and I told him that I was in town. He immediately knew my predicament and told me that at sundown (which fortunately was early in the evening in January) I was to come to his place and he would see that I had something to eat. In fact, when I got there it was more like a feast. He also told me that he had invited a guest over after dinner, a medical friend of his, to meet this Canadian. We had a wonderful time. And as long as I was in Zagazig I went to his place every evening for dinner.

The two areas in the Eastern Delta that I wanted to spend some time examining were the region a few kilometers north of the town of Faqus, specifically Qantir and Tell ed-Dab'a, and the great excavation site of Tanis (San el Hagar), some 15 kms further north. In the Egyptian histories dealing with that period scholars made rival claims for Qantir and Tanis as the site of the ancient city of Pi-Ramesses, the capital built by Ramesses II. The reason for my interest in this debate was because it had a direct bearing on the results of my dissertation on the Hyksos, which I had just completed. The literary and epigraphic evidence for the location of Avaris, the ancient capital of the Hyksos dynasty, pointed to a spot close to Pi-Ramesses. I had spent a chapter of my study trying to demonstrate that Qantir, and not Tanis, was the site of the capital city, Pi-Ramesses, and that Tell ed-Dab'a, a short distance to the south, was the location of the ancient city of Avaris. So I had to see these places for myself.

On my first full day in the Eastern Delta region I set out by bus with the assistant inspector of antiquities, Ibrihim, for the region from Zagazig to the town of Faqus, following the Bahr Faqus canal and what was once the ancient third branch of the Nile (the Pelusiac branch). From all of the literary evidence it seems clear that Avaris and Pi-Ramesses were situated on this eastern Pelusiac branch. When we arrived at Faqus we were joined by the chief antiquities guard of the region whose job it was to show us the various sites, between Tell ed Dab'a and Qantir, both on the road that runs beside the Bahr Faqus canal. The whole area north of Faqus to Qantir is covered with fertile vegetation and groves of trees, broken up by low mounds with a few houses. To the east of this wide strip of fertile land beside the canal was the desert. Walking around the region of Tell ed Dab'a one saw great quantities of potsherds scattered on the ground, all witnesses to the regions ancient history. There was also a large flat depression bare of vegetation with part of it containing water. Next to it was a tell or mound that was 2–3 meters higher than the surrounding vegetation. The low flat area looked as if it could have been an ancient harbor for the occupation site, which in the past was fed with water running off of the Nile River. All of this fitted very well with my theory that this was the site of Avaris, capital of the Hyksos. From Tell ed Dab'a we drove on to Qantir, which is the largest village of several small farming communities. Qantir, along with its elevated grave yard, was situated on a large ancient tell. Some of its houses were built with ancient carved stone blocks, with the inscriptions largely erased. In the fields around Qantir were the remains of pieces of broken monuments. The whole region was just crying out for archaeological investigation, but a major deterrent was the fact that so much of it is farm land with villages occupying the remains of the ancient tells. Time did not permit us to go on to Tanis that day so I had to leave that trip for another day.

The next day Ibrahim of the Antiquities Department showed me around the archaeological excavations of Tell Basta (ancient Bubastis) on the outskirts of Zagazig. It is a large site and had received a lot of archaeological attention, with a large number of interesting structures from the Old Kingdom, Middle Kingdom, New Kingdom, and later periods. There are remains of many fine temples and tombs. There is also a cat cemetery in honor of the goddess Bast. After inspecting this site we took a taxi on the road to Ismailiya and the Suez Canal. This road runs east from Zagazig alongside the freshwater canal through the Wadi Tumilat to the Suez, and we visited important sites along the way. We stopped first at Saft el Henna. This was once a major city of the region, but now the modern town sits on top of the site with only a small part of the ancient tell preserved in the middle of the town. Our primary destination, however, was the large site of Tell el Maskhuta (Pithom). This had been excavated about a century earlier, and traces of that earlier dig were still obvious from the exposed walls of ancient buildings. There were a few broken monuments and blocks of limestone and granite visible on the surface, all indications of a place of major importance. A modern village covered part of the low mound, which arose above the level of the surrounding fields that were covered with crops, watered by irrigation ditches. I was to return to this site as part of an archaeological expedition, about fifteen years later.

The following day I took a bus alone to Faqus and from there, with my official guide Sheikh Abdel Monan, made a trip by taxi to Tanis. Sheikh Monan, who was on loan to me from the Antiquities Department, spoke only Arabic, and my use of the language was rather limited, but we got along well. On the road to Tanis a few miles to the north of Qantir the road turns off and runs along another canal, which links up to a different branch of the Nile that leads to Tanis. In antiquity there were only three main branches of the Nile River, but now the Nile splits up into many branches and canals in the Delta region so that none is very impressive as compared with the great river that flows past Cairo. On the way to Tanis my guide had us stop at an apartment building in a small town. I wondered why we were doing this, but I could not get an explanation. He just told me everything was fine, I would see. It turned out that this was his home and that he was going to offer me something to eat. As I said earlier, this was the time of Ramadan and it was only mid-morning, but when I went in, there was a plate of sweets and something to drink, but only for me. My guide and his wife were Moslem so they were fasting, but they could see no reason why I had to and for them hospitality to a stranger was more important. I was deeply touched by this.

Tanis was a site being excavated by the French and had been for several years, and they did not permit anyone on the site without permission. Of course my guide knew the Arab guards employed by the French, so after a few brief words of exchange between them, I was given the complete run of the place. It is a huge site with many impressive monuments, including a number of Ramesside period statues, building blocks and inscriptions. A large statue of Ramesses II now stood at the entrance and there were statues of deities in another area. There was a large obelisk with the name of Ramesses II, lying on its side. Of particular interest were large stone-lined wells with pools at the bottom and steps going down into them. I was reminded of the pool of Gibeon with its staircase. One could easily understand why the French archaeologists had insisted in the scholarly debate that this must be Pi-Ramesses. The sheer size of the site was quite overwhelming.

Nevertheless, there were some disturbing features about the place that just did not make sense with that identification. First, I could now see for myself one curious feature that I had noted in the French publications of the archaeological finds. The inscribed building blocks were not in their original positions. The lines of inscribed hieroglyphs of one block did not match with the one next to it. It was as if the only purpose of the blocks had been their use as secondary building material. All the blocks had been reused and not in their original location, and the archaeologists were never able to find a specifically Ramesside stratum beneath the layer of these blocks. That meant that all of the Ramesside monuments and building blocks had to have come from another location. In my view that place was Qantir. Second, it was also clear that Tanis was not located on the Pelusiac branch of the Nile, whereas Qantir, on the Bahr Faqus, clearly was on the ancient eastern branch of the Nile. Third, the many literary descriptions of the lush vegetation in the vicinity of Pi-Ramesses do not fit with the very sparse vegetation and almost desert-like soil around Tanis. This is certainly not farming country as one finds between the town of Faqus and Qantir. Fourth, there are no other ancient mounds around or to the south of Tanis that could be identified as Avaris. The land is flat and barren for a great distance.

On returning from Tanis, I stopped again at Qantir and examined the area on the west side of the road opposite Qantir as far as the Bahr Faqus. In the field there were numerous building blocks and traces of the old mound now under vegetation. I also saw the white limestone foot of what had clearly been part of a colossus (no doubt Ramesses), previously observed and commented on by an Egyptian scholar, and a large block of red granite, perhaps part of a monumental doorway. I walked along the Bahr Faqus for some distance towards Faqus, and all along the banks there was an abundance of potsherds and ancient building debris. All of this seemed to me strong confirmation that my location of Avaris in the vicinity of Tell ed-Deb'a as argued in my dissertation was correct. I took a number of pictures at both Tanis and the region of Qantir. I now had a first-hand image in my head of the whole region of the north-eastern Delta of Egypt that I had been dealing with in my dissertation and could reflect this in my final revision in book form.

One more comment must be made about this area, and it has to do with the name Faqus, both for the town and the Nile branch, the Bahr Faqus. The name Faqus can best be explained as "the city of Qus" and Qus is a late short form for the name Gesem. This older form occurs in the Greek Septuagint as the name for Goshen, the form of the name that occurs in the Hebrew Bible. This region stretched all the way from north of Bubastis to Qantir and it is identified in the Joseph story as the land of Rameses. The name Goshen does not go back to the time of Ramesses but arises as the name of this region only in a much later period, no earlier than the eighth century BCE. This lush strip of vegetation irrigated by the canals of the Nile, runs along the eastern edge of the Delta down to the Saft el-Henna, identical with the 20th nome of Lower Egypt. To the east of Goshen lies the desert and it is for this reason that it was known also as the Arabian Nome. [Note: It is surprising how many scholars try to draw biblical maps of Egypt and describe the movement of the Israelites out of Egypt without ever having traveled in the region or become familiar with its geography. The maps thus produced are quite impossible and meaningless.]

The day after my trip to Tanis and Qantir I returned to Cairo and my family. While I was gone Elizabeth had gotten it touch with the Egyptian family that we had met on board ship from the USA, and they had made a great effort to entertain Elizabeth and Peter. We all got together again and visited the new home of one of their friends in the suburbs, which was very nice. In the evening we had a final celebration in our friends' apartment that overlooked the city of Cairo. It was very enjoyable. But there was still one last project that I needed to do and that was to get in touch with the Egyptian scholar, Labib Habashi, whose archaeological research and finds in the region of Tell ed-Dab'a had been so important to me. But how was I to find him? Fortunately, his wife Madame Habashi was the secretarial person in charge of the office at the American Research Center so there was no trouble in making arrangements for a visit to their home in Heliopolis, just north of Cairo. I went out there by train and Labib brought me from there to his place. I told him all about my dissertation on the Hyksos and how my views on Qantir as Pi-Ramesses and Tell ed-Dab'a as Avaris supported his position. He was, of course, delighted and proceeded to show me many photos of additional finds that he had made that were not yet published. I suggested that I should try in my survey report to interest Kelly Simpson and the Yale–Pennsylvania Expedition to dig at Tell ed-Dab'a, but he replied: "You are too late. There is a young scholar from Austria, Manfred Bietak, who has already gotten the concession from the Egyptian Department of Antiquities to dig at this site." Later when I returned to North America I wrote to Bietak and congratulated him on his choice because he was going to find Avaris at that site. His response was: "I hope you and Labib are right." We were right and he did indeed find this most remarkable city and has made a whole career out of his work there. After my visit to Labib Habashi we returned the next day to Jerusalem.

Before leaving this subject of my first Egyptian adventure, I want to make a few additional comments about our experience and some important lessons that I learned from it. In addition to the academic enrichment that this time in Egypt gave to me in terms of visiting archaeological sites and geographic regions so important to my research and scholarly development, as I hope I have made clear in the above, there was something else about life that was equally, or even more, important. My family and I were in Egypt at the very height of the President Nasser era, when there was a strong feeling of animosity between Egypt and the United States and the passions of the general populations of both countries were swept up in this fervor. It is true that I was a Canadian but Elizabeth was still an American at that time and my son was both, and few Egyptians were inclined to make any distinction between the two North American countries. Both countries supported Israel, which was a serious threat on its border. The Russians instead of the Americans were building the Aswan Dam. Yet in spite of all this, the hospitality, the assistance, the kindness and friendship that we received from so many in the Egyptian government service, from academic scholars, yes and even from my guide in the Delta, Sheik Monan, was just overwhelming. I was not yet an established scholar or a person of means and influence, just a struggling graduate student, but I was treated with far more respect than most foreign scholars gave to their Egyptian colleagues. I could not help but observe the stark contrast between Paul Lapp, who was so secretive about his archaeological work, and Labib Habashi, who was so eager to share with me all of his materials and help me in any way he could in the areas in which our interests overlapped. Our new Egyptian friends treated us for who we were, not for our politics and religion. I was determined never to forget that lesson and I hope that I never have. I would return to Egypt again a decade and a half later.

Archaeology in the Jordan Valley

Shortly after our return from Egypt I spent two months (mid-February to mid-April) on an excavation with Professor J. B. Pritchard and the University of Pennsylvania team, digging at Tell es-Saidiyeh (biblical Zerathan?), which was located on the eastern side of the Jordan valley at the end of the Wadi Kuffrinja. The tell or mound sits beside a spring that feeds the steam which flows a short distance down to the Jordan River. Tell es-Saidiyeh is also about 5 kms north of another archaeological site, Deir Alla on the Zarqa (or Jabbok) River. Although I had done a lot of armchair archaeology during my doctoral work, this was my first experience in the field. The amount of instruction and direction in digging technique by Pritchard was rather limited. However, there was a young German fellow, Stephan Kroll, fresh from the excavations at Kamid el Loz in the Beka valley of Syria, who was very helpful. Kroll later became a leading authority in Iranian archaeology.

Pritchard relied heavily on a select crew of Palestinians from Jericho who had been trained by Kathleen Kenyon during her excavations at Jericho. One such person and an area supervisor were allocated to each excavation square. The rest of the workers who were used to do the digging and removal of dirt were hired locally from the village. Our archaeological base camp was in a former engineers' camp at Wadi Yabis about 15 kms north of the tell site. (Wadi Yabis is the biblical Valley of Jebesh and is to be associated with biblical Jebesh Gilead. There was an ancient mound close to our camp, generally identified with this biblical town.) We took our breakfast and evening meals at the base camp and ate lunch at the excavation site. On weekends we traveled back and forth to Jerusalem where I rejoined my family for a couple of days. Needless to say, I became very familiar with the route through the Jordan valley and up to Jerusalem.

From the top of our tell at Sa'idiyeh one could look over the Jordan valley south to the Dead Sea and north to Mount Tabor and the Sea of Galilee, with the highlands on either side rising sharply from well below sea level to over 3000 feet. The Palestinian Arabic that I had learned at Princeton University also came in handy in my communication with the local workers on the excavation. One also experienced the change in seasons, from the winter rain (which was rather sparse in the valley) to the great show of spring flowers and the migration of birds going north through the valley, especially the great flocks of cranes gliding up the Jordan valley on the wind currents. The vast irrigation system had been built by the Italian engineers in the Gore valley on the east bank of the Jordan, from the Yarmuk to the Jabbok, and it made the whole region very fertile. It was also a short and easy hike from the dig site to the Jordan River itself.

Another member of the dig, who became a good friend, was Magnus Ottosson. He was from Sweden and had studied under the biblical scholar, Ivan Engnell at Uppsala, and later in his career Ottosson also occupied the chair in Old Testament studies at Uppsala. His doctoral dissertation had been on Gilead, and when it later appeared in publication he gave me a copy. This was his first excavation with Pritchard and he later worked on a number of other digs with him and then had his own archaeological excavations in the Gilead region. During the 1965 season at Sa'idiyeh we had time to discuss the pros and cons of the Engnell approach to Old Testament studies. The subject of oral tradition, on which Engnell had made his reputation, was a matter of considerable debate in biblical criticism of that era. Many years later we would have a wonderful reunion when, during a speaking tour of Scandinavia, he invited me to Uppsala to give a lecture there. More on this later.

The Trip Home

A few weeks after the end of the dig we had to pack up our belongings and prepare for the long journey home. The plan was that we would enter Israel and spend some time there and then proceed to Greece and Rome and from there through Europe to the Netherlands, where I had family, then on to London and finally fly from there to New York. Some of these connections we anticipated with correspondence, others we would make plans as we went along. We had no agent to work out our itinerary for us. We took all our belongings, including a big trunk, and went through the Mandelbaum Gate between East and West Jerusalem, not far from the YMCA (which was just about on the border). We had been informed about a wonderful hostel connected to a convent on the south side of Jerusalem and we booked in there. It was a real delight. I made contact with an American archaeological institute in West Jerusalem, where Ernest Wright was staying during a sabbatical. I had met him earlier at ASOR at Christmas time. I was introduced to some Israeli archaeologists, in particular Ruth Amiran, who also had an interest in Middle Bronze material and was most willing to help me in every way that she could. In my later publication on the Hyksos I made use of pottery drawings from her handbook on Palestinian pottery.

Shortly after I arrived in Jerusalem I ran into Malcolm Clark, who had been a graduate student at the same time as I at Yale. He was in Israel on a research leave with his wife. He also had a car of his own there and offered to take us on some trips in the region. So we went to some sites nearby, most notably, Lachish, which was a very impressive site. However, we did not stay long in West Jerusalem. I had some Anglican friends, Rev. and Mrs. Adney, who lived on Mount Carmel, overlooking Haifa; they had invited us to stay with them for a few days. So we set off by train for Haifa, where they met us and took us up to their place on Carmel. Rev. Adney was a clergyman with a little chapel and manse. His wife, Lora, an old family friend from college days, set about planning an excursion of archaeological sites in the Galilee region. We set out by car through the Esdraelon plain up to Nazareth, then on to the Sea of Galilee and north to Capernaum, where there were the fine ruins of a Roman period Synagogue. From there we went north to Hazor, a very large site by Palestinian standards. It had been recently excavated and the ruins were quite impressive. To the north-east was the lofty and imposing peak of Mt. Hermon and beyond that lay Damascus. On our way back from Hazor we stopped in Tiberius, a very pretty town on the Sea of Galilee, and spent the night in a Presbyterian hostel. The next day we went south and across the Esdraelon Plain again to the large archaeological site of Megiddo on the south-east slope of the Carmel range. We explored the extensive excavations that had taken place there, especially by the University of Chicago, and which have since been renewed by Israeli scholars. So many of these sites had been included in my archaeological studies at Yale and it was good to see them first hand. From the hot temperature of the plain we ascended to the top of Mount Carmel, which was much more comfortable.

Soon it was time to leave Israel for Greece. Mr. Adney had helped us to ship off our trunk to Canada and through his travel agent to get an inexpensive flight on Olympics Air to Athens. So from Lod airport in Israel we flew to Greece and stayed in a small hotel not far from the center of the city, and from there we could easily walk to the Acropolis. We explored the Parthenon and other temples, the museum, the Roman theatre, and other interesting antiquity sites in the region, as well as the wonders of central Athens. We also booked a four-day bus tour that included a marvelous circuit of great historic sites such as Corinth, Epidaurus, Mycenae, Olympia, Delphi, and several others. The tour package included coach travel, three nights in fine hotels and meals, and all of this for less than $125 for all three of us. The weather was warm but not hot and the countryside in spring was very beautiful. Once again my classical studies came alive in such a landscape.

From Athens we flew to Rome. While still in Jerusalem I had become acquainted with a couple of young priests who were students of Professor Patrick Skehan of the Catholic University of America, a scholar and specialist of the Dead Sea Scrolls. When I told the young priests of our plans to visit Rome on our way home, they immediately told us of an inexpensive place to stay. It was close to the school where some friends of theirs were living and they would inform them of when we were coming and they would be happy to show us around. So when we arrived in Rome, we went to the recommended pension, booked in and then called the young American priests who were studying in Rome. Their residence was just across the street so one of them came right over and the planning began for two rather busy days of sightseeing. They also took us to some good eating places that would fit our pocketbook. We toured St. Peters, the Vatican museum, and Sistine Chapel. We went to the Pantheon, walked through the Roman forum to the Coliseum, and the many ancient remains around it, drove around Rome in their small car, and visited one of the catacombs not usually open to visitor. They gave us a wonderful time and with their familiarity of Rome and the places visited, it was a great learning experience. Even my four-year old Peter was having a great time with the priests, who gave him their special attention.

From Rome we took a train north through Italy to Lausanne, Switzerland. My sister, Philippina, had an apartment in the city because she was working there, and although she was away at the time we had use of the apartment. A friend of hers, who also lived in the same apartment building, met us at the train station and after settling in, she showed us around the city. After a few days there we went on to Basil, and stayed a couple of nights in a hotel. I especially remember the visit to the zoo which was not far from the train station. We also visited the famous cathedral. The cities of

Switzerland, including Lausanne, would play a very important role later in my life, although I could scarcely imagine that at the time.

It was now time to board the train and head for my relatives in the Netherlands. I had never met any of these uncles, aunts and cousins before, and there were a lot of them. First we went to those on my father's side of the family in Apeldoorn and Ede and made the rounds there. Then after a few days we went to my mother's sister, aunt Jo, in Narden on the outskirts of Amsterdam, and she gave us our first taste of the big city and all its sites as well as many other interesting places in the region. After being spoiled by family for several days it was time to take the ferry across the North Sea and then the train to London. We booked a bed and breakfast in Russell Square near the British Museum. We spent some time in the museum, especially in the rooms of the Near Eastern and Classical artifacts and monuments. We also did a turn around London on a tour bus. We set aside a day to visit by train some of Elizabeth's relatives who lived near Chesterfield. While this was our first trip to England and London, it would certainly not be the last.

On the first of June we took an Icelandic Airline flight from London to New York where members of Elizabeth's family were waiting for us. After all the travel it was good to be back home. We were also broke. I had been given a grant of $4000 to cover my expenses and with an additional $1000 of our own money we had made that stretch to support the three of us, including all of our travel, food and shelter and incidental expenses. We had been responsible for all of our own planning and decisions, although as I indicated, we were given so much good advice and aid from so many persons all along the way. The entire year was a life-changing experience, with new horizons constantly opening up that would affect us for the rest of our lives. Those at Yale who made this possible knew how important such a year abroad would mean and trusted me to make the most of it. The sad fact is that within a very short period of time and down to the present day, which we could never have anticipated, it would be impossible for a family of modest means to duplicate what we were able to do in that year abroad.

Graduation

A few days after I arrived back in New Haven I graduated with a doctorate from Yale University, with members of my family from Toronto joining in the celebration, along with Elizabeth's family from New Haven. During the procession to the graduation ceremony, marching in alphabetic order, the person beside me was Vera Vanderlip, my former Latin teacher from High School days. It just so happened that she had decided in 1962 to return to graduate school for her doctorate in classics and I had met up with her again when she was registering at Yale Graduate School at the same time that I was returning to Yale after my time in seminary. It is likely that I would not have been in that graduation procession at all if it were not for the fact that when I changed by course of study in high school and needed to do two years of Latin in one year, Vera Vanderlip agreed to tutor me and help me to catch up the extra year. So it was a pleasure to march beside her on that day. It was also a great joy for me to have my parents there to see me receive that doctoral degree in the courtyard of one of the finest graduate schools in the world.

First Academic Appointment—Waterloo Lutheran University

After graduation and the celebration of that event, it was necessary to return to the reality of moving on to my employment in Waterloo, Ontario. I had made arrangements with my new colleague, Norman Wagner, to rent an apartment on Hazel Street, not far from Waterloo Lutheran University, so we had a firm destination. I rented a U-haul truck and we loaded all of the furniture and our accumulated possessions on board and set out for Waterloo, with me driving the truck and Elizabeth and Peter in our car, a "vintage" Plymouth. Everything went quite well crossing the border, and Norman Wagner helped us to move in when we got there.

Within a few days I was to begin teaching summer school and I obviously had had little time to prepare my course outlines, lectures, reserve reading etc. Furthermore, the subject was an "Introduction to the New Testament," which was not exactly my specialty. There were always a lot of students in the course because at that time there was a religion requirement of at least one course for every student in WLU. With Norm teaching Old Testament Introduction and with me teaching NT Introduction, and a great many students in each of these courses, this Bible teaching fully justified the existence of our two-man department. Whatever else we taught was up to us. Over the two years and three summers that I was at WLU, I taught NT Introduction five times. I also taught a portion of a survey course on ancient history, together with the Classics Department. My one-third covered the whole of Near Eastern history before Alexander the Great, while my classics colleague covered the histories of Greece and Rome. This course was a favorite of history majors and quite popular. In my other courses I could offer more specialized study of Near Eastern and biblical history and literature, and some classes in biblical Hebrew. The teaching load was quite heavy and I also did some weekend teaching to part-time classes. Needless to say, this did not leave any great blocks of time for research, to say nothing of non-academic activity.

Nevertheless, I was involved in two research and publication projects. The one was to finish the final stages of my work on the Hyksos book, which was at the copy-editing stage. The book was published by Yale Press in 1966 under the title: *The Hyksos: A New Investigation*. The book was very well received and I heard from a number of scholars, especially Labib Habachi, and some Egyptologists who considered me one of them. After fifty years this book is still available in paperback. My other research project was more long-range and involved carefully going over all of the evidence that had been presented by scholars in their support of an early second millennium BCE dating of the patriarchal traditions. As indicated earlier, I had become skeptical of such an early date during my graduate studies and I began to build on that with strong support from my colleague Norman Wagner. Elizabeth and I, with Peter, also made it a habit of visiting her family in New Haven once or twice a year and this gave me a chance to make use of the Yale library and especially the Babylonian collection with which I was so familiar. But with teaching summer school and a heavy load during the rest of the school year, my research progressed rather slowly.

A word should be said at this point about my relationship with Norman Wagner. He was a good colleague and friend, and our families got on very well. But more than that we had much in common in terms of our approach to biblical studies and discussions between us were stimulating and important to my future development in the field. Norm had been a graduate student of Prof. Fred Winnett at the University of Toronto and had done his dissertation with Winnett. The title of his dissertation was "A Literary Analysis of Genesis 12–26" and in it he very much espoused Winnett's views as reflected in the latter's 1964 Society of Biblical Literature presidential address, "Reexamining the Foundations" (*JBL* 84 [1965] 1–19). I was not at that meeting because I was in Jerusalem at that time, but I became aware of it soon after it appeared in print, and I was persuaded by its arguments. Winnett's thesis argued that there was a second Yahwist whose work was much later than the older stories of the Patriarchs, but this late Yahwist was limited to the book of Genesis. Winnett's much earlier treatment of the Moses stories (*The Mosaic Tradition*, 1949) was quite different in approach from the standard Documentary Hypothesis, and rather saw the Mosaic Tradition and the Patriarchal tradition as developing quite independently from one another. Thus he regarded the connection between Genesis and Exodus–Numbers as a much later development and ascribed this connection to the Priestly writer. All this was a quite radical reexamination of the Documentary Hypothesis on the Pentateuch that was the reigning compositional theory of the day. Norm's dissertation on Genesis 12–36 was an attempt to spell out in great detail the literary basis for this late Yahwist (which he called C for compiler). Norm gave me a copy of his dissertation and needless to say we had a lot of discussion about it. Unfortunately his dissertation was never published in any other form and remained quite unknown to Pentateuchal scholarship.

It should be pointed out that this was not the reflection of a "Toronto school" as some have suggested. Indeed, Norm had a lot of difficulty with getting his dissertation accepted, because the outside examiner at the orals, Prof. Simon DeVries, who was a close friend of John Wevers, was a diehard supporter of the Documentary Hypothesis and strongly resisted the dissertation's acceptance. It had to be revised in various ways to tone down its remarks against the Documentary Hypothesis. Needless to say, there was no love lost between Wagner and DeVries over this matter, and this was only the beginning of Simon DeVries's fight against the "revisionists," which in later years was directed at me. It was through Norm that I also became more closely associated with Fred Winnett from that time on, as well as with Donald Redford, who was also finishing his dissertation in Egyptology at Toronto at the same time, and came down to Waterloo from time to time to visit with Norm and me. Another scholar who became part of that Toronto group was Robert Culley, who had done his dissertation under John Wevers on the problem of oral tradition in the Old Testament, using the work of A. B. Lord (*The Singer of Tales*) and Milman Parry, long before it became the fashion at Harvard. All of these persons, but especially Norm, got me thinking about the basic literary questions relating to the book of Genesis and the Patriarchs, as well as the other research project in which I was actively engaged, that of the questionable second millennium dating of the Pentateuch. These two lines of investigation would eventually culminate in the two parts of my later book on *Abraham in History and Tradition.*

While in Waterloo, my family and I were active in the Presbyterian Church there, and I also consented to give an adult class on the book of Genesis, trying to introduce in a gentle way a more critical and mature approach to the stories of creation, the flood, and the Patriarchs. They were not to be understood as scientific or historical by modern standards but a reflections of the way in which Near Eastern cultures understood the world and their own remote origins. By means of these stories the authors (there was more than one) also attempted to articulate their own formulation of Israelite religion. I expected a certain amount of opposition and resistance to this kind of approach in a church Bible class, but to my surprise the response was one of eager acceptance and lively discussion and a certain relief by the participants that they were being treated as adults. Throughout my career, not only in churches but in other contexts as well, I did quite a few of these "not-for-credit" lecture and discussion presentations on biblical topics, and invariably it was an enjoyable experience.

Norm Wagner and the Canadian Society of Biblical Studies

Norm had a great gift of organizational skills from the very outset of his career and it eventually led to a very successful presidency at the University of Calgary. But that was some time down the road. One of the early tasks that he took on was the reorganization of the Canadian Society of Biblical Studies (CSBS) that had slowly dwindled to near extinction. Already before I arrived in Waterloo he, as president and Robert Culley as secretary, began to pump new life into CSBS by active encouragement, cooperating with other societies for joint meeting times and venues and some joint sessions, and publicizing the society to attract graduate students. It also established a connection for a time with the North American Society of Biblical Literature (SBL) as the Canadian regional meeting of SBL so that it attracted members from across Canada and even some from the US. Norm, Robert Culley and I all gave papers on a regular basis. Eventually, when SBL reorganized its system of regional meetings CSBS joined the Canadian Learned Societies Congress as part of a much larger gathering of associations of the humanities and social sciences, as it is today. Even when I taught in the United States I tried to maintain my membership with CSBS, although not always with my presence; but for a time it did lapse and was renewed again after an interval.

It was during a meeting of the Canadian Society of Biblical Studies together with the Canadian Church History Society in 1966 that I met a professor of Church History from Andover Newton Theological School (Newton, Massachusetts). Although he taught in the US, he was a Canadian. We got into private conversation and he asked me if I would be interested in teaching in a theological seminary and at Andover Newton Theological School specifically. I told him that I would seriously consider it, if the opportunity arose. It was not unusual at that time of very rapid expansion in post-secondary education for young academics, just coming out of graduate school, to be sought after by several institutions. The rapid expansion of the established universities and the building boom of new ones created a high demand for faculty members to staff them. Before accepting the job at WLU and later during my two years there I had been approached by a number of different institutions, including McGill, University of British Columbia, the University of Michigan, and the University of Toronto. While all of these were attractive, the offers came at times when other plans and commitments had already been made and I could not consider them.

In the fall of 1966 I did get an invitation to visit Andover Newton (ANTS) for an interview. I was favorably impressed with the quality and vitality of the younger faculty and the facilities of the seminary and I seemed to make a good impression on them. They made me an attractive offer and I accepted. When I notified Norm Wagner at WLU, he told me that WLU would match the offer from ANTS and I soon had a letter from the President that would make me an associate professor after only two years of teaching and would have raised my salary to a level above ANTS's offer. That is the way things were done in those days. It was tempting to take this counter offer, but I did not accept it for two reasons. First, I was not happy with the idea that one would go through the whole process of interviewing for a position only for the seeming purpose of getting more money from one's present employment. This happened frequently at ANTS and later when I was a chair at the University of North Carolina. Second, I still felt strongly that my calling was to teach in a theological school and I would not know if I would be happy there unless I tried it. And while I was very happy with my colleague Norm Wagner, I was not so happy with the current President of WLU. As it turned out, a lot of others felt the same about him and he was soon replaced after I was gone.

Years at Andover Newton, 1967–1970

The move to Newton Massachusetts was not an easy one; making an international move of this kind never is. Long before the move I had to get a packet of instructions on all that would be necessary for immigrating to the USA, including police records from places where I had lived, proof of employment and much else. This took months to track down. Since I had contracted to teach summer school in Orillia, Ontario, as an extension of WLU summer school, we had to hire a place to live there, put all of our furniture in storage and arrange to have it moved to our new address in Newton, MA just when we planned to get there from Orillia in mid-August. It also happened that Elizabeth was seven months pregnant with our second child. When we finally got to our new address in Newton, we expected the mover to show up at noon. Instead it was not until about 8 p.m. We lived on Cabot Street, Newtonville, and apparently in greater Boston there are many different Cabot Streets and it took the driver a long time to find our particular one. It was a very long day.

We lived in an apartment on the second and third floor of a large duplex, with an older resident living below us and the landlord living in the other half of the duplex next door. It was a pleasant neighborhood with a good school for Peter and convenient to the seminary, but we stayed there only a year. We bought our own house in Needham, Massachusetts, the following summer and enjoyed suburbia there. Peter adapted well to the new school and had friends in the neighborhood, especially the three brothers who lived across the street, one of whom was Peter's age. The suburbs of Boston consist of a large number of independent municipalities of varying sizes with their own governments, schools, police and fire departments, etc. In terms of population, Needham was one of those smaller, fairly homogeneous (mostly white) communities. There was a Presbyterian Church in Needham in which we were fairly active. There were now four of us, with Deborah arriving in mid-October, 1967. I set up my study in a sunroom off the master bedroom overlooking the back garden. We did quite a bit of redecorating the place, including the building of a recreation room in part of the basement. It was a habit of mine throughout my career to get involved in projects of gardening, remodeling, redecorating, repairing, and building. This I inherited from my father, and my brothers were all very good at this too. However, I was supposed to be a scholar and these handyman projects took up a lot of time. Yet with modest salaries many scholars also picked up these skills as well.

There was an episode in Needham in which we were personally involved during the last few months that we lived in there, which illustrates attitudes characteristic of such small towns in the suburbs of Boston at that time. In the spring of 1970, in anticipation of our move to Toronto, we sold our house privately to a new faculty member, Eddie O'Neal, who was coming to Andover Newton in the new term. The O'Neals were an African American family who would be quite exceptional in a solid white neighborhood. When the deal was made I decided to inform my neighbor next door. (There was no direct neighbor on the other side of the house, only an open field.) As soon as my neighbor opened the door, I sensed that he already knew all about the sale and was not happy. I tried to tell him that he was getting a wonderful family as neighbors, but he would hear none of it. He first accused me of not using a local realtor, by which he meant that such a person would have prevented this "disaster" from happening. I told him I was under no obligation to do so. He then told me that he would lose much of the value of his property on which he depended for his retirement. I argued that I was sure that this was not the case and would get evidence that would put his mind at rest. He told me that was not possible. In fact, just a few days later I happened to mention this episode to a member of the church whom I knew who was also vice-president of a company and who told me that he wanted to relocate in Needham where his firm had now relocated. He would be happy to buy my neighbor's house for whatever it was worth. I told my neighbor this, but it was immediately dismissed and he did not want to see me or any of my family again. They even lowered all of the blinds on that side of the house and rarely came outside in the backyard. Our little girl Deborah, who had been so friendly with this older couple, could not understand where they had gone. In stark contrast to this news of the new owners of our house was the young family of Peter's friends across the street. When I went to speak with them, wondering what the reception would be this time, it was entirely different. They were happy to have such a family as I had described and the color of their skin was of no concern to them. They wished us well and their boys continued to play with Peter until we moved.

Andover Newton Theological School was located on Herrick Road in Newton Centre, on a large piece of wooded hill-top property, but still near the center of town. It had several buildings with some of the teaching facilities and faculty offices quite new. One could hardly ask for better facilities. In 1931 Andover Theological Seminary, a Congregationalist seminary became affiliated with Newton Theological Institution, a Baptist school, and moved from its location on the Harvard campus to NTI's property in Newton; yet each retained their own faculties. However, two years prior to my arrival there, these two separate faculties now combined to form a new fully integration faculty with common facilities, under the name of Andover Newton Theological School. This was an interesting time at ANTS, which also seemed to be a combination of an old guard on the verge of retirement and a new crop of young scholars under a new young dean, George Peck, and the younger scholars were bursting with energy and innovation. This group of Max Stackhouse, Earl Thompson, Meredith Handspicker, Joe Williamson, and myself often met together to discuss issues relating to both theological education and the direction of the school specifically. We had the ear of Dean Peck, as well as his support, and we were given a lot of responsibility from the very start.

I had no sooner arrived on the scene at ANTS when I was asked to give an address to the faculty and student body at its opening convocation for the academic year 1967–68. I chose as my subject, "History and Myth in Biblical Interpretation." This may appear as an odd kind of talk to give to seminary students who expect to be told how they will learn to give Sunday homilies and run the affairs of their churches, but I was concerned that they become fully involved in the current theological debates of the day as they relate to biblical interpretation, and the issue of "myth" in the Bible, particularly in the treatments of Bultmann and the "new hermeneutic" scholars. For me theology was myth and myth theology, and it would not do to make biblical myth into something called "salvation history" and in that way confuse it with history while dismissing all other myths as unhistorical. It would be too easy for these pastors in the making to stand before their future congregations and simply say that the Bible was the revealed Word of God and therefore fundamentally different from all of the myths of other religions. This was when I realized, in the preparation and presentation of this statement, just where my studies and reflection had taken me. Brevard Childs at Yale could see where I was heading when I showed him my research paper from Princeton in 1962 and he rejected it and the possibility of my working with him. My address to the students was followed up by a fall convocation a month later (Oct 18, 1967), also dealing with the role of myth in biblical interpretation. Presentations were made by Professors Morton Enslin, Professor of Religion at Bryn Mawr and Helmut Koester, Professor of New Testament at Harvard Divinity School. I was appointed as one of two respondents to these lectures and it resulted in lively discussion, in which Koester, a disciple of the Bultmann School, and I had particular and basic differences. All of this came at a time when things were rather hectic for me and my family because Elizabeth gave birth to our daughter Deborah the very next day.

My teaching program at ANTS was entirely different from that at WLU, which meant that I had to develop a whole new set of courses from scratch. But I was now teaching more particularly in the field of my primary interest: Old Testament Introduction, Old Testament Theology, Biblical Hebrew, and various exegesis courses. This gave me more chance to reflect on the problems of literary criticism, particularly the Documentary Hypothesis and to test the ideas of Winnett and Wagner. In Old Testament Theology I paid particular attention to G. von Rad's theology, which was now available to students in English. It was the history of the biblical theological traditions that especially interested me. These interests I now added to the historical research that I was deeply involved in with my on-going critique of the Albright School. The early results of this latter activity were two articles: "The Problem of Childlessness in Near Eastern Law," *Journal of Biblical Literature* 87 (1968), and "Jacob's Marriages and Ancient Near East Customs: A Reexamination," *Harvard Theological Review* 62 (1969). Regarding the first article, since Morton Enslin was the editor of *JBL* and we had met at ANTS in the fall of 1967, he accepted my article very quickly and it appeared in a rather short period of time. The second one, which I submitted to *Harvard Theological Review*, went through the hands of Frank Cross, and he was not so quick to act on it. However, with a little prodding he handed it over to his colleague, the Assyriologist William Moran, who went over it together with me and suggested a number of improvements. I, of course, accepted these changes and the article was published shortly afterwards. From that time onwards Moran and I were on friendly terms and I had the greatest admiration for him. I had already encountered Moran's work when I studied Assyriology under Goetze at Yale, and the latter had highly praised Moran's scholarship.

This brings me to make a comment here on my wider relations with Harvard and my colleagues in Near Eastern Studies there. Andover Newton had a special connection with Harvard because Andover Theological Seminary was originally affiliated with Harvard and located on Francis Avenue where Harvard Divinity School is now located. Andover Hall, the library of HDS, is actually the old library of Andover Theological School and the collection was never moved to the Newton campus. So ANTS faculty and students have the right of access to the HDS library.

Regarding the faculty of Harvard's Near Eastern Studies, I had met Ernest Wright previously at ASOR in Jerusalem and had corresponded with him on a number of matters and he was familiar with my work on the Hyksos and had made it known to some of his doctoral students. He also wrote a favorable review of it for the Andover Newton Quarterly. While I was at ANTS he was always most cordial towards me and invited me often to seminars that might interest me. When there were special speakers he would not only invite me to attend but also to join him and others at a Harvard faculty club reception and dinner afterwards. On one such occasion he invited Ted Campbell of McCormick Theological Seminary, a very close friend of Wright who worked with him on the Shechem dig. This also gave me a chance to reconnect with Ted and it was quite enjoyable. On another occasion Roland deVaux was the speaker, which gave me the chance to meet this venerable scholar from the Ecole Biblique in Jerusalem. He told me that he had read my book on the Hyksos and regarded it highly, which pleased me very much. On the other hand, my relationship with Frank Cross was always cordial but never very close. He did not particularly approve of the direction that my historical research was going, as reflected in my *HTR* article mentioned above. Later I would become a major critic of the Johns Hopkins (Albright) and Harvard (Cross) schools of biblical studies that so dominated biblical scholarship in North America.

There was, however, something slightly ironic in my relationship with Harvard. When considering the various graduate schools while I was in Toronto back in my senior year (1957–58) I scrutinized the programs of both Harvard and Yale. The most prominent scholar that I recognized at Harvard was Robert H. Pfeiffer. I was quite familiar with his learned *Introduction to the Old Testament*, but at that stage in my thinking his work was much too liberal for me and I could not see working with him. On the other hand, at Yale I knew the work of Millar Burrows on the Dead Sea Scrolls and owned both of his books on the subject and had worked on the scrolls material in my senior year. I even wrote to him and he said that I would be most welcome at Yale but that he was retiring. Yet he was sure that I would be happy there nonetheless. What I did not know was that Pfeiffer at Harvard was also retiring, and that he would be succeeded in 1958 by Ernest Wright from McCormick, and that Frank Cross had also come to Harvard from McCormick in 1957. As an undergraduate I was very much attracted to Wright's book, *God Who Acts*, and would have enjoyed studying under him. And I would also have been strongly attracted to work under Cross on the Dead Sea

Scrolls. I just did not know, at the time I made my decision, that they would be there in 1958 and would have so completely suited my interests and theological orientation at that time. There are many today who could not imagine me as a member of the Harvard School, but looking back, it was a very close thing.

In addition to my teaching duties at ANTS I was involved in administrative obligations and other activities. The dean was keen on undertaking a revision of the curriculum and course offerings and I was made chair of the biblical department with the task of streamlining our offerings. My colleague in Old Testament, Prof. John Scammon, was in his last year of teaching and we would need to search for a replacement, and the New Testament had also recently experienced a similar retirement. Furthermore, Prof. McLean Gilmore, a quite distinguished senior scholar in New Testament, took his own life after suffering numerous bouts of deep depression. This meant that by default I was rather heavily involved in the searches to fill these positions. The whole department of biblical studies would receive a radical makeover in a very short time. Beyond this formal seminary business I discovered another matter that was the cause of some discontent among my colleagues, particular the more senior ones, towards the administration (the president and dean), which called for some attention. It was over the question of faculty salaries. There was no salary scale related to rank and each person's remuneration was directly negotiated with the dean and president in private. Consequently, through casual conversation with my colleagues I learned that I was not only making more than my fellow junior colleagues but even more than some of the much more senior full professors. The system at WLU had been radically different. Your rank of assistant, associate, and full professor reflected your worth and therefore your salary range within that rank. So, after some conspiratorial discussions among the younger activists, in which I explained this model of compensation and about which they had no prior experience, we held a general meeting of the faculty, without the dean, on this issue. We put forward a proposal to be presented to the administration and the board of the seminary whereby they were asked to implement a set salary structure and to move towards rectifying the inequities of the past over a set period of time. Needless to say there was overwhelming support from my colleagues for such a proposal and I was chosen as "shop steward" to meet with the board.

We informed the president of our intentions and requested an audience with the board and a date was set for the meeting. I went to the John Hancock building in Boston to its executive suite to join the board of the seminary, who were also its principle benefactors as well as senior managers and owners of various companies. To many of them the whole process seemed like a union negotiation and they were not happy with it, but apart from asking for a little clarification of the details they said little in favor or against it. They merely thanked me for my presentation and then informed me that the meeting was over and they were going to lunch, to which I was obviously not invited. When I reported back to my colleagues about the meeting, they were not pleased and communicated this displeasure to the president and dean. The result was that a committee of the board and the administration and financial officer worked out a fair and transparent pay structure that seemed reasonable to us and then inaugurated this with a large catered dinner of faculty and board members together. This was a very smart move on the board's part and did wonders for creating a bond between the faculty and board. The change to the new system was going to cost the seminary a good sum of money to set the system right and it was agreed that they would have to spread its implementation over three years. But it was a victory and greatly improved the esprit de corps of the faculty. For me personally it was an omen. Unlike at WLU where I could leave this kind of dealing with senior administrators to Norm Wagner, in future I would inevitably become involved in such mundane matters at the expense of being engrossed in pure scholarship.

There was another project in which I also became involved. The theological seminaries in the greater Boston area had recently formed a loose cooperative union known as the Boston Theological Institute, in an attempt to share resources, facilities, and programs. One attempt at this by the various biblical studies programs was to appoint Professor Philip King of St. John's Diocesan Seminary in Brighton, Massachusetts, and me to organize a special event to which all the Old Testament faculty and students would be invited. The two of us met together and discussed various possibilities. There had been a recent publication by Brevard Childs, *Biblical Theology in Crisis* (1970), which challenged the current modes of doing theology in biblical studies, particularly of the kind reflected in Ernest Wright's very popular book, *God Who Acts*. The idea was for Childs to come and give a public lecture to be held at ANTS in late afternoon and then all attending faculty of the BTI would retire to the lounge and banquet room for drinks and an evening meal together after which there would be an open discussion on the issues raised in his paper, based upon this lecture. I was delegated to approach Childs personally about this. Childs was a little reluctant to do it because he believed there might be a confrontation with Wright on this issue. I assured him that all would go well and he accepted (Childs was not yet that well known). The lecture was superb and was well received and at the dinner I arranged that Childs and Wright sit together because I knew that Wright was a very gracious and courteous person, along with the equally gracious Philip King, who chaired the session. Once the lively discussion got going, it soon appeared that Wright and Childs (both followers of Karl Barth) had more in common than Wright and his colleague Frank Cross. The latter was strongly committed to a history of religions approach, which was very problematic for Barthians. At any rate the program was a success and Father King and I had done our bit for BTI. We also got to know each other through this process and were long-standing friends afterwards.

Reflecting on that meeting, I recall that I did not say much. I was a junior scholar in that crowd with no published position in Old Testament theology. Much of Childs's original criticism of my Princeton essay was based upon his former commitment to a salvation-history theology, which in this latest work he was now giving up. Yet I could not accept his new "canonical" approach, which came to dominate his work for the rest of his life, because from a historical-critical point of view the notion that the canon was divinely inspired was a myth, and all myths are phenomena within the purview of the history of religions. He could never have accepted what I had said in my convocational address, if he had ever read it. I enjoyed the lively discussion on that evening, but I was in a theological wilderness. This event took place towards the end of my ANTS period and I was ready for a change.

Furthermore, the period from 1967–70 was one of great upheaval in America, which had a big impact on life in the seminary community. This was the period of the Vietnam War, and as a landed immigrant in the USA I had a draft card, although it was never likely that I would be called up to serve. But one way for young men to avoid the draft was to go to seminary and thus get an extension. So seminaries such as ANTS were inundated with applications, and in examining them it was very difficult to discern the motive of the one who applied. There was, among this student group, as there was with some of the younger faculty, a high level of activism on this issue. But I was a foreigner and felt that my role should always be a rather moderate one, although I certainly had no sympathy with the war. Some students expressed this opposition by insisting that the study of Marx should be an option or even compulsory while biblical studies should not be required. Also important at this time was the concern for greater equality and opportunity for blacks with an attempt to admit and support more black students and reflect their concerns within the curriculum. And then there was the women's liberation movement, with more admissions for women and more of the theological program geared to reflect their concerns. Alongside all of these pressures was the movement at many institutions to hold "town meetings" to reflect and debate all of these issues and to rate faculty members by one's presence or absence as to how committed he or she was on these matters.

While all of this was going on, I began seriously to consider what I was doing in a seminary at that time. Certainly, there were many enjoyable aspects to my work and teaching at ANTS, not least of which was a fine group of colleagues and friends. But I was there to try to help students prepare for ministry in their future churches and I was not certain enough at that point that I was really helping them. I decided I was a scholar and I had to do that, and it was too easy to become completely distracted in this environment with a lot of other concerns that were not related to my own scholarly interests. The general atmosphere was not conducive to a very scholarly way of life, so I began to think of other possibilities. Professor Ronald Williams, chairman of the Near Eastern Studies Department at the University of Toronto, had originally approached me about whether I was interested in a position at Toronto at the time that I was already committed to coming to ANTS. Now I got in touch with him to see if that position was still open. The result was that he offered me a position at Toronto beginning in the fall 1970, at the rank of Associate Professor and I accepted.

It should be noted that at that time many institutions did not have search committees, reviewing the merits of multiple candidates. The department chair or the dean simply offered a position to a particular person and if one was interested then one could negotiate the terms. Thus, while I was at ANTS I also had a completely unsolicited offer from UCLA that included a salary figure. However, I had no real interest in moving to California at that time, and I immediately declined. Williams actually made a number of appointments about the time that I arrived in Toronto, and many members of the department did not even realize that they were coming until they arrived.

2

Toronto Years, 1970–1977

The long-distance move back to Canada was something of a disaster. The movers loaded up our belongings, one of three different households on the same truck and set off. We stayed long enough to transfer ownership of our house to the O'Neals and then set off for Toronto. My brother Richard had found us a temporary place to stay in Willowdale, North York, in greater Metropolitan Toronto, and not too far from where my parents lived. We rented this furnished home for a couple of months while we looked for a house of our own. My brother had also arranged for storage of our furniture whenever it arrived, until we could move into our new place. That was the plan. A few days after we arrived back in Canada we received a phone call from the moving company that there had been a fire on the moving van in New Jersey and that some of our load of goods was destroyed. When it finally arrived at my brother's storage facility it was a very depressing mess. There followed a long, drawn-out process with the insurance company as to what could be saved or repaired and the replacement cost of what were lost. Among the items lost were most of the mementos that we had collected during our stay in the Near East and travels through Europe, and a large part of my library, as well as files from my years at Andover Newton. It was not a very pleasant way to start our time in Toronto.

First let me deal briefly with domestic and family affairs during the Toronto years before turning to the ivory tower of academia. Of course these two realms were never so neatly divided with frequent overlap, although my family often made reference to my life in "another world." We bought a new home in east Scarborough, in the Port Union region at the end of the Go Train line, near Lake Ontario. Of course it had the bare minimum of landscaping so it needed fencing, trees and shrubs, and flowerbeds and the interior needed a lot of decorating. All this we did ourselves in our spare time. I commuted by Go Train and subway to the university on a fairly regular schedule, like the 8 to 5 crowd. We joined the local Presbyterian Church, but even so we never became too deeply involved or rooted in this community, and I can scarcely recall any close connections made there. We only stayed two years. Our main connections with friends and acquaintances were with other members of the faculty who were Toronto people and lived within the heart of the city, and being on the very edge of Toronto we seemed out of touch.

So we sold our house in Scarborough and bought an older and a little smaller house in Leaside on Bessborough Drive. It was very convenient to everything, to the schools, to the Presbyterian Church, to shopping and public transportation, even to the hospital, where they had an excellent family medicine group that had someone on call 24 hours a day. In this community we made many friends and connections that lasted for years, up to the present. Our children made close friends in the neighborhood and became involved in lots of groups and activities, some through the church, others through the school. Of course there were also some renovation projects to keep me busy. The old galvanized plumbing need to be upgraded, so I tore it all out and put in new copper plumbing in its place, after getting a few pointers from my father about soldering. Of course it meant a big hole in the kitchen ceiling to get at the pipes in the floor of the bathroom, which meant a new ceiling and some remodeling in the bathroom. And with the new plumbing we decided to upgrade the kitchen sink and counters and new doors and handles on the kitchen cupboards. And there was the refurbishing of the basement bathroom and new ceiling tiles in the basement recreation room. It is remarkable how one thing led to another.

The last refurbishing job that was done on the house was to tear down the sunroom at the back of the house off the dining room and to rebuild it entirely with new walls and siding, new sloping roof, new windows and door, new wiring and baseboard heating, new floor. This also meant taking out a door in Deborah's bedroom that lead to the outside onto the flat roof of the old sunroom (a very bad idea) and replacing it with a window. The result, I am happy to say, produced a very nice little room.

Of course, besides all of this extracurricular work we as a family liked to do what so many other Toronto families liked to do and that is to escape to the lake district of Muskoka or Haliburton for some holidays and to have our own little place on a lake. So the first few years, while on vacation, we would take some time to look for a piece of property for a cottage, and we found and bought a site on Lake Potash in Haliburton. The next step was to put up a building on the site. We cleared the site for the building and the lane into the property. We then bought a Viceroy cottage building kit that consisted of all the necessary construction components with instructions about how to put it together. I hired a person with a backhoe to dig out some trenches for the footings and then constructed footing posts in them with concrete blocks. Then, while the four of us camped on the site, a big truck delivered the building kit all in one giant package and we began to build. Elizabeth and I, with a little help from the children, put up the whole three-bedroom cottage in less than two weeks. We had the roof on and shingled just before the rain came. The next season I completely wired the cottage. All of this took place over several seasons and a lot of travel back and forth with a trailer behind the car hauling materials, furniture, etc. Of course, we enjoyed the many activities of such a summer place, swimming, canoeing on the lake and fishing. Peter and I love fishing after dark in the canoe, listening to the hoot of the owls and the cry of the loons, with the myriad of stars, the milky-way and the meteors overhead. And there were so many places to hike and explore in the whole region.

What has all of this to do with being a biblical scholar? Nothing directly, but a great deal indirectly. There is always the challenge of creating a balance between two worlds, with the often conflicting demands and joys of each. And I was certainly not alone in attempting to negotiate the tension between these two spheres of activity. One can understand the basic demands of teaching and class preparations, grading papers and exams, office hours for students, department meetings and committees, etc. These can all be done at the office, the department, the university during specific times allotted for them. But what about the time for research and writing at one's home study or in the library? And not just during the school year, but in the breaks between semesters? That supposed free time was viewed in one way by the family and one's commitment to them and another way by the expectations of academic colleagues and administrators as to the level of one's scholarship and productivity. I have tried to give a brief summary of the kinds of things I did in those ambiguous spaces of time, over and above all of the usual family activity, in order to set into context what I attempted to do in the academic world of biblical studies. This will be a recurring theme in what I recount throughout this piece.

Turning now to that academic world, my first year in 1970–71 was something of a fill-in year while things were still very much in transition within the department. At that time there were two independent undergraduate departments in the two colleges, University College and Victoria College, which were part of a joint program under a common coordinating chair. After my first year I served for a time as the coordinator of this program, under the title Chairman of the "Combined Departments of Near Eastern Studies," which simply meant doing all the committee and paper work while the real college chairs, Professors Ronald Williams of UC (my boss) and Ernest Clark of Victoria had all of the power. My primary teaching responsibility was in the area of Old Testament Introduction and History of Israel, and the teaching of 2nd year Biblical Hebrew with emphasis on grammar and syntax. Ted Lutz of Victoria College and I organized the OT Introduction course in such a way that I would teach the first half, starting with the broader issues of interpretation and then focusing on the Pentateuch and Historical books, and Ted would deal with Prophesy, wisdom literature and poetry in the second half. In addition to our lectures both of us would split the class into a number of sections and conduct discussion tutorials with the students. The class was quite successful as a student draw such that the two chairs, Clark and Williams decided to take it over, although it was not really their areas of expertise. But they were the bosses. Williams even plagiarized my course outline with only minimal changes.

The chair of the graduate program was John Wevers, which he organized and ran with great skill. In addition to the faculty from both colleges, there were also members from the Royal Ontario Museum who had adjunct status or joint appointments, so that the total for the program as a whole was about 14 members and this gave us a number of fields in the history and archaeology of Mesopotamia, Egypt and the Levant (including Israel), Septuagint, Aramaic, Syriac and Targumic studies, and Jewish studies. Islamic studies, which had once been a part of Near Eastern Studies, had in the 70s a department of its own. One of the requirements of all incoming graduate students is that they had to take an introductory course in the civilizations of Mesopotamia, Egypt and Israel, with Kirk Grayson teaching Mesopotamia, Donald Redford teaching Egypt and I taught about ancient Israel. In this way the three of us could pretty well judge the levels and comparative excellence of all the incoming students each year. And all the students shared the experience of surviving or enjoying this course together. In addition to this course I also taught graduate seminar courses in the Pentateuch and the Historical books of the Hebrew Bible.

During my first year at the University of Toronto I was asked by the University College Lecture Committee to open the college lecture series, and I chose the topic "The Social Function of Tradition in Ancient Israel." (It appeared some years later in print.) The sociology of tradition was a theme to which I returned frequently throughout my career. I was especially influence by the great Chicago sociologist, Edward Shils and his book *Tradition* (1981), as well as others outside the field of biblical studies. In addition to giving this lecture for the college I was soon involved in other college matters, such as a committee headed by the college Principle, Hollis Hallett, along with five other college members, to select a new Chairman for the Near Eastern Studies Department. I was one of three from Near Eastern Studies, the other two being Kirk Grayson and Cuyler Young, Jr, an adjunct member from the ROM. Ronald Williams was finishing his fifth year as chair in 1972, so we were to choose his replacement. For the three of us the choice was obvious, that of Professor John Wevers. Among his many gifts he was a superb organizer with experience in running things of all kinds. Thus Wevers became the chairman and a new era began for the department.

On the level of graduate studies Wevers continued on as chair to reshape it into an effective program with a marked increase of students and a new reputation of excellence. People began to refer to it as the "Toronto School," which was quite misleading because while Wevers certainly dominated the area of Septuagint, along with Albert Pietersma, his former student (who actually had strong opinions of his own), the other areas of research had a lot of methodological independence. There was nothing like a Harvard School or a Johns Hopkins School at Toronto. During my first three years at Toronto, Kirk Grayson was the graduate secretary under John Wevers and did a wonderful job of organizing the administration of the student files. For this I was especially thankful because Wevers chose me to succeed him in the fall term of 1973. Even before this I had often made the practice of having lunch with Wevers in his office. We both brought bag lunches, and while I was graduate secretary we talked about many subjects regarding the department, especially the Graduate program. Before each graduate studies meeting we would review all of the problems and issues to be discussed, so that all of the business could be completed within an hour.

In contrast to these formal meetings, however, there was a long-standing practice of all the members of the Near Eastern Studies faculty having lunch together once a week at the faculty "high table" in the college dining room in the Sir Daniel Wilson residence, and after lunch retiring to the senior common room. It was in this open and unregulated atmosphere that vigorous discussion and debates took place about a whole range of subjects, including matters pertaining to the department, the university, guest speakers and the like. And we got to know our colleagues much better this way. John Wevers was a very strong advocate of this practice because it separated this kind of informal discussion, which often came up with good suggestions, from the more formal business of the departmental meetings. Unfortunately, when we moved out of University College in 1975, we no longer had access to the college dining room and we found no workable substitute for it.

As graduate secretary I was also involved in the humanities division of the University of Toronto Graduate School and this meant some involvement with administrative duties on this level. One such duty was occasionally to chair a doctoral orals examination in another department. It was the custom in the Graduate School for all such orals exams to be chaired by a member from outside of the home department conducting the examination, and graduate secretaries who were supposed to know all of the rules of the Grad School seems like a good source from which to choose such persons. Another committee of the Grad School was the one which met periodically to review petitions for deadline extensions on thesis completions and other such matters. At the same time I was also asked by University College to serve on college committees, one of which was to review and recommend revision to departmental governance and other such matters. It is possible that at a social event of the college I might have mentioned to Principle Hallett that I thought the way in which chairman in some departments made appointments with little input from the rest of their colleagues should be reevaluated. So I got put on the committee. The chair of the committee was Professor Shepherd of the Classics Department, who had been one of my undergraduate professors, and after many meetings discussing many things he wrote up a huge report that was delivered to the principle and presented to the members of college. However, by that time the university was engaged in reorganizing the whole college system and the relationship of college departments to university departments. This meant that the report was shelved. We became a university department in 1975 under a quite different set of guidelines. Needless to say, all this administrative experience and exposure gave me considerable expertise in administration, whether I wanted it or not. My ambition was to become a good scholar, not an administrator.

When I arrived at Toronto in 1970, Professor Fred V. Winnett was in his last year of teaching. (After he retired I was lucky to inherit his fine office.) Winnett, Wevers and Williams had all been my teachers during my undergraduate program. The rest of my teachers of Hebrew had all retired by then. During Winnett's last year, he and I took many coffee breaks together and of course we discussed issues relating to our common interest in Pentateuchal criticism. Prior to this we had had conversations from time to time at the Society of Biblical Literature, together with Norm Wagner, and in his final year in the department we became good friends. I was working on some articles related to Pentateuchal criticism, which I had started at ANTS and it was helpful to bounce them off of Winnett. The first of these articles, "The Terms 'Amorite' and 'Hittite' in the Old Testament," I submitted to *Vetus Testamentum* in the fall of 1970 and it was accepted and published in early 1972. The editor of this journal, P. A. H. (Pete) de Boer, was a good friend of a number of persons in the department and he became a friend of mine also. The point of this article was to demonstrate that the way in which this geographic terminology was used in the Pentateuch corresponded to its use in Assyrian and Babylonian texts no earlier than the seventh century BCE, and this anachronistic use would date these texts as no earlier than the seventh century and some parts of the Pentateuch could be much later. Against the Albright school, these names of peoples could not be used as historical references to political entities of the second millennium BCE.

The second article, "The Conquest of Sihon's Kingdom, A Literary Examination," I submitted to the *Journal of Biblical Literature* in January of 1971. I had a lot of respect for the editor, Joseph Fitzmeyer, but this piece was controversial and challenged the status quo on its dating and historicity, and the editorial board was heavily stacked by those who would likely oppose it. The process was a long drawn out one with a split decision, which Fitzmeyer resolved in my favor. It was eventually published in late 1972. Up to this point most scholars, particularly those of the Albright School, regarded the battle by the Israelites against the "Amorites" of Heshbon in Trans-Jordan as described in Num 21:21–31 as a memory of an actual battle against a major city of the region in this area in the late second millennium BCE. Shortly after my article was published, excavations were conducted at Heshbon hoping to find this second millennium city. Instead all they found were traces of a village for the early period, and archaeology revealed that it was only much later, in the second quarter of the first millennium BCE that a city of any size became established on the site. My analysis was completely vindicated. As it turned out, my article was frequently cited for years afterwards by British and European scholars.

The third article, "Confessional Reformulation in the Exilic Period," I also submitted in early 1972 to *Vetus Testamentum*, because I knew that Pete de Boer was sympathetic to the approach that I would take in it. He not only accepted it but rushed publication so that it appeared about 6 months later. With this article I clearly set out for the first time the direction which my literary criticism of the Pentateuch would take. In it I argued that what was generally regarded as the oldest literary source or author in the Pentateuch, the so-called Yahwist, found in portions of Genesis, Exodus and Numbers, was actually later in date that the book of Deuteronomy. This was a position that I would frequently argue and defend for the rest of my scholarly career.

During this period from 1970 onwards I was also actively involved in both SBL and CSBS, giving these studies in the form of papers to the societies. Professor Rolf Knierim of Claremont was the chair of one of the groups in which I regularly gave papers. He had been a doctoral student of von Rad in Germany, so we had this von Rad connection in common. We had a long and close friendship within SBL. In February of 1972 I received a letter from Professor Patrick Miller of Union Theological Seminary in Richmond, Virginia, announcing that at the forthcoming SBL meeting in Los Angeles in September, there was going to be a special session with "a major paper by George Mendenhall on the Abrahamic narratives and traditions," and I was asked to be one of three persons responding to the paper. The other two were Frank Cross and Loren Fisher. The curious thing about this arrangement was that the deck was stacked in favor of the Albright School. Cross and Mendenhall had both been students of Albright and Fisher's position was close to their views. Miller, who arranged the whole program, had also been a student of Cross at Harvard. From my recent papers at SBL, they all knew where I stood. Of course I knew what to expect, so I told them I would be happy to do it. A copy of Mendenhall's paper was promised for April but did not arrive until August. I never saw such an incoherent mess. It was also full of factual errors. And Mendenhall was a professor at the University of Michigan, Ann Arbor. So in my fifteen-minute response all I had time for was to point out all of the factual errors and some of the obvious weaknesses of the argument. Of course, Mendenhall was quite unhappy and made some brief dismissive remark to me and then spent all of his time in conversation with Cross on subjects that seemed to have little to do with the paper. Mendenhall never forgave me for those fifteen minutes for the rest of his life. This conference was still three years before my own book on Abraham appeared, but the lines were already drawn between the Albright followers and myself.

While my primary focus of activity in academic associations was within SBL, I was also reengaged with the Canadian Society of Biblical Studies (CSBS) in which Norm Wagner played a leading role and in which Robert Culley was the society's secretary. While Wagner eventually moved on to other things, Culley remained a bulwark of support to CSBS throughout his career and a close friend. I regularly offered papers at the CSBS. I was also a member of the American Schools of Oriental Research (ASOR), whose primary focus of research was Near Eastern archaeology, especially Palestine. ASOR in Jerusalem, where we spent that wonderful year in 1964–65, was renamed the Albright Institute and this organization was dominated by Johns Hopkins and Harvard graduates. ASOR soon held joint meetings with SBL on the national level and often on the regional level as well. This was convenient for many biblical scholars who were active in both societies and who could therefore attend sessions in both meetings at the same time and location. For me membership in ASOR was a way to keep up with archaeological information and those engaged in it. I occasionally offered a paper to this group as well. My Toronto colleague, John S. (Jack) Holladay was particularly active in ASOR and in archaeological research in Palestine. His Harvard mentor, Ernest Wright, along with Ted Campbell, were major figures in the organization, and Wright's archaeological students, including Holladay, played a major role in ASOR. They were all adherents of biblical archaeology and its defense of the biblical tradition concerning the historicity of the patriarchs, the exodus story and the conquest of Canaan by Joshua. My own work in archaeology as it related to my history of the Hyksos and in my subsequent studies made me something of an outsider and suspect to many in this organization, in particular to Prof. William Dever, a student of Wright. Dever became a major spokesman and leader of this group.

In 1969 Donald Redford and a number of his Egyptological students in Toronto decided to form a Canadian Egyptological society, *The Society for the Study of Egyptian Antiquities*, with its own journal, and the following year with the aid and financial support of Geoffrey Freeman, a businessman and amateur Egyptologist, they drew up a charter and I was invited to join the original group and become a charter member, along with Ronald Williams and members of the Egyptian department of the ROM. It was a remarkably successful venture, with an active program of both scholarly meetings for academic papers and public lectures. The SSEA also attracted a number of scholars from other parts of Canada and from the USA, and additional chapters were eventually established in other Canadian cities. While I was primarily a spectator at its meetings, it nevertheless allowed me to remain in touch with the field, with considerable benefit to my future work, especially when I had to deal with issues related to the biblical tradition of the Israelites in Egypt.

By my third year at Toronto I had been teaching eight years without any sabbatical leave, so it was agreed that I could take off the second semester of my third year to complete my research and writing of a book dealing with historical and literary problems relating to the biblical traditions of the patriarchs. The plan was for me to go to New Haven alone for the winter and spring of 1973 where I could work in the libraries of Yale, particularly the Babylonian Collection in the main university library, and the Divinity School library. I was very familiar with these collections and I had complete access to them. I would stay with my in-laws there while Elizabeth and the two children, who were in school, would remain in Toronto. During the fall semester, 1972, in anticipation of my spring leave I had been in contact with Profs. Marvin Pope, Brevard Childs, and William Hallo, curator of the Babylonian Collection, about my plans to do research at Yale. As a result I received an invitation to give a Woodward Lecture in the Graduate School in April of 1973 on the subject "Was There Ever a 'Patriarchal Age'?," which I did. Of course I argued in my lecture that there was no credible evidence for any such period in Israel's prehistory. Two Yale professors at the lecture who had argued in print in favor of such a patriarchal age were Hallo, who chaired the lecture, and Prof. J. J. (Jack) Finkelstein, an Assyriologist of some distinction. I had in fact dared to offer arguments against one of Finkelstein's articles on the subject. In the question period that followed Finkelstein was the first to respond and he immediately said that he accepted my critique completely, not only of his own article on the subject but the whole endeavor to make historical figures out of the patriarchs. I was amazed and delighted. This admission, of course, left Hallo speechless. Later when Hallo took me to lunch he told me that he was not convinced by my lecture but that he would need to be a little more careful in what he had to say on the subject. We continued to be on good terms, in spite of our differences, for many years after that. I also got in touch with my mentor, Harald Ingholt, who had been retired since my graduation, and we had a pleasant and prolonged lunch together. He strongly supported my research as always.

For the first couple of months at Yale all went very well and I made good progress on my research and writing. There was, however, a serious family crisis in the spring that interrupted the best laid plans. My mother-in-law, where I was staying, had a serious coronary episode in which her heart stopped beating in the middle of the night. The paramedics came and managed to get it going again and she was rushed to the hospital where she remained in critical condition for several days. As a result Elizabeth had to take the two children, Peter and Deborah, out of school and bring them down to Hamden (a suburb of New Haven) to help her father cope with the situation and the care that her mother would need when she came home from the hospital. The children were put into Hamden schools for the rest of the school year, which was most upsetting to them. Furthermore, Elizabeth could not bring our dog, a lovable Airdale, to the USA on such short notice, so with great reluctance she had to give him up to the humane society animal service, who found a good home for him elsewhere. All of this was a major disruption in our lives.

When matters had settled down a bit and Elizabeth's mother was home again, it was decided that I should return to Leaside so as not to leave the house empty too long and Elizabeth would stay with the children until the end of the school year. Most of the research was done on my project, and it was a matter of getting the writing done which I could do as well or more easily in Toronto. So I drove the family car back to Leaside and returned again to pick them up at the beginning of the summer. Even while I was on leave I was not entirely out of touch with my NES department home at Toronto. Already in the spring of 1973 John Wevers, along with Grayson, Redford, and members of the Classics department had been planning a joint faculty seminar on ancient historiography for the winter term of 1974 and they wanted me to participate. I was, of course, keen to be involved, but this meant that no sooner would I be finished with one major project than I would become involved in another, this one focused much more on the historical books of Joshua to 2 Kings.

By this time in mid-1973 word was getting out through my articles in scholarly journals and in papers read at SBL and other meetings that I was challenging the status quo regarding the historicity of the patriarchal narratives of Genesis, and this led to a number of invitations from various societies to give more lengthy presentations on the subject. In the summer of 1973 I received and accepted an invitation from the American Oriental Society through Professor Jack Sasson of the University of North Carolina, Chapel Hill, to give a special presentation at the annual meeting in Santa Barbara, CA, in March of 1974. The program of this venerable society covered studies dealing with the whole of the ancient and modern "orient," divided into three units, Ancient Near East, East Asia, and Islam. Within the Ancient Near East division there was a strong emphasis on Ancient Mesopotamia and cuneiform studies in which North American Assyriologists played a prominent role and some of whom had a keen interest in biblical studies as well. Among the latter was the very active young scholar, Jack Sasson, who became a major figure in this society in later years, especially in program development.

I had been associated with AOS in the 60s but my membership had lapsed. So it was a surprise to get this offer from Jack. The suggestion had actually come from Hallo, who was also active in AOS, as a result of the Yale lecture a few months earlier. The topic for the session (one and a half hours) would be "Dating the Patriarchal Traditions," with my talk taking forty-five minutes and the rest of the time would allow for a response by Professor Dean McBride of Yale Divinity School—a Harvard grad and member of the Albright School—and questions from the floor. I would also provide a detailed outline of my talk two months prior to the meeting, which could be distributed beforehand. Bill Hallo was, in fact, the one who chaired the session, and because of that fact he sent me comments on my paper, based on the outline I had provided ahead of time. The meeting itself went very well and the text of the meeting was widely distributed long afterwards. In addition to McBride, another scholar very prominent in the Albright camp, Professor David Noel Freedman, was there, but he said little.

In November of 1973 I received a second invitation from Professor Gene Tucker of Candler School of Theology at Emory University, Atlanta, Georgia, inviting me to the meeting of the Colloquium for Old Testament Research in the summer of 1974 at Yale University as a guest of Dean McBride. The paper and its discussion would take up a full morning or afternoon session. The Colloquium consisted of about a dozen of the younger Harvard students of Wright and Cross (with the exception of Tucker, who had been a fellow student with me at Yale), and it was like going into the lion's den. My Toronto colleague, Jack Holladay, was a member. Of course I accepted the invitation. The family would be visiting Elizabeth's parents anyway, so it was easily done. For this meeting I would deal with the literary critical aspect of the Abraham tradition which I had been working on for my book. This would not duplicate the talk that I had given to *AOS* since McBride would attend both meetings. Needless to say, I enjoyed this vigorous exchange of views, which was beginning to become a habit. It should also be noted that although the Yale doctoral graduates in Old Testament studies did not have a corresponding colloquium, we did tend to correspond with each other and send offprints and notices of our activities. There was a striking difference in interests between the two groups, with the Yale group little affected by the Albright School.

In January, 1974 I received yet a third request for a long paper from Robert Culley of McGill, representing CSBS. I had submitted a proposal for the usual 20-minute paper for the CSBS spring meeting, but in place of this Robert suggested that I expand my presentation and they would give it a full session with two respondents, who turned out to be Professors Sean McEvenue of Loyola College, Montreal, and Norm Wagner of WLU. I would, at least, have one person in my corner for a change. My paper, "Hagar's Flight (Genesis 16) and Expulsion (Genesis 21), A Discussion of Method," would deal with the literary problem of explaining the presence of texts representing parallel episodes in the Abraham narratives. Both of my respondents were interested in this issue but from quite different perspectives. This meeting took place at the end of May, 1974. (In the fall of 1974 I received yet another invitation from Professor Jeffrey Tigay of the University of Pennsylvania, again at the suggestion of Bill Hallo, his former teacher at Yale, to make a presentation at the east coast regional meeting of SBL, similar to the one that I had done for AOS. By this time I was now focused on other things and I turned it down.)

In the spring of 1974 I completed the revisions of my manuscript on *Abraham in History and Tradition* for Yale University Press. This study had served as the basis of all those papers that I had been giving during this period. Shortly after I had submitted the manuscript to Yale, I received a letter from Piet de Boer of Leiden, telling me that he had just received a book for review in *Vetus Testamentum* of which he was the editor, titled *The Historicity of the Patriarchal Narratives: The Quest for the Historical Abraham*, by Thomas L. Thompson (Berlin, 1974). It would appear that I had been "scooped." The reason why de Boer wrote to me so soon was that he had visited the University of Toronto a few days earlier where he had a number of personal friends in our department, and I had had a chance to speak with him about my work in which he had a strong interest. So it was little wonder that he wrote to me immediately on his return to Leiden. I also got hold of the Thompson book as soon as I could and looked through it. Thompson clearly took the same skeptical view towards the historicity of the biblical patriarchs and the "quest for the historical Abraham" that I did, and there was some overlap in material that I dealt with in the first half of my book. Indeed, he was aware of a few of my earlier articles. However, there was nothing comparable in Thompson's book to the literary study that made up the second half of my book. His position on these matters seemed to follow more closely those of his German mentors at Tübingen. So I decided, being at the copyediting stage of production, to take some note of his book, but not to pull the manuscript back for a more detailed revision at this stage.

At the same time that I was engaged in all of these endeavors, and my regular departmental teaching and administrative responsibilities, the winter semester was taken up with the activity of the historiography seminar, chaired by John Wevers. Kirk Grayson covered the various genres of Mesopotamian historiography; Donald Redford focused on the king-lists, annals and day-books of Egypt; Professor Harry Hoffner, an invited guest from the Oriental Institute in Chicago, dealt with historical texts of the Hittites, and I concentrated on the historical tradition of the biblical books from Joshua to 2 Kings. Contributions from the Classics department were by Professors Peter Derow on Polybius and Timothy Barnes on Eusebius. There was one paper given in each weekly seminar covering six weeks, and in addition to presenting a paper, each participant was also responsible for offering a critique and leading the discussion on one of the other papers. It was a remarkably successful and stimulating experience as well as a lot of work. All of the papers were eventually published in one form or another, whether as lengthy articles in journals or expanded into monographs.

I did publish my paper in the journal *Orientalia*, along with those of Grayson and Hoffner, but more importantly I entered on an important new phase of my scholarship, that of ancient historiography in general and biblical historiography in particular. For me, the biblical study of this subject would always be within the larger comparative context of both classical and Near Eastern forms of history writing. This is the project that would lead to my next book and, indeed, to much of my work for the rest of my career. This new field of study also re-awakened in me my past undergraduate training in the classics, and especially in the Greek historians, and I made it a point to be closely associated with classical scholars both at Toronto and later at UNC, Chapel Hill.

The mid-70s was a time of particular ferment in academic disciplines, such as biblical studies and the larger field of religious studies, and I found myself very much involved in both. In German biblical scholarship there had been a very strong movement in the development of a new method of literary criticism called "form criticism" (*Formgeschichte* or *Gattungsgeschichte*). In the history of Old Testament studies the major figures were Herrmann Gunkel and his followers, Albrecht Alt and Hugo Gressmann. Gerhard von Rad, a student of Alt, had introduced me to form criticism at Princeton. In New Testament studies the major figure was Rudolf Bultmann, whose students dominated the field both in Germany and America. In my own field of Old Testament studies, this movement was belatedly making an impact, in which the Yale students of the German trained Childs, such as George Coats, Burke Long, Malcolm Clark, Gene Tucker, and Bruce Birch, played a prominent role, as well as the Heidelberg scholars, Erhard Gerstenburger and Rolf Knierim. All of these persons were close friends of mine, so it was only natural that I was involved with them and some others in creating a form criticism study group within SBL.

My own interest, arising out of the Toronto historiography seminar, was in the contribution that form criticism could make to the study of biblical historiography. There were both positive contributions that this method could bring to biblical studies as well as serious weaknesses and dangers that were not always avoided. On the positive side, the benefits of this method are obvious for such collections as the book of Psalms, Proverbs, and the prophetic books where the variety of different forms or genres and their diverse social settings is quite apparent. Within the Pentateuch the variety of legal genres in the law codes has also long been recognized. With respect to the narrative portions of the whole corpus from Genesis to 2 Kings, the matter becomes much more debatable. On the one hand, the form-critical method provided a much needed antidote to the biblical archaeology movement of the Albright School that seemed to treat all of the biblical texts in the same way, as if they were historical documents. Indeed, they viewed the whole German approach of Gunkel and his followers to biblical narrative as nihilistic towards early biblical history. Nevertheless, form criticism demanded that one try to understand the genre or form of any particular narrative unit and its use in its original social setting, before one passed any judgment upon its usefulness in constructing a national history. Stories judged to be folk tales or ancestors legends or myths of origin and derived from the traditions of individual local tribes, could not be used to reconstruct a history of Israel in the modern sense of that term.

On the other hand, there was an implicit danger in the German concept of *Formgeschichte* which attempted to use the method to understand the history or evolution of forms to correspond to the evolution and sophistication of thought and rationality, and to social evolution from primitive tribes to statehood, the apex of what was often deemed to be the time of the "Solomonic Enlightenment." The irony is that while Gunkel read everything in the historical narrative, from the patriarchs of Genesis to the time of David and Solomon in the books of Samuel and Kings, as leading progressively to this highpoint of historical thought and rationality, what follows in the rest of the books of Kings was viewed as corrupted by the theology of Deuteronomy and therefore a degeneration of the form in Dtr to the end of the monarchy. It was this method of wedding the critical analysis of form to an ideology of historical development that could be just as destructive and misleading as the simplistic historical methods of biblical archaeology. Needless to say, I did not figure all of this out immediately. My remarks regarding these dangers are made retrospectively. The advantages of form criticism in the study of comparative historiography seemed obvious to me from the start and I began to offer papers in the Form Criticism group of SBL.

Another development in academia at large in the 70s was the scholarly study of religion as an academic discipline in its own right, often under the rubric of the Comparative Study of Religions, within its own department. Many colleges and universities, particularly those that were church related, had undergraduate departments of religion, with a compulsory course requirement, invariably in biblical studies but sometimes in "other religions" as well. One could always borrow faculty from other disciplines to teach one of these courses, as we did at WLU when I was there. But the notion that religion should be treated as an academic discipline in its own right was slow to develop. In the late 60s the American Academy of Religion was formed to advance the study of religion in colleges and universities and hold annual meetings and these meetings were arranged in combination with the meetings of SBL. At the University of Toronto, those colleges within the university that still maintained church connections, such as Victoria, St. Michaels, and Trinity, all had required courses in "religious knowledge." The effect of all of this new ferment in religious studies was to develop a combined graduate program as a Centre for Religious Studies with its own director, quite independent of the college programs. It would draw its graduate faculty from a wide range of university departments, and that meant that Near Eastern Studies was involved.

One of those behind this ambitious development was Willard Oxtoby, professor of Religious Studies at Trinity College, University of Toronto. Willard had started his career in biblical studies, and that is where I first met him many years earlier, but then he decided to do a post-doctorate at Harvard in comparative religions. Now as member of an interim executive committee to gather possible adjunct faculty for this proposed center and as a friend who knew my work, he asked me to join this group. This meant a whole new set of meetings and planning sessions, as well as discussions on the academic study of religion. At the time, of course, I did not realize that I would belong to such a department of religious studies, just a few years down the road. My interest in ancient historiography would need to include the historiography of religious studies in general and of Israelite religion in particular.

At long last, in June of 1975 my book, *Abraham in History and Tradition,* was published by Yale Press. The two books, Tom's and mine, became known as the Thompson-Van Seters attack on biblical history, and the Albright School and its sympathizers went on the counter attack. The very popular textbook, *The History of Israel* by John Bright, a student of Albright, went into a new edition after the appearance of our books; he noted them but dismissed them without discussion and with the brief comment that "it is to be doubted whether their positions will gain general or lasting acceptance." In fact, he was quite wrong. It was not long before other histories and introductions appeared in which our position was readily accepted. The last holdouts were the biblical archaeology crowd who sold their archaeological endeavors to lay supporters largely on the grounds that they were indeed uncovering biblical history, and anything that undercut the amount of historical content in the Bible was bad for business and fund-raising for their activities. Conservative Christians and Jews, who made use of biblical archaeology in support of their belief in the historicity of the Bible, tended to vilify me, even though they knew little about me or my evangelical past.

In the summer of 1975 there was a major change in the University of Toronto colleges, in which individual college departments in Near Eastern Studies and Classics became consolidated into single university departments within the Faculty of Arts and Sciences. For us this meant a move out of University College and Victoria College and into new quarters in the newly renovated "Borden" building on Huron St, which also used the first floor as a textbook store. The property of the former Borden's Dairy had been taken over by the university some years earlier. This building had once been the repair shop for the dairy and my father had actually worked in this building when I was a child. Our move to these newly renovated quarters did not go well. We were ready with all of our books packed the last week of August, but the building was not quite ready and it was not until mid-September after the beginning of classes that we finally got in. It was not the best way to start a new school year. However, Near Eastern Studies now occupied the third floor with all members of the faculty located in the same place. John Wevers was chair of the whole department as well as chair of graduate studies. John Revel took charge of the undergraduate program so that between the two of them the department was run very well.

In response to my book on Abraham and my articles I began to get a lot of correspondence, not only from North America but also from Europe, particularly the Netherlands. Pete deBoer and I corresponded about my book, of which he strongly approved, and also about my developing views on Israelite historiography. He was trying to organize a European study group on biblical historiography and wanted me to be part of it, but the group did not work out. Nevertheless, in anticipation of my next sabbatical, which was expected in a couple of years, he invited me to come to Leiden, and I was keen to do so. However, my move to Chapel Hill in 1977 did not permit that. I also had considerable correspondence with another Dutchman, C. H. G. de Geus of Groningen. He was hoping to come to Toronto on a sabbatical leave but it did not work out. He had sent me a copy of his book, *The Tribes of Israel*, first in the Dutch edition and later in the English edition. It was a thorough critique of what was at that time a very popular notion, especially in Germany, regarding the organization of the Israelite tribes in pre-monarchic Israel. The thesis, advocated by Martin Noth, was that the twelve tribes were united in an amphictionic league around a central sanctuary and in this way shared their traditions and commitment to a single deity. De Geus's work, to my mind, completely demolished this thesis, and I told him so and subsequently cited him in my publications. This led to correspondence on other historical matters. The fact that I had a Dutch name seemed to attract notice and give me affinity with an increasing number of Dutch and Flemish scholars.

I also had a lot of correspondence with Robert Culley. We shared publications and discussed his studies on oral tradition, a topic that was very much used and abused in biblical studies, but in contrast to many others, his work was solid and well-grounded in the latest sociological research, and I made much use of it. We remained close friends throughout my career. On the American scene, in addition to my Yale friends, my new research in historiography put me in closer touch with Professor Max Miller of Emory, whose writing was primarily on Israelite history and who chaired a section in the SBL program on this subject. I began to submit papers for this group and we became close friends and have remained such over the years.

In the fall of 1975 I had an appendicitis attack, and this put me in Sunnybrook Hospital for a few days. In the process of getting my appendix removed I acquired a stitch infection which meant that they had to open the wound up again and have a grain inserted with daily dressings for an open wound until it gradually closed. This was quite a bother, especially since I was slated to give a paper at the SBL meetings in Chicago, and while at the meetings I had to change the dressing everyday myself. Elizabeth thought that I was a little "off my rocker," but I survived. I missed very few classes with health problems and the students did not seem to mind the break.

During this year I was in touch once again with a former friend and fellow student of Yale Graduate School, Stanley Walters, who was now a professor and Chair of the Department of Religion at Central Michigan University. Stan had received his doctorate in Assyriology, although his main interest was in biblical studies. Both Stan and Adrienne, his wife had been friends with Elizabeth and me while in New Haven, and for a time they were also connected with the Evangelical Free Church in New Haven, where Elizabeth's father was the minister. Their background was quite as conservative and evangelical as ours. Now there was a position open in Old Testament at Knox College in Toronto, the Presbyterian seminary on the University of Toronto campus and Stan was considering applying for the post. He assumed that I would be familiar with the position, which I was, and I encouraged him to apply. I also volunteered to give him other necessary information on housing in the Toronto area and on immigration matters. The result was that he was given the position and moved to Toronto. Knox College was only a short walk from our department offices, so I would see quite a bit of Stan for the next couple of years.

In April, 1976 I was informed by John Wevers that I would be promoted to full Professor of Near Eastern Studies as of July 1st. This was based in large part on the publication of my book, *Abraham in History and Tradition*, as well as several articles and other writings. At the same time Wevers was leaving town for a two-month research trip to Göttingen, Germany, where he was involved in a major project in the editing of the manuscripts of the Septuagint, to produce a new critical Greek text. While he was gone he informed the Dean of the Faculty of Arts and Science that I would serve as signing officer for the department. This, of course, was no great chore except for one particular item. While Wevers was gone the new salary evaluations would need to be made and I would need to sign-off on them. Before he departed therefore, we met in order to anticipate this task of setting salary increases. The scheme that I was instructed to use was quite simple. On the merit or discretionary portion of the increase, all would be the same. Wevers was quite averse to making these kinds of judgments and I was happy to comply.

In March of 1976 I was invited by Professor A. L. Basham, Head of the Department of Asian Civilizations at the Australian National University, to participate in a session of the 30th International Congress of the Human Sciences in Asia, to be held in August in Mexico City. The University of Toronto would cover my airfare, and my subsistence expenses would be paid for by a grant from the Australian government. The theme of the session was to be a comparative study of kingship in Asian civilizations, and I would represent those of the ancient Near East, including Israel and Judah. The Mexican government contributed much to the hospitality for the congress, so that we had a great banquet and a few sightseeing trips, including one to a pyramid temple site. The Anthropology Museum was also quite spectacular. The whole was a very memorable experience.

While the congress was quite large, those representing the ancient Near East and Egypt (which was somehow also included within Asia) did not make up a very large group. Many of them were at the session in which I gave my paper and this gave me a chance to become acquainted with international scholars whom I had not met before. A couple of these scholars stand out in my memory. There was an Egyptologist, Professor Säve Söderbergh of Uppsala, Sweden. He had written on the problem of the Hyksos, taking a position against the majority view and I had made use of his work in my thesis and book. So when he met me he treated me as if I were a fellow Egyptologist and was delighted with what I had written. I told him that I was no longer working in Egyptian studies, but he would hear none of it. What I had written on the Hyksos was qualification enough, especially since the archaeological evidence that was now being dug up in Egypt was proving us correct and we could laugh at those scholars who had so easily dismissed our work. This would not be the last that I would see of him.

Among the Old Testament scholars at the congress, whom I met for the first time, was Gösta Ahlström of the University of Chicago. He was a Swedish scholar from Uppsala and a former student of Engnell, as was my old friend Magnus Ottosson. Ahlström was actually much better qualified to speak on the subject of Near Eastern kingship than I was, and I told him so. He did not get a chance to comment on my remarks during the session because one pompous scholar (Werblowsky), who was not qualified in the field, took up all of the time with his comments, and I did not get the chance to speak with Ahlström again at the congress. Nevertheless, he wrote me a long letter afterwards and that was the beginning of a long-standing friendship. We were both considered outsiders and mavericks at SBL so we often got together for at least a dinner at the meetings whenever we could. His Chicago students also considered me as one of their gang. They had little sympathy with the dominant Albright–Cross contingent.

Another scholar with whom I spent considerable time at the Mexico congress was Professor Mitchell Dahood of Rome. He was a former student of Albright and an expert of Northwest Semitic languages, and of course an avid follower of the Albright School. He was a most amiable person and we got on very well together. What made our discussions interesting was the fact that just a short time prior to this congress there was a great archaeological discovery that members of the Albright School claimed would prove that Thompson and Van Seters were wrong about the biblical patriarchs. Italian archaeologists had excavated a huge site in Northern Syria, which turned out to be the ancient city of Ebla, and in the debris they had found a very large quantity of cuneiform texts, very well preserved, dating from the late third millennium BCE. Most of the texts were written in ancient Sumerian, the literary language used in Southern Mesopotamia at that time, demonstrating a strong cultural and commercial link between Ebla in Northern Syria and the cities of southern Iraq, such as Ur. Some texts appeared to be written in the local Northwest Semitic language of Northern Syria, using the Sumerian system of cuneiform writing, which made them very difficult to translate. Nevertheless, this did not prevent rather wild speculation about their content and connections with the figure of Abraham. It was even being suggested that Abraham had undoubtedly passed through Ebla, coming from Ur and Harran on his way to Canaan.

Mitch Dahood was at the very center of the debate because he, as an expert in Northwest Semitic, was the one in Rome who was working together with an Italian scholar of Sumerian in an attempt to translate these texts, and it was his sporadic reports appearing in the press, that gave rise to the suggestions about biblical connections. Here was my chance to get the goods on this find from the horse's mouth. So I got together with Dahood, along with a few others, and I said, "OK, Mitch, tell us about these texts and how you set about to decipher them. What kind of texts are they and what are they about?" He explained that at this point they did not know what kind of texts they were or their overall content, only that they think that they have identified a number of individual Semitic words. But even this was extremely doubtful because they first assumed that they were dealing with a particular Semitic dialect that was similar to the language of the region a millennium later and the cuneiform syllabic script made it difficult to even tell where a word began and ended. So I confronted him with a news clipping containing claims that the texts contained the biblical story of the Flood, references to the names of biblical figures, such as Abraham, and the like. He had to admit that all of these claims were based upon his tentative suggestions regarding a few Semitic words that he thought he could identify in the texts.

Needless to say, Mitch took a ribbing about his discoveries, but he was very good natured and enjoyed the fun. He was quite convinced that he would still be proven correct, and there were many who continued to follow him in this. In later years when I encountered Dahood at SBL meetings we would have a chat as old friends and reminisce about our time in Mexico City. Unfortunately Dahood's career ended in an untimely death, and I was one of many who missed him.

One scholar who made a great fuss about the Ebla texts and Dahood's treatment of them in support of biblical historicity was David Noel Freedman, and he continued to champion them for some years. However, virtually nothing of all that so-called evidence has survived. What I learned from that all too short friendship with Dahood was that we could accept each other for who we were, in spite of our conflicting views. He was completely honest with me about what he knew and did not know concerning the material he was trying to decipher, and I was always up front with him. That is the way academic dialogue ought to be. However, there were many in the Albright camp who were quite dishonest and vitriolic in their attacks on Thompson and me, and we lived with those consequences for many years.

At the annual meeting of SBL three scholars from Sheffield University in England began to show up on a regular basis, David Clines, David Gunn, and Philip Davies, and I got to know them quite well. David Gunn and I were in a regular program section on biblical narrative. Both of us were interested in the Saul and David stories, although from somewhat different perspectives, so we carried on a lively debate about these issues, reflected in some of our published papers of that time. These three scholars also started a new journal, *Journal for the Study of the Old Testament*, published by Sheffield University Press. They asked me to contribute an article for the first issue, which I did: "Problems in the Literary Analysis of the Court History of David." This was a review of David Gunn's writings on this subject, so our discussion over the literary analysis of the David story continued for some time. For *JSOT* this was the beginning of what proved to be a very successful publication venture.

At the same time that I gave *JSOT* a piece for their first issue, they asked me to contribute to a scholarly discussion, along with several other prominent Old Testament scholars, dealing with an article by Professor Rolf Rendtorff on the Pentateuch: "The 'Yahwist' as Theologian? The Dilemma of Pentateuchal Criticism." This was an English translation of a German article published in 1975, at about the same time that my own book on the Abraham tradition appeared. The second half of my book also dealt with the problems of Pentateuchal criticism, although from a somewhat different perspective. Then, in 1976, another book appeared by the Swiss scholar, Hans Heinrich Schmid, titled *Der sogenannte Jahwist*, which also dealt with "observations and questions regarding Pentateuchal research." So Schmid was now brought into the discussion. Likewise included in the list of contributors to this *JSOT* issue were George Coats, my good friend from Yale who had done his dissertation on the Pentateuch, Norm Wagner, my former colleague from Waterloo, and Norman Whybray of Hull, UK, a senior British scholar. This made for a memorable issue very early in the life of this journal and one that was frequently cited.

What was significant for me was that this new development in the discussion about the Pentateuch was a major shift away from the American obsession with the concerns of the Albright School over historicity to a largely European and Germanic interest in literary criticism. Wagner was, of course, a student of Winnett, who had started the ball rolling with his SBL presidential address of 1964, and Wagner's dissertation on Genesis would make heavy use of German scholarship. George Coats, while studying at Yale under Childs, actually wrote his dissertation in Göttingen under Walter Zimmerli. But it was particularly Rendtorff, Schmid, and I who were increasingly identified as the "revisionists" in Pentateuchal criticism, and the North Americans who were "reactionaries" and defenders of the older methods of literary criticism. That is not to say that there were not significant differences amongst the three "revisionists." I did have some serious reservations about Rendtorff's approach to the problems in Pentateuchal criticism. But more on that later.

The one thing that happens when you become a scholar advocating a controversial position is that you get a lot of correspondence and invitations to give lectures, which can be both a blessing and a problem. There was still interest in the archaeological questions and I was invited to fly down from Toronto to New York and do an interview for BBC television on their program, "The Age of the Patriarchs," which I did in November of 1976. About the same time I was invited by Professor Jonas Greenfield of the World Union of Jewish Studies, to attend their Seventh World Congress in Jerusalem in the summer of 1977, to give a paper on the religion of the patriarchs. I had also made plans to attend the International Organization of Scholars of the Old Testament Congress in Göttingen that same summer to meet my European counterparts. However, both of these summer engagements needed to be cancelled, because of my change of employment and move to North Carolina, in the summer of 1977.

Before I move on to this next phase of my career, let me make a few comments about my colleagues at Toronto. They were a superior group of energetic scholars, mostly young with great energy, and they created a wide range of research projects that offered both permanent and temporary employment, in addition to dissertation subjects, to a large number of graduate students. Toronto in a short time rose to be one of the premier programs in Near Eastern studies in North America, with an international reputation. Much of the leadership credit for this goes to John Wevers, who encouraged and facilitated it. During my last two years in Toronto, when we were in the Bookstore Building, Don Redford, Jack Holladay, and I made it a habit of meeting together for morning coffee and talk about topics of mutual interest. Both Don and Jack were enthusiastic about archaeology, Jack with his work in Palestinian archaeology and Don with his digs in Egypt. Of course I had my own interests in the archaeology of the Egyptian delta, because of my work on the Hyksos, which covered both these worlds. Jack had always worked under someone else at Shechem and Gezer, but he wanted to have his own dig and run it his way. Both Don and I had visited Tell el Maskhuta in the Eastern Delta region of Egypt in 1965 and we were enthusiastic about having this large site excavated. The site was identified as the historical location of Pithom, which was mentioned in the biblical story of the Israelites in Egypt, as well as in Herodotus. It was situated in the eastern end of the Wadi Tumilat. Jack was a strong proponent of biblical archaeology, while Don and I were not, and usually we gave him a hard time about his views. However, on this site our strategy changed. We suggested to Jack that this site could be an important test for the historicity of the Moses story. Let's dig it up and see just what it can tell us about this city in the time of Ramesses the Great, who was considered by the biblical archaeologists as the Pharaoh who had enslaved the Israelites in Egypt to build Pithom. Jack bought the suggestion and began to make plans and raise money for the project. I was planning to accompany him on the initial survey of the site in the summer of 1977, but a change in my summer plans meant that I would join him on the Egyptian dig in 1978. (More on that later).

3

The Move to UNC Chapel Hill

Let me begin by going back to the set of events that led to my move from Toronto to Chapel Hill. I received a letter from Professor Giles Gunn of the Department of Religion at the University of North Carolina, Chapel Hill, in January of 1977. He was chair of a committee conducting a search for someone to fill the James A. Gray Professorship in Biblical Studies. This was an endowed chair with an attractive salary and additional funds for research and travel. The previous occupant of this chair, Bernard (Bunny) Boyd, had died of a sudden heart attack, after occupying the position for about 25 years. On behalf of the department, Gunn invited me to apply for the position. There were two people in the department whom I knew from previous contact, Jack Sasson and John Schutz. I knew Sasson from my membership with, and involvement in, AOS, and John Schutz was a graduate from Yale Graduate School in New Testament, and we had interviewed him to fill a position at Andover Newton, but he went to Chapel Hill instead. Both had something to do with my name being suggested for this search, as did the recent publication of my book, *Abraham in History and Tradition*, which was quite familiar to Sasson. I decided that there was no harm in taking up the invitation to visit Chapel Hill in order to talk about the position and what it would entail.

I flew down to North Carolina in early February and was met at the Raleigh-Durham Airport by Ruel Tyson, the department chair, and Charles Long, the department's Kenan Professor and formerly of the University of Chicago, with an international reputation. We had a light supper and talked together at Ruel's place for some time, until I turned in for the night at the Carolina Inn. I met other members of the department the next day and I gave a public lecture that was intended to be appropriate to a Department of Religion. Because of the short notice, I used the lecture that I had given at the University College assembly my first year in Toronto: "The Social Function of Tradition in Ancient Israel." It had not yet been published and it suited the orientation of the department very well.

After the lecture I met with the entire department alone and they peppered me with lots of questions about my methods and approaches to biblical studies and the study of religion in general. My work with Erwin Goodenough at Yale, under whom John Schutz had also studied, and a course in the Sociology of Religion at Princeton, had given me a good background for doing biblical studies within the context of contemporary religious studies. Their major concern was to establish a clear break with the previous pattern of biblical studies by Bunny Boyd that had been dominant for many years. He taught large classes in both Old and New Testament and was very popular. He was hardly a fundamentalist by southern standards, but he was very homiletic in his style. He also worked together with Israeli archaeologists and supported their excavation projects with fund-raising, although he was not himself an archaeologist. He was certainly within the "biblical archaeology" tradition. He had a large and avid student following, but many in the rest of the university regarded his teaching with some suspicion. He never published anything scholarly, although he was known far and wide throughout the state. It was not difficult to convince the religion faculty that I was not another Bunny Boyd.

One of my major concerns was that the department did not have a graduate program, although with the recent new appointments they were hoping to move towards establishing one. There was already at least an MA program proposal in the works, but getting a PhD program would be a bigger hurdle. However, even with such a program, it seemed to me that it would be difficult for Jack Sasson and me, with some help from David Halperin, a rabbinic specialist, to compete adequately with other programs for good students, let alone train them satisfactorily. The answer to this, it was suggested, was cooperation and coordination of our program and faculty with Duke University, just ten miles down the road. Charles Long already had a joint appointment with both UNC and Duke, and there was a special joint program in Judaic studies between the two institutions, which had enabled Halperin to come to UNC. There was also a draft document laying out the guidelines and principles by which the two institutions would cooperate on the graduate level to make the best use of the resources of both institutions. This was already the case with some other programs. All of this seemed very encouraging to me and I could see real possibilities.

There was, however, one fly in the ointment, and I should have taken it more seriously. This was the fact that all of those in the Old Testament field at Duke were either former students of Albright (Orvel Wintermute and Roland Murphy), or Harvard (Eric Meyers), or Brandeis (Carol Meyers). However, I scarcely knew any of these persons before I came to Chapel Hill, and I was perfectly content to work with them, but I discovered over time that this sentiment was not shared, especially by the Meyers. Of course, I was given no indication that there would be any problem with developing a working relationship with them. Sasson, indeed, was very optimistic and the whole atmosphere at Chapel Hill was quite euphoric. It was clear after the few days that I was there, that they wanted me, and very soon after I returned I received an offer of the endowed chair. Still, after much discussion with Elizabeth, we decided against it and turned it down. Yet they said that we did not need to make the decision so soon, and so we kept on debating the pros and cons (during some very cold February weather), and changed our minds about it.

I called Tyson back some days later and said that I would accept the offer. Plans were immediately made for Elizabeth and me to fly to Chapel Hill for a visit during winter break. The weather in Chapel Hill was like spring with flowers blooming, robins singing, and mild temperatures. We were treated royally, introduced to all kinds of university officials and faculty and given instructions relating to immigration. We also did some looking at real estate and found a house on Hoot Owl Lane that would soon come on the market, and we could make a deal on it. It was much larger than what we had in Toronto, with a lot of land with many mature trees, and it was not far from the university. Yet it would cost less than what our present house was worth. We were now firmly committed to moving once again.

Once I had made the decision to accept the position at Chapel Hill, I informed John Wevers about it. We discussed the pros and cons. He knew that I was not happy about the prospect of having no graduate students doing their doctoral research with me in the immediate future. I could not compete with either Wevers or Clark and that would likely be the case for some time. He told me to be patient and that I would certainly have them in due course. He also notified the Dean of Arts, Robert Greene, who wrote to me and asked me to come and see him. He was very gracious and friendly and wanted to talk me out of it, but I had made up my mind. There was no chance of Toronto matching Chapel Hill's offer, and I never liked the common practice of using an offer from another institution to bargain for a raise in salary.

Thus I began the huge task of preparing for this international move to the American South. The paper work for such a move was extensive, and there was no longer time enough to go through the whole process of receiving immigration status as a permanent resident. Instead I had to obtain an H-1 visa with a three-year limit, during which I could file for permanent residence. I had no idea at the time what a headache all of this would be, and I received very little good advice from the office for foreign nationals at UNC. It took me four months just to get my H-1 visa and about two years for Elizabeth and me to finally get our "green" cards. Both Peter and Deborah were born in the USA so they were already US citizens. We did the whole process ourselves, although I have known others at UNC who paid special immigration lawyers thousands of dollars to do it all for them, although even that does not prevent the need to visit a government immigration office in Atlanta and go through the final bureaucratic process of getting one's Green Card (which is actually blue).

Another major step in the process was to sell the house and the cottage. I had to finish quickly the construction of the new back sunroom and then put the house and cottage on the market. There was a very active market in housing in Toronto at that time and following real-estate advice we put it up for what seemed like a very large amount. At the open house we received an offer, that was very close to the asking price and we took it. We had lived in the house for five years and had admittedly done some upgrading. Nevertheless, in that period of time the value had more than doubled. The cottage was not so easy to sell and when it did we recovered the cost of the land and the materials and expenses that went into its construction, but little for all of the labor expended in building it. We could not have kept the cottage for summer use because it was too far to travel from North Carolina to Haliburton to make good use of it. We never did invest in another one.

This move was the most difficult one that we had made or would make, and I suppose that we have thought about it endlessly since that time. The fact is that there was so little time, from the invitation to visit Chapel Hill to the acceptance of the offer and the rush to get everything done in time that it was scarcely possible to get all of the necessary information about such a move and to consider everything properly. Those who had the least say and who may have been affected the most were our children, Peter and Deborah. They would now part with friends and the familiar environment of school and church and have to adjust to a whole new setting and new schools, make new friends and find their way.

There is always a certain time lapse of a few days between the time that the moving van loads all of your possessions into the van and the time that it gets unloaded at its destination. We stayed overnight in Toronto and the next day, after the sale of the property we set out for the border at Queenstown-Lewiston, just east of the eastern end of Lake Ontario. The crossing and immigration took some time with more paperwork, but we were finally on our way. Since we had time to kill, we decided to go south by way of the Skyline Drive and Blue Ridge Parkway, which begins in Virginia and runes along the top of the mountain ridge and watershed, through Virginia and North Carolina to the Great Smoky Mountains National Park. We would take our time on this road, stopping at some of the scenic lookouts and trails, and stay overnight at an inn. Traveling in August, this was all very pleasant until we came down from the mountain at the North Carolina border into the hot humid air of a Carolina summer. The reality of what it means to live in this part of North America for several months of the year hit us full blast, and the euphoria of the mountain air quickly dissipated. In a few days after we arrived in Chapel Hill, the mover arrived and this time there had been no fire on the way. So we moved into our new home, and turned on the air conditioning.

Settling into a New Life in Chapel Hill

When we arrived in mid-August, the school year was upon us very quickly; it starts early in the south. Deborah started in the local public school, quite close by and soon made new friends, although she also stayed in touch with some of her Toronto friends and never lost her love for Toronto. She did very well in Junior High and Chapel Hill

High School, all of which had high standards as one would expect in a university town. Peter was in his fourth year of high school so we decided that instead of putting him into the large high school, we would enroll him in a private school, Durham Academy, where he could get more help for preparing him for college. This prep school, with its rather elitist student body, was quite different from Leaside High School, and although he made some friends there, he never did fit in very well. After that year he became an undergraduate at UNC Chapel Hill.

I do not want to deal with all of the personal details of family life in Chapel Hill, so I will limit my remarks to a few observations about life in this city as it relates to the academic environment in which I worked. UNC Chapel Hill was founded in the last decade of the eighteenth century and is the oldest publicly owned university in the nation. The town was created because of the university and has always been its *reason d'etre*. Chapel Hill was a city of about 30,000 residents when we arrived and into this city came about 15,000 students, most of them non-residents and living in dorms on campus or in housing in town. Needless to say, the city was dominated by people connected with the university in one way or the other. Consequently the fathers of Deborah's friends were almost all my colleagues in the university, and the same applied to those of Peter's friends who were from Chapel Hill. Most of our friends and those of our children were part of the academic families of the university.

The city also consisted of a collection of local neighborhoods, and each neighborhood often developed its own little organization, with a governing body and sets of rules and regulations. Our little neighborhood, called Hidden Hills, had a number of faculty members in different disciplines, whom one got to know through various socials and other activities. The same was true of churches and any number of other communal activities. The hospital was the teaching hospital of the university's faculty of medicine, so that my physician, Dr. James Briant, was also Professor of Medicine, as well as the father of one of Peter's friends. The only sports in town of any consequence were the university sports, the Tarheels, with gigantic facilities. The football stadium holds over 60,000 seats and the Dean Smith Center over 20,000 for basketball, and there are several other sports venues on campus. The Tarheel basketball team is one of the most famous in the history of the NCAA and their archrival is the notorious Duke Blue Devils, just ten miles down the road. Many members of the faculty may have resented the dominance of sports in the university, but it was a fact of life in Chapel Hill.

When we arrived in Chapel Hill it was natural for us to attend the Presbyterian Church in the heart of town, since we had been members of Presbyterian churches in all of the places where we had lived in my previous appointments, Waterloo, Needham, and Leaside. So we went there for a while. There was, however, a drawback, and that was the fact that my predecessor, Bunny Boyd, had been a prominent figure in the church and active in biblical instruction there, and it was expected that I would also do the same. But my style was far different from that of Boyd and I resisted any such role. Furthermore, Bunny's widow, Thelma Boyd, was also very prominent, and while she was a pleasant person and very friendly towards us, I did not want to get into a situation where comparisons were being drawn between her late husband and myself. So we went to the United Church of Christ, a liberal denomination with strong ties to New England. A young couple who were graduates of Yale Divinity School shared the pastoral and preaching duties equally. It was a much smaller and less assuming church and we were active there for several years.

A couple of decades before we arrived in Chapel Hill, UNC Chapel Hill had formed a consortium with Duke University and North Carolina State University in Raleigh, to create a Research Triangle Park on a large track of land within the triangle created by the three cities of Chapel Hill, Durham, and Raleigh. This was anchored by some pharmaceutical companies, Northern Telecom, the Federal Environmental Protection Agency, and many other research facilities, all taking advantage of the expertise to be found at the universities. With Nortel prominent in RTP at that time, there were direct flights between Toronto and RDU (Raleigh, Durham, Chapel Hill) airport, which was very convenient for travel between the two. Shortly after I arrived, the National Humanities Center was also set up in the RTP with the building set in beautiful wooded grounds, which allowed scholars from the rest of the US and some foreigners to spend a year at the center, supported by the National Endowment for the Humanities, using the libraries and other resources of UNC Chapel Hill and Duke. This was a great boon for the scholars themselves and for those in the humanities at Chapel Hill and Duke. As the Research Triangle flourished to become the largest in North America, there was a significant impact on Chapel Hill because it soon became the residential location of choice. So the upscale locations in town soon became populated with those working in the research triangle.

It is easy to see from these brief remarks that Chapel Hill was a great place to raise a family and most academic families thrived in this environment. However, our two children, Peter and Deborah did find it a little parochial and small town after living in a big city like Toronto. There was, in fact, no city of comparable size and with the same kind of attractions as Toronto in the whole of North Carolina, so that one would need to travel north to Washington or south to Atlanta to find the same big city life. We once took Deborah and a friend of hers from Toronto to Washington for a visit, and Elizabeth and I went a number of times to the Capitol for a weekend when the hotel prices were low, because all of the government workers left town on the weekends. We would take in some entertainment at the Lincoln Center or visit the museums on the Mall. Nevertheless, from the perspective of what Chapel Hill could offer, it seemed to represent a pretty good future for my family and career.

Teaching in the Humanities at a Major American University

I want to begin the discussion of my academic career at Chapel Hill by presenting my personal perspective on the task of teaching in a top ranking American university, such as Chapel Hill. I confess at the outset that this perspective is largely conditioned by my own experience as a student at the University of Toronto and by my seven years of teaching there, which were radically different from teaching at UNC. Without going into too much detail, let me mention a basic undergraduate liberal arts requirement. In addition to a major field of study, that took up a third of ones courses, there was a distribution requirement of perhaps a third of ones courses that had to be taken covering a broad range chosen from the humanities, the social sciences and history, the physical sciences and mathematics, the life sciences, and the arts, with two or three from each field. These would be selected from a range of offerings that were predominantly introductory in nature. These distribution requirements were serviced by very large classes and there was always a great demand for these courses, so that students often begged at registration time to get into the course merely to fulfill that obligation. This choice had nothing to do with the subject matter to be covered by the course, in which the student might have little or no interest or aptitude, but only to get it out of the way with the least possible amount of time, energy and expense. The rest of the required number of courses could simply be free electives according to one's interests. The rational for such a system that was widespread throughout the educational system of the USA was to create "well-rounded" students prepared for life.

Frankly, I never believed in this system, and nothing in my twenty-three years of experience at Chapel Hill changed my mind. On the contrary, it only convinced me of its futility. My own experience as a student at Toronto was perhaps the other extreme. I chose a challenging four-year honors program in Near Eastern and Classical studies, (following a fifth year of high school graded according to a wide Ontario perspective), with few options within that program and the only college requirement outside of that program was one full year course in English literature. I did not have a single large course, not even the English course, which was outside of my field of interest. All my courses went for the full year with up to nine exams at the end of each school year. I was very well prepared for graduate studies at Yale and did not need the usual amount of course work there. Even though the system at Toronto was modified in later years and became less programmed, it never went to the American liberal arts model.

What effect did these two models have on the teaching mission and practice at the two institutions and for me in particular? This American system had a great impact on the nature of the department, its offerings and its funding, and on the individual faculty member, his or her style of teaching, and on their value to the department, i.e. their tenure. Shortly before I arrived at Chapel Hill there had been a revision of the curriculum to redraw the lines of the distribution requirements and what courses from each department could be used to fulfill these various requirements. Members of the Religion department had actively engaged in the various committees drawing up these lists so that courses from Religion would qualify for several different fields: humanities, social sciences, arts and literature, etc. This meant that we could mount several of these large courses to fulfill liberal arts requirements and have over a thousand students a year. That would be enough to get sufficient funding for a good size department and do all of the other more specialized courses within the field of Religion.

What was the general effect on undergraduate teaching? The teacher was faced with the fact that a large portion of the students were not there because they had an interest in the subject, but how to get an adequate grade in the quizzes and exam with the least amount of effort. So the instructor had to attract and retain a respectable number of the large group of students (about 150–300) in a large auditorium, and this meant learning to entertain as well as instruct, and use a variety of teaching devices to get a modicum of information across on which to evaluate them. These students were also required at the end of the semester to fill out a questionnaire that ranked the teacher in a number of different categories. These would then be used by the chair to evaluate the teaching performance of the faculty member, especially in these large classes, in yearly evaluation reports and by tenure review committees. The big classes always carried far more weight (because they were more valuable in terms of departmental financing) than the small courses. And they were very important for teaching awards. A side effect of this whole process was that of "grade inflation." It was common practice after quizzes and exams to post the grades without names, only identified by the *id* numbers of the various students. It soon became apparent that many of those who taught these large courses also gave high grades with very few marks below a "B" grade. This, of course, encouraged their popularity and high teaching evaluations. Our department did win a number of those teaching awards and because I visited some of these classes I can say that their teachers were indeed skillful at this kind of "popular" communication. But I was far from convinced that it was in these classes that the best teaching was being done.

When it came to the matter of majors, the lack of serious concentration in the field of study made for rather weak results. This was strongly resisted by the science departments who found ways around this requirement and usually got their way. Departments that tended to embrace multi-disciplines, such as Religion, were most vulnerable to this trivialization of the field. Someone doing a major in religious studies was subject to an internal distribution requirement within the department so that someone interested in biblical studies could only take a few courses but most of the rest were spread over several other areas of study, which were largely introductory in nature with few prerequisites or skill requirements. It was virtually impossible for someone with a major in Religion to qualify for a graduate program in Near Eastern Studies at Harvard or Yale, no matter how bright they may be. Students in the USA who wanted to go on in Near Eastern Studies invariably had to go through a seminary program first, and that was far from ideal, to get into such grad programs. Yet I could go from my BA program at Toronto into Yale and be ahead of all those who had to take the longer route. The very fact that majors in Religion were spread among several fields also led to internal department rivalry for the best students for the very few small seminar courses. It was an inherently bad system, and there was almost no way on the individual or even departmental level that one could fix it.[1]

What did all of this mean to me and my teaching at Chapel Hill? In a word it meant "frustration" with the system and "disillusionment" with the vaunted American higher education. While teaching at Toronto I had my courses at various levels from introductory to advanced, and all of the feedback I controlled with my own system of anonymous evaluation, and not a silly computer generated "fill in the squares" form of rating controlled by the university. While the system at Toronto had been modified since my undergraduate days, students graduating from our department program still could go directly into the best graduate schools, and I was happy to see some of mine take that route.

When I first arrived at Chapel Hill I had to confront the ghost of Bunny Boyd and his very popular courses and entertaining style of teaching. It took some time for me to change my style, develop aids and materials that would spoon feed the weak and occasionally challenge the bright, but poor students still got poor grades and word got around. Unlike junior faculty, however, because of my status I was quite immune to serious criticism. Ironically, I wrote many recommendations in favor of awards for junior faculty, and visited many of their classes for that purpose, and most of those that I supported got the money. This was blatantly hypocritical, because I loathed the system, but these colleagues could use the money and I clearly did not need it, so I held my nose and did it successfully. Ratings for my introduction course took two extremes. Students loved it or they did not with few in between.

I did attract a number of the better students into my other, more demanding smaller courses. These usually had my introductory course as a prerequisite, and there was a limit on the size of the class. These were much more like my Toronto courses, and these students I got to know and have pleasant memories about a number of them. My prize was bright students choosing one of these courses and then learning to produce a very good piece of work. A number of them went into Law school, and I wrote recommendations on their behalf. It should also be said that teaching Bible in the American South included a very large percentage who were conservative Christians and fundamentalists, since most of the students at UNC Chapel Hill came from the state itself. They often chose the course because they thought that they already knew what it was all about and knew all of the answers. When they were confronted with the high degree of their own ignorance, they could become angry and disgruntled. Yet it was important to lead them step by step to broaden their perspective by relying on the great diversity of the biblical text itself, the problems it raises and the ways in which scholars have come to terms with it, and then let it percolate for a while, without clobbering them with the right scholarly explanation, i.e. my own views. It is a fine line to challenge the student out of his/her complacency but also to be sensitive to the difficulty that such a rethinking involved for them. Sometimes they would come to my office after class and chat with me. I can vividly remember one freshman southerner with a great drawl coming to my office after a lecture on David. "Mighty interestin, what you were sayin bout David this mornin, sir," he said, "mighty interestin, but I wouldn't say that in my town." And he smiled.

I would compare this experience of teaching these large Old Testament Introduction classes every year (even while I was department chair) with a quite different teaching experience, with which I became involved. About the time that I arrived at Chapel Hill the Philosophy Department there had developed, in collaboration with the university alumni association, an extracurricular program in "Humanities and Human Values." For a modest fee a person who was not a student would attend a weekend of meetings on Friday afternoon and evening and Saturday morning (3–4 sessions) with lectures by faculty members on a particular academic theme or deal with a subject of current interest. The range of subjects was very large, but in a state such as North Carolina it is not surprising that subjects related to the Bible would be included. So once I was installed as the new James A. Gray Professor of Biblical Literature, and the fact that so many in the state had taken a Bunny Boyd course as undergraduates, I was approached to see if I would do something for such a weekend with one or two other faculty. Thus I became involved in these weekends on a regular basis. Sometimes I would be teamed up with others from other departments, at other times I would take the whole weekend alone.

I was under no obligation to do these programs, although I did get a modest honorarium as an incentive, which was hardly necessary, because I loved it. The director of the program was also under no obligation to use me. He had to be concerned about whether the topic would draw an audience of about 70 persons, for all of the sessions. His staff conducted their evaluations after every program so they had a good idea about what persons and what subjects had a good draw and were highly rated, and I seem to score well on both accounts. I was particularly gratified to be included in their rather select "distinguished Professor" series, and even to be asked to repeat it. Each session would be about an hour with 30–40 minutes talk and the rest for questions and discussion, and there was no hesitation in these folks jumping right in and carrying the discussion to the end with the person in charge bringing it to a halt. Even during the break for coffee and cookies, one would get into interesting conversations with individual participants. They were given recommended reading lists, which they appreciated and they often offered their personal thanks. Of course they were older adults with no grades to be concerned about. They were there simply for the enjoyment of it and so was I. I often recognized some who had been at a previous series in which I had a part. There were quite a number who were regulars at these weekends.

There were also auditors in some of my regular classes, usually in the Introduction to OT and most often they were retirees. I remember a couple of them who always came for the large class and sat together. They even repeated it the following year, because they enjoyed it, or so they said. Sometimes they treated me to lunch at the posh Alumni Club, and they would comment on the lectures and even suggest something that I could do a little differently or a bad habit that I could change, and of course kid me about it. When I was lecturing, I could always tell if I had slipped back into it, just by the look on their faces. They gave me lots of good tips and I enjoyed having them there. And there were others as well. (I will make some remarks later on my graduate teachings and the graduate program, after I deal with the development of the doctoral program in the Department of Religion and my own role in its inauguration.)

Scholarly Research at Chapel Hill

Let me now turn to the narrative of my life as a scholar and my first year at Chapel Hill. As mentioned earlier, late in 1976 Hans Heinrich Schmid of the University of Zurich publish a book, *Der sogennante Jahwist: Beobachtungen und Fragen zur Pentateuchforschung* (The So-called Yahwist: Observations and Questions concerning Pentateuchal Research) and when I became aware of it through a review in *JSOT* in late 1977, I got hold of a copy and after reading through it I realized that we had come to many of the same conclusions about the Pentateuch in general and the late dating of the Yahwist in particular. So I wrote to him and told him: "I cannot say how much I enjoyed it [the book] or how deeply I feel in fundamental agreement with you. On matters of detail there are of course some differences. But on so many issues on content and method we have come independently to the same conclusions. My own seminar notes on Exodus [the major area of his focus in the book] are filled with just such observations as you have made which now seem obvious when they are so clearly stated as you have done. Yet they will be stoutly resisted I am afraid." I expressed the hope that I would hear from him and that some scholarly contact would be established that would involve me more in continental scholarship, because I had little hope for change in America, based on the response that I had received up to that point. With the letter I also sent him some recent offprints.

Hans Heinrich sent me a warm and friendly letter in return that was a harbinger of a deep and enduring friendship. He thanked me for my letter and said that he could say the same things about my book on Abraham that I had said about his book on the Yahwist. He went on to say that during the past summer he had read my book along with two detective stories and found my book much more exciting (*viel spannender*) than the two novels, which was high praise indeed. He went on to discuss at length the possibilities of getting it translated into German, which would require getting some funding and permission from Yale Press, or doing an 80-page summary that he could get published in Zurich. He expressed the hope that we would maintain contact and get together some time in the future. In a separate parcel post he sent me two additional books of his, which I also enjoyed.

I did follow up on his suggestion about a German edition of my book with Yale Press, and after some months they indicated that they would not get involved with the expense of a German edition. They did not object to Hans Heinrich's other proposal about a summary version in German, but I was too involved with other commitments that I could not stop to write such a work. I was committed in the coming summer to two months digging in Egypt and just could not do it. So that chance slipped away. Nevertheless, Hans Heinrich and I stayed in close contact, which would eventually lead to personal encounter in Switzerland.

About the same time that I wrote to Hans Heinrich, I also wrote to Professor Rolf Rendtorff of Heidelberg. The issue of *JSOT* that included a translation of Rendtorff's article on the Yahwist and various responses to it, including mine, and Rendtorff's responses to his critics had just appeared. In his response to my comments, I could see that he rather scolded me for criticizing him on a misquotation that he had made of von Rad. He stated that the misquotation had been the fault of the printer and would be corrected in his new book which greatly expanded on the thesis of his article. That said, he felt that he did not need to deal with the substance of my critique. In my letter I wanted to do two things: the first was to mend fences that would make possible a dialogue with this important senior professor and successor of von Rad, and second, to set the record straight regarding the way in which I felt he had misrepresented von Rad's viewpoint on the Yahwist. This may seem like trivial academic quibbling, but the issue would survive in German biblical scholarship for years.

I began my letter by saying: "Let me apologize to you if I seemed too polemical in my approach or in any way misrepresented your position or intention. I am more interested in fruitful discussion than in public debate," and I also ended on the same note that I hoped in the near future for more direct contact with continental scholarship and for continued dialogue, especially concerning these new directions in Pentateuchal studies, and made reference to the new work of Hans Heinrich as well. Regarding the second point, I insisted that the misquotation could have nothing to do with a typesetting error, because his argument depended entirely on the misquotation and not on von Rad's original German text, which I cited. The misquote was used to suggest that the great scholar and his mentor had suggested that the Pentateuchal source called the Yahwist should not be understood as an author and this left open the possibility of other scholars treating it as a mere collection of traditions. However, any unprejudiced reading of von Rad could not reasonably draw this conclusion from his work, and certainly Hans Heinrich's book on the Yahwist mentioned earlier did not follow this line.

It took about a year before Rendtorff sent a reply, and for this delay he apologized "very much." He then went into a long response of what can only be described as special pleading on the points I raised, and the fact that his argument still held true, even with the correct quotation of von Rad. He also blamed part of the problem on German terminology, for which there is no adequate English equivalent, which is true simply because the Germans have never been clear about what they meant by their technical terms. Rendtorff, however, was no better in this respect than the rest. He even praised the ambiguity of the language he used so he could never be pinned down. He closed the letter with the hope that we would stay in contact and that one day we would meet personally, and we did years later in Heidelberg.

I have highlighted my initial contact with these two scholars because our three names were commonly linked together in European circles as "the three revisionists" in Pentateuchal studies, just as in North America it was the Thompson–Van Seters revolution. The remarkable thing is that both Europeans and Americans were referring, in my case, to the same book, *Abraham in History and Tradition*. The first half, on the issue of historicity, was the major concern of American scholars, the second half on issues of literary criticism, was the obsession of the Europeans. By the time I received Rendtorff's letter, I had been asked by Jack Sasson to do a review article for the *Journal of the American Oriental Society* on the books of both Hans Heinrich and Rendtorff, and this gave me lots of space to lay out the areas on which we were in agreement and those in which we differed. It was quite clear, at least to me, that Hans Heinrich and I were much closer and Rendtorff quite different on some fundamental issues of Pentateuchal criticism.

After I had read Hans Heinrich's book, *Der sogenannte Jahwist*, I wrote to Piet de Boer in December of 1977 about the book and my strong approval of its conclusions that were reached independent of my own book. I stated: "It is very exciting for me and I am sure both you and Hoftijzer [a Leiden scholar and former student of de Boer] would be delighted with it." I also wrote: "I am more anxious than ever to get to Europe for my sabbatical which I have had to postpone until 1979–80. I hope that something can be worked out." De Boer was quick to respond and agreed with me that Hans Heinrich's book was an important contribution, but that "the leading group of German scholars is still unfavourable to this new approach but I am sure that this will change." He also indicated that as editor of the journal, *Vetus Testamentum*, he had asked Dr Ernest Nicholson of Cambridge to review my book on Abraham. He further announced that he was retiring as professor at Leiden in the fall of 1978, but would continue as editor of a major international project on the publication of the Peshitta, the Syriac version of the Old Testament. He also hoped that my sabbatical plans would bring me "in personal contact, now in Europe." As it turned out, those sabbatical wishes to go abroad in 1979–80 did not materialize and would be postponed for a few years. De Boer's retirement at Leiden, where he had been such a dominant figure for so long, marked the end of an era for the program there, and it never quite recovered the prestige and reputation that it had as a great center in the discipline of biblical studies.

A quite different reaction to my *Abraham* book is reflected in an invitation I received in January of 1977, which involved conducting a "celebrity seminar" and giving a public lecture at Dartmouth College in New Hampshire in May of 1978. I was being invited to do this task for the Department of Religion at Dartmouth by the young assistant professor, Robert Oden Jr., an Old Testament scholar in that department, and the program would revolve around at six-week seminar, highlighting my book, *Abraham in History and Tradition*, in both its historical and literary aspects, as well as many additional works with whom I had been in dialogue. The seminar would end with four successive sessions in three days in May during my visit, in which the eleven students would each offer papers on various aspects of the seminar and I would comment on, and respond to, questions on the issues raised. I would receive copies of all the papers after I arrived at Dartmouth, the day before this last series of sessions, which gave me very little time to read and prepare for each paper. During the evening of the first day I would also give a public lecture, which further squeezed my time to prepare responses for five papers on the second day. And the Department members were all encouraged to arrange having one of their meals with me during my stay. Naturally I accepted the honor and challenge of the occasion.

Rob Oden, who organized this seminar, was an interesting person. He was a graduate of Harvard and student of Frank Cross, and was given a quite different story from mine, as he told me, but in reading my *Abraham*, he was strongly persuaded by my arguments against Albright. However, he had also done a few years study at Cambridge, UK, between his undergraduate and graduate studies at Harvard, and while in Cambridge University he had taken in lectures from Edmund Leach and was very much attracted to anthropological interpretations of myths and religious texts, particularly in the Claude Lévi-Strauss tradition of Structuralism. It was also the case that the chairman and senior professor of the Department of Religion at Dartmounth was Hans Penner, who was also a Structuralist. Readings for the seminar included some essays by Leach and his treatment of biblical narrative so that I would need to do some homework on this work. At that time literary structuralism was very popular in the humanities at Chapel Hill, so I would need to gain some familiarity with it at any rate.

On the 7th of May I flew up to Lebanon, New Hampshire, where Rob met me and took me back to Hanover, a beautiful little college town. Rob was an amiable and hospitable person and clearly made very careful preparations for this seminar with what proved to be eleven very bright "Ivy League" college students. The faculty had been encouraged to sit in on the sessions as well, and Penner in particular was at most of them. On the Monday evening after the first seminar day, I gave my lecture—another updated version of my "Tradition and Social Change in Ancient Israel," which would fit well with Oden's sociological interests. There was a reception afterwards, which meant a late night to prepare for the next day. Every day was rather full with both student and faculty interaction. Penner in particular was a quite intense person. He had studied under Mircea Eliade at Chicago with my colleague Chuck Long, so I learned a little about him before I went to Dartmouth. As soon as I returned to Chapel Hill I wrote to Hans Penner, as chair of Rob's department, with high praise for the whole experience and for Rob's hard work and wonderful personality in making it such a success. I closed with the statement: "This letter has too many superlatives in it, I know, but that is the way I feel at the moment." At the same time that I was writing to Penner, Rob was writing to me to thank me for all the work that I had put into the seminar and compared me favorably with all of the other previous "celebrities." He closed his remarks by stating: "I cannot think that any of the students will forget, and I am certain that I will not forget, all you have done for us."

Let me make here a few additional remarks about Rob Oden. We occasionally met at SBL and exchanged greetings but we did not engage in the same sessions, so we did not maintain any close contact. Nevertheless, I was asked on two occasions by the dean of the Faculty of Arts and Sciences at Dartmouth to evaluate Oden for promotion. The first time it was for promotion to Associate Professor and tenure, with a quite respectable list of articles and monographic studies, the latter primarily of a technical nature, so I had no difficulty with supporting his advancement.

In the spring of 1978 I attended the Southeastern regional SBL meeting and began my long association with this group. It frequently met in Atlanta and brought me into close association with Max Miller and others of the program at Emory University, as well as other major universities of the South. This SBL group also met with a local chapter of ASOR and their biblical archaeology program, led by Professor Joseph (Joe) Callaway of Southern Baptist Seminary in Louisville, Kentucky. I had told him that I would be participating in a dig in the Wadi Tumilat in the summer of 1978, so in the fall after I returned he invited me to give a report on the season's excavations at the next regional meeting in New Orleans. I was happy to do so. Although Joe was a conservative Southern Baptist, we got on very well, and I regularly gave papers in both the SBL and the ASOR portions of these meetings. Joe Callaway was a wonderful person and very honest about his reporting of archaeological data, even when it seemed to go against his conservative convictions. He was director of an archaeological dig at et-Tell, biblical Ai (both the biblical name and the modern Arabic one mean "the ruin"), and was hoping to find the city that the Bible says was destroyed by Joshua. Instead, he had to confess that there was no such ruin of that period at this site. He was a very good archaeologist and one could always talk archaeology with him, as I did, without prejudice. We were once asked by two different journals to review the same book on the historicity of the exodus by a very conservative scholar. When I told him that I thought it was a bad book, he agreed and suggested that I choose a few of the major problems with the book and then send him a copy of my draft review so he did not need to repeat them and he would concentrate on some of the rest. That was Joe.

In the spring of 1978, the second semester of my first year at Chapel Hill, I was also engaged in making preparations for the first excavation season at Tell el Maskhuta in the Delta region of Egypt. This was in addition to all of the work that I had been doing for the "celebrity seminar" at Dartmouth. Five days after I returned from Dartmouth I was on my way to Egypt on May 15th. One hurdle, among others, that had to be overcome before I left for Egypt was the fact that Elizabeth and I had applied earlier in the year for permanent residence status, and one of the requirements of that process is that one could not leave the country until the whole process was complete. So I had to make a special appeal for "parole" status on my visa application so that I could be out of the country from May 15 to July 20, in order to engage in this excavation which was being funded by the Smithsonian Institute and sponsored by ASOR. My parole was granted, which meant that on reentering the country I had to report to Immigration at the airport on arrival to be cleared. Elizabeth, who had also applied for "parole" because she wanted to take Deborah to a Canadian summer camp where she would be with some of her former friends, was denied. Both of us did get permanent residence status during the coming year.

First Egyptian Expedition

The mounting of a multi-year expedition to Egypt required a massive effort and became the major preoccupation of the director, Jack Holladay. He had the support in Toronto of Donald Redford, who had experience with his own excavations and all of the red tape involved. He also received help from two curators in the Egyptian department of the Royal Ontario Museum, who had experience with digging in Egypt. Jack had to apply for funding from Canada Council and the Smithsonian that would ultimately amount to a few hundred thousand dollars over the course of the dig, a good piece of it in the first year of start-up. That required detailed plans and presentation to be submitted to ASOR and the American Research Center in Egypt, as well as the funding agencies. He would have to gain the permission and contracts from the President of the Egyptian Department of Antiquities and the necessary security clearance. The latter was no small matter because Egypt at that time was still in an uneasy truce with Israel and our site was only fifteen miles down the road from the city of Ismailia, on the Suez Canal and across the canal was the Israeli Bar Lev line. The UN forces maintaining the truce were stationed in Ismailia, which was also the provincial capital.

In addition to this there was the problem of a rival application from the Egyptologist, Professor Hans Goedicke of Johns Hopkins. In his application he wanted to lay claim to the concessions of both Tell el-Maskhuta and Tell el-Rataba in the Wadi Tumilat, and he wrote Jack to tell him in so many words to back off. Furthermore, he also was making an appeal for funding to the Smithsonian and whoever got that funding would call the shots. In response, Jack pointed out that the information Goedicke had received about Toronto's plans was out of date. He had already been in the field at Tell el-Maskhuta that summer and his permission to do so included the request for further archaeological exploration at that site. The whole planning process had been in the works for some time, long before Goedicke had expressed any interest in the region. As it turned out, Jack, with his meticulously detailed plans and obvious expertise, easily won out on the funding from the Smithsonian and this reduced Goedicke's dig at Tell el-Retabah to a very limited operation. Jack offered Goedicke our cooperation and sharing of information, but Goedicke would have none of it. Goedicke was not an archaeologist but an epigrapher, looking for inscribed monuments, and the archaeologist on his team who would actually run the dig was not very experienced. He was also a fundamentalist Christian looking for evidence of the exodus.

Armed with all of Jack's instructions, plans, and procedures, and the necessary visa from the Egyptian authorities, the team flew to Cairo. From there we could not go directly to the dig site, because we had to first receive individual security clearance, and for this we had to go into the city and stay at the Garden City hotel, the same one that Elizabeth, Peter, and I had stayed in back in 1965. Jack had come to Egypt some weeks earlier with a few others and they had gotten their clearance by that time and were out at the dig site. So I was left in charge of the group in Cairo. The first thing to do was to go to the office of the American Research Center in Egypt on Tahrir Square, a short distance from the hotel and get the forms that we needed for this purpose. One of the pieces of information that needed to be supplied was one's religion. This was no problem for most, but there were two Jews on our team, and given Egypt's current relations with Israel we decided to make one a Presbyterian and the other a Quaker. It took several days before government clearance came through, and we could not go very far from the hotel until it did.

Two episodes during that waiting period in Cairo stand out. A few days after we arrived in Cairo I had a call from Professor Manfred Bietak of the University of Vienna inviting me to come to the Austrian embassy in Cairo to see him. You may recall that earlier in this narrative I had mentioned the fact that Bietak was the director of a Viennese expedition to Tell ed-Dab'a in the eastern Delta, the site that Labib Habashi and I had identified as Avaris. I had corresponded with Bietak at the time but had not been in touch with him lately or ever met him personally. So I was delighted with this opportunity to do so. As it turned out, the Austrian embassy also housed the headquarters of the Austrian archaeological mission in Egypt, including that of Bietak's excavations. Consequently, after his most cordial welcome he escorted me through all of their work rooms, which were very impressive indeed, and the envy of any serious excavation endeavor, with all of the latest equipment. It is little wonder that he had been exemplary in getting out his publications on his archaeological finds very quickly.

After the tour he told me that I should return to his place that evening for dinner, and I gladly accepted the invitation. What I did not realize at the time was that I would not be the only guest. When I arrived and was shown into the dining room, there was Hans Goeticke who was also having dinner with us. Goedicke was Austrian, although he was now connected with Johns Hopkins, and was a friend of Bietak, and the latter certainly knew all about the dispute between Goedicke's expedition and ours. I do not know whether this was an effort on Bietak's part to mend fences between the two groups, but the occasion was somewhat awkward. Goedicke did not help matters any by frequently reverting in the conversation to Viennese German, which I could not follow, even though Bietak spoke fluent English and there was no obvious reason for him to speak Viennese. I had the sense that Bietak found it embarrassing and he continued to speak English throughout. The attempt at cordial reconciliation between the two expeditions clearly was not working and the whole matter did not come up. This would not be my last encounter with Goedicke.

The other episode that occurred while the group was in Cairo, had to do with a night of entertainment in the western desert. Not far from our modest hotel there was a very fine souvenir shop as part of the Semiramis Hotel, and various members of our group went there to do a little souvenir buying, but mostly to kill time. They became quite friendly with the owner, and when he learned that we were not well-heeled tourists but poor academics from the Garden City hotel, waiting to go on a dig, he decided to entertain us. He had a big tent on the desert plateau, just beyond Gizah and the pyramids, where he regularly entertained wealthy tourists for a fee. So he invited all of us to his tent completely free of charge and provided the transportation. The taxis picked us up in the early evening and drove us out to the tent in the desert. What amazed us when we approached the tent is that there were a large number of them, all rather large, and they were laid out on this flat sandy area just like a fancy suburb would be, with streets and driveways to each tent. These tents served as summer retreats because it was always cooler up on the desert plateau at night than in the hot city below.

Our group joined the more sedate tourists inside this large, brightly light-up tent. The first act was the whirling dervish, a very artful and acrobatic dance. Then came the belly dancer and she was also very professional. But then the owner requested us to supply a volunteer to join the belly dancer. Well I should have known what to expect, and I am sure that this was something dreamed up by the young members of the group and the shop owner. Before the tourists had any chance to enter into the spirit of the occasion, my group began to immediately volunteer me to do a dance with this voluptuous dancer. Of course I refused their suggestion but they would have none of it, and I was more or less hauled to my feet and thrust into the circle and I made the best of it. Soon everyone got involved in a kind of conga dance with typical Arabic music in the background. And a few made sure that some incriminating photos were taken of the whole episode. There was also a great spread of delicious native Egyptian goodies after all this exercise and then a ride home in the moonlight with the Giza pyramids light-up with spotlights. It was an unforgettable evening with no cost to the expedition.

Eventually, after more than a week's wait we did get our security clearance and headed out to join the others at Tell el-Maskhuta. The archaeological site is situated on the south side of the modern fresh-water canal that leads from the eastern branch of the Nile River to Lake Timsah, which is part of the Suez Canal system. The distance from Tell el-Maskhuta to Ismailia on the north shore of Lake Timsah and the Suez Canal is about 15 miles. There is a road and a railway line that run east-west alongside the canal on its north side, and one can reach the site only directly from this road by using a raft with a cable attached to put yourself across the canal. Vehicles must go down the road a mile or two and cross the canal on the only bridge in the vicinity and then drive back on the south side over an unpaved track. On the north side of the canal and a short distance away was a large military base. At that time the UN Peace keeping base with Canadians (the largest group), Poles and Australians was stationed in Ismailia. One convenient aspect of this base was that it supplied us with excellent medical assistance when we needed it, which unfortunately was quite often.

Our living quarters consisted of using the rather rudimentary rooms of the school with cots replacing desks in some rooms and with work tables set up in others. The largest room was used for the refectory. The toilets were also of the most basic "Turkish" variety, with no running water and no electricity that first year, so that we had to use our own generator. Once we made contact with the Canadians of the UN they began to supply us with treated fresh water and other services. The fact that our staff included a number of young women perhaps had something to do with their generosity. While there were two or three houses of the villagers close to the canal, the main part of the village was located at the south east corner of the site half a kilometer away. The site and the village were all part of a large flat area that rose one to two meters above the surrounding landscape, which consisted of farmland made possible by irrigation from the canal system of the region. Beyond this strip of vegetation was the desert. Along the south side of the canal was a long ridge of tailings from the constant dredging of the canal, and this rose to three or four meters. One could climb up the slope of this ridge and walk along the top for some distance with a view over the whole area of the excavation site and the village and farmland to the desert's high sand dunes. In 1978 it was unwise to do too much picture taking on this ridge, especially to the north, in the direction of the military base.

The work schedule was based upon the principle of making use of as much of the early daylight as possible, when the day was the coolest. So we would rise at 4 a.m. and have a light first breakfast and be in the field before 5 a.m., with an adequate supply of water with us and all of our tools. The villagers that we hired to do the actual digging and those that carried the baskets of dirt to a dump location, many of the latter were young girls, would all flock to the mound and be there my 5 a.m. to greet us (in Arabic or very simple English). Each area of excavation had a particular team, which we tried to keep together. There were also some experienced Egyptian workers that had developed their digging skill as a profession in the region of Luxor and we imported these, along with a general foreman (the *mukhtaar*). We would work until 9 a.m. and then take thirty minutes for a hearty breakfast, prepared by the cook, and then work until about 11:30 a.m., by which time it was too hot to continue. Dehydration was always a risk, which could make one quite ill, as I can attest from experience. After we came in from the field work and cleaned up, we joined the staff, who had been working undercover in camp, for the largest meal of the day.

From 2 to 4 p.m. was siesta time and the chance to avoid any activity or sunshine. The best way to keep cool was to take a sheet, soak it with water, remove all your clothes and rap yourself in the sheet and lie down to rest. By the time you had taken your nap, the sheet would be completely dry and you would have been quite comfortable and ready for more work. If you did not drop off immediately then you could watch the geckos racing up and down the walls inside the room, getting rid of the mosquitoes. About 4 p.m. we would head out to our particular area and try to make some sense out of what we had dug up in the morning. Usually, when digging, we would begin our area by opening a trial trench, ideally about 10 meters long by 1½ wide, and this would gradually produce a long wall of dirt on both sides, which we kept as straight and smooth as possible. These dirt sides were known as baulks, which would produce a profile of the way in which the various occupation layers had accumulated over time, the history of occupation. So it was necessary to draw carefully each layer on graph paper to scale and mark each layer. In this way all materials from a particular layer could be identified with a precise period of occupation and its history. This was not easy work. The sun was still hot and usually the wind had picked up so that particles of dusk and grit were bombarding us. The baulks had dried out since the morning, and we had to scrape them with our trowel to make then fresh again. It was also hard to keep the clip board clean. Often one worked in two's, helping each other, one measuring while the other drew, and so on.

For the first part of the dig season I worked with Carol Redmount. She had had a lot of experience on various expeditions in a range of different sites and was very good at dirt archaeology. In fact she seems to love dirt. My field experience was rather limited to one rather poor dig in Jordan, as I mentioned above, so I learned a lot from her. One has to be a little crazy to do this sort of thing for two months. At the end of the day we tried to clean up as best as we could for supper. It was dangerous to bath in the canal, because one could get a serious disease, although many of the locals did anyway. After supper we would relax and watch the sun go down. There was rarely a cloud at this time of the year.

Once a week we got a half day off. This meant that we went into Ismailia, often to visit the Canadians at the UN base where they had a swimming pool under a canopy and the water was a cool 85 F, compared with over 100 F outside. With the showers and the pool at least one felt clean for a change. Often we went for a swim in the Suez Canal, but the drawback was that it was salt water with no way to rinse off. One could not do any shopping before the end of siesta, which was about 5 p.m., because all the stores were closed. We also visited the Australians. They were a much smaller group and were not on the base itself but in the top two floors of a hotel. They did not have a pool but they did have showers and there was a line-up to use them. They also had lots of beer and other beverages "on the house." They were happy to have company, both male and female, and we learned a lot about the UN operations and experiences in the region. We often went to Harry's Restaurant in Ismailia, where there was great Red Sea shrimp.

In the middle of the dig season we took a four day break and some of the group used this chance to go down to Luxor by train. Jack and Phyllis, along with a few others and myself needed a good rest, so we went to Alexandria by train (first class), and stayed in a hotel on the edge of town, located in a large park that was once the grounds of a royal palace. It was right on the Mediterranean, with a great beach, which made a big curve out to a long peninsula, at the end of which was President Sadat's summer place. However, it was well guarded and one could not just wander out there to have a closer look. The hotel location was a very relaxing place. One could wander around the gardens and buy an ice cream treat. We took a ride to a neighboring fishing village that had a restaurant with a great reputation for sea food. The idea was to look around the various displays and pick out a selection of fresh caught fish and other sea food. These would be prepared for you and then brought to one long table on platters, along with all the trimmings and one would just keep passing the platters around until it was all gone. While you ate you could watch the fisherman bringing in their catch of the day and replenishing the supply. It was wonderful. After this pleasant period away, however, it was back to the dig.

One of the things that we needed to do in this first season was work out how to enlarge our working space, to allow for more staff and the increasing load of artifacts in subsequent years. Rather than build a separate dig house, which was customary for many well financed expeditions, our plan was merely to add on some rooms to the school in a new wing of the main building, which could then be used for needed classroom space when we were not there. But all of this had to be negotiated with the local officials in Ismailia. Jack, of course, did not want to leave the site to do this job because he was all too aware of how time-consuming and frustrating it could be. So he delegated the task to me. Why else was I the associate director? I drove into town in the dig vehicle and went to the office of the superintendent of education in the regional government. After the usual wait I was ushered in to see him and he provided me with the customary tea and we chatted for a bit. Then I laid out just what we had in mind. We would add two large classrooms, two European style washrooms with showers and a secure storage room for the objects that we found and some of our equipment. He seemed quite pleased with our suggestions and said he would support it when it was presented to the governor.

The next step was to give the governor's office a copy of the proposal and arrange for a meeting. They told me that he was not here today but to come back tomorrow (*bukra*), and they gave me a time. I came back the next day at the appointed time and I waited, and waited. As time went by I asked, "Is he coming today?" The responded, "Perhaps (*mumkin*)." After another 30 minutes I asked again. This time they told me that he was not coming that day. Come back tomorrow (*bukra*). The next day when I came, I was told that he had arrived and they showed me into a large office full of people being very busy, but the large governor's chair was still empty. They were serving tea and the Superintendent of Education was there and smiled at me. I asked him what our chances were of getting his approval. His answer was "If God wills (*nshaalla*)." These three Arabic words, *nshaalla, mumkin, bukra,* one encounters constantly when dealing with Egyptian government officials. The governor did arrive in due course, a very impressive figure, and after being informed of the matter and questioning the Superintendent of Education, he approved the plan, we shook hands, and that was it. The new classrooms, washrooms and the rest were built the following year.

I will not go into all of the archaeological details of the summer's work. They can be found in the excavation reports. I only want to highlight a few details significant for my own academic work. In a probe trench that Ed Bleiberg and I were digging we worked through a thick layer of debris with no clear structures or floors, dating roughly to the sixth century BCE, judging by the pottery sherds. Then we came to sand without any debris at all. We continued on down until we came to a curious cluster of bricks sticking out from the baulk, but all around it was just sand. It was not sitting on any floor! What it was would have to wait until we extended that side of the trench at a later stage. We continued on in the rest of the trench and it looked like we had a similar structure at one end of it. At this point I had to leave, just when things were getting interesting, to go into Ismailia to see those government officials. When I finally got back I was greeted by Jack who hurried to me and said: "Guess what we found in your trench while you were away? The Hyksos!" I thought this was some kind of joke, but he rushed me over to where Ed was sitting in the square beaming and pointing to what they had found just below the spot where we were working when I left. It was a typical Palestinian burial of the period contemporary with the Hyksos rule in Egypt. It had some well-preserved pottery offerings, a dagger, and most telling, the skeletal remains of a donkey at the entrance. The grave had been dug into virgin sandy soil, the brick tombs constructed at the bottom with the dead and the grave gifts placed in the tomb and then closed with a corbelled roof construction and a sacrificial donkey placed at the front. The hole was then filled in. What we had seen in the side of the baulk elsewhere in the trench was the corner of another such grave. In the following season a few more of these graves would be found.

There was nothing Egyptian about these burials. Instead they strongly resembled those that had been found many years earlier in Gaza and other southern Palestinian sites. They were also found at Bietak's Tell ed-Dab'a, the capital city of the Hyksos! The great debate about who the Hyksos were was over and the mystery solved. Furthermore, the theory that the Hyksos had gained control of Egypt through a massive invasion using horse-drawn chariots to overthrow the Egyptian armies, could also be relegated to the dusk-bin. This group used donkeys and reflected a gradual migration into the region from Southern Palestine during a period of political instability in Egypt. They settled at a place where there had been no settlement previously. Both the Hyksos identity and the way in which they had come into the delta region were just as I had proposed in my thesis of 1964, and I had been completely vindicated.

The other matter that was settled in these early stages of the excavations at Tell el-Maskhuta was the debate with biblical archaeology over whether excavations at this site could clarify the historicity of the biblical story in Exodus regarding the building of Pithom in the time of Ramesses the Great. This goes back to the challenge that Don Redford and I made to Jack to get him involved in the whole enterprise. It was also the unstated reason why Goedicke was interested in this region and why he enlisted the help of fundamentalist Christians on his team. The steady accumulation of archaeological evidence pointed indisputably to the fact that the city, with its massive brick walls, was built by Pharaoh Necho II (ca. 600 BCE), in conjuction with his construction of a canal through the Wadi Tumelat to Lake Timsah and then south through the Bitter Lakes to the Red Sea. The account of this canal building is described in the Greek historian Herodotus, and traces of Necho's canal can be found running on the south side of the site. This system provided a valuable link between the Mediterranean and the Red Sea, the ancient precursor of the Suez Canal. The city remained an important trading center into the Roman period.

If this archaeological reconstruction is correct, and nothing discovered since the excavations has suggested otherwise, then it meant that the biblical account of the Israelites building of Pithom (Tell el-Maskhuta) must belong to the sixth century BCE, as I had advocated in my earlier studies. The model for the Pharaoh who enslaved the Israelites was none other than Necho II. It was also the case that the wars by the Assyrians and Babylonians had resulted in the migration of many Jews and other Palestinians into the eastern Delta region (i.e. Goshen). These refugees were all regarded as Hebrews because they all spoke the same Hebrew language, and it was from this group that Necho undoubtedly drew his labor force for digging the canal and building Pithom. The old traditions about the Israelites coming originally from Egypt (the Phoenicians had similar traditions) were greatly embellished by this recent experience of Necho's rule in Egypt. There was, of course, a great amount of valuable additional information on the history of this vital trade route between the eastern Mediterranean and the sea route to India, which was gathered in the successive seasons of the expedition, and I will say more about this after my experience in the 1981 season.

Back at Chapel Hill, 1978–1979

The return to Chapel Hill after the dig was uneventful, although I did have to meet with a parole official in the immigration office at the airport, to be admitted back into the country. The family took a few days of relaxation up in the Blue Ridge Mountains, away from the summer heat. Then it was back to work, catching up on the correspondence that had accumulated while I was in Egypt. I also had to finish writing up reports on the excavation areas that had been under my supervision, and this meant a good deal of correspondence with Jack to get the materials from him that I needed to finish the job. There was also the matter of preparing for classes that began at the end of August. At the same time, Elizabeth and I had to make a trip to Atlanta to finally get our "green cards" as permanent residents of the USA. In addition to teaching and developing new courses, and attending meetings and committee work, there was always a flood of others matters, mostly unanticipated, that seems to more than fill up my time.

First on the agenda was to plan for my leave in 1979–80. While I was promised a leave for this year as part of my agreement to come to Chapel Hill, the university still expected me to raise some of the cost for replacement teaching for that year. This meant that I had to make application to a number of organizations for a research grant, as well as ask established scholars such as Bervard Childs, John Wevers, and others to write recommendations for me, which was time consuming. At the same time I was being asked by others to write on their behalf as well. In addition to letters of recommendation for my own students, I was also writing in support of former Toronto students, such as Claude Cox, with whom I had stayed in touch. I also received a request from the dean of Yale Divinity School to write an evaluation of the scholarship of Robert Wilson, who was being considered for tenure. I had met and chatted with Bob Wilson during one of my frequent trips to do research so I knew his work very well, and I could write a strong letter in his support. During this term Yehoshua Gitay from Haifa, Israel was living in Chapel Hill with his family. Gitay was doing some post-doctoral work with Professor George Kennedy of the Classics Department, who was a noted authority in ancient rhetoric, so our department hired Gitay to do some Hebrew teaching and as a teaching assistant for my large Introduction course. At the same time Gitay was also looking for a permanent position in the US so I was writing letters of recommendation for him as well.

Naturally there were academic papers to prepare for SBL and other meetings, and needless to say, I did not have the summer to work on these. I was preparing one for the national SBL meeting in New Orleans in the fall and had to submit a topic for the spring meeting of the regional SBL. I also had a request from Joe Callaway to give a report on our Tell el-Maskhuta dig at the regional ASOR spring meeting. There was a long review of my book on *Abraham* by Professor Nahum Sarna of Brandeis in a recent issue of the popular journal, *Biblical Archaeology Review* and its owner and editor, Hershel Shanks invited me to write a reply, which I could hardly refuse. I had also been doing some final editing of the long paper on Israelite historiography, which was now being published by *Orientalia*. Kirk Grayson in Toronto was coordinating all of that and we were in close touch on that matter.

The Society of Biblical Literature had developed their own publishing house, Scholars Press, for scholarly publications in competition with other publishers, in addition to producing the society's journal. One of the SP series of studies was Sources for Biblical Studies, and its editor, Burke Long of Bowdoin College, a former Yale graduate whom I knew very well, sent me a proposal for this series, having to do with creating a kind of handbook on "Pentateuchal Parallels," much like the handbooks on

Gospel Parallels. The one-page proposal was submitted by Professor Kent Richards of Iliff School of Theology in Denver, and Burke wanted me to evaluate it. I responded to Burke's request in detail, indicating that I was opposed to it and laying out all of my reasons for doing so. It was never done. It is not surprising that Richards never produced any significant scholarly work, preferring to become a dean in his institution and eventually the chief executive officer of SBL. I strongly suspect that Richards knew I was the one who rejected this proposal. We never did get along and I blame Richards as one of the major reasons for the scholarly decline in SBL and the wide embrace of shallow biblical studies of every kind.

I also developed a connection with Professor James VanderKam at North Carolina State University in Raleigh, and we corresponded about matters of mutual interest. I also went down to Raleigh to give a lecture to his class. VanderKam was a graduate of Harvard and became a leading specialist in the Dead Sea Scrolls. We got along very well. Another scholar from NC State was Professor Ron Sack, an Assyriologist in the History Department. He came up to Chapel Hill frequently to see Jack Sasson and me and we became good friends. I have some of his publications. He seemed to be constantly at war with his department about one thing or another. But he was an interesting person.

During the fall semester the department had, as a guest speaker, a scholar who was making quite a name for himself, Professor Hayden White of the University of California, Santa Cruz. I was not particularly impressed with his lecture, which seemed to be a few remarks jotted down on a sheet of yellow note paper, probably written during his flight east. I later read one of his books to try to figure out what he was talking about. The whole discussion at the lecture and in a following faculty seminar seemed to be an attack on doing any serious historical research. I did have a more private chat with him, which seemed much more productive and I later sent him some bibliography on biblical narrative and ancient historiography. He thanked me and we had some pleasant correspondence and made some vague statements about keeping in touch, but that was very unlikely as we never went to the same academic societies.

One of the broader consequences of my archaeological work in the Wadi Tumilat project in Egypt was that I was drawn increasingly into the orbit of American archaeologists working in the Near East and into the organization of ASOR in particular. One of the first moves that I made in this regard was to petition UNC to become a corporate member of ASOR by contributing a modest fee to support its operations. Duke had long been a member and the Meyers were very active in the organization, so it was appropriate that UNC should also be included. This was especially so because ASOR was one of the sponsors of Jack's dig and Ted Campbell, who had signed off on the project, was a good friend of mine since the days in Jerusalem together, and he had been the president of ASOR. The current president was Phil King, my old friend from Andover Newton days. We had worked together in the Boston Theological Institute, and he knew me well, perhaps too well. The first thing that I knew was that I was elected to the Board of Trustees of ASOR for a two-year term. Then I was appointed to the Editorial Committee of the *Annual of the American Schools of Oriental Research*, chaired by none other than Joe Callaway. So that would mean more meetings and correspondence.

It was within this context of ASOR that I received from Jack Holladay as Associate Director of the Wadi Tumilat Project a copy of a report by ASOR's Committee for Archaeological Policy, evaluating the work of the excavation and offering a list of some criticisms. Some of the criticisms I felt were quite unjustified, and I sent to the chair of that committee my own thoughts in support of Jack, with copies to Jack, Ted Campbell, and Phil King. The chair of the committee responded to Jack by downplaying the criticisms and commending Jack's work, as did a long response by Ted Campbell, with a copy to me. It was becoming clear to me that for at least as long as I was involved in the WT Project I would have to balance my involvement in both SBL and ASOR.

Another archaeological society that had a much broader scope that ASOR was the American Institute of Archaeology (AIA), and there was a local branch of this society in the Research Triangle Area, with most of the members in a number of different departments at Duke and Chapel Hill. This regional AIA group developed plans for a special symposium on the theme, "The Archaeology of Trade in the Eastern Mediterranean," with ten papers ranging from the second millennium BCE to the medieval Islamic period. I was asked to contribute and I offered a paper on: "What Is Trade? The Nature of Egyptian Trade in the East Mediterranean during the Second Millennium B.C." The topic took me out of my biblical work and back to the historical and archaeological studies of my Yale days, which was an enjoyable academic diversion. One of the benefits of this conference was to draw me into a wider context of scholars at Duke, NC State, and Chapel Hill. One scholar in particular, Robert Broughton, who gave a paper "Remarks on the Roman Empire and Mediterranean Trade," was a distinguished Roman historian, one of a group of retired outstanding scholars connected with the Classics Department at Chapel Hill. Broughton was a Canadian who had graduated from Victoria College in Toronto in the 1920s, and this connection with the University of Toronto gave us a bond. He was also a good person to consult on matters of classical historiography.

One of the sources that I had written to for funding support for my sabbatical in the coming year was the Guggenheim Foundation, and in March of 1979 I had received notice that I had been awarded a Guggenheim Fellowship. My primary concern had been to have enough funding so I could have the whole year free to work on my project. However, an added bonus that I had not really thought about was the prestige that this award gave me. It was the practice of the Foundation to announce it widely so that I began to receive congratulatory letters from many different quarters. From those such as Peter Ackroyd of King's College London, Brevard Childs, and John Wevers, who had written in support of my application, such notices were expected and I could express my gratitude to them for their help. With Ackroyd it gave me a chance to be in closer touch with him, and we became good friends. Other letters of congratulation, however, were more surprising. There was one from James I. (Jim) McCord, president of Princeton Seminary. He stated: "I have followed your career with a great deal of interest and pride, and am happy to recall our days together when you were in Princeton Seminary." He also expressed the wish: "I hope we can entice you back to the campus of Princeton for a lecture one of these days." This had not been the only note that I had had from him, but I had not heard from him in quite a while. In fact, I never heard from anyone else at Princeton again.

I also had a letter of congratulations from the Attorney General of North Carolina, Rufus Edmisten. He had written to me previously when I was first appointed as James A Gray Professor, and I put that down as just a political gesture. But this seemed more personal. He had spotted the notice in the university's "Carolina Notebook" and was very fulsome in his remarks towards me and the university. This time I wrote him back to thank him and express my gratitude that public officials like him took a strong interest in our institution. I also heard from others around the university. A few months after the Guggenheim award I was informed by *Marquis Who's Who in America* that I was selected to be included in the next edition (1980) of this work. There is little doubt that the publicity of this award had an influence on my being selected for *Who's Who*.

University presses also check such published lists of Guggenheim fellows, which include the title of the scholar's project, and I heard from some, including Cornell, Chicago, and Yale presses. The new editor at Yale University Press, Charles (Chuck) Grench, who had succeeded Jane Isay at that position, wanted to know when they could see me and talk about the project, even before it was begun. So I made a date for when I would be in New Haven on a visit to Elizabeth's family, and we had lunch together. It was the beginning of a long friendship. Another result of this publicity over the Guggenheim within the university was that the James A. Gray Professorship of Biblical Literature was no longer defined in terms of the Bunny Boyd era. I would be taken seriously as a scholar and not just a popular Bible teacher. There was an elite club of Guggenheim fellows at UNC that I never even knew existed until I became one of them. That was also good for the department which aspired to develop a graduate program.

There was another obligation that I somehow had to deal with and that was my relationship with the Gray family, the offspring of James A. Gray. They did not control the Gray fund, but Bunny Boyd had maintained a close relationship with them, and I received correspondence from Howard Gray, the spokesman for the family. He suggested that perhaps I could come to Winston-Salem and give an archaeological presentation to the Rotary Club regarding my archaeological work in Egypt. It had been the practice of Boyd to do this sort of thing from time to time in connection with his involvement with Israeli archaeologists. His talks were of a quite popular kind with emphasis on the biblical connections with the excavated finds. So I prepared a talk and made it as "popular" as I could, by trying to point out some of the important consequences of our work. But with the dig at such an early stage, there was nothing very spectacular to show them. They were very polite and Howard wrote me a nice thank you letter afterwards, but there was no other recognition in the way of an honorarium for the work put into it and the travel to Winston-Salem from Chapel Hill and back, not even a meal or a drink after the presentation. It was as if this rich family thought they owned me. Well, there was little further contact with the Gray family. I had paid my dues.

As if I had nothing else to do, I was approached to write two *Festschrift* articles. The one was a volume of articles in honor of Marvin Pope, a former teacher of mine who was soon to retire at Yale, to be put together by John Marks of Princeton University. It was to be on the theme of Love and Death and all papers had to conform to this theme, so it could not be on something that one was already working on. I tried to make it as close to my current interests as I could, so I wrote a piece on "Love and Death in the Court History of David." The deadline for submission was in early 1980 although as it turned out, the volume was not published until 1987! A second *Festschrift* was being organized by some students of Gösta Ahlström for this good friend of mine, and again I had to find a topic that was appropriate to Ahlström's interests but not too far from my current research. This piece was also finished long before its eventual publication in 1984.

In late 1978 John Bartlett of the University of Dublin had published an article in *JBL* on the story of "The Conquest of Sihon's Kingdom," in response to my earlier views on this episode in the biblical book of Numbers, published in *JBL* 1972. I wrote to the editor of *JBL*, John Hayes, and asked him to allow me to make a short response under "Critical Notes," that would allow for speedy publication instead of the usual three-year delay. The request was granted. In addition to the literary arguments, the trump card in my favor was the recent archaeological evidence of excavation at Heshbon in Jordan that argued entirely in my favor of a late dating and made Bartlett's position impossible. Even before my response to him was published we had been in correspondence about our differences and I sent him a copy of my article before it appeared in print. I met him a few years later in Oxford and we became good friends.

My position at UNC in a Department of Religion meant that I had to be concerned with issues that dealt with the field of the history of religions and I took this obligation seriously, for which my training under Goodenough had prepared me. This brought me into some conflict with the history of religions approach reflected in the work of Frank Cross, on the one hand, and the theological/homiletical approach that dominated the scholarship in SBL. I did a study on "The Religion of the Patriarchs," which took issue with the followers of Cross in particular. I presented it at the SBL national meeting and then submitted it for publication to *Biblica*, the journal of the Pontifical Biblical Institute in Rome. The Jesuit scholar, Dennis McCarthy, the Old

Testament editor of the journal responded by stating that they were happy to accept the article for publication. He did pass along some comments by readers, with the comment that I may wish to clarify certain points to forestall any objections of readers, but that was entirely optional and he was prepared to accept it as it is. McCarthy was a very good scholar and I would make good use of his work. However, we never met because he died prematurely. He was one of a number of Catholic scholars who had thrived as a result of Vatican II, which encouraged study of the scriptures in the original languages.

In September of 1979 I received a letter from Carol Redmount Bryant (she was now married), who was at the Oriental Institute in Chicago, telling me all about the past dig season. They had been digging up more of the Hyksos period graves and she hoped to get a doctorate out of this material, which she did from the additional material of the small Hyksos settlement found in subsequent seasons, to which these graves belonged. From an extensive surface survey she found traces of many small "Hyksos" settlements in the Wadi Tumelat region. All of this was in confirmation of my own Yale thesis, which of course pleased me. She said that it was a good season with everyone getting along very well. My former Toronto colleague Albert Pietersma was a great help in maintaining the sanity of the group. She also wrote to ask me if I would write a letter of recommendation on her behalf, because she was job hunting, and I did. It was for the head of the Albright Institute in Jerusalem (formerly ASOR and my home in 1964–65), and we both knew that she had little chance of getting it. But it was important for her to begin to get her name and credentials noticed, for future jobs consideration. This would not be the last reference that I would write for her, and eventually she landed a very good position in California.

With the end of the semester in May of 1979, I was ready to dive into my research on biblical historiography. This was going to be a broad comparative study and for this purpose I already had the material from the Toronto historiography seminar of 1974 and copies of the expanded papers by Grayson and Hoffner that would form useful study guides of a wide range of ancient Near Eastern texts. After I worked through all of these materials I sent copies to them for their comments. I also received a paper on "The Historiography of Ancient Egypt" from Don Redford and corresponded with him about these issues. On the historiography of ancient Greece, the two classicists at Chapel Hill, Philip Stadter and William West, were most helpful with their suggestions and scrutiny of what I had written. Jack Sasson, Bill Moran of Harvard, and Bill Hallo of Yale all helped me with the comparative material, and that took up more than half of the book. With my previous work on the Toronto seminar paper and various papers that I had given at academic society meetings I had a large part of the rest done. I had a wonderful assistant in Teresa Smith to check on bibliography. Teresa was a major in history and had taken one of my courses, so I was familiar with the quality of her work. She later got an editorial position with the UNC Press.

First Term as Department Chairman

During the spring semester, while I was on leave doing my writing on biblical historiography, Ruel Tyson's term as chairman was coming to an end. This meant that the dean of the College of Arts and Sciences, Sam Williamson, set about to interview all of the members of the Department as to their choice of chairman for the next five years. It was quite clear that there was little sentiment within the Department to have Tyson serve as chair for a second term, although he certainly wanted to do so. In spite of the fact that I was on my sabbatical, I was not exempt from this process. Williamson asked me for my views of the various prospective members and I gave them, based on my limited experience of only two years. He also asked me if I would be willing to do the job, should that be the consensus of the Department. I told him straight away that I did not want it, that I did not come to Chapel Hill for that purpose and that, in any case, the rest of the department hardly knew me after just two years. My views were duly noted and that was the end of the first interview, but it was not the last. Perhaps a week or so later I heard from Williamson again. This time there was only one thing on his mind. He indicated that I was the overwhelming choice for the job, and now it was clear that he would not take no for an answer. The Department had gone through a rough patch, involving a lawsuit against two former chairs, including the most recent one, and the dean wanted both stability and greater democratic accountability and harmony within the department. Usually the dean has something to offer in order to entice the more senior scholars to take the job, such as his support for an endowed chair, but I already had one. The best I could do was the promise of another sabbatical at the end of the five-year term. He was also aware of my recent recognition with the Guggenheim Foundation and my publication record, and the fact that I was working on a project in ancient historiography. He was also a historian. I quickly got the sense in our conversations that Sam and I could deal with each other quite candidly and with mutual respect. He talked me into the job as chairman, beginning in the fall semester of 1980.

There was a very modest "administrative supplement" to my salary for being chairman, which hardly compensated for the time spent on this part of the job, the rest was coming out of the Gray chair endowment fund. I made sure that he was aware of the fact that he was getting a bargain in the deal. Anytime I needed a little more for the Department budget I reminded him of that fact. I took time to examine the departmental spreadsheets and learned the math and economics of the system, something that many chairs did not bother to do, to their department's detriment. I developed a good relationship with Sam's financial secretary, and would always make it a habit to go over financial matters with her just before I went in to my conferences with the dean. It saved time and was more efficient, which deans liked, even if he knew that I would get for the Department all that was coming to it. Deans loved to find ways that they could save a bit of the college budget at departmental expense for their own discretionary spending.

There were, of course, a host of other matters that involved new appointments, promotion and tenure reviews, annual salary increases, program development, guest lectures, temporary appointments and teaching assistants, and many of these included not only departmental discussion but also review by the dean's office. The chair organized all of these activities as well as running the monthly departmental meetings, appointing committees, writing up five-year planning reports for the college every two years (or so it seemed). To make time for all of this administrative activity, I was relieved of half my teaching load, but I still retained my large introduction course (which was the most work) because this was what the Gray Chair was all about. I had two offices, the one that was off the administrative secretary's office and the other was my academic office and study, with the major part of my library, and a division of labor was associated with each. All the files relating to departmental business were kept in the administrative office and were the property of the university, and still are.

I had a very good and loyal administrative secretary and office manager in Maxine Underwood, and she and her husband, Harvey, remained good friends long after she retired. She helped me maintain my sanity by keeping track of my commitments, assignments and deadlines, appointments, and my administrative files. And she typed up all of my correspondence and documents. There were others in the front office staff, which often involved hiring new personnel, especially Maxine's replacement, and this could be a tricky business, but while I was chair the morale was always very good and many of these staff members became lifelong friends long after I was no longer chair. There was, of course, the important responsibility of hiring new faculty members and tenure decisions that could be very controversial and had to be negotiated with great care by the chair. During my first term there were no new appointments, but we did have three young faculty members that came up for tenure review. Fortunately they had good teaching and scholarly publication records and they there given permanent faculty status.

I will not burden this narrative with all of the petty little hassles that constantly beset the department chair or all the other interruptions to the time spent in scholarly pursuits. However, one of the more meaningful activities was the monthly meeting of department chairs, run entirely by the chairs themselves, in which they occasionally invited administrators in order to interrogate them about their policies and plans, but more important was for the chairs to share their own thoughts and ideas on a range of subjects. There was a sense of comradery within the group and it was very helpful to know those with experience and good sense whom you could consult and share your ideas. I made a number of good friends within this group.

4

Second Trip to Egypt and Visit with H. H. Schmid in Switzerland

Plans for the third season of excavation at Tell el-Maskhuta in the summer of 1981 were being made during the academic year, the fall of 1980 and spring of 1981. There had been no excavation in the summer of 1980 in order for Jack Holladay and his research team in Toronto to put together a detailed preliminary report on the first two seasons, as a requirement of obtaining funding support for further work in the field, and this they did in fine style. I kept in touch with Jack and had him down to Chapel Hill in February of 1981 to give a talk to like-minded archaeologists at the university. This also gave Jack and I a chance to talk over in detail all of the plans and aspirations for the coming season. The situation in Egypt had changed a great deal since the first year, because Egypt had signed a peace treaty with Israel, so there would be no UN forces in Egypt and no military base in Ismailia. There would also be the chance of having much freer movement around the Eastern Delta.

At the same time that I was making these preparations, I decided to get in touch with Hans Heinrich Schmid in January of 1981 to see what he thought about my visiting him in Zurich, Switzerland on my return home from Egypt. If that was a possibility, then I would also plan to have Elizabeth and Deborah fly over from America to meet me in Zurich and we could use the occasion to have a holiday at the same time, if we could find some appropriate accommodation in the vicinity of Hans Heinrich's home. In previous correspondence Hans Heinrich and I had talked about exploring the chance to meet each other and this seemed like a good opportunity to do so. I was quite delighted when, in a few days-time, I received an enthusiastic response encouraging me to make plans for such a visit. He would also make plans for the accommodation and help with suggestions about the vacation part of our visit. I would precede Elizabeth and Deborah by a few days so that Hans Heinrich and I could have all the time we needed to talk about academic matters of mutual interest. So along with the season of excavation in Egypt this was going to be a very busy summer.

The date for the flight to Egypt was May 15th and most of us who were involved in the dig made a rendezvous in New York. However, weather conditions in New York were so bad that incoming flights, including our plane, were being diverted to Washington, with the result that they ran out of gas and needed to refuel all the aircraft and planes had to wait until more supplies came before our plane could fly back to New York to pick us up. The result was that instead of leaving in the evening, we spent the night in the airport lounge and left at 5:30 a.m., ten hours late. This also meant that we arrived in Athens at 9:30 p.m. local time and missed our connecting flight to Cairo. As a consequence we had to spend the night in a cheap hotel in Athens, and then kill time the next morning by visiting the acropolis and other landmarks in the city center. The afternoon flight to Cairo was delayed until 7 p.m. and we were split into two groups. We arrived in Cairo quite late, hoping that in all this mess our baggage would somehow also arrive when we did. I was lucky with my baggage but some others were not and did not get theirs for a few days. From the airport we were supposed to go directly out to the dig site at Tell el-Maskhuta, but instead we went to Ismailia in our own hired bus, because we did not yet have military clearance to go to the site so close to a military base. It was 12:30 a.m. by the time we arrived at the hotel. Jack went to Cairo to deal with the authorities, while Ted Lutz, the camp manager (and my former colleague at the University of Toronto), organized matters in Ismailia, i.e., rooms, meals, etc. He was superb at that and proved quite indispensable to the whole operation. We remained in Ismailia the better part of two days. On the second day we went swimming at a beach on Lake Timsah (salt water) belonging to the Suez Canal Company, which catered to the middle class. It was very pleasant with umbrellas supplied and a view of the ships passing through Lake Timsah where it leads into the Suez Canal. Our stay at the beach was interrupted by Ted Lutz, who told us to get back to the hotel as soon as possible because we now had clearance to go to the dig site. After quickly packing, we piled into some taxis, and off we went to Maskhuta, 25 kms west of Ismailia. Thus, we arrived at the dig site three days later than originally expected.

The little village school that served as our camp had now expanded to include the new wing of rooms that I had helped to negotiate during the first season, which had been built during the second season in 1979. There was also the addition of electricity in the village, courtesy of the Aswan Dam Power project, and this improved matters considerably for us. It seems that one of the first acquisitions made by the villagers when electrification arrived was to purchase an inexpensive television set and a simple antenna that was stuck into a metal container filled with sand, which sat on the flat roof of their simple abodes. In the evening one could stand on top of the high ridge made of canal waste and look over the village in the distance and one would see these numerous spots of blue glowing from all of the television sets. The village also acquired a new health clinic, which was located next to the school, with its own young doctor. This meant that we had medical help very close by when we needed it. The doctor often shared an evening meal with us. He was, of course, fluent in English and we had interesting conversations with him. We also had our own nurse on site as well. The weather in May is still quite pleasant and the nights are cool but the mosquitoes are abundant at night and nothing can stop them.

There is no need for me to go into any great detail about the excavation itself. By the end of the third season we had opened up a number of areas on the site and followed them down to virgin soil, so that the history of occupation of the site was quite clear. We could not possibly excavate the whole site; given the size it would take several years and great expense to do so. However, we did run a trial section though the center of the mound, from one side to the other, which gave us a pretty good profile of the settlement phases. Of special interest to me was the discovery of the small un-walled village that had belonged to the earliest phase, which corresponded in time with the period of the so-called Hyksos donkey burials that had been discovered in the previous seasons. These migrants from southern Palestine had moved into the region and settled there without any evidence of conflict or conquest during the time that Egyptologists call the Second Intermediate Period, ca. 1750–1550 BCE, a time of decentralization of royal authority, corresponding to the period of the Hyksos domination of the Egyptian Delta. This village, together with the graves, completely confirmed my doctoral thesis on the Hyksos, quite radical at the time, and that position has scarcely been disputed since then.

At the mid-point of the season we took a break of four days, and I opted to go to the same hotel resort as before, the Salamelek, at Montazah, about 20 kms east of Alexandria. The trip by train (first class) was not expensive and quite pleasant. Ted Lutz and I shared a large corner room with private shower and bath, on the third floor, and a big rap-around balcony on two sides, so that you always had a choice of sitting in sun or shade any time of the day. It was also great for panoramic pictures of the beach and beyond. Ted and I also shared the same ideas about our time here, relax, write, read, swim, and relax again. We did make one side-trip out to that marvelous fish-food restaurant that we discovered the first time that we were here.

During the second half of the season we had a visit from Ted Campbell and Phil King, representing ASOR, along with two of its trustees. So Jack and I took them on a tour of the whole site, explaining what was going on in each of the fields where we were working. This was very useful to me because, working in an area on the eastern side of the tell the whole time with all of one's attention on that one spot, it is hard to keep up with what is going on in the other areas, so it gave me a very good over-all review. The ASOR group was quite impressed with the whole operation and amazed at the problems that an excavation such as this represented. I was also glad to see my old friends, Ted and Phil, again and pleased that they were happy with what Jack was doing.

On a free day towards the end of the dig a few of us rented a couple of taxis at 6:30 a.m. in order to visit Manfred Bietak's archaeological site at Tell ed-Dab'a, the region on the eastern branch of the Nile that I had explored back in 1965. I had given a talk to the group about the site and its historical significance, and also what to look for in terms of the similar Hyksos settlement and graves on our site. We did not take the main travel route, which would have been to follow the canal road to the western end of the Wadi Tumilat and then turn northeast, following the eastern Nile branch and the eastern edge of the Delta. Instead, we took a short-cut from the Wadi Tumilat directly north-west on the desert road to the town of Faqus, which is where the desert meets the lush vegetation that runs beside the eastern branch of the Nile, which extends to the Mediterranean. Following this road north from Faqus beside the Nile a few kilometers we arrived at Bietak's excavations at Tell ed-Dab'a, the ancient city of Avaris and capital of the Hyksos rulers. We were met by a member of his team who showed us around. Bietak himself was not there. He wisely prefers to dig in the cooler part of the year. He had built a very fine expedition house with field research facilities, and his excavation was meticulous. We carefully wandered around the site looking at the latest exposure. We could identify the remains of the same type of Hyksos burials, pottery and other features that we had at Tell el-Maskhuta. For me it was a personal thrill to realize that the barren low mound that I had identified as Avaris sixteen years earlier, against the views of so many other scholars of the day, was now being so thoroughly and carefully excavated. From Tell ed-Dab'a we proceeded further north along a side branch of the canal up to Tanis. This was familiar territory for me from my previous visit in 1965, but the others had never seen it, and the great size of the site with its monuments never ceases to impress the visitor. But aside from some archaeologists few visitors ever go there because it is so far off the beaten track. After wandering over this site for a while it was time to return the way we came, once again by way of the desert route rather than following the longer route, namely, the river road from Faqus south to western end of the Wadi Tumilat road, which I mentioned earlier.

Let me pause and say something about the historical geography of this region. In antiquity there was no such desert road, which runs through an area of high sand dunes and must be constantly maintained or it is soon buried by the desert. All ancient travel routes stayed within the great Delta triangle of lush vegetation created by the branches of the Nile and its many canals. The area on the eastern edge of this triangle from Faqus to the western end of the Wadi Tumilat was the ancient district of Goshen. The Egyptian form of this name was Gesem or Qesem, from which the modern name of the town of Faqus is derived. The Wadi Tumilat is a shallow valley running east from the Delta to the Suez, and in antiquity this valley contained a long narrow fresh water lake that served as a drain from the Nile during the annual inundation and this created some vegetation along this lake region in the western end of the wadi. It also attracted the Bedouin into this region from the Sinai with their flocks in the dry season to this fresh water supply. That was a pattern that lasted for many centuries. Then in ca. 600 BCE Pharaoh Necho II dug a canal from this lake at the western end of the Wadi Tumilat to its eastern end at Lake Timsah, which was the ancient northern extension of the Red Sea, in order to have commercial access by ships from the Mediterranean to the Red Sea and beyond. (This was the precursor of the Suez Canal.) This extended the growth of some arable land alongside of the Wadi Tumilat Canal, as it does today. (Include map of the region).

The Bedouin still come into the region with their animals, but not to a lake at the western end, which no longer exists. Now they encamp at any convenient spot along the side of the fresh water canal while there animals graze on the vegetation beside the canal. We periodically had them set up camp on part of our site away from the excavation area and the village, with their donkeys, sheep and goats and chickens, and a few camels. Some groups were small, others quite large. When they moved along the canal road the larger groups could block traffic for quite some time. They were just accepted as a fact of life in this region. The local villagers always refer to them as "*arab*," which means Bedouin, the true Arabs, and not Egyptians. The villagers are *fellahin*, farmers, and regard the Bedouin as foreigners from Arabia, which historically always meant the desert region east of the Nile, including the Sinai. Even though everyone in Egypt spoke Arabic, i.e. the language of Arabia, they were not Arabs in the real sense of this term and would tell you so.

In the story of the Israelites' departure from Egypt, they could not take the northern coastal route towards Gaza (the land of the Philistines), so they had to take the only other route, the long road south to the west end of the Wadi Tumlat and then east to Succoth = Pithom (Tell el-Maskhuta) and the northern end of the Red Sea (= Lake Timsah). Biblical atlases that show the Israelites going in a straight line from Qantir (= Rameses) and Faqus (Goshen) through the desert to Pithom make no geographic sense. The story also tells us that a group of "*ereb*" went with them (through the Wadi Tumilat) along with a large number of domestic animals and birds. Who are these *ereb*? Translators have made some vague guesses, with the meaningless rendering "mixed multitude," but the answer is quite simple. The Hebrew *ereb* refers to the *arab*, the Bedouin, and the description of them with their sheep, goats and birds could not be more obvious. That is exactly what one would expect to encounter going through the Wadi Tumilat, the Bedouin with their flocks heading for the Sinai Peninsula.

Furthermore, in the biblical story of the Israelites in Egypt the model for the Pharaoh is none other than Necho II of the late seventh early sixth century BCE. It was he who built those massive brick walls at Pithom with the very large labor force drawn from the foreigners of Goshen, many of whom were Jews. The description of the great city wall's construction in Exodus 5 matches the remarks that Herodotus makes about this building activity, in which many lives were lost in the process of its construction. All of this fits exactly the Yahwist version of the events and is completely missing from the Priestly version of the story. This evidence strongly confirms my dating the Yahwist to the mid-sixth century BCE and not to some later time as is now commonplace in German biblical scholarship today.

The point that I am trying to make is that what I learned from first hand travel in this region of Egypt is that geography and archaeology are very important for understanding history, and indeed for understanding ancient stories such as the Israelites in Egypt and the exodus. I used this in both my study of the Hyksos and in my biblical studies and I have written a number of pieces on these issues during my career. The same need for understanding geography of a region applies to the whole of Palestine where my time spent there during the better part of a year was invaluable for me. In the latter case, however, the land of Palestine, particularly Israel, is so well traveled by biblical scholars that they are less inclined to make the same errors than they do with those parts of Egypt that are rarely seen by tourists or even other scholars.

I do not intend to report on the excavations in detail or all of the many interesting episodes that happened during the two months on the site. However, a couple of them stand out and may be of interest here.

1. *Buried Treasure.* It is common for excavations to report the discovery of a treasure trove of silver or gold coins or the like to the local authorities. But sometimes it is the case that one makes a discovery one would rather not have made, and it is a puzzle as to what to do about it. It turned out that in the excavation we came across a large block of brown vegetable matter, weighing perhaps a kilo, but obviously of no great age. We called the foreman of the workers to get his opinion. He smiled and said "hashish!" Well Jack and I conferred and decided that we had to inform the local police about this, or there could be trouble. Well the police came and we handed over the forbidden trove to them. They then talked for a while with the foreman and then left. I later spotted the foreman and called him over for a chat. I asked him what had happened to the hashish. He put his hand into the pocket of his long gown and pulled out the block of hashish. I asked him why he still had it and not the police. He said with a smile: "I told them it was found in the ruins of this very old city. So it was too old and no good any more. So he gave it back to me." He could hardly keep from laughing. I told him to put it away in a safe place and get on with the work. My guess is that it had been hidden on site by one of the Bedouin passing through and then had failed to retrieve it at a later date.

2. *The Great Robbery and the "Scotland Yard" Detective.* This next event was so bizarre and unusual, and yet so typical of what could happen on a dig like this that shortly after it happened I wrote down a journal of the event in detail. The following is a summary account of this journal. Events in camp at Tell el-Maskhuta had been very dull during the recording days at the end of the dig season. In fact, for myself there was very little more to do and time was rather dragging by. Thursday, July 9th, was not much of an exception. Even though it was an off day, which meant that some went into Ismailia for the day, I was tired of the hassle, so I stayed in camp. After a simple meal with only six of us I then turned in around 9 p.m. The next morning things began to

change rather dramatically. About 5 p.m., shortly after we got up, it was discovered that the camera room, which is also the room where important finds of objects are recorded and repaired and where the money box is also kept, had been broken into. Someone had broken through the screen on a window of the room at the back of the building. Outside, a short distance from the building, the camera case and the cameras were scattered about. The only things that were missing were a small light-meter in a leather case and an antiquity—a large ceramic Bess-figurine—quite fragile. It had been temporarily restored but could easily break into several pieces again without special care. No attempt had been made to take the money box, which was chained to the shelf and not easy to find in the dark. It was clear that one of Maskhuta's new "street lights" must have helped the thief see the large ceramic and the camera case, and that is all. It was immediately apparent that we had been negligent. Although we had locked the door on the compound side, we had left the windows unlocked on the backside of the building. In fact they were open with only thin screens to prevent entry. It was rather easy to come through the window from the back, about four to five feet from the ground. But where was the guard? One was always posted every night at the back of the building, but on this night he was not there at 5 a.m. and had not been there during the entire night. He would pay dearly for his negligence.

I had finished my breakfast by about 5:45 a.m., a little late, but on Fridays things are a little slower. Word about the theft had spread rather quickly and the other guards had assembled at the back of the building to do their own investigation. The chief guard, Abdel-Aziz, and one of our camp workers, Fuad, were following the rather clear tracks of a bare-footed person from the location of the window away to the east. Even though the sand is full of footprints of every kind, after a good fall of dew fresh prints are quite clear and easy to follow. The thief obviously had large feet, was flat-footed, with a heavy tread on the right foot, which dug deep into the sand, and his stride was fairly short. We followed the tracks for 100 yards and then a fresh set in shoes, apparently a young boy, met the other. They appeared to go on together for a little way in the direction of the town of Abu-Suwer. The bear-footed thief stopped, put down the camera case, the imprint in the sand is quite clear on this. Perhaps he changed his mind about this plan because he picked it up again and took it back the way he came and just dumped it where it was later found behind the school building. But the small light-meter and the ceramic Bess-figurine were still missing. Further scrutiny seemed to indicate that this person had originally come from south of the school around the front of the medical building and had returned in this same direction going around the back of the clinic towards the western edge of the village. All of this was ascertained rather quickly and it was decided that the authorities had to be notified. Of course the local antiquity inspectors were informed of the details because all significant objects found on the site had to be reported each day so that if any went missing, such as the ceramic Bess-figurine, it had to be accounted for. The police in the town of Abu-Suwer, a couple of kilometers away were informed, but they told us that no investigation could be conducted without special forms from Ismailia. So our party had to go to Ismailia to get these papers, and that took most of the morning. In the meantime the guards had roused Suliman, the unfortunate negligent guard, and began to interrogate him, slapping him about. He confessed that he had not been on duty during the night. It was observed by others that he had had a number of visitors the night before and was seen entertaining them outside, in front of his house well past the time that he was supposed to be on guard. In fact, he never did go to his post.

The police finally showed up about 2 p.m., eight hours after the attempt was first made to bring them to the scene of the crime—incredible! And there were many of them. They asked some questions about the details of the theft and looked at the room. They were told about the two objects that were missing and they briefly looked at the tracks, which were hardly very fresh any longer. However, they had no special personnel to do foot-print casts, tracking, fingerprints, etc., even though they brought out to the site a special detective from Cairo who just happened to be visiting in Abu-Suwer. He told Jack and me that he had been trained by Scotland Yard. We tried very hard to keep a straight face. One wonders in what he was actually trained. The police began a rather perfunctory interrogation of the guards and the camp staff. It was obvious that it had to be someone familiar with the camp and that room. They made various persons walk barefoot in the sand but did no more than just glance at the impressions.

Their main attention was directed towards Suliman, the guard. They began to yell at him and push him about, in a very threatening manner, but he protested his innocence of the theft, while confessing his negligence on the job. His son was also called for questioning—a boy in his early teens. It was obvious to Suliman's wife that her husband was in for a rough time. She was dressed in black and had five little girls, her children, around her. She began to wail and to beg the police to go easy on her husband, and all the children were crying as well. The police merely told her to be quiet and to go back to her house. After considerable questioning they decided to take Suliman into Abu-Suwer, along with his son, in one of our vehicle. They did not even bring a paddy wagon. This action, of course, drove his wife to the point of hysteria, but they paid no attention. She believed that it would be the end of him. They also took along one of the kitchen boys, a dark-skin chap who was not too bright. The reason for including him was that the chief guard had put the finger on him as a suspect, for the simple reason that he was not from the village and would make a good scapegoat. This charge points up another method of the local police. They would ask everyone who they think did it, and the locals would respond by suggesting persons whom they did not like and not based upon any real evidence. Since the two Antiquities Department personnel attached to the dig did not relate well with the locals, they were also named as suspects. And so it went.

Amer, one of our Egyptian staff, had driven Suliman, with police escort, to the police station. There he witnessed the interrogation, which was rather brutal. We received a graphic description of it when he returned. The two boys apparently were not touched, but they wanted either to get Suliman to name accomplices or just to teach him a lesson. Suliman was returned to his home late Friday night by Amer, and our nurse, Evelyn, gave his wounds first aid. He looked a mess. The police also brought in a tracker late in the afternoon, who traced the footprints to a house in the village, and took a suspect away for questioning, but the matter does not seem to have been taken very seriously.

The photographer's equipment was insured so Jim made a request to the police that they give him a statement to the effect that his light-meter had been stolen. That request was a mistake! The "Scotland Yard" detective made some remark to Jack and I that this would be bad publicity and that instead he would write to say that it had been "lost in the desert." If the matter had simply been left at that, it would still have been alright. Jim still figured that he could collect without such a statement, so he was not greatly concerned. But the request set the detective thinking, and he came up with a new motive for the crime. As he explained to Jack and me: "What do these locals know about light-meters? Nothing! Why were the cameras not taken, merely scattered? Why was no money taken by these poor people? The figurine plaque was of little value in his opinion and therefore not the point of the theft. All of this came to one conclusion. The whole thing had been engineered by Jim or someone in camp in order to collect the insurance ($180)—about the cheapest item of all the equipment! It did not occur to "Scotland Yard" that the thief probably mistook the case for a transistor radio, which was all the rage in the village. Suliman's release from prison was probably the result of the move to this new theory.

All of this focus on the light-meter led to a police raid on the camp at midnight. One by one the rooms of our sleeping quarters were searched. It was both ludicrous and very disturbing. Our room was the first and Ted Lutz, the camp manager, came in with a few officers, of course without a search warrant. They began at one end of the room, looking through everyone's personal possessions. They must have assumed that we had electricity in these rooms—we did not—and did not come equipped with any flashlights, so they had to borrow ours. Naturally, they looked through Jim's stuff and found nothing of interest. I got out of bed (in a foul mood) and showed them my cases and other things I had out in plain view, including my light-meter next to my camera. When their light shown on the light-meter, they asked me what it was: "Shoo hatha" (what is that?). I told them: "a light meter." So they asked me if Jim's light meter was like mine and I said yes, but his was in a leather case. This answer seemed to please them because now they knew what they were looking for. Then they moved on to the next room. By this time the whole camp was awakened and some were treating it as a lark. The women, of course, had to be duly warned so they would be respectable. The total operation took more than an hour and by that time everyone was in a state where little sleep was possible for the rest of the night. After what had happened to Suliman, there was little humor in the whole business.

Saturday morning we learned that we were confined to camp and the excavation site and could not leave the area. Little explanation was given as to why or just how restricted we were to be, but we played it safe, to appear as cooperative as possible. During the morning we had a staff meeting to discuss what we would do if they tried to detain us longer, since some of us were scheduled to leave by plane the next day. My flight was not until Tuesday, but the irrational behavior of these people made me very nervous. Ted and Carol offered a review of our situation, suggesting that the police were still playing with so many different options. It was best to just "keep cool." Ha! If the police gave us any trouble when they came later in the morning then we would contact our embassies.

The police did arrive in two groups, the local police and the security police, and the same questions and details were repeated. At this point they also took fingerprints. They also asked us for two plastic basins to place over a couple of the footprints—a little late. The senior antiquities inspector from Zagazig, the boss of our two local inspectors, also showed up conveniently and he offered the police a statement, suggesting that the two junior inspectors were obviously responsible for the theft. This now seemed to change the whole complexion of the affair. Soon after this we were informed that we would be allowed to leave as scheduled. The young inspectors, of course, looked very upset with this development. However, apart from some mild interrogation, they were permitted freedom of movement. No one actually thought that they had done the deed themselves or how they hoped to get anything out of it. They were merely there to take the blame.

Saturday night had been planned some days earlier as a bit of a party, and now by late afternoon there was a little more to celebrate. Appetites picked up and the spaghetti was devoured, washed down by Egyptian white wine (I don't recommend it). We even had a little sing-song after supper. It should be pointed out that through all of this distraction, some people at least had still a lot of work to do, particularly with processing pottery and working on field reports. Saturday night I slept like a log.

Sunday morning was rather quiet. The police now seemed totally disinterested in us, and we saw nothing more of them. The chief inspector of the whole Eastern Delta region, the boss of the Zagazig inspector, now appeared to review the situation. He was an able person and quite reasonable. It appears that he was visiting not primarily because of this theft but because there had been some problems between the junior inspectors and their immediate superior (the one now accusing them of the theft) before this present episode. So he also became involved in the investigation. He and Jack had a good discussion about the situation. It appears that the two junior staff members, who had been rather "unpolitical" in their actions towards superiors for some time, were being demoted to lowly functionaries for the time being. As for the investigation of the present situation, the Antiquities Department had its own police force and would carry out its own investigation.

On this day, Sunday, members of the dig started their long journey home. The first car, a red Nissan, loaded with luggage, left at noon for the Sheridan Heliopolis hotel, along with Amer, the driver, Carol and Bryant Wood. Then at 2 p.m. the white dig car along with two taxis and the rest of those leaving that day, set out for the Sheridan where they were going to stay that night and fly out in the morning. They left without incident, which seemed a good omen. The camp was greatly reduced in numbers—some still working on reports before they had to leave the next day. Jim Peacock, the photographer, and I were taking a nap, what every sensible person did in Egypt on a summer afternoon. About 3:30 I heard voices—Ted Lutz and Jack Holladay—just outside the room door. One of them said, "Perhaps Jim could do it," so I whispered to Jim, "Start snoring, I think they have some work for you," and he immediately carried off a pretty good imitation as soon as they came through the door. They asked me in a whisper, "Is he asleep?" This broke us up. They then explained that Magen Williams had gone off to Cairo without her purse and passport. The idea was to send someone after her with a cab. After much deliberation, it was decided that both Jim and I would go in a cab. We would stay overnight at the Sheridan, I would stay at the hotel while Jim would come back with a taxi the next day. They set off to get the taxi while I made a very quick job of packing. I even had a wet pair of socks which I had to stick in a plastic bag. The taxi sounded the horn from across the canal and I became the ferry man for the raft across the canal. We negotiated a rate for the trip and set off in his Peugeot.

There was one slight problem with this plan. It was easy to imagine that once Magen discovered her loss of purse and passport, one of the cars would be persuaded to return and we would probably meet them—or rather pass them—on the road. The desert highway to Cairo is a four lane divided road and cars travel at least 60 miles an hour so that on-coming cars are approaching at 120 mph. The sand is very bright and the sun is getting low in the west, the direction we were heading. To make matters worse, the government was trying to beautify the highway and provide a screen between the opposing lanes of traffic by planting trees in the divider. All this provides little time to see an oncoming car and clearly recognize it. I tried to explain to the driver in my limited Arabic that we were looking for a white car going in the opposite direction and when we saw it we would have to stop. He looked at me as if I was crazy, not because he did not understand the Arabic. Every other car on the road coming at us was white. I was guessing that it would be Richard in the white car and not Amer in the red Nissan. I also tried to calculate the time that we would probably meet. We set out about 4 p.m., but it would be close to 5 p.m. before we would see them. At best we would have about three seconds to roll down the window and wave frantically. What a hope! There was no way it would work and they would just go by all the way to T. el-Maskhuta and then would find out we had it back at the hotel. At 20 minutes to 5 I said to Jim: "It's got to be sometime between now and 5 o'clock." Well, a short piece down the road for some mysterious reason the engine in the taxi conked out and he just pulled over. He tried to start it again, but it would not go. He got out and lifted the hood, at which point we got out also. To make sure we had a view of the other side of the highway, Jim suggested that we actually cross over to the median, just in case. We no sooner got there and a couple of cars went by, when Jim said: "I think that's the Jeep (our red Nissan)." He was right! As it approached we started waving our arms as close to the edge of the road as we dared. I can still see the look of disbelief on Richard's face as he passed us. But our signaling did register and 100 yards down the road he stopped, turned around over the meridian and came up behind the taxi. We shouted to Magen in the front seat, "we've got it," and she came out to give us a big hug. Well, a few minutes of very fast explanation and then, what to do with the cab? The cabbie tried to fix the problem with our screwdriver, but with little luck. So we paid him off and gave him the screwdriver as well to let him keep trying. We all hopped into the Jeep and headed to the Sheridan. We booked into this luxury Sheridan Heliopolis Hotel and rejoined the others who had preceded us and who were taking a flight early the next morning. After changing into more civilized apparel we all met for a final celebration dinner.

The next morning, Monday, I saw them off. I could not leave until Tuesday morning because there was no flight to Zurich on Monday. My original intention was to come out to the Hotel on Monday, so I now had an extra day to kill in the lap of luxury. I did a little swimming in the pool, but the company of the rich, lounging at the pool-side sipping drinks and bragging about all the other luxury hotels in which they had stayed around the world, was so tedious that it drove me away. Instead, I went to my room and spent the time writing up the adventure of the last few days while they were still very fresh in my mind, which accounts for the details that are contained in it. I also did a little preparation for the talk on the Maskhuta dig that I was going to give in Zurich in a few days.

I was up early the next morning because my flight to Zurich was at 7 a.m., a four-hour flight, and I was the only one of our group taking this flight. The Sheridan was very close to the Cairo airport, a short taxi ride. I checked in with lots of time to spare and eventually went by a bus out to the plane on the tamarack. After identifying my suitcase before it was put on the plane, I boarded the plane and found my seat. Everyone was on board and it looked like we were ready to go, when a voice came over the speaker, "Would Mr. John Van Seters report to the front of the plane." Given all that had happened the previous few days, I could imagine that the little "Scotland Yard" detective had come up with another crazy idea to make trouble for us. I went to the front where the door was still open. The stewardess asked for my passport and then gave it to a man in uniform, who then went down the steps, got into a car and headed back to the main building. The time for take-off passed and we waited. I am sure that the rest of the passengers were cursing me, or they were familiar with Egyptian ways of doing things. After perhaps ten to fifteen minutes the car returned, the official got out and came up the stairs. He smiled and gave me my passport. I went back to my seat, the door closed, the engine started and away we went. I was finally on my way to Zurich and an entirely different world.

Before I begin to narrate my activities in this different world, I would like to add a few remarks on my Egyptian experience and my work in the field of archaeology in general. This was my last trip to Egypt and my last experience in archaeological field work. This decision had nothing to do with the adventure of the last few days of this season, which were not likely to be repeated in any subsequent season. The primary focus of my research in historical and literary criticism would not be advanced by time spent in field work. I have the greatest respect for Jack Holladay and his dedicated team. They worked very hard under quite uncomfortable conditions. The massive amount of data collected and processed was very impressive, with twice the number of staff working on analysis than digging in the field. This was a far cry from my experience with Pritchard where the object was to "move dirt" and the analysis and recording was slim. With this experience I could understand the language of archaeological reports and evaluate the merits of the evidence presented as it related to historical problems and debates. The biblical archaeology movement had held much of biblical studies hostage to their supposed expertise, but I was immune to their claims. My future association with the field of archaeology as it related to historical studies would move in quite a different direction. The shift from Near Eastern Studies in Toronto, with its many fine archaeologists, to the Department of Religion at Chapel Hill with no niche for archaeology also made the choice of my research and interests in other directions inevitable. Even though there was a strong archaeological component in the Duke Religion program, the Meyers were quite hostile to my work and cooperation was minimal. I did retain my connection with ASOR for quite a while, especially when their meetings were held together with SBL, and tried to follow the developments in the field. But my primary interest and scholarly passion was in that other world to which I will now turn.

Welcome to Switzerland, Gateway to the World of European Scholarship

My plane from Cairo landed safely at Zurich airport and I quickly went through passport control and then to the baggage area to pick up my suitcase and clear customs. Even though the plane had left a little late on my account, as mentioned earlier, it arrived in good time. I had arranged with Hans Heinrich Schmid, who was meeting me there, that I was fairly tall and would wear a particular outfit. So when I came through from customs, he spotted me and did not hesitate to approach me and introduce himself. I can still recall that great smile as he warmly shook my hand. At last, after four years of correspondence, we finally met each other, the beginning of a long and deep friendship. We had so much to talk about. I had hoped that Elizabeth could get a flight in a few days, but the only one available was the flight on 22nd, arriving on the 23rd, nine days later. So there was time enough for us to discuss a number of subjects about which we had been corresponding with each other. He had also told me about his doctoral student, Martin Rose, who had written a doctoral dissertation on the problem of the relationship between the Yahwist and Deuteronomist, with a special focus on Joshua, and I was keen on meeting him and seeing the work.

We drove to Hans Heinrich's home in Schwerzenbach, which is a small town to the east of Zurich, on Lake Greifensee. There I met Christa, his wife, and his four children, their daughter Regula, the oldest, their sons the twins, Konrad and Ulrich, and daughter Verena, the youngest, all in their teens. In addition to their home, there was in the same housing complex an apartment building in which Hans Heinrich had a large room for his study and library, and he gave me a tour of it. It was already a very impressive collection and he was younger than I was. What especially impressed me was the extensive collection of books dealing with the critical study of religion and history of religions. This concern with *Religionsgeschichte* as it related to Near Eastern antiquity and Israelite religion within this world is clearly reflected in his book, *Altorientalische Welt in der alttestamentlichen Theologie* (1974), a copy of which he had sent to me earlier. It was a major challenge to the Heidelberg school of von Rad, which dominated German biblical scholarship at that time. This interest and challenge I shared, especially now that I was in a Religion Department in Chapel Hill and we would discuss this subject a great deal in the coming days. Since Hans Heinrich did so much of his work in this study, he had a secretary come to this office a few days a week to do his correspondence and other matters of this kind for him. Also within this apartment block was a small apartment which he had arranged for our use, which was only a few steps from his home.

Hans Heinrich was eager to show me around Zurich of which he was very proud and for good reason; his roots were deep in this place and it is a very beautiful city. It was quite convenient to get there by train from the station in Schwerzenbach to the main station at the north end of the city center. The Limmat River flows through the city from north to south and empties into the large Zurichsee at the south end, dividing the city into the east side and west side. The first stop of our tour was obviously the theological seminary where he could check his messages, introduce me to others on the faculty and his graduate assistants, then see his office and tour the building in general. The seminary had an important role in the founding of the University of Zurich, and had a certain pride of place in the institution. Hans Heinrich was always active in the politics of the university, as he was in the life of the city in general. (more on this later). The seminary was built as an extension of Grossmünster Cathedral, one of the most venerable churches of Zurich, so of course we did a tour of the church. Of particular importance for Hans Heinrich was its fine collection of old Bibles which he showed to me. He had just published a little book on them which he gave me.

Across the river from Grossmünster on the west side was Fraumünster Cathedral and Hans Heinrich was keen to show me the magnificent stained glass windows in the choir and south transept by Chagall. Later, with Elizabeth and Deborah we would attend a concert in this place, a marvelous experience. Hans Heinrich and I also visited St. Peter's Church, the oldest church in Zurich and famous for having the largest clock on a church tower in Europe. The church itself was much simpler in design and appearance, compared with the others, but it had a special attachment for Hans Heinrich because his father had been pastor of this church. He pointed out many other features of significance in Zurich on both sides of the river. We visited one of the guild halls, not generally open to the public, and the *Rathaus*. On a later occasion we would visit the *Rathaus* while the city government was in session. An added bonus for this detailed tour was that I could later act as a guide for Elizabeth and Deborah when we did the rounds of the city. On another day Hans Heinrich and I took an excursion up to Schaffhausen, which is a city north of the Rhine and almost completely surrounded by German territory so that one needs to pass through a German checkpoint to get there. It is a very attractive city, but its main attraction is the Rhine Falls, which is quite impressive. It was definitely on the list of places to visit with Elizabeth and Deborah, and an easy train ride up from Zurich. Years later Hans Heinrich and I would again make a trip back to this spot.

A couple of days after I arrived in Zurich Hans Heinrich had his final seminar of the term for advanced students. On this occasion it was attended also by his assistants and some faculty, because I was to give a presentation on the excavations at Tell el Maskhuta (biblical Pithom) and then to say something about the relevance of our findings to biblical studies. On this occasion I also met Martin Rose, who gave me a copy of his recently published doctoral dissertation, *Deuteronomist und Jahwist*, which was a study of the parallels and interconnections between Deuteronomy and the book of Joshua on the one hand, and the Yahwistic corpus of the Pentateuch on the other hand. This work was done under the direction of Hans Heinrich, and we all agreed that its conclusions were very close to what I had advocated in my book on *Abraham*, and on my research materials for my later book, *In Search of History*, dealing with the so-called Deuteronomistic historian. I had been sending copies of my studies to Hans so that both he and Martin Rose were well aware of the direction my own work was taking. I was quite pleased to have this copy of Rose's book, hot off the press.

After receiving his doctorate, Rose became a pastor of a small church in the village of Dinhard in the countryside, and he invited me to come for a visit and overnight stay, which I did. It was very enjoyable being entertained by Martin and his wife in this beautiful historic church. The only drawback was that the guestroom was in the bell tower right beneath the bell and it rang all night, so I did not sleep that soundly. Nevertheless, we kept in touch for a time after he received a more permanent academic appointment at the University of Neuchâtel. From there he sent me his commentary on Deuteronomy, published in 1994. However, he rarely attended any international conferences and consequently I saw little of him, and his work did not receive the attention that it deserved. Another book that I received from Hans while in Zurich was a doctoral dissertation by Hans-Detlef Hoffmann, also a student of Hans Heinrich, published the year before as *Reform und Reformen*, which was an investigation of the basic themes of Deuteronomistic historiography. I did not meet Hoffmann, as I did Rose, because he was now in Bielefild-Bethel, Germany, in an academic position previously held by Hans Heinrich. His book was a superb, high quality piece of scholarly work and very useful for my current historiographic studies, and I made good use of it. What these two dissertations, those of Hoffmann and Rose, showed was that Hans, his students and I were together moving in a quite new direction in this area of study. To these books of Rose and Hoffman I will return later.

A few days after I arrived in Zurich, Hans Heinrich and Christa invited Prof. Odil Steck and his wife to dinner. Odil Steck was a colleague of Hans in the theological faculty of the university. After a great dinner on the patio, the two women went off to leave the three of us to our "shop-talk." Hans Heinrich had a good supply of his great Italian red wine on hand and we had a very enjoyable evening. Steck did not speak English, although he understood it, and I did not speak any German although I could manage fairly well with understanding the conversation and Hans Heinrich helped both of us out. Steck had been a student of von Rad, while Hans Heinrich was not, and had been critical of von Rad on some important issues, so it was interesting to see the dynamic between the two. Later, after Elizabeth and Deborah arrived, the Stecks invited us to their place, which was in a small town not far from the Schmids. Steck's wife was fluent in English and very outgoing, much like Christa, so there was no difficulty in communication and the occasion was quite enjoyable.

One of the important things that had to be done before Elizabeth and Deborah arrived was to get some advice and information on our sightseeing trips around Switzerland. Here the twins were the experts, Konrad in particular, I believe. He explained the whole system, the time table charts, and the amount of time needed between trains, 3 to 5 minutes, depending on the size of the station. Time-tables were completely dependable. With the size of Switzerland, one could usually reach most places of interest and return back to home base within a day. From Schwerzenbach to Zurich was a short trip by train and from Zurich main station one could travel in all directions, and with the Swiss holiday card there was no need to even queue up to buy tickets. It all seemed so easy, and it was. Before Elizabeth and Deborah arrived, the Schmid family was going to go for their vacation to a place in the southern Ticino region. However, they insisted that the three of us should come down and stay with them for a couple of days and see that part of the country, so plans were made so that they could meet the right train to take us to their place.

After the Schmids had left for their summer place in Ticino, I had some time to relax and take some strolls through the nearby woods and along the shore of Lake Greifensee to the next town and back. I also set to work, planning a series of day excursions and a longer overnight trip to Geneva. I also called home to Elizabeth and consulted with her about all of the plans that we had been making and assured her that all was set for a good time. On the day that they arrived, it was not difficult to take the train via Zurich all the way to the airport and meet them there, and then to return to Schwerzenbach the same way. We took a day or so to get adjusted and see a little of Zurich, and then we were off to the Schmids' place in Ticino. It was in the little town of Vira on the northeast shore of Lake Maggiore opposite the city of Lacarno. Their summer house is on the side of a mountain overlooking the lake. We were met at the train when we finally arrived and introductions were made all around, and soon we were all like family. It had rained hard on our way down and during the night, but the next morning was bright and clear. After breakfast Hans Heinrich called our attention to a spot on the hillside above Lacarno on the opposite shore, where there was a high power dam. There one could see a huge flood of water poring over the dam. It was quite spectacular and Hans Heinrich could not recall having seen anything like it before. So plans were made quickly and everyone piled into the Schmids' large family car, and we drove around the top of the lake through Lacarno and up the mountain road along the edge of the deep valley to the power dam. There is a bridge that runs over the top of the dam above this great waterfall, and some of us walked out onto the bridge to get this remarkable view of the waterfall and the whole valley down to Locarno. From the dam we drove further up into the mountains to some beautiful villages of this region. This is Italian-speaking Switzerland and has its own character, and we could experience this when we later walked around Locanro. The Italian border is about 10 km down the road and the city of Milan is not very far away.

For our return trip, after visiting the Schmids, Elizabeth, Deborah and I decided that we would not go by the more direct route that we had taken coming down. Instead we changed trains at the Gottard Pass and followed the Lower Rhine valley below a great range of mountains to the city of Chur, nestled in the valley surrounded by impressive peaks. We disembarked and wandered around the city center for a little while, then returned to the station and took the next train to Zurich. The frequency of the trains and the convenience of the holiday pass allowed one a great deal of flexibility in getting around the country. I will refrain from trying to describe each trip that we made in detail, and mention only a few highlights. Of course we went to Shaffhausen and Rhine Falls, but on the way we also stopped at Winterthur, where there is an art gallery just north of the city that has a marvelous collection of impressionist paintings. Another day trip was down to Lucerne, which straddles the one end of the lake, known in German as the Vierwaldstättersee, and a beautiful wooden covered foot bridge cuts across the lake, where it flows into the Reuss River, to connect both parts of the city. We also took a boat tour around the large lake while they served a wonderful lunch on board. Berne, the capital of Switzerland, was also a favorite, with its old buildings, a church tower that you can climb for a wonderful view of the city and beyond, and it's very old main-street with numerous fountains. We took another day trip to Basel, a large city on the Rhine where France, Germany and Switzerland all meet. The things to see there are more spread out here. We did make a return trip to the Basel Zoo, where we had taken Peter many years before.

On a beautiful sunny day we went to Interlaken and the Bernese Oberland to see the mountains and it became clear that others had the same idea. From Interlaken we ascended by special train to Lauerbrunnen, and from there by cable car up to Murren. From there the view of the Jungfrau and related mountain peaks was very beautiful, and a great setting for a little lunch. From Zurich we also made a trip to the northeastern part of the country, to St. Gallen, famous for its old monastery, and then onto Appenzel, a very picturesque place with beautifully painted houses. The landscape is also known as one of the most beautiful in the country. Finally, we took the longer trip to Geneva, going down one day, spending the second day sightseeing, and returning on the third day. Geneva is more spread out than Zurich, with a great deal to see. We also took a boat ride on Lake Geneva, and we visited the park with the monuments to the great reformers, most notably, John Calvin, because this was his city. Of course we did not neglect Zurich, and I already knew where to take Elizabeth and Deborah from my previous tour with Hans.

The Schmids returned home from Ticino in time for the national holiday on August 1st. There was a celebration with the local band at the center of town, with Hans Heinrich delivering a patriotic speech. In the evening we had a festive dinner and then watched the fireworks over the lake, just as one would do on the 1st of July in Canada. A few days later we said our fond farewell and expressed the hope they we would have the chance to entertain them at our place in Chapel Hill. Just such an occasion would come about in the years to come. During this visit what we came to realize was that the Schmids were a very remarkable family. In addition to his academic life, Hans Heinrich was also the conductor and leader of the Zurich youth orchestra in which all four of the children played instruments, and Christa was a concert pianist and accompanied the orchestra in their concerts. They even played for us a recording made of their latest concert. Christa had a grand piano in their home. In addition to this and other hobbies too numerous to mention, Hans Heinrich was also very much involved in the politics of the university. As he explained to me, they were revising the whole university system away from the rector of the university as a token and ceremonial figure to that of a chief administrator with a longer term of office, more on the North American pattern. As dean of the Theological School he had become very much involved in this whole process, and since I was now the chairman of our Department of Religion, we had considerable discussion about the pros and cons of comparative administrative structures. I was not yet aware, however, just how far this would take him in the future.

With this rather fortuitous visit to Zurich and the bond that developed between Hans and me, Switzerland now became my future gateway to Europe. Hans Heinrich was very highly regarded in the other universities in Switzerland, and also among many scholars in Germany. Later, my name was always included together with that of

Hans Heinrich Schmid and Rolf Rendtorff as the three "revisionists" of Pentateuchal criticism, and Hans Heinrich even showed me a recently published article in one of the major German newspapers on this movement in biblical studies, created by the three of us together. I had originally hoped that I could get an entrance into European biblical studies by way of Leiden and Piet de Boer, but that had not happened. With Hans Heinrich's help and determination, this Swiss gateway now showed great promise.

Back to the Book In Search of History

Landing in New York, after the Swiss adventure, was a return to reality of a kind similar to what had started here almost three months earlier. There was the famous air-controllers' strike in the Reagan era which created some havoc at the airports. To make matters worse, we were stopped at immigration because Deborah had tried to enter the country on her mother's Canadian passport, whereas, having been born in the US, she needed her own US passport, even though she was a citizen of both countries. This created a delay and a fine, which meant that we missed our connection to Raleigh–Durham airport. Consequently, we rented a car and because it was getting quite late, we stayed overnight in a motel room on the New Jersey turnpike. We finally arrived back in Chapel Hill with the new school year looming all too soon.

When I arrived back in the department office at the university there was a pile of mail waiting and administrative matters to be attended to, which kept me busy. I will pass over most of this and mention only items of some significance to the recent archaeological work in Egypt, to my visit with Hans Heinrich, and above all, to my work on biblical historiography. It was soon after I returned that I heard from Carol Redmount, a very fine archaeologist on Holladay's dig. She wanted me to write on her behalf for funding support for another season of excavation, and in particular, to write a cover letter to Manfred Bietak, about the possibility of getting a place on the Tell ed-Dab'a excavation next season, which I did. I could speak, not only to her superior qualities and experience as a "dirt" archaeologist, probably the best we had besides Jack, but more important to the value of her knowledge about out the Middle Bronze Age "Hyksos" materials at Maskhuta. I told Bietak that Holladay had given Carol the primary responsibility for preparing the MB materials for publication and that they would constitute the basis of her doctoral thesis so that cooperation between Bietak's dig and ours at Maskhuta were vital.

He wrote me a long and cordial letter in return, expressing the fact that he could not take her on because of obligations he had to using persons from his own University of Vienna, as well as Heidelberg and Amsterdam. Nevertheless, she would be more than welcome to visit the site and to discuss all relevant matters with him. He went on to give me a rundown on his excavations thus far and his interpretation of the material. He also sent me a copy of his recent publication, *Avaris and Piramesse.*

After I received the latter and read it, I gave him a more detailed description of our finds, including those of the most recent season and how they related to the particular examples of graves and the like that he had published in his book. I emphasized that the two sites, ours and his, had to be considered together. Since he was planning a trip to Toronto, I assured him that Jack Holladay would be happy to show him in greater detail the materials that we had from Maskhuta. As far as my role in the Tell el-Maskhuta expedition was concerned, it had been a supporting role from the start, and that would gradually wind down, especially as I was no longer in Toronto. I would not be involved in any of the publications.

I also had a letter at the beginning of term from Professor James (Jim) VanderKam, who taught Old Testament at North Carolina State University in Raleigh, NC, requesting that I give a guest lecture to his OT class on Israelite historiography. I was happy to agree, and we set a date in mid-October. Jim's specialty was text criticism, and he had trained in this field under Frank Cross at Harvard. He later became a noted member of the team of scholars editing the Dead Sea Scrolls. But in 1981 he was a young scholar and this gave me a chance to get to know him better. The event went off very well. I was pitched as a celebrity by this Harvard man, and the students seemed to enjoy the occasion. I gave Jim an offprint from my historiography article in *Orientalia* and we had a pleasant lunch together before I headed back to Chapel Hill. Jim, a graduate of Calvin College in Michigan, also had a conservative religious Dutch background, so we had a lot in common, and we got along very well and stayed in touch until he took a position at Notre Dame, and we lost contact with each other.

There is a popular periodical called *Biblical Archaeology Review* that was founded and edited by a Washington lawyer, Hershel Shanks, which seeks to present news of archaeological discoveries in the Holy Land to a lay readership and to be a forum for debates and controversies among biblical scholars. I had met Hershel at ASOR meetings, which he always attended to pick up stories. And he frequently tried to get me, as a controversial figure, involved in writing for his periodical, which offers I mostly resisted. Of course my books were usually given extensive, but seldom favorable, reviews in *BAR*, to which I was invited to respond, which I did. However, his rather high-handed editing was a constant irritation and heated disagreement. In the September/October 1981 issue of *BAR*, there was a report by Shanks on "The Exodus and the Crossing of the Red Sea according to Hans Goedicke," and I felt compelled to respond. Goedicke's original piece, which I had seen previously, seemed to be a rather wild piece of speculation involving a volcanic eruption in the Aegean, producing a tsunami, all of which was somehow made to fit the exodus story of the plagues and sea crossing. I sent my response to Goedicke's article in as a "letter to the editor," primarily because we now had solid archaeological evidence about Pithom, which directly related to the story of the exodus, particularly its late dating almost a millennium later than that being proposed by Goedicke. This was all part of the rather silly rivalry between Goedicke's effort to whip up conservative support for his dig at Tell el-Retaba in competition with our dig. At any rate, it was easy to demolish the piece. Goedicke was no biblical scholar and even in his use of Egyptian texts he was playing fast and loose with their interpretation. Shanks was very interested in the piece I wrote, but wanted me to expand it into something a little bigger, so I sent him a revised version and he printed it with minimal changes. As will become apparent, this would not be the last time that Goedicke and I would cross swords on scholarly matters, but our relationship was always a very odd one.

Let me now return to the primary focus of my research during this period, i.e. my book on Israelite historiography, which I now called *In Search of History: Historiography in the Ancient World and the Origins of Biblical History*. By the end of my research leave in the summer of 1980 I had the manuscript in rough draft form and so, with some additional research funds, I hired a doctoral student in English Literature, Flora Taylor, to work through it during the academic year of 1980–81 in order to make corrections and suggestions for style improvement. At times, with all of the red pencil markings on the page, I thought that she was overdoing it a bit. In the end, it did get quite a thorough rewrite. A few weeks before I left for Egypt, I sent the manuscript to Yale University Press to get into the queue moving towards approval and publication.

At the same time as this drawn-out process was taking place, I offered papers on the content at SBL and other meetings to get feedback. In particular, I had the two books by Martin Rose and H-D. Hoffmann, that would call for some important revisions, and in October of 1981 I sent off to Hans Heinrich my introductory chapters of the history of German scholarship dealing with historiography, as well as the chapter on the books of Samuel, in which he had a particular interest for his own current research. It was not until the end of December that he had a chance to send me a response in a long and detailed letter in English for my benefit. He began his remarks by stating: "I have received and just read the second part of your historiography manuscript. Thank you very much for it! I have never seen such a profound critique of its indeed sometimes curious and even confused theories." This was high praise indeed, coming from a very astute European scholar who was well read in all of this literature. However, he then went on to suggest that I should have taken my critique further back to Wellhausen with his "foundation in the 'historistic' movement of his time." In this he was entirely correct, but it would have taken a lot of time to do all the necessary reading of German scholarship on Wellhausen and his era to extend my survey back to that era, and so I did not take him up on this. It would be many years later that I would look at the whole issue and in fact begin at a point long before Wellhausen. (More on that later.) Hans Heinrich also was somewhat reticent in accepting my late date for the bulk of the David story, although he offered no specific arguments against my view. He only wanted to reserve judgment on that question. This also would be a subject to which I would return in the future.

In addition to Hans Heinrich, there was one other scholar in particular at this time with whom I had a lot of discussion about by project, and that was Burke Long in the Department of Religion at Bowdoin College in Maine who was also a Yale graduate. He was involved in a major publication project that had to do with genre studies, specifically with the forms of literature employed in the books of Kings. So we agreed to exchange substantial blocks of material from our respective studies as a basis for further discussion. In addition, he asked me to write a recommendation for an ACLS grant to give him more free time to work on it and I did my best, but he did not get one. Nevertheless, the process of scholarly dialogue constantly sharpened my thinking on these matters.

By December of 1981 I finally received from Yale the reader's comments on my book, which were favorable, although there was some discussion about reducing its length. On this I was quite adamant that it was all or nothing. The decision to accept it was made in January of 1982, and it was put into the schedule with a copy editor assigned in May, followed by the long drawn out task of revisions and corrections that lasted until the end of the year. The book finally appeared in April of 1983, about two years after the work was originally submitted. Of course, Yale University Press does a meticulous job of editing and publishing, so there is a trade-off.

Standing between Two Different Worlds of Scholarship

In January of 1982 I received a letter from Professor Otto Kaiser of the University of Marburg, as the new editor of the *Zeitschrift für die alttestamentliche Wissenschaft* (*ZAW*), inviting me to consider contributing articles to this journal. This was no form letter sent out to drum up business but an appeal sent to me personally. He stated that naturally this appeal arose out of his familiarity with my book, *Abraham in History and Tradition*, which he had found most stimulating and had forced him to extensively revise one of the chapters in the fourth edition of his widely used *Introduction to the Old Testament*. (In fact, I had been making use of the English translation of his third edition and had not yet seen the new fourth edition.) He also mentioned the fact that his student Hans-Christoph Schmitt in his doctoral dissertation has come to similar conclusions in his work on the Joseph Story, and that this new and somewhat controversial direction in biblical studies was now receiving a lot of attention in Europe. He also commented on how deeply I had gone into the European scholarship, and he offered to publish whatever I presented to him in a very timely fashion, including the journal's monograph series. The whole character of the letter was very friendly and personal. I should mention here the fact that a few years later I met Hans-Christoph Schmitt and we became close friends. He told me the story that when he first presented his work on the Joseph Story, Kaiser regarded it as too radical and controversial, but then Schmitt produced my book on *Abraham*, as support for his own thesis, which Kaiser had not yet seen, and after Kaiser read it, he was persuaded to support Schmitt's work. So Schmitt thanked me for saving his career and allowing him the freedom to be different from the majority view in Pentateuchal criticism.

I immediately responded to Kaiser's letter, thanking him for his kind remarks and invitation to publish with *ZAW*, telling him also that I had been using the English edition of his *Einleitung* for my classes. (Although Kaiser's letters were always in German, I responded in English and this arrangement produced a flood of friendly correspondence between us.) I told him of my work on the historiography project, which was already under contract with Yale University Press, and I mentioned the wonderful visit I had with Hans Heinrich Schmid and his colleague Odil Steck in Zurich, and how much I prized this personal contact with continental scholars. I also mentioned that once I had finished my historiography manuscript I would be writing four pieces on the Exodus stories, based on my work in a Pentateuchal seminar over the next few years. Kaiser immediately responded that he wanted any article of mine on the Exodus and if I could tell him when I would have it ready, then he would reserve a spot in a particular issue. He also expressed great interest in my historiography project and praised my choice of Hans Heinrich Schmid as a frank and appreciative dialogue partner. Any time I was in Zurich visiting Schmid, I should count on making a side trip to Marburg for a visiting lecture and a chance to meet personally.

In the correspondence that followed I did submit an article which was quickly published as promised. In addition to this I also sent him some recent offprints and this led to some long letters in which we exchanged various viewpoints and differences of opinion, but always in the most respectful fashion. Kaiser was, after all, about sixty years of age, a student of the noted scholar, Karl Elliger, and had had a quite distinguished career and, as he himself freely admitted to me in one of his letters, at this stage in his life he was not about to change all of his views about the Pentateuch. Nevertheless, he admitted that "for the careful researcher there is gold lying in the street," and he loved the give and take of lively discussion. So we enjoyed our association in spite of our differences and this friendship would last many years.

In contrast to this European world in which I was being treated with respect, there was the American world back home. At the same time that I had this correspondence with Kaiser, I received a request from David Graf, an associate editor of the *Biblical Archaeologist*, which was a semi-popular journal put out by ASOR, asking me if I was interested in submitting a recent paper that I gave at SBL on "Herodotus and the Old Testament," a session that he himself had attended. He set a deadline for submission of less than a month by which to get it in to make a publication deadline. This would mean I could do little more than make some minor additions and revisions and add only basic documentation to the text. But given the semi-popular nature of the piece, that hardly mattered and I sent it off within two weeks. My much more detailed treatment would appear in *In Search of History*. After submitting it to their editorial board for review, Graf informed me regretfully two months later that my paper was turned down, not on the basis of its merits, but on the appropriateness of the essay for an archaeological journal. This explanation did not make any sense to me, since it had been solicited after Graf had heard the paper and already knew its content and persuaded me that it was for the journal's special issue on historiography, in which a quite un-archaeological article by Arnoldo Momigliano would also appear.

Consequently, I wrote to him and told him that the reason for this rejection was just a lame excuse to cover up the fact that the biblical archaeologists of the Albright School, including the editor David Noel Freedman, for whom Graf was working, did not want it for ideological reasons. They had no right to play games with me and waste my time in this way. Graf then felt compelled to contradict the earlier letter and give all kinds of other reasons, most of which were to suggest that I should have written a quite different kind of paper with much more documentation, which the popular style of *BA* does not permit. The time constraints imposed on me also would not have made this possible. I flatly rejected these excuses and told him I would let my book *In Search of History* speak for itself. It was slightly ironic that after my book was published I met Momigliano in Chapel Hill and he personally praised the work, and particularly my comparison between Greek and biblical historiography, as did other classical scholars.

I mention this contrast between my acceptance within German scholarship of my contribution to the field by so many major scholars, on the one hand, and the constant opposition and pettiness against me in the two major American organizations in which I had been so deeply involved, that of SBL and ASOR, and in which I had given so many papers. Whenever I gave a paper at SBL or ASOR, I could easily fill a room, often to overflowing, because people expected something new and interesting, and probably controversial. However, those who had gained central control of these organizations, SBL in particular, were deeply opposed to my playing any significant advisory or governing role in the organization, and at no time did they ever give any recognition of my scholarship. Often, at the regional level, however, matters were quite different, as reflected in my active role in the Southeastern region of SBL, perhaps the largest of all the regional meetings.

During these early years in Chapel Hill I tried to continue my connection with the Toronto-based Society for the Study of Egyptian Antiquities, of which I was a chartered member, because of its connection with Jack Holladay and the Tell el-Maskhuta dig, and all the other Toronto Egyptologists who were close friends. In February, 1982, I received an invitation to participate in a symposium open to the public on the theme of "Egypt and the Bible," to be held on a Saturday in November. The symposium would be an all-day affair, with a number of lectures and for my plenary lecture on "The Semites in Egypt—Moses and the Exodus" I would receive a modest stipend and my travel expenses. These public symposia were always a popular draw and the modest attendance fee covered expenses, such as mine and other outside speakers. In addition to the symposia, the society also held its annual meeting of scholarly papers and business meeting on the previous day, so I offered to attend that meeting and give a paper there as well.

The reason why I was eager to present a paper on an Egyptological subject was that in the course of my study of Egyptian historiography, there was a particular text that intrigued me, called by scholars "The Report of Wenamun." The text has to do with the travels of a high Egyptian official to Byblos to procure cedar timbers for the ruler of Egypt, and this story is regarded by many scholars as a rare historical source for relations between Egypt and the Levant during the obscure eleventh century BCE. My own study called this interpretation of the text and its dating into question and so I proposed the topic: "The Report of Wenamun: Fact or Fiction." One of the major recent studies of this text was done by Hans Goedicke and my paper questioned his treatment of the text as a historical document in particular. Now it so happened that after I moved to Chapel Hill I had not been able to attend most of these society meetings, but in the interim, and unknown to me, Hans Goedicke had become a member, and thus to my surprise he attended this meeting. Of course he challenged my understanding of the text and my criticism of his study after my presentation and this continued later during the social hour following the meeting. Nevertheless, there did not seem to be any animosity in the exchange, as I had expected, given our previous history.

This, however, was not the end of the story of my strange relations with Goedicke, a typical European transplant from Austria. In 1984 I received a most remarkable letter from him, which took me completely my surprise and I take the liberty to quote it in full:

> My dear colleague: The Johns Hopkins University received recently a major grant to establish a William Foxwell Albright Chair in Biblical Studies. I would like you to apply for this position because I respect your scholarship, and I think it would be very good for the Department to bring in a new voice and break away from the continuation of traditional lines. I just received your recent book [*In Search of History*], and I am reading it with great interest. You might be surprised that we have more in common than comes out in most of our heated discussions.
>
> Yours sincerely, Hans Goedicke

Attached was the flyer with the announcement of the Albright Chair and details for making application by December of that year.

To say that I was completely stunned by this letter was putting it mildly, not only because the invitation to apply had come from Goedicke, but also that it was the Albright Chair. On the one hand, the invitation was quite attractive because Johns Hopkins' Ancient Near Eastern Studies program was a major doctoral program in the field with great research facilities within a quite elite university. On the other hand, there was no way that all of the illustrious graduates of that program, especially Frank Cross, would ever permit me to desecrate the memory of Albright by my occupying that position. So, as a contrarian, I applied. Jack Sasson also had a good friend on the faculty of the same department at Johns Hopkins, who persuaded him to apply as well. Jack was as realistic about our prospects as I was and we would joke about it, and even speculated which one of Cross's students would get the chair. Apparently the four finalists were all Cross's students and we guessed that Kyle McCarter would get to job, which he did. In December, after the choice was made, Goedicke again wrote to me, telling me that he had tried his best. He stated: "Despite my repeated forays, my Biblical and Assyriological colleagues have not agreed to invite you for a lecture or anything else. It seems to me that the new appointment will go the way which was easy to anticipate, and we will be blessed with another seminarian proclaiming to pursue academia in the interest of spreading religious beliefs. I am sorry about this development." This was, perhaps, an overstatement in McCarter's case regarding the matter of religious beliefs, but the continuity of the dominant Albright tradition through Cross to McCarter was certainly maintained. I wrote to Goedicke and thanked him for all of his support in spite of our previous differences and suggested to him that it would have been too ironic for me to have been named the W. F. Albright Professor. I also assured him that McCarter was not as doctrinaire as he thought and he would probably do a good job. The fact is, however, once McCarter arrived in that secure position he did very little besides publish a few popular works of a quite conservative nature and had few graduate students of note in his career.

Another scholar with whom I began to develop a close association was Professor Peter Ackroyd of King's College, London. I had first met him when he was on sabbatical leave as a visitor to our department in Toronto in 1973 and then later at the SBL, which he visited from time to time. We always made some time at SBL for some interesting conversation, especially since we shared a common interest in biblical historiography. It was therefore entirely appropriate for me to suggest to Yale Press that they ask Ackroyd to do a prepublication review of the book, *In Search of History*, which he did. Ackroyd was one of the most respected scholars in the UK and a very careful scholar so that any discussion with him was always interesting and helpful. In our correspondence in 1982 I told him about my meeting with Hans Heinrich Schmid and Odil Steck, and of the publications of Hoffmann and Rose. I also told him about my correspondence with Kaiser. He knew Steck but he did not know Hans Heinrich, and he had not seen Hoffmann's work, which he was now anxious to get hold of. He also had an invitation from Kaiser to contribute to *ZAW*, which did not surprise me, so I was in good company. He also announced that he was retiring and would do some traveling to America for lectures at various places. I expressed the hope that we could get him to come for a visit and lecture at Chapel Hill. In the end, however, plans for that visit did not materialize because he accepted visiting teaching obligations at Notre Dame and Emory for 1983–84 and Japan for 1984–85. However, while at Norte Dame he did get to the SBL meeting in New York in late 1983 and as arranged, we spent some time together, and we discussed my next major project on the Pentateuch and plans for my next sabbatical in 1985–86 to be spent in the UK.

The James A. Gray trust fund, from which my salary was being paid, was accumulating a surplus such that I thought that we could do some additional things with it, and in the spring of 1982 I raised the question of whether we could create a James A. Gray Lectureship in which distinguished scholars could be brought in from time to time to give a set of lectures, and hopefully their lectures would then be published in book form by the University of North Carolina Press. The idea was discussed and accepted in a departmental meeting and a committee formed to consider the details and likely candidates for such an invitation. I was one of four members of the committee, but not the chair for the obvious reason that the chair must appear unbiased and the one least in a position to make suggestions about a candidate, and I definitely had someone in mind. The only other person that would have a strong opinion about a different candidate was Charles Long and his views would carry a lot of weight. As I recall, and I do not have the minutes of those meetings, there were at least two or three candidates put forward and brought before the whole department for a vote. I made a persuasive case for Hans Heinrich Schmid, set forth in a fulsome memorandum, as one who had strong scholarly interests in both biblical studies and history of religions, and his candidacy won. So the invitation went out to Hans Heinrich from Ruel Tyson, the chair of the committee, in June of 1982, laying out the terms of the lectureship and indicating that as Department chairman I would be in touch with him about the details.

This invitation did not come as a complete surprise to him because we talked about finding ways in which I might help him make such a trip to America while he would help me with a tour in Europe. So this whole scheme of a lecture series at Chapel Hill and a visit to other universities and seminaries did not come out of the blue. Now the ball was in my court to take care of all the details of time and travel as well as negotiate the precise topic of his four lectures at Chapel Hill. Around this I would also arrange an extensive lecture tour across the US, with all of the details that this would involve. This would all take place in March and April of 1984, during the period between terms in Swiss universities. I could, of course, be accused of manipulating the system, but the fairly modest expenses for this were coming out of the James A. Gray Trust Fund and the lectureship was still intended for the enrichment of the department as a whole. Its faculty had the ultimate say in it, and could have done otherwise. My predecessor in the Gray Chair had no qualms about using Gray funds for pet Israeli archaeological programs so he could make his trips to Israel, even though he had no credentials as an archaeologist whatever; nor did his projects benefit the department as a whole. So I was quite satisfied with this outcome.

I will not get into the fine points of the arrangements for the Gray Lectures and the lecture tour, but merely focus on some of the main outlines of the itinerary and the basic principles of the lectureship, as well as some of the high-points of the visit itself. What we did not want in the lectures was a series on Old Testament Theology in the guise of Hebrew religion, reflecting a strong Barthian dichotomy between Near Eastern religion and biblical theology, such as was typical in European universities, as well as in America. Hans Heinrich had seriously challenged that Barthian approached in his book, *Altorientalische Welt in der alttestamentlichen Theologie*, and we wanted him to expand on this theme in terms of the broader discipline of the history of religions. I pointed out to him:

> In America the Barthian dichotomy between religion and theology is still very strong with theology understood as confessional and associated with theological seminaries whereas religion is the proper study of the university. To argue as you do that this division is false, and to actually use *Religiousgeschichte* as a necessary method in the presentation of major themes of Old Testament theology constitutes an interesting challenge. I would like to see what some of my American colleagues do with this.

In this connection I pointed out to him the recent work of his colleague at Zurich in the Classics Department, Walter Burkert, who had given a series of lectures at both UCLA and Harvard on the application of the history of religions to classical sources, and I had heard a fine lecture recently from him in Chapel Hill on Greek mystery religions. Hans Heinrich, of course, knew Burkert very well, so I told him to be sure to chat with him both about the subject and about his experience of giving such a series in America.

In subsequent correspondence Hans Heinrich mentioned that his oldest daughter Regula was graduating from Gymnasium (High School) and wanted to do her collage work in America, and in anticipation she was going to a language school in California in 1983. He suggested that he would accompany her to San Francisco and then he could return by way of Chapel Hill for a visit and a direct discussion of plans for the following year. All this sounded very good but it came to nothing because he was having a serious problem with his hip, which was diagnosed as having necrosis in the thighbone and would need surgery, putting him in the hospital for 7 weeks followed by 6 months on crutches. This would cancel his trip to America in 1983, but he assured me that this would not interfere with the plans for 1984. Nevertheless, he would need a cane and his hip would bother him for years to come. While he was laid up I kept him occupied with off-prints and other publications, and of course he received a copy of my book in April of 1983.

Early in 1983 while Hans Heinrich was convalescing from surgery he was working on two lists of topics, the one list from which a selection would be made for the four lectures given at Chapel Hill, the other a list of subjects that would be distributed to the various university departments and seminaries that I would be contacting. The first group of lecture topics were discussed and negotiated with the departmental input. With the second list I began to contact a number of persons whom I knew in the various institutions to sell the lecture tour. Harvard and Yale need so much advanced notice that there was little chance of getting something there. At the University of Chicago Divinity School I worked through my good friend Gösta Ahlstrom, and for Princeton Seminary I contacted President James I. McCord, who passed it on with his support to the biblical department. For Vanderbilt University I worked through James Crenshaw. I did not know Jim very well, at that time, but I knew his specialty was wisdom literature and I could play on Hans Heinrich's work and strong interest in this area. Patrick Miller was now the dean of Union Seminary in Richmond, Virginia, and I had had a lot of dealings with him in the past, so it was fairly easy to get a commitment from him. In Iliff School of Theology in Denver, Colorado, I contacted Kent Richards who was only too happy to have their school included within this distinguished list of institutions. Finally, on the west coast there was Claremont School of Theology in California, with Rolf Knierim, a good friend for several years and former student of von Rad. Mixed into the itinerary were stops at Pittsburg Theological Seminary and Provo, Utah, which were separately arranged by Hans Heinrich and fitted into the schedule. In addition, since I was the president of the Southeast regional SBL that year, which was meeting in Williamsburg, Virginia, I arranged with the program committee to have a special evening session that would feature both Hans Heinrich Schmid and Peter Ackroyd, who was visiting that semester at Emory. I also had my own presidential address to give on that occasion.

All of these lecture stops were fitted into an elaborate schedule, with some sightseeing in New York and Washington thrown in, twelve stops in all. The stops covered the period from March 1 to April 21, extending from Chicago to Chapel Hill and the east coast, and from there to the west coast, and were arranged in such a way as to minimize the travel time and distance between stops. Each participating institution would be responsible for local hospitality and a modest honorarium, which would easily cover any expenses above those for which Chapel Hill was responsible for its own lecture series. All of the schools would also correspond directly with Hans Heinrich to issue the invitation, agree on the lecture topic from a selected list of titles, and the other arrangements, with copies of all the correspondence sent to me. Hans Heinrich also managed to get a very reasonable travel pass, which allowed an unlimited number of flights for two months. Once he was out west his family flew out to California and did some sightseeing in San Francisco and the Rockies. While the rest of the family flew straight back home, Hans Heinrich and Christa flew to Chapel Hill and spent a few days at Easter visiting with us, before they too headed for home.

I will not go into any details of the meetings themselves, except to say that they went very well. There was some difficulty with some of the public audience understanding Hans Heinrich's English, which is not surprising, and the attendance tended to drop off a bit after the first lecture, although the discussion following the lectures were certainly lively, especially when he got away from the formal script of the text. However, let me recall one interesting aspect of his visit. The housing that we were able to provide for Hans Heinrich was a suite of rooms in the residential wing of the beautiful Planetarium building on the UNC campus. Not only did he have a luxurious bedroom and private bath, but a very spacious sitting room with the latest newspapers, etc. and a stock of assorted drinks. Furthermore, there was a valet who would pour him a drink and offer him sweets in the evening and a made to order breakfast in the morning, and anything else that he might want. I remember meeting him there for breakfast one morning to go over the day with him, with the valet nearby to refresh our cups of coffee when needed. Hans Heinrich was the only guest in the whole complex at that time, so it really was the royal treatment, which he talked about for a long time afterwards. In fact, for some strange reason, the charge for this service was quite reasonable at that time although in the subsequent years it became very expensive, so that we never used it for such visitors again.

The Williamsburg regional SBL meeting in my presidential year was also another highlight for many reasons. Not only did we have both Hans Heinrich Schmid and Peter Ackroyd there giving major papers, but to my surprise, another European scholar from Sweden, Professor Tryggve Mettinger, was there as well. I had not expected him and had never met him before. He later sent me two of his books. Elizabeth had come up to the meeting in Williamsburg with me so we could also do some sightseeing at the historic Williamsburg National Park along with Hans Heinrich. At the end of the meeting on our way home we drove him back to Richmond from which he could take the flight to his next stop in Nashville. Given the location of the meeting place and the distinguished foreign scholars, there was a large turnout and a very successful conference.

The Inauguration of the PhD Program

In addition to these scholarly lectures and meetings and all of the preparation for them, there were also other important matters with which, as a department chair, I had to give special attention. There had been a lot of talk and planning for some time on the development of a graduate program, without which the department was never quite regarded as a serious academic entity. We had been granted an MA program in 1978 as a first step, but the real hurdle was to get the PhD. The big push was made in 1983. As chair of the Department of Religion I had to take the lead in this process, and with my credentials now recognized by my colleagues in the administration and within the faculty in other departments, I had some credibility. After the department mapped out five major programs and laid out our case for the serious academic and non-confessional study of religion in the university, we made a presentation to the executive committee of the Graduate School. Important in this pitch was the fact that within the last decade or so, a number of public universities, such as the University of Virginia, had developed just such graduate programs. This presentation won the Graduate School support.

However, any new program of this kind needed the approval of the General Administration of UNC, which was the governing body of all of the 16 senior institutions within the UNC system, of which the Chapel Hill campus was only one. So with the support of the Dean of the Graduate School I sent the proposal on to General

Administration, also known as "Raleigh Road" because of its location in Chapel Hill, to Raymond Dawson, Vice President for Academic Affairs. This was followed up by a visit to his office in late 1983 in which I laid out the case for the program, and the fact that our program could easily compete with the one at University of Virginia. He was favorably impressed and put the proposal on the agenda for the next meeting of representatives from all the campuses in the system in the spring of 1984. They were all supplied with the proposal. Of course I went down to make the case at the meeting, but I also took Charles Long with me, because when he was at his best, he could be very persuasive. And he was superb. The proposal sailed through and we had our program to begin in 1985.

As the Department's "point man" this had been a lot of work for me. The irony was that of all the senior colleagues within my own department, I had perhaps the least to gain from it. The area of study that included Old Testament and the ancient Near East (Jack Sasson and I), Early Judaism (David Halperin) and New Testament and Early Christianity (John Schutz) was included within the common field of Ancient Mediterranean Religions. To make it work all of the sub-fields within AMR would need the cooperation of resources and faculty of the Duke Department of Religion. However, after seven years at Chapel Hill it was clear that I could count on minimal cooperation with the Meyers at Duke. By contrast, John Schutz had established a good relationship with Duke and this was only strengthened when Elizabeth Clark came to Duke. Nevertheless, over the course of time I did manage to establish some inroads into the Duke graduate program, in spite of some opposition to my work, but it was never a major part of my career at Chapel Hill.

In late1982, Melvin Peters, a former graduate of the Toronto Graduate program and student of John Wevers, had made application for the position of associate professor with tenure at Duke University and I was asked by Professor Kalman Bland, chairman of their Department of Religion, to write up a detailed evaluation of his scholarship for this position. I had known Peters well from my Toronto days even though he had never been my student, although he had sat in on some of my classes. As graduate secretary of the Toronto program I had often talked with him about his career and various appointments, and about his struggles with his conservative religious (Adventist) background. Duke gave him the position, but they deferred granting him tenure, which would be cause for some problems down the road. However, Melvin and I established a close relationship.

Also in the spring of 1983, Richard Bjornson, a professor of Comparative Literature and a fellow at the National Humanities Center in the Research Triangle Park, called me about a former student of his, Stuart Lasine, who was trying to move into biblical studies from his comparative literature background and was encountering some difficulty doing so. One of his articles had been submitted to *JBL* and rejected, and he was discouraged. Could I perhaps look at his articles and offer some advice? I was very reluctant to get involved, given all of the other commitments that I had at that time and the prospect of this developing into a long-term commitment. I had never even met Lasine up to this point. However, I agreed to look at the pieces and offer my advice on them, and so he sent them along with a cover letter.

What I did not realize at the time that he spoke to me and what he could not have known was that I was one of the readers of the article sent to *JBL*, as a member of the editorial board, and that I had actually approved it and said that I saw very little need to make any changes. The other two anonymous readers voted against it, and from their comments I said that it was clear that they had very little literary sense, but the way the system works neither I nor the editor could do anything about it. After additional comments on the second article with only a few suggestions on minor changes and some remarks on the difficulties in applying the comparative lit approach within the discipline of biblical studies, I nevertheless urged that the articles be published and I made some suggestions about where he should submit the articles with a better prospect of their acceptance. I said that I would be happy to meet with Lasine at the SBL annual meetings, should he attend them. Bjornson past along my comments to Lasine, which he said greatly encouraged him.

Shortly thereafter Lasine himself wrote to me a long and thoughtful letter about his articles and his projects, and it was clear that even though he was not formally trained in biblical studies, he had made himself familiar with a large body of it and had read some of my work. All of his remarks were very thoughtful and the beginning of a long habit of exchanging views on literary questions. He followed through on my suggestions about journals and in fact he did get both articles published. I also supported him in ultimately finding an academic position. It was the beginning of a long and fruitful relationship.

One of the graduate students in the Near Eastern Studies program at Yale, with whom I had shared a number of classes in 1962–64, was James (Jim) Muhly. He had come out of a strong undergrad program in Classics and Near Eastern Studies at the University of Minnesota. He also had a strong interest in archaeology, but not in the tradition of the biblical archaeology school and he eventually gained a position in Ancient History at the University of Pennsylvania and became active in ASOR. It was in this connection, after a long interval, that we finally were in touch again, in the early 1980's. Jim Muhly and Max Miller were organizing a joint ASOR-SBL session at the annual meeting in Dallas on the theme of "Biblical History and Archaeology," so I was in touch with both of them with a proposal on "Joshua's Campaign of Canaan and Near Eastern Historiography." Needless to say, it was accepted and reflected a new attitude towards the use of archaeology in historical studies in opposition to the biblical archaeology movement. I was also glad to get caught up with Jim again.

The National Endowment for the Humanities in Washington, D.C. sponsored a program at a number of major research universities that allowed a senior scholar at each university to select twelve junior faculty members to participate in a seminar on a particular theme for eight weeks in the summer. In addition, the leader of the seminar would offer advice and assistance on a participant's particular research project during the course of those eight weeks. The senior scholar would be paid a certain lump sum for his time spent in developing and conducting the seminar and for processing the applications and selecting the 12 participants. In early 1983 I applied for the opportunity to run one of these seminars during the summer of 1984, on the theme "History writing in ancient Greece, the Near East, and Israel: a comparative study," in anticipation of the publication of my book, *In Search of History*. I was duly awarded the directorship of this seminar, which was one more thing to occupy my time during this very busy time when so many other things were going on as well. In addition to receiving and vetting all of the applications, I also had to make a trip to Washington to the headquarters of NEH for an orientation program for seminar directors on running their program and handling all of the paperwork involved. The university also received a sum of money for housing the seminar and others expenses, so they were happy to get them and it was good publicity for the Department. The experience was a very enjoyable one for all concerned, and I was to repeat it a few years later.

One of the applicants to the summer seminar was Fred Cryer, who was a doctoral student at Aarhus University in Denmark, studying under Professor Niels Peter Lemche. Fred was originally from the city of Chapel Hill, where his mother and brother still lived, and had been a student at UNC before my time, but he was well known to Jack Sasson. On one of his visits home he came to see me and we had a long conversation so that he was certainly known to me and I would have loved to have him in that seminar, but as I pointed out to him, the Humanities Summer Seminar rules did not permit him to participate and I could not persuade the head of the program in Washington to make any exception. In spite of this rebuff, we had a lot of correspondence, especially because he was reviewing my book, *In Search of History*, for *Vetus Testamentum*. Both he and his mentor Lemche regarded my views as a little too extreme. I had never met Lemche, but he told me that Lemche followed my work closely, and there was an open invitation to visit Aarhus and other Scandinavian universities. It would be several years before I could take them up on that. Nevertheless, this was the beginning of a long and interesting relationship with the Danish school of biblical studies, especially after Lemche moved to the University of Copenhagen.

5

End of First Term as Chair and Sabbatical at Oxford

The school term of 1984–85 was to be my last year as department chair, followed by a sabbatical in 1985–86. At least I thought it was my last, but the Dean of Arts and Sciences had other ideas. The usual procedure was that the dean would canvas the opinions of the other members of the department about their choices for chair, with the result that in the dean's interview with me, she indicated that I was the overwhelming choice. As a compromise, I agreed to take it for only two years beyond my sabbatical and then they would need to find a replacement. During my year on leave, John Schutz would fill in as chair, which suited me very well. I was planning to be away in England that year and I was sure that with John in the chair I would have little bother with administrative matters. However, as we shall see, it did not quite go as planned.

With all the preparations I would need to make for that sabbatical I tried not to take on too much in addition to my regular duties. I had one particular weakness, however, and that was giving a talk for the weekend "Program in the Humanities for the Study of Human Values" to an audience of alumni, school teachers and friends of UNC. So when Warren Nord, the director, asked me to do a "Celebrity Seminar" of four lectures on "The Old Testament as History" during one of the weekends in October, I could not resist this flattery. I did have a good time especially when one can sense that your audience is also very much into what you are saying and the questions come pouring out at the end of each session. I received a letter from Warren soon afterwards, in which he stated: "I want to thank you again for the superb seminar you led last weekend. I was very pleased with the way it went." He went on to say that "there were no criticisms of your talks at all, and many compliments," and he proceeded to give me a number of examples, which included the following comments from participants: "The overview of the material was marvelous. The seminar was thought-provoking and extremely informative," "at times entertaining," "this has been delightful!" "Question and answer periods were a 'plus' time. Dr. Van Seters was at his best during the 'on-the-spot' answers he gave," and many more. Warren closed with the remark: "Be assured that we greatly appreciate your efforts and contribution to the Humanities Program." Some years later the Humanities Program made an anthology of a selection of about 15 seminar talks over a ten year period, and the opening talk of my seminar was included. I did several more of these seminars, whether alone of with others. And for me it was always a most gratifying experience.

After my book, *In Search of History*, was published, I began to hear from a number of scholars, some of whom I had never met. One was a Dutch scholar, Klaas Smelik of the Rijksuniversiteit Utrecht, who had written a dissertation in the field of Israelite historiography, in Dutch of course, and also some articles in a Dutch periodical, none of which I had seen. He had come independently to some of the same conclusions and was eager to share his publications with me and to enter into scholarly discussion on these publications. So we began to exchange off-prints. I also told him of my plans to spend the next academic year in either England or the Netherlands and perhaps we would meet and spend some time together. As it happened, I did go to Holland on a trip from Oxford and gave a talk at the University of Amsterdam where Smelik was then teaching, and Elizabeth and I did visit with his family in Harlem. So we became good friends and tried to keep in touch.

Another letter that I received was from Bruce Trigger, Professor of Anthropology at McGill University. I had known Bruce casually from my student days at Toronto because he lived in the same residence at University College. He was a year behind me but he also went to Yale to do his graduate studies there, and even though he was in Anthropology, his doctoral research had to do with the so-called "pan graves" of Upper Egypt in the early second millennium BCE. This meant that he was doing a lot of work with the Egyptologist, Kelly Simpson, just as I was working with Simpson as well on the Hyksos. So it was natural that I would become familiar with his work and with all of his archaeological materials from Egypt, housed in the research rooms of the Anthropological Museum at Yale, and Bruce and I became good friends. But after my graduation in 1965, being in quite different fields, we soon lost touch. So it was quite a surprise to get this letter from Bruce out of the blue. In it he states:

> I have just finished reading—belatedly but with much pleasure and admiration—In Search of History. I want to tell you how much, as a non-specialist in biblical studies, I enjoyed the book. In setting Hebrew historiography into a regional context, it is a splendid piece of anthropological research, although it requires skills that few real anthropologists possess. My warmest congratulations.

I was delighted to hear from Bruce again after twenty years and thanked him for his kind remarks. He was now a distinguished scholar in his own right and I was on the lookout for his books. In 1989 he published *A History of Archaeological Thought* (Cambridge University Press), which I bought and read with pleasure and great appreciation. Bruce was, in fact, a prolific and much decorated scholar and a joy for me to have known him.

In November of 1984 an interdepartmental committee, including some from our department, invited Professor Arnaldo Momigliano of the University of Chicago to come to Chapel Hill to give a lecture on "Ancient Bibliography and the Study of Religion in the Roman Empire." I was not on the committee but I was delighted with the choice, because I had made use of his publications in my research of *In Search of History* and held him in very high regard. In fact, the committee asked me to introduce him before the lecture and I was happy to do so. I also had the chance to spend a little time with him on that visit and he told me that he had read my recent book and liked it very much, and that he had a copy for review on his desk in Chicago. Needless to say, I assumed that I could find it in some journal but was not successful. Later, when I won the James Breasted Award for the book, I was reasonably certain that he was referring to his role on the award's committee, since Breasted had himself been a distinguished ancient historian of Chicago. Many years later, I was in touch with Professor Anthony Grafton, a scholar of distinction, who had been a student of Momigliano, and he told me that the latter had introduced the book to him and they had discussed it.

In March of 1985 it was time for our daughter Deborah to make a decision about where she would go to university after graduation from High School that year, and we had encouraged her to consider a school in Canada because she was a Canadian citizen and could take advantage of the lower fees for Canadians. So Deborah and I drove up to Ontario during "spring break" in North Carolina, which of course meant that we arrived in a big snow storm in Toronto, which limited the number of places that we could visit. I took her down to the University of Toronto to give her a tour of the campus, and University College in particular. Wandering through the halls of UC, my old college, I suggested that we drop in for a visit with the Principal. Deborah was a little reluctant to do this, but I assured her that it was OK and went in to the office to ask whether he was in, told the secretary who I was, and asked if he could see us. Peter Richardson, the Principal, an old family friend whom I had known since childhood, came out and greeted us warmly and ushered us into the inner sanctum where we proceeded to catch up on family and other news. He then turned his attention to Deborah, asked about her interests and ended by accompanying her personally to the registrar's office, where she could get all the rest of the information she needed for application and all questions answered from the highest authority. It was obvious that no other school could compete with that kind of attention, and while we did visit some other places, in spite of the snow, it was clear that the City of Toronto and the university had a special attraction for her. And this is where she went on graduation from Chapel Hill High School.

While in Toronto at that time I had hoped to catch up with some of my old friends and I had the chance to do so by attending the final dinner meeting of the Oriental Club, a group to which I had belonged during my Toronto years. Its members included many from my former department as well as some from Classics, Islamic Studies, and others. I had hoped to see both John Wevers and Fred Winnett there but they were out of the country at the time. Nevertheless, I had a good time. I had received a long letter from Winnett a few weeks earlier and so when we returned to Chapel Hill, I wrote to him, telling him about my plans to spend my leave in Oxford, working on some new approaches to the Pentateuch, of which I thought he would approve. I sent him some recent articles which would indicate the direction that my research was taking me, the ones on the religion of the patriarchs, on the Passover and on Joshua 24. Winnett wrote to thank me for the letter and the offprints. He then continued:

> After reading the [offprints] I felt like throwing my hat in the air and shouting "Van Seters has done it! Van Seters has done it! He's solved the Hexateuchal problem!" Each of the three studies is a classic in itself and moves inexorably to the conclusion which you present: the placing of the Yahwist after D. This is a stroke of genius and opens the way to the solution of a great many problems. I recall the trouble I had trying to explain the presence of D materials in the Exodus tradition.

After wishing Elizabeth and me the best on our sabbatical in Oxford, he stated: "I hope I live to see your proposed book on the Yahwist as historian. I believe it will be an epoch-making work."

I have taken the liberty of quoting this flattering letter from Winnett because many years later German scholars, who discovered Winnett only after I introduced his studies on the Pentateuch to them, have in a curiously perverse manner tried to use Winnett's views against me, as if I did not know what he had written. These remarks by Winnett speak for themselves. He fully supported my work, even when it meant that he had to revise his own earlier held positions. He did not live to see the day that I published by book on the Yahwist as historian, but I am sure that if he had, he would have been no less enthusiastic about it than he was of the articles that I had sent him at that time. Of course I wrote back to him immediately and thanked him for the "boost to my ego" and only wished "that others were as enthusiastic about my ideas as you are." Since I had two more articles on Exodus in the works, I sent him copies of these as well. I also wrote John Wevers on the occasion of his receiving an honorary doctorate from Leiden, telling him how pleased Elizabeth and I were for him and bringing him up to date on the latest news and plans. Since we were going to Oxford the same year that Deborah was going to Toronto, it was comforting to know that there were family members and many friends there, should she need them.

In the Spring of 1985 the Department arranged for a visit of the leading scholar of the Hittite language and civilization in North America, Professor Hans Güterbock of the Oriental Institute of the University of Chicago. It was at an American Oriental Society meeting that I had met him and he expressed an interest in visiting Chapel Hill because he had some old friends there. So I told him I would see what we could do. I was very interested in his work because he had written on "the historical tradition and its literary form among the Babylonians and Hittites in the 2nd Millennium BCE," and I had made great use of it for by book, *In Search of History*. His study was regarded by many as the definitive essay on the topic up to that time, so we had lots to talk about. I also knew his colleague and successor in Hittite Studies at Chicago, Harry Hoffner, very well from the historiography seminar in Toronto. So I organized interested parties in our own and other departments to bring Güterbock for a seminar. We had the usual dinner with selected colleagues and a very good seminar session. He had read my book in preparation for the seminar, which gave us lots to discuss.

In addition to these activities, however, Elizabeth and I had arranged some time for him to meet with his old friends. Güterbock was one of a number of mostly Jewish refugees who had lost their academic positions in German universities before WWII and had come to America, many by way of Ankara Turkey. My own teacher at Yale, Albrecht Goetze, also a distinguished Hittite specialist, had likewise been an academic refugee from Marburg University, and although not a Jew himself, he spoke with great admiration about these fellow refugees at the Oriental Institute. There were indeed quite a number of these scholars at University of Chicago, which made it a world class institution. Chapel Hill also had its share of such scholars, and this gathering of Güterbock's friends was just such a group from the "Ankara days." It was a heart-warming experience to see this reunion of old friends, from quite different academic fields, but sharing this very important history. Some of these Chapel Hill scholars whom I had met through Jack Sasson or as a department chair were also good friends of mine as well. After his visit Güterbock sent a very personal thanks to Elizabeth and me from both himself and his wife for this Chapel Hill experience.

I had also been in touch with Gösta Ahlstrom at the University of Chicago. In the fall of 1984 he had asked me to write for him in support of a Guggenheim Fellowship for 1985–86 and in the spring of 1985 he informed me that he had won the award, for which he thanked me for support. I had also asked him for recommendation for a National Council for the Humanities Fellowship for 1985–86 and I too received the fellowship, for which I thanked him. That is the way the system works. A record of good awards and the confidence of the fellowship of good scholars brought more awards. And one could not find a better friend than Ahlstrom. His project was a fairly massive *History of Israel*, which, when it appeared was far ahead of the very popular *History of Israel* by John Bright. However, views on the subject were changing so fast that it could not survive as long as the other. Nevertheless, for a time at least it was the best.

In making my plans for Oxford and my year abroad I was in touch with a number of scholars with whom I had become acquainted, Piet de Boer, Peter Ackroyd, and James Barr. Barr informed me that he would not be in Oxford for most of that academic year, but he suggested that I get in touch with Professor Ernest Nicholson of Oriel College, who could help me. I had never met Ernest Nicholson before, but I wrote to him and received a most warm and encouraging reply, giving me advice and suggestions about securing information on accommodation and getting me a membership in Oriel College to the Senior Common Room with lunch and dinner privileges at the beginning of term in October. He also invited me to participate in the Old Testament seminar of faculty and grad students which he organized. Finding temporary accommodation in Oxford is not an easy matter, but after a lot of correspondence and several failed attempts, Ernest was able to find an apartment for me in North Oxford, just off the Banbury Rd, not far from his own place, and convenient to bus service and shopping in Summertown. He himself would be in Australia from August to early October so he would not be there when I arrived. In anticipation of our meeting I sent him some of my recent offprints, for which he thanked me. I felt that we were going to hit it off very well.

I informed Piet de Boer of my plans and he strongly approved of the arrangement with Oriel College, adding that "the Nicholsons are very nice people," which indeed they were. He assured me that he expected a visit from us, while in the UK, to Holland and to Leiden in particular. Peter Ackroyd had already paved the way for an invitation from his successor Ronald Clements to visit Kings College in London and I was in touch with Clements about a visit in the fall term and the selection of a lecture topic. The final details would be completed after my arrival in Oxford. I also had an invitation from the British Society for Old Testament Study (SOTS) to give a paper at their December meeting, which would be a great way to meet those in OT studies in the UK. I already knew the Sheffield scholars because they were by now regulars at SBL and I had mentioned to David Clines the possibility of my coming to Oxford for the 1985–86 academic year and a possible visit to Sheffield, on which he seemed keen. So I was in touch with him again after the Oxford arrangements were finalized and we nailed down a date for the visit to Sheffield and a topic for the lecture.

There was much correspondence and planning for a European tour between Hans Heinrich and me during the spring semester of '85. He was quite determined to keep me as busy in Germany and Switzerland as I had done for him in America. My various presentations would revolve around the theme of my studies in biblical historiography and the "Yahwist as historian" in particular. Hans Heinrich had arranged with Professor Albert de Pury of the University of Geneva for me to give two public lectures in Geneva in February of 1986, as well as participate in a colloquium of scholars later in May of that year on the theme of "History and Historical Consciousness in the Civilizations of the Ancient Near East," to be held at a retreat center near Geneva in Cartigny, Switzerland. This would involve two trips to the continent, and around these two trips other talks would be arranged. During the February trip I would also give two papers to the Swiss Society of the Ancient Near East at their meeting in Fribourg, one in the morning and one in the afternoon, each followed by extended discussion, on the theme of the Yahwist as Historian. It would basically cover the whole program. I would also then go to Zurich and give a paper and conduct a seminar there. Needless to say, I had a detailed invitation from Professor Albert de Pury about the Geneva lectures and the Cartigny seminar followed by extensive correspondence on subjects and details. In addition to all of this Hans had also approached Professor Klaus Koch of Hamburg and Professor Jörg Jeremias of Munich about trips to their universities and I was in touch with both of them with invitations secured. I also contacted Rolf Rendtorff of Heidelberg and Otto Kaiser of Marburg, with whom I had virtual open invitations for visits already. All these lectures and the itinerary were then coordinated with the two Swiss trips. This meant that even before I left for the UK all my European itinerary was largely arranged.

In addition to all this scheduling of my lectures and papers Hans Heinrich was eager to translate, and eventually publish, my lectures on the historiography of the Yahwist in German, along with a German translation of one of the papers that I would give in Geneva: "Myth and History: the Problem of Origins." He also wanted these sufficiently early so that he could distribute the translated versions ahead of time for the conference at Fribourg and the lecture and seminar in Zurich. That meant that I would be particularly busy during the summer before I left for Oxford and in the early weeks while I was there. At the same time Hans Heinrich was reminding me of the fact that he was still busy working on the manuscript of the Chapel Hill lectures, not as a burden but as a continuing fascination with the subject.

Preparations for a year abroad require a massive number of practical details, and even with the best of plans, things can go wrong. Nevertheless, the rewards of the experience are abundantly worth the risk. Arrangements were made for forwarding necessary mail from home and office, and my administrative assistant, Maxine Underwood, could contact me in case of any necessity. We also rented our home out for the duration that we were away. One complication was that in order to claim a rather generous tax benefit for working abroad, one had to spend 330 days overseas without returning to the USA. This meant that I would need to leave in mid-August and not return until the end of June. However, Deborah would not be going to the University of Toronto until the first week in September, so Elizabeth had to stay behind and then drive her up to Toronto alone, without my help, get her settled into residence at Knox College (where many of the rooms were used by undergraduates). She then had to drive down to her brother John's place in Milford, Connecticut, leave the car there and fly from Newark, New Jersey, to London. On paper the plan looked fine, but in reality it was quite an ordeal for Elizabeth to undertake all of this by herself.

In mid-August I flew to London by way of New York and then took a bus to Oxford, found the agent for the department rental who took me out to our apartment in

North Oxford. The apartment building was in a quiet cul-de-sac next to a park on the edge of town with farmland beyond. I had a letter from Ernest Nicholson welcoming me to Oxford, who was at that time in Australia until early August, but explaining that Hazel, his wife, would be happy to help me with any advice and assistance I needed, and gave me their local phone number. He also supplied me with the necessary papers to gain access to the Bodleian Library and any other library that I might use around Oxford. He also informed the librarian of the Faculty of Theology Library at Pusey House on St. Giles Rd about my stay in Oxford, and when I called there she was very helpful in showing me my way around. Before I had a chance to call Hazel, she showed up at the door of my apartment with her oldest daughter and invited me to dinner on Sunday. I soon became well known to the Nicholson family.

The best way to get around Oxford is by bicycle because most of Oxford is quite flat, so I bought one and after Elizabeth arrived we bought her one too. I could easily ride down Banbury Rd. all the way to St. Giles in the heart of Oxford, lock up my bike on a rack with a myriad of others, and from there easily get to where I wanted to go. In bad weather there was always the bus service, which was excellent. The center of Oxford is always very busy with students, tourists and locals, because, in addition to the many colleges, there are the Covered Market of fresh food, the main shopping center and public library, the theatres and museums, and much more. It takes time to master all of this, but the rewards are great, and I tried to at least get familiar with the basics before Elizabeth arrived.

At the Chapel Hill end of things Elizabeth was left with the heroic task of taking care of last minute details, and then on September 1st, driving the two day trip to the University in Toronto. After much shopping for supplies and furnishings, etc. and visiting with my family for a few days, she finally got Deborah moved it, and then headed down to Hamden, Conn. to her folk's place. She then left her car at her brother John's place in Milford and took a plane out of Newark to London. I met her at the airport and we took the bus to Oxford and taxi to the apartment. She was completely exhausted. It was now Sept 9th and she had been going the whole time. The next few days we explored Oxford together and did some shopping, including the purchase of a typewriter. During the time in Oxford, Elizabeth did a massive amount of typing for me, all the academic correspondence, the manuscripts for my public lectures and papers, my research and so much more. This was before the age of the portable computer.

In addition to exploring Oxford, we gradually ventured out of town to Blenheim Palace and toured the palace and grounds, and the town of Woodstock. A few days later we took a bus down to Winchester, to the magnificent cathedral, to Jane Austin's house and the other great sites of the city. Then we took on the intimidating challenge of London and were quite won over by it. This had not been the first time, because we had been there twenty years earlier. But now we had the time to learn its ways and how to get around. We would return many times. About ten days after Elizabeth arrived,

Hazel Nicholson invited us to dinner, and this time included John and Mary Barton. John Barton was also in the field of Old Testament studies at St. Cross College. We later visited with them in their home in Abingdom, south of Oxford. Elizabeth and I became good friends of the Bartons, a friendship that would last for many years. It was also a common practice for us that if Elizabeth was in downtown Oxford doing some shopping or visiting the library or the Ashmolian Museum, we would often meet at noon and go to lunch together at a local restaurant or pub. Browns restaurant was a favorite.

Our first major excursion was a five-day trip to Scotland. We took the train from Oxford through Birmingham and Carlisle to Edinburgh, and stayed in a nice B&B there. The next day, we did a tourist tour of the city, but also stopped in at New College on our trip to the Castle. There I met Graeme Auld, Professor of Old Testament, and he invited us to his place for the evening before we had planned to return home. In the meantime we took one day to make a trip up to Aberdeen, spent some time there sightseeing, then on to Inverness, a beautiful little city in the north of Scotland. We then took the train south past Lochness through the highlands, with a stop at Pitlochry, where Elizabeth did some shopping for her birthday, and finally back to Edinburgh, all in one day!

The next day we took another train excursion to St. Andrews on the North Sea, a beautiful spot with old ruins of church and castle. I also looked up another Professor of Old Testament, William McKane, whose work I knew but I had never met personally. We were invited out to his place where we also met his wife Agnes. We had a pleasant time over tea, but we little realized that we would later meet again in Chapel Hill and they would become very good friends. When we returned to Edinburgh we went out for a special birthday seafood dinner for Elizabeth; she still speaks of that dinner. This was followed by a pleasant dessert and coffee at the Aulds' place. The following day we returned to Oxford.

At the end of October I received a phone call from Ruel Tyson that John Schutz had suffered a serious injury to the head in a bicycle accident. It had now become apparent that Ruel had been put in charge as acting chair in John's place, at least until he recovered, if he did. John and Barbara Schutz had a daughter Amy who was studying in a University in the UK and we were given her telephone number. We made contact with her about her plans to return home and arranged to meet her at Heathrow airport, to see that she made her flight connections and for some moral support. There were, of course, regular reports by phone from Chapel Hill as to John's progress, which was very slow. We also tried to keep in touch with his family, who had become close friends.

By this time we had settled into our routines in Oxford. With the fall semester started I was becoming more involved in the college and university life and in speaking engagements, about which I will say more later, and Elizabeth had developed her own associations and activities. Sometimes we traveled to London together, and sometimes she went alone. She soon knew the city better than I did. By mid-December both Deborah and Peter flew in from different directions to be with us for the holidays, so that there were two trips to the airport to meet them. Once they settled in they too needed a tour of London, the National Art Gallery and a comedy at the theatre. We also made a day trip to Stratford and took in "Taming of the Shrew." On Christmas Eve afternoon we went to the carol service at Christ Church Cathedral in Oxford. This is a major religious and social event for which tickets are usually quite scarce. However, the dean of the cathedral also happened to be a biblical scholar and he gave me a gift of four celebrity tickets, among the best seats in the church. We enjoyed it very much. We celebrated Christmas in our little apartment. Peter had met a friend of his from Chapel Hill who was traveling on his own so he joined us for Christmas and stayed over a couple of days, sleeping in the living room. Peter returned to Chapel Hill on boxing day, but Deborah stayed on for another week. Between Christmas and New-Years there were trips to London and Bath and we took in a play at a theatre in Oxford, Oscar Wilde's "The Importance of Being Ernest," a splendid performance.

After we saw Deborah off on her flight to Toronto on New-Years Day, we were back to normal, well almost. With all of the dinners and teas that the Nicholsons and Bartons had given to us, Elizabeth felt it only appropriate that we ought to respond with a social event in our apartment, however humble. This was easier said than done, because with very limited dishes and cutlery, we had to rent extra supplies, order flowers, etc. everything done my bike. Then a couple of days before the party while out shopping Elizabeth stepped off the curb of the road and injured her foot. It was quite painful, but she thought it was only a sprain and went on with her activities, including the party for the Nicholsons, the Bartons, and another faculty couple, the Morgans. Actually, when she finally went to the doctor about ten days after the accident, and then had an X-ray taken, it was discovered that Elizabeth had a fracture in her foot. She was fitted with an elastic boot support and keep off her feet as much as possible for four to five weeks! I went to the Red Cross office and got a cane for her to use. At the same time as this was happening we received word from my mother in Canada that her cancer was spreading with little prospect of remission.

What was also troubling about Elizabeth's freak accident was that it came at just the time that I had to leave for Zurich to begin a ten-day lecture trip in Switzerland and Germany. This had been planned for a long time and could not be rescheduled. But it left Elizabeth alone with only a limited amount of groceries and stuck in the apartment with very little to do. The weather also turned cold and it was hard to adequately heat the apartment. Just the day before I returned Elizabeth actually had a house call from the doctor, who proceeded to strap her foot for more support. While I had a great trip (more about that later), it was tainted by the constant thought of how Elizabeth was making out. The day after I got back Larry and Miriam Slifkin from Chapel Hill came for a visit. They actually lived in the same neighborhood that we did in Chapel Hill. Larry was a Physicist on a half year sabbatical from UNC and they had bought a second-hand car. So they took us out for tea, which was great for Elizabeth. We made a number of outings with the Slifkins and became great friends. We also had an invitation, along with the Bartons, for dinner at the home of James and Jane Barr who were now back from abroad.

By mid-February the foot was finally able to withstand more normal activity, so that when I took off for a speaking trip to Scotland, she made her own excursion to Salisbury and Stonehenge. The Slifkins had a great affection for the Cotswolds, so on a Saturday in mid-March we drove out with them by car to explore this beautiful region. This would be a common practice so that we became familiar with a large part of this area. It often included some hiking, another of their favorite sports. Later in March Elizabeth and I took a four day railway trip to Penzance, stayed in a wonderful seaside Hotel, from which we made side trips to Lands-End, the artists' haven of St. Ives, and on the way home, a stopover in Exeter with its beautiful Cathedral. We made a similar British Railway trip to Windermere, staying at a hotel in Lakeside at the southern end of Lake Windermere, from which we explored a large part of this beautiful Lake District region. We also did a four-day bus trip to Caernarvon and the rugged North-western region of Wales in May. Elizabeth also made a number of one and two-day trips on her own while I kept my nose in the books. In most of the cases involving these trips around the country Elizabeth was the master planner, arranging schedules and getting good deals on train tickets to make the most of our time in the UK.

There was one trip with a dual purpose that we were both keen on making and that was a trip to Holland. In addition to our seeing the sights of Amsterdam and visiting the museums, I had promised Piet de Boer that we would look him up, so we took the short train ride to Leiden, and de Boer met us at the station. He gave us a tour around the heart of the city and the university and then left us with Professors of Old Testament and Near Eastern Studies, Mulder, Hoftijzer, and Dirksen for lunch. It was a pleasant occasion. After lunch we took a taxi to de Boer's home and met Mrs de Boer and spent a pleasant time there until tea-time, after which we headed for Amsterdam. Piet de Boer's friendship and encouragement so early in my career had meant so much to me and now he was retired and at the end of his own illustrious career in scholarship. We also made contact with Klaas Smelik, as I had promised, and visited his family in Haarlem, and had supper with them. A couple of days later, while Elizabeth made a trip to the city of Delft, I met with Smelik and his colleagues at the University of Amsterdam, conducted a small seminar on biblical historiography and had an enjoyable lunch with them. We also had time on the final day to take in the beautiful bulb gardens of Keukenhof before we returned to England.

While I was off on my second trip to Geneva and a European tour, Deborah arrived back in England after the end of classes at the University of Toronto. As usual Elizabeth had organized a number of excursions for the two of them, to Penzance and Winchester as we had done, and to Cambridge. They also did a seventeen-day sight-seeing tour by bus through Europe at the end of May and first half of June. A few days later they flew back home while I stayed on another month in Oxford. Larry Slifkin was also left behind by his wife Miriam, who had likewise returned to Chapel Hill, so the two of us occasionally drove out to the Coswolds in his car for a day of hiking and enjoyment of nature, and Larry's search for "Roman roads," which was an obsession of his. He was always a lot of fun.

It is true that I thoroughly enjoyed all that this almost year-long residence in Oxford afforded Elizabeth and me and which I have so briefly and inadequately described, and I make no apology for it. But this memoir is primarily about my work and activities in the world of academia, which was the reason for my presence in Oxford in the first place. I was at the door of any one of the libraries as soon as it was open, which was never early enough to suit me, and I worked steadily. I was a regular participant at the Old Testament seminar, and gave a paper to the group on my current research. In addition to Ernest Nicholson and John Barton, I got to know John Day, Rex Mason and others. Early in the fall semester Rex Mason asked me to go along with him to sit in on a seminar on ancient historiography, chaired by the distinguished classicist Professor Fergus Millar, because Peter Ackroyd had been asked to give a presentation on the subject of my book, *In Search of History*. Obviously, I was most interested to hear what he had to say. When I got there Peter was rather surprised to see me, although he knew that I was in Oxford for the year. At any rate he began by pointing out to the seminar that the author of the book that he was going to discuss was present in the audience and that it was I and not him that should make the presentation, but I said that I was eager to hear what he had to say. In fact, Peter was very gracious and complimentary in his remarks and most eloquently described what I was trying to do in that work. The consequence of this was that Fergus Millar asked me to join the group as a full member at the seminar table and I came to a number of the subsequent sessions.

I want to comment on one of these sessions in particular. Millar invited a young scholar, Rosalind Thomas of the University of London who was working on the problem of oral tradition and its relationship to the writing of history in Athens. She would finally publish this dissertation in 1989 as *Oral Tradition and Written Record in Classical Athens*. This issue was very important for my own work on biblical historiography and I would follow her work very closely, which included a much broader treatment of the subject, and a real classic, in her book, *Literacy and Orality in Ancient Greece* (1992). After the seminar session Millar and a few others, including Rosalind Thomas gathered for drinks at a pub and continued the discussion. He also wanted me to have dinner with him and Thomas at his college that night but on such short notice I had to decline. Nevertheless, it was most gratifying to me that I was involved with this seminar in classical historiography at the same time that I was doing research in biblical historiography.

The primary focus of my research during this period in Oxford was to extend my study of biblical historiography, as reflected in my book, *In Search of History*, to include a place for historiography in the Pentateuch, and in the writings of the so-called Yahwist in particular. It was my conviction that this source in the books of Genesis, Exodus and the latter half of Numbers was a kind of antiquarian historiography that was also reflected in a similar form of archaic history of ethnic, social and institutional origins that one finds in ancient Greek historiography. Most of the many talks and lectures that I would be giving in the UK and in Europe would be dealing with various aspects of this larger study. As I mentioned earlier, in preparation for some of the presentations in Switzerland Hans Heinrich wanted me to furnish him with a two part manuscript that he could then translate into German and be ready for distribution to the Swiss Old Testament conference in Fribourg in February. So from August to December I had my work cut out for me.

Prior to my departure for Oxford I had already arranged to give two lectures in the fall term, the one at King's College London in the Strand and the other at Sheffield. I went to King's College in November and met Ronald Clements, Ackroyd's successor, for the first time. My lecture there was on "History as National Tradition," and it was well received. After the lecture Clements and a few of his colleagues took me out to dinner at a little restaurant in the Strand and we became good friends. In his note to me a few days later he stated: "Many thanks for giving your time and thought to our Theological Seminar last week. It was a very valuable occasion for us, and I greatly benefited from what you had to contribute and the conversation afterwards." Ronald Clements and I developed a very close relationship after that. My Sheffield lecture was in early December and David Clines was my host. The topic of that lecture was "Joshua's Conquest of Canaan and Near Eastern Historiography," which was eventually published in 1990. The Sheffield group of John Rogerson, David Clines, Philip Davies and David Gunn, were something of an odd collection. Their graduate program seemed to cater to foreign students who were quite conservative theologically, and who produced very conservative dissertations, even though the "Sheffield School" was gaining a reputation for being "minimalist" in its approach to biblical history and not very strongly committed to literary criticism of the type practiced in Oxford or Cambridge. Within the rest of British Old Testament scholarship, Sheffield seemed to be the "odd group out."

Also in early December just two days before the Sheffield trip I had another talk to give at Ripon College, an Anglican theological school affiliated with Oxford but situated in the countryside in Cuddesdon. In late November Professor Paul Joyce, who taught at the school and was a member of the Oxford OT seminar where we had met, asked me if I could speak at the final session of their college seminar, in the place of John Rogerson of Sheffield, who for some reason had to bow out of his commitment. As this was the final session they were reluctant to cancel it and could I help them out. I agreed to do so, and as I was totally dependent upon Paul for transportation, I would be there for the whole program, which included tea at 4 p.m., followed by the seminar until 5:30. The talk and response went fairly well, more like an undergraduate lecture.

This was followed by a "Sung Eucharist" at 6 p.m., a church service in a separate unheated chapel, for which I was not prepared. There was a college dinner at 7:30 (a farewell dinner for the Principal, who was leaving to become a bishop in the Church of England). Needless to say, the dinner also went on for some time so that I finally arrived home quite late.

Beginning in the summer before I set out for Oxford and throughout the fall term after I arrived, I had considerable correspondence with Willemina de Filippi, a student at Toronto working on a doctorate under Kirk Grayson. I had met her previously when she was student during my time at Toronto. She had been reading my books on *Abraham* and *In Search of History*, and was so enthusiastic in her appreciation of them that she wanted to translate them into German for the German-speaking students and public. She sent along a few pages of my Abraham book in German as a sample of her work to demonstrate her skills. I replied, thanking her for her interest and the sample and told her that I would take up the matter with Professor Hans Heinrich Schmid of Zurich to see what he thought of taking the matter further. I knew that she could not do this work for nothing and it might be difficult to find a German Press that would support such a venture, as Hans Heinrich was soon to inform me after he had consulted presses with which he was familiar. Suggestions were made about producing a more abbreviated version in German, which I was reluctant to do. That would only divert my time and efforts from my current program. With all of my commitments for the spring term I felt reluctant to pursue the matter very diligently. In hindsight, I should have taken up the matter with Otto Kaiser who was looking for publications for his monograph series (BZAW), but I let the matter slide. This was clearly a mistake, because I could not compete with German publications by relying entirely on my English publications to reach the German audience. With some effort, I could have found the funding, but I was too preoccupied with all of these engagements for the spring term.

During the fall term at Oxford I was invited by Professor Adrian Curtis of Manchester and Secretary of the Society for Old Testament Studies (SOTS) to attend their winter meeting in London. It was held after term at Halliday Hall, a small college on the south side of the city and we would stay overnight in the college residence. Ernest Nicholson and I went down together. I had also been asked to give one of the major papers relating to my current work on the Yahwist, and the title was: "Mountain-climbing with Moses: Some Observations on Exodus 19–24." This meeting was also an opportunity to meet many British, Scottish, and Irish scholars whom I had previously only known by name. One such scholar was John R. Bartlett of Trinity College in Dublin. We had engaged in a lively exchange of views in *JBL* regarding the story of the conquest of Sihon's Kingdom by the Israelites in the book of Numbers. He greeted me warmly and conceded that in my final response to his arguments against my views, I had convinced him of my position. I thanked him for his graciousness and then he proceeded to tell me that he was going to be in Oxford on leave for the spring term.

We agreed to get together, which we did, usually in a pub for lunch, and we became very good friends over the years. Bartlett had never actually earned a doctorate, but there was a system at Trinity College whereby one could be rewarded a doctorate on the strength of one's publications, and some years later the administration of that institution asked me if I would be willing to give my critical assessment of his various publications, which they sent to me, for just this purpose. I was, of course, delighted to do so, and he duly became Dr. John R. Bartlett and fully deserved that honor.

Another scholar that I met at the London meeting was Lester Grabbe, a young American scholar who had been recently appointed to a position at the University of Hull. He informed me that he had read my books on *Abraham* and *In Search of History* with much appreciation and that he was not a follower of the Albright School. Lester and I would maintain a close association throughout our careers. Professor John Emerton of Cambrige University was also there and this was the first time that I actually met him. He was the new editor of *Vetus Testamentum*, succeeding Piet de Boer, and I believe that he was in charge of the SOTS program on this occasion. At any rate, during this meeting we made some arrangements for a visit in the spring to Cambridge for a lecture there. Adrian Curtis of Manchester who had invited me to the meeting was also there, and he spoke to me after my talk about coming to Manchester, and this was followed up later by correspondence to set a time and topic. Those colleagues from Sheffield and King's College and the others from Oxford, and Graeme Auld from Edinburgh, were all there so that I felt that I was already among friends. That atmosphere was quite characteristic of SOTS as compared with the increasingly mammoth size and fragmentation of SBL. It was a very enjoyable experience and by no means my last. For a time I even took out membership in SOTS and received their materials.

With the Christmas and New Year's holiday festivities past, January was a very busy month making all the preparations for a very full lectures schedule in February. As indicated earlier, I was particularly concerned about Elizabeth's broken foot and the ten days in early February when I would be in Europe and she would still be largely immobile. On the morning of the 30th of January I flew down to Geneva where I was met at the airport by Professor Albert de Pury, with his sign containing my name. This was our first encounter, and the beginning of a long and valuable friendship. At the university I met de Pury's young assistant, Thomas Römer, who was working on his doctoral dissertation under de Pury. In conversation I learned that Römer had been a student at Heidelberg under Rolf Rendtorff, but they had had some disagreement over the dissertation, so Römer had come to Geneva and he thrived in the Switzerland environment. He was also very much aware of my work and had taken up some suggestions that I had made in an article in the early 70's about the theme of Israel's forefathers in the biblical tradition, and he engaged in an exhaustive treatment of this issue. So we had lots to talk about.

In the late afternoon, 6:15 to 7 p.m., I gave the first lecture: "Myth and History: The Problem of Origins." This was directly related to my larger subject on the historiography of the Yahwist in Genesis, because I understood this biblical author as constructing a history of the origin of the Israelites similar to the antiquarian histories of the classical world. The method of the Greek historians was to "historicize" myths and legends of origins and to fit them into a chronological framework down to the time of the rise of their own nation. On the following afternoon I took up the theme of "Tradition and History: History as National Tradition," in which I focused on how this history of the archaic past is presented in such a way as to formulate a conception or understanding of national or corporate identity. This was basically a sociological approach to tradition, following the University of Chicago scholar, Edward Shils, in his book *Tradition* (1981), and applying it to biblical historiography. Previously, the preoccupation of scholars had been either on trying to find bits of history in Genesis and Exodus, with disastrous results, or they had emphasized a kind of theology of sacred history, *Heilgeschichte*, which was no longer in vogue.

With the second lecture late in the day on Friday, this left the early part of the day free, so de Pury suggested an open discussion with his class of advanced students on the subject of the Yahwist. For this session Hans Heinrich came down from Zurich and joined in so that the students had two of us to fire away at, the students having been prepared by reading our books on this subject as part of the course. The whole session was completely unscripted and the students were thrilled with their chance to go after these two controversial figures. Hans Heinrich and I had a great time, but de Pury was not finished with us yet. After lunch we went to his apartment and he set up a recording machine with microphones. The three of us, Albert, Hans Heinrich and I spent a couple of hours debating a range of issues related to our work. They then let me have a little time to relax and recover my voice so that I could give the second public lecture as planned.

The next day I was off bright and early to Fribourg and the Swiss Society for Ancient Near Eastern Studies, so that we would be there to start the session at 10 a.m. and continuing to 4 p.m., with a break for lunch. The theme of the whole day was "The Yahwist as Historian," with two hour sessions in both halves, in which I would present one aspect of the subject in one and a different aspect in the other. These were introduced in the following manner:

> Since the time of Wellhausen the J source has often been described as a historical work (*Geschichtswerk*), but little consideration has been given to the *form* of an ancient history, how historians collected and made use of oral and written traditions, and what constitutes literary and thematic unity in such works. The first part of the paper will present a survey of views from Wellhausen to the present on how scholars have dealt with the matter of J's literary form. The second part will look at comparative historiographic materials from

the Near East and ancient Greece which include primeval myths and heroic or ancestral legends as part of a larger national historical tradition.

Each presentation would be followed by discussion, and Hans Heinrich had prepared for this by translating a text of each presentation into German and distributing them to those who wished to participate in the discussion. Albert de Pury, as president of the society, would chair the sessions.

Needless to say, with all of the material they were given ahead of time, they came well prepared with all of their questions, and they hardly stopped at lunchtime, so that by the end of the session I was drained. It was another chance to meet Swiss scholars and to be absorbed in the European atmosphere and perspective of the discipline. A very close friend of Hans Heinrich's was Professor Othmar Keel of Fribourg. His primary interest was in the religion of ancient Israel within the context of the other Near Eastern religions, and he had accumulated a large collection of archaeological artifacts, particularly, seals, scarabs, amulets and bullae. So following the afternoon session, Keel gave Hans Heinrich and me a tour of his collection. Over the years he had quite a prodigious output in publications, along with his junior colleague Christoph Ühlinger, and they developed a very important monograph series, *Orbis Biblicus et Orientalis*, a joint Swiss-German venture that was very successful.

After supper and a farewell to Albert and Thomas, Hans Heinrich and I took the train to Zurich and on to Schwerzenbach. It had been the plan that Elizabeth would fly down to Zurich on the Saturday, and we could spend a few days together with Hans Heinrich and Christa, and then she would return to Oxford when I had to leave for Germany. However, Elizabeth's broken foot forced a change in those plans and they had to put up with just me instead. Sunday was a day off and a welcomed break before the next round of activity. Monday I gave a lecture in German, translated from the English by Hans Heinrich, to a large class to students that was also open to the public. I met Professor Fritz Stolz of Zurich at that time. He had published a commentary on 1 and 2 Samuel, which Hans Heinrich had given me earlier, so I was familiar with his work.

The following day, I set off for Heidelberg by train and arrived in the late afternoon. I was met by Professor Rolf Rendtorff with whom I had had considerable correspondence about the visit. We went to a very nice Greek restaurant by the river, just the two of us, and I had a chance to get to know him better. We got on very well. I stayed in a small hotel in the middle of Heidelberg near the cathedral. The next day Erhard Blum, Rendtorff's assistant came by to collect me. The lecture was at noon and, as Rendtorff was tied up for the morning, Blum showed me around Heidelberg. Because it was wintertime the castle was closed, but as we walked around town we had lots to discuss. His dissertation had just been published and I was in the process of reviewing it, a quite remarkable work of over 550 pages presenting a new approach to the composition of the patriarchal stories. While the influence of Rendtorff was quite obvious in this work, what struck me was that it was an attempted compromise between Rendtorff's views and my views on the Pentateuch, along with a very large spectrum of relevant scholarly studies. He followed up this book with a sequel a few years later, expanding his literary studies to include the rest of the Pentateuch. It was quite obvious to me then that he was an exceptional young scholar. After my lecture in the afternoon, I had lunch together with a number of the biblical faculty, including Manfred and Helga Weippert, together with Rendtorff and Blum, and this was followed by a discussion of my paper, which had been distributed to them earlier, along with other aspects of my work and its relationship to the recent work of Blum. After some time to relax in the afternoon, there was a social at the Weippert's place with much the same lunch group in attendance. I was a little surprised when Helga Weippert greeted me in Dutch at the door. The Weipperts had spent some time early in their careers in Utrecht so they were quite fluent in Dutch. The social was a wonderful occasion with great food and conviviality. The Weipperts were very active in the German-Palestine Society, the German equivalent of ASOR and worked primarily in the areas of history and archaeology, but they were hardly in support of the American biblical archaeology movement. One of Manfred's books translated into English as *The Settlement of the Israelite Tribes in Palestine* (1971), which was a critical appraisal of the Albright position, was very well received and quite influential in North America.

The next day it was off to Marburg. Professor Otto Kaiser met me at the railway station, and even though we had never met before, it was not hard to guess who he was. We already felt that we knew each other because we had corresponded frequently and I had been sending him articles to be published in *ZAW* of which he was the editor. My lecture was not until evening so he showed me around Marburg. The university itself is built on the slope of a large hill, so one soon gets a lot of exercise traveling up and down. On the way to the lecture that evening, I was surprised to encounter Erhard Gerstenberger, a newly appointed professor at Marburg. I had known Erhard when I was at Yale because during that time he was working on a post doctorate there and doing some teaching at the Divinity School. The evening lecture was a public one and I was instructed beforehand to make it simple, even for beginners.

The next day was open with nothing scheduled formally. After a little more sightseeing Kaiser and I had lunch with some students, with lots of lively conversation. It was characteristic of Kaiser that he always seemed to be surrounded by students and young scholars and they loved him. In the afternoon Kaiser took me to visit with Professor Ernst Würthwein, an emeritus professor of Marburg, who lived on the south side of Marburg. Kaiser left me there and said that he would pick me up later. Würthwein was a highly respected German scholar, who had spent a lot of time in Oxford so he was fluent in English and a very congenial person who was keen on what I was doing and quite familiar with my latest work. So we had a good time. At 4 p.m., following the British custom his wife brought in some tea for us. Then he asked me what I would like in my tea and I told him, "a little cream and sugar," but he had another suggestion. "How about a little Cognac?" I must say it was very good tea. Later Kaiser came around again and we all had supper together with Mrs Würthwein, along with a daughter who taught in the Law School.

On Friday evenings Kaiser was accustomed to having a small group of graduate students over to his place for a symposium to discuss philosophy. This was one of Kaiser's major interests and he was scheduled to talk about Fichte, but instead he told the group that since I was in town they would turn the meeting over to me. I had a number of talks on various subjects that I had prepared for this trip so it was no great strain to lay out a topic for discussion. Kaiser also had a great wine cellar so we had a little wine to lubricate the discussion. Kaiser's other interest, besides biblical studies, was classics and in his large personal library was a remarkable collection of classical literature. This trip was a wonderful opportunity to get to know this scholar personally and we would have a close relationship for many years. The next day I flew back to Oxford. It was quite a remarkable and productive trip.

It was good to be back "home" in Oxford and to see that Elizabeth's foot was on the mend. As mentioned above, the doctor had paid a house-call the day before and had strapped her foot for more support so she could start to put more weight on it. The Slifkins also came by on a Sunday to give her an outing so we had high-tea at their place, which was very thoughtful of them. I did some shorter guest lecture trips during the rest of the month. One was a two-day visit to Cambridge where Graham Davies of Fitzwilliam College was my host. I gave a paper to their colloquium of scholars and graduate students, just as I had done at Oxford. Professor R. Norman Whybray, recently retired from Hull University, was also there. I was familiar with his writings and was glad to meet him in person. I was invited to dine at high table at St. John's College, which was very pleasant, with lots of wine to wash down the dinner. Then when my host and I with a few others retired to the "combination" (senior common) room, there was another selection of after-dinner drinks. I was a little dizzy when I left the college but the walk to Fitzwilliam College in the cold February air managed to clear my head. The Cambridge trip was a taste of things to come.

Towards the end of the month I made a four-day trip to Scotland, with a stop in Glasgow to give a popular lecture in the morning to undergraduates and then a more challenging paper to a seminar in the afternoon. I should say at this point that the lectures to the wider audience were ones that I had worked on in my lectures for Warren Nord's Humanities weekends, which I knew had been effective so I had no reason to refrain from using them again. From Glasgow I took the train to Edinburgh in the evening where I was met by Graeme Auld and he and Sylvia, his wife, put me up for the night at their place. My task for the next day was a seminar in the morning and a class lecture to undergrads in the afternoon. This worked out very well and following the afternoon lecture we had a tea in the senior common room of the Divinity Faculty of New College, to which Professor John Gibson, the Head of the Department of Old Testament, together with Gaeme Auld, had invited some former retired colleagues.

One such retired professor that I was quite surprised to see and meet was Professor Norman W. Porteous, a distinguished Scottish scholar, who was getting up in years, but still very sharp. He insisted that we sit together at tea and we had a pleasant chat. After a light supper with Professor Gibson and his wife at their home I took an overnight train to Oxford and was home before 9 a.m., not the best way to get a good night's sleep. Nevertheless, the trip was a very enjoyable time and Graeme's gracious note to me a few days later suggested that the talks were well received. The same was the case with the letter from Professor Alaster Hunter of Glasgow who thanked me for the contributions and further stated: "Not the least important thing [about the talks] was that you succeeded in communicating with people of a wide range of experience and academic interests." That compliment and feedback was much appreciated.

During the months of March and April I had a break from giving talks on the continent. This was largely because this is also the period in Europe when there is a break between school terms. So I used this time to catch up with my library work and research, as well as make some sightseeing trips with Elizabeth, which I have mentioned above. The second nine-day lecture trip to Europe was scheduled in conjunction with a large colloquium of scholars on the theme of "History and Historical Consciousness in the Civilizations of the Ancient Near East" to be held at a conference center in Cartigny, Switzerland, near Geneva. The lectures that I had given earlier in Geneva were part of a series on this theme. They would be made available to the group in printed form, while others would be presented for the first time at the colloquium. There would also be time for discussion on both sets of papers. The whole conference was in French and I had some difficulty understanding the oral presentations, except for the distinguished German scholar Professor D. O. Edzard, whose French I could understand. There were few other non-francophones at the conference. Professor Edzard's field was Assyriology, and quite distinguished in that field, and I did have the chance to speak with him during one of the breaks. Another scholar whom I met there was François Hartog. His interest was in how the Greeks viewed the east. I later discovered a translation of his very stimulating book, *The Mirror of Herodotus, the Representation of the Other in the Writing of History*. The convention center site was very pleasant with a magnificent view of the French Alps, and in spite of my language limitations, it was quite enjoyable.

After the colloquium I left Geneva and my good friend Albert de Pury and proceeded to Zurich for an overnight visit with the Schmids. That evening we had a great party, as Hans Heinrich had promised. They were disappointed again that Elizabeth was not with me, but I explained that Deborah would be coming to Oxford from Toronto while I was gone and Elizabeth would be there to meet her. The Schmids and I had an enjoyable, albeit all too short, visit. Plans were made for the publication of my preliminary study of *The Yahwist as Historian* in German, along with a German translation of my Geneva lecture on "Myth and History," which appeared the following year by a Zurich publisher as *Der Jahwist als Historiker*.

I traveled by train from Zurich to Munich the next day and was met by Professor Klaus Baltzer. Jorg Jeremias was to have been my host but a sudden death in the family meant that he had to leave town and would not be there for my visit, so Baltzer was my host for this visit, and a wonderful host he was. As the time permitted we did a tour of the city center and some of the university. I had never met Baltzer before, but he was a student of von Rad and had produced his doctoral dissertation at Heidelberg on a form-critical and comparative study of the covenant formulary in the Old Testament. I remember von Rad at Princeton mentioning this study of Baltzer's to a small group of us in his seminar on form-criticism before it appeared in print. Later it was translated into English and I owned a copy of it. This work, along with that of George Mendenhall, sparked a great deal of attention in "covenant theology" at the time in the sixties and seventies, although by the late 80s it had tapered off. Needless to say, my familiarity with his work and background in this study created a close point of connection between us.

At the lecture later in the day there was a young scholar, Hans-Christoph Schmitt, who had come from a nearby theological school at Augsburg for my talk. He introduced himself to me and then proceeded to tell me that he had become familiar with my work on the story of Abraham, and particularly my revolutionary work on the Pentateuch at the time that he was working on his own doctoral dissertation under Otto Kaiser at Marburg. He had also been working on the Pentateuch and had attempted something quite different from the standard documentary approach, and when Kaiser objected to it as too radical, Schmitt had showed him my book: "If you think I am radical, look at what Van Seters had done to the Documentary Hypothesis." Kaiser saw that there was a lot of change in the air and so accepted Schmitt's thesis, and he was eager to give me credit for helping him at that important stage in his career. Naturally I was delighted to meet him and to hear his story, and we became good friends, as we are to this day. Our paths would cross many times in the future.

The next day I took the train from Munich to Hamburg and was met at the station by my host Professor Klaus Koch. We had become acquainted fifteen years earlier in Los Angeles at an SBL meeting so it was a pleasant renewal of our friendship. Koch was also a student of von Rad, as were so many in Germany. He had also produced a very useful handbook on form-criticism which had been translated into English, and I have made extensive use of it. He was a gracious host and showed me around some interesting parts of Hamburg. I gave a lecture and also had a session of "shop-talk" together with some of his colleagues. The whole experience was a very pleasant one. The next day I flew out of Hamburg to Heathrow and then by train on to Oxford where both Deborah, who had arrived a few days earlier, and Elizabeth were waiting for me. I had one more academic trip, an overnight to Manchester, to give a lecture and meet with faculty in biblical studies. For the rest of the time until late July I kept at my research, while Deborah and Elizabeth made their travels together until they returned to the US in mid-June.

I had become rather anxious towards the end of my stay in Oxford and eager to get home because the news from there was that my mother in Toronto was failing fast. So a few days after I arrived in the US I made a quick trip up to Toronto to spend a weekend there. She was still at home and was glad to see me, but it was obvious to all that the end was near. I said my final goodbye and about a week later she died in hospital of her cancer. Then Elizabeth and I drove back up to Toronto for the funeral and a visit with my dad and the rest of the family. Then it was back to Chapel Hill to tackle the backlog of work in the front office of the Department.

6

Second Term as Department Chair and the Interim Years, 1986–1992

My second term as Chair of the Department lasted from 1986 until mid-1988. That brief tenure was my decision and I was not going to be persuaded to do otherwise. During this time there were still a lot of things to get done, among them being the making of new appointments to fill a certain amount of turnover in the faculty, and all of the searches and administrative paperwork that that entailed. Most difficult in this regard was the matter of finding someone to fill the void created by John Schütz's accident. For some time it was not immediately clear the extent to which John would make a full recovery, so I tried to find senior retired faculty of some stature to come on temporary appointment to give the new graduate program some boost, but to no avail. Over the course of the year that I was back it became apparent that John would not be able to teach again and so we received permission from the dean's office to make a search for a new position in New Testament studies in 1987–88. The result was the appointment of Bart Ehrman, a doctoral graduate of Princeton Seminary with four years of teaching experience at Rutgers University.

Since I was not only chair of the department but also the most senior in biblical studies and knowledgeable in the area of the New Testament, I obviously had a lot to say about this appointment. While Ehrman came from a conservative educational background with a doctorate under Professor Bruce Metzger in textual criticism at Princeton, he already had a good publication record with more projects in the works and a very strong teaching recommendation from Rutgers. I was sure that he would get along well with Elizabeth (Liz) Clark in New Testament at Duke and compliment that combined graduate program very well. Ehrman certainly proved to be one of the best junior appointments that we made during my time at UNC. In time he was to become quite prolific in his publications and after my retirement he would succeed me in the James A. Gray chair.

During the time that I was chair of the department there was little that I could do by way of developing the Near Eastern/Old Testament side of the graduate program. It was all that I could do to maintain my undergraduate teaching responsibilities, with the occasional graduate seminar. Indeed, for the first few years we did not even attempt to get involved in such a program. For the rest, the graduate program slowly grew and in a few areas had some real success. For the most part my stimulus in academic matters came from outside the department.

Within the university I was sometimes involved in the affairs of other departments. By virtue of my record in archaeological activity I was also appointed by the Dean of Arts and Sciences to the Advisory Committee for the Research Labs of Anthropology. This was not an odious task, with very few meetings, but I was always invited to the Anthropology Department's Christmas social and became acquainted with some members of this department. I also had a close association with the History Department. This department had a long standing tradition of offering undergraduate courses in ancient history, and the professor responsible for these offerings was retiring at this time. There was the strong possibility that he would not be replaced by someone in this field. So Professor Philip Stadter, Chair of Classics and a close friend, asked me if I would help them get support for such a senior appointment in ancient history in the History Department by writing to the chairman of that department, which I did. I could use my recent award for *In Search of History* by the American Historical Association as a way of suggesting that I was qualified for being concerned about this issue and involvement in such an appointment. This kind of cooperative effort with Classics paid off with just such an appointment and I was always closely associated with these scholars in classical history.

Indeed, what constantly surprised me was how familiar those in classics and historical studies were with my book and how little recognition it received in biblical studies, especially in North America. In 1986 the American Academy of Religion established three book awards for excellence, one of which was in historical studies, and I was notified in December of that year that I had received this award for *In Search of History*, together with Wayne Meeks for his book, *The First Urban Christians*. In addition to this award there was a special session held at the annual meeting of AAR, which met jointly with SBL, in which the recipients of the book awards were publicly honored and some remarks made about their particular publication. SBL had no such book awards, but they often recognized a special publication in the field of biblical studies with a special session focused on this work. This never happened with *In Search of History* or any other of my publications. All additional honors for my work in biblical studies would come from Europe and not from North America.

My major preoccupation with SBL at this time and over the next few years, as mentioned earlier, was with the development of a new section on the Pentateuch, which had been entirely missing from the annual program for some time. In 1984 the executive of SBL had approached Rolf Knierim (the last doctoral student of von

Rad) and me to hold two consultation sessions in 1985 and 86 to get the section off the ground. These were intended to produce a proposal that would outline the format of the section, the chair person(s) and the planning committee who would be responsible for lining up the program for each year. There was, however, a basic problem and this was the fact that I would be on sabbatical in the UK for the first of these sessions in the fall of 1985 and Knierim would be on sabbatical for the second one in the fall of 1986. The way that we dealt with the program part of it was that he would make a presentation and chair the session, as well as canvass the group on their views and line up those who were committed to participate in it. Knierim was of the firm opinion that it should have the seminar format with a committed group of members around the table with the rest in attendance as an audience. I had some reservations about this because it would restrict the section on the Pentateuch to a small group and still give the serious critical study of the Pentateuch only a very low profile. Knierim, however, was quite determined to push this very European model, so I went along with it.

Rolf and I were under the impression that following the two years of consultation we would be able to draft a program plan and submit it for approval, but I was informed by Kent Richards, the Executive Secretary of SBL, in mid-August that it was overdue in September and that we should submit our report immediately. Because Rolf was away on sabbatical and left me no forwarding address I could not get a hold of him. He had told me that he already had a meeting set up with the consultation steering committee at the SBL meeting for November 21st. So if SBL wanted this section or seminar on the Pentateuch to be established they would just have to wait for that meeting. That is exactly what we did and we had our seminar for the next five years. I was made chair of the steering committee, which meant getting the whole process started, drafting the proposal, and vetting requests for membership. Regarding the steering committee, in addition to Rolf and myself there was my good friend from Yale days, George Coats; also John Gammie of University of Tulsa, another friend whom I met through SBL. Knierim insisted that his friend Simon De Vries also be on the steering committee, even though he knew that De Vries and I did not particularly care for each other. My most recent gripe was that Knierim had chosen him to respond to my paper in the 1986 meeting and he was supposed to send a copy of his response to me well before the meeting, but he did not do so, and offered a very lame excuse.

The showdown came in the following year when the steering committee gave Simon De Vries the task of presenting the major paper on the history of Pentateuchal research while I was asked to chair the meeting. This put me in a real bind because the paper that he produced was 85 pages long and this was much too expensive to send out to all of the membership. They would have to buy the volume of seminar papers to have a copy and few would have done that before the meeting. The whole piece was very one-sided against the new approaches of the "revisionists," Rendtorff, Schmid and myself, and as chair of the meeting I would have little chance to respond. So in a letter to the group membership I explained the situation and urged them to also read a "different perspective" that could be found in the resent publication of R. N. Whybray, *The Making of the Pentateuch* as preparation for the discussion. However, I was getting a little tired of this contest between myself and De Vries, backed by Knierim, and so even before this meeting I sent a letter to the steering committee indicating that I was tired of being undermined by De Vries and I was prepared to step down as chair and the new chair could decide whether to have me on the steering committee or not. The result was that I got the vote of confidence. As John Gammie stated in his letter to me: "Why should you step down from being Chair? I would hate for one position to put itself in the driver's seat without some countervailing dialogue." By this he meant De Vries and Knierim. He continued: "You have very definite views but you do respect informed disagreement."

That "informed disagreement" not only with me but also with the views of De Vries came when I submitted the new names for membership that I had received, including Jacob Milgrom of UC Berkeley, Ellis Rivkin of Hebrew Union College, Cincinnati, Thomas Thompson, and Thomas Dozeman. A few years later Rolf Rendtorff also began to come on a regular basis. I was on very good terms with all of these scholars so that De Vries had very little impact within the seminar after that. After five years I wrote up a report reviewing all of the sessions for that period. In the evaluation I pointed out the value of the smaller seminar format (which Knierim had so strongly supported) but also the fact that it was not reaching the much larger constituency of those interested in participating in a Pentateuch section. Consequently, I indicated that the steering committee advocated changing the format to that of a section with a new chair, Thomas Dozeman, and a new steering committee. It would be up to Tom to submit the proposal for the new section format, together with my report. This time around everything would be on time and in order.

Because I was going to be on sabbatical leave in Cambridge at the time of the final meeting, I would not be able to participate in it. However, the steering committee decided that there would be two papers with responses. The one by Knierim would be his swansong, and a second paper would be presented by Thomas Dozeman reviewing the previous twenty years of my work on the Pentateuch. He sent me a draft copy of his paper six months in advance of the meeting and asked me to make some additional comments to be included at the end, which I did. He also included a complete bibliography of my work up to that point. I could not have been more pleased with his effort. Thomas Dozeman was a young and very energetic scholar and I served as a mentor not only in getting the new Pentateuch group off the ground but also in his research. That is not to say that he was a disciple by any means. He also had a good relationship with Rolf Rendtorff and was determined to be open to considering seriously all sides in the Pentateuchal debate. We had a long and fruitful association. Dozeman was open to the new developments in European biblical scholarship and eagerly invited their participation. Knierim, the last assistant to von Rad, on the other hand, was dedicated to a major form criticism project in keeping with an older era of

German scholarship in which George Coats and De Vries were also involved, and it was slowly becoming obsolete, especially as it had to do with the Pentateuch. I continued to offer papers in this section from time to time, happy to see that such a section now thrived in this new format, while leaving the organizational chores to a younger generation of scholars.

One of the scholars whom I met early on in the Pentateuch group was Professor Ellis Rivkin of Hebrew Union College in Cincinnati. He belonged to the liberal or "Reformed" branch of Judaism, quite different from that of the conservative Rabbi Jacob Milgrom. In mid-1987 he invited me to come and present a paper to his history seminar at HUC in the coming fall term. We agreed on a date and I gave him the option of a somewhat controversial topic or a rather bland review of recent histories of Israel. He, of course, chose the former: "Myth, Legend, and History: the Creation of a National Tradition." He suggested that I fly up on a Sunday, the day before the lecture so that he and his wife Zelda could show me the sights of the city of Cincinnati and in the evening after the lecture they would take me out to a favorite eating place with some of the colleagues "for dinner in my honor." I already knew a number of the faculty, one of whom, D. J. Wiseman, had been in the same year and program as me at Yale and who had specialized in Assyriology. Needless to say, I had a great time. In a letter to me after the visit Rivkin wrote, "By throwing down the gauntlet and compelling all of us to take a new look at our unanalyzed assumptions, you put us all in your debt. There was not a single class that did not reverberate with heated give-and-take in the wake of your lecture. A very rare tribute indeed." I am sure that if I had tried the same lecture at Princeton Seminary I would not have had such a positive response. Rivkin and I were good friends after that.

With the very limited graduate studies program in the area of the ancient Near East and Old Testament at UNC, I had very limited prospects of having many graduate students of my own. However, having acquired some notoriety with my books on *Abraham* and *In Search of History* I did have some contact with a number of younger scholars, both in the process of writing their dissertations or recent graduates of other doctoral programs. One such young scholar was Patrick van Steenis of the Catholic University in Leuven, Belgium. He wrote to tell me that he was working on a thesis for this institution on the subject: "Professor Van Seters' Vision on Old Testament History-writing," and he asked me for a bibliography of my publications, which I gave him. This correspondence began while I was on sabbatical at Oxford and continued for a few years. Because this thesis was only for a licentiate in Religious Studies (undergraduate) and subsequently in Sacred Theology, it would have been easy to dismiss this assistance as of little consequence. But that was hardly the case. He was clearly very enthusiastic in digging up all the information about me and my academic background that he could and thus informing those in the Department of Old Testament Exegesis about me through his thesis. This undoubtedly was a factor in the faculty of Leuven extending an invitation to me to make a major presentation at the Congress of the International Organization for the Study of the Old Testament (IOSOT) in Leuven in 1989. (More about this congress later.)

Earlier in this narrative I mentioned Fred Cryer, a doctoral student of Niels Peter Lemche, who was originally from Chapel Hill and who liked to keep in touch with Jack Sasson and me. I heard from him again in late 1986. He was now in Bochum Germany at the university serving as assistant to Professor Siegfried Herrmann, a scholar who was well known in America for the English edition of his *History of Israel*, a work very much in the tradition of Martin Noth. When Herrmann's work was first published in German in 1973 it was viewed as at the cutting edge of this field of study, but now Cryer writes that due to the work of Lemche and me, he and Herrmann's former assistant "are lightyears away from his positions," which in a little more than a decade indicates how quickly the discipline was changing. Fred continued to correspond from time to time and to send me samples of his work for feedback.

One of the Old Testament graduate students whom I met at Oxford and got to know through the Old Testament Colloquium was Brian Schmidt, an American. We also frequently had lunch together in Oxford and talked about his work and his future plans. Shortly after I returned from Oxford he began writing to me about his plan to move back to America, to Durham NC, after his Oxford residence requirement was fulfilled in September of 1987, and to complete his dissertation in Durham, using the resources of Duke University. Brian was a doctoral student of John Day, but he regularly referred in his correspondence to Nicholson as if he were the one primarily responsible for his work and the one in Oxford to whom he most frequently appealed for assistance and recommendation. He was, of course, hoping for some part-time teaching while he worked on his dissertation and I was able to supply him with some teaching of Biblical Hebrew for a couple of years. Needless to say, once in North Carolina I saw quite a bit of him in Chapel Hill and I ended up reading parts of his dissertation and offering him some advice and counsel, probably more than his more distant director, John Day. I also wrote at least two dozen job recommendations for him. (I lost count after that.) Brian did eventually get a very good position at the University of Michigan where he remains to this day.

I also had a letter from Ernest Nicholson soon after I returned from Oxford which contained a lot of family news and university politics, which strongly suggested that he would move increasingly into an administrative role, much like Hans Heinrich Schmid did at Zurich. Nicholson also kept me up-to-date on his current research and writing projects and ended with the remark: "I shall miss you around here, your knock on the door at lunchtime and the chance to see you and have a talk. . . . Keep in touch." That last sentiment about remaining in contact was always easier said than done. We did keep it up for a while. I wrote to him about Brian Schmidt's work in our department, teaching language and sitting in on my graduate course in biblical exegesis. In his response Nicholson indicated that he too had been writing letters on his behalf and felt a little awkward about it, especially because he had not asked John

Day, his thesis supervisor to write any. Also, in anticipation of Nicholson's sabbatical in 1989 we had some correspondence about the various possibilities as to where he would spend it. Because he only had a half a year leave, he could not take advantage of the National Humanities Center in the Research Triangle. Instead he accepted an offer from Southern Baptist Seminary in Louisville. With this in mind we arranged with Duke for a lecture at Duke and a seminar with grad students at Chapel Hill. Elizabeth and I also had him with us for a Sunday dinner and gave him a tour of Chapel Hill and the region before taking him to the airport. His wife Hazel did not come with him on this leave and it was the last time that we had such close personal contact with each other. At subsequent international conferences, if he was there, it was always a brief and polite greeting and little more.

I also kept in touch with John Barton and his family and this has continued up to the present time. When my book, *In Search of History*, came out in paperback in 1987 I sent him a copy and we had some correspondence about what was going on in Oxford and his own research projects. His preferred location for sabbatical research was Germany and he did not travel much to America, so I saw him only on trips to the UK or conferences on the continent. He remained a good friend. I also sent a copy of *In Search of History* to John Bartlett and tried to catch up with him since Oxford. He immediately replied with a letter recalling our pleasant times together and promised to send me a copy of his forthcoming book on *Edom* as soon as it was out. It appeared in 1989. John Bartlett had a close association with Max Miller at Emory and spent some time there, which meant that I would run into him at the Southeastern regional SBL meetings, if he was in town. There were also some young scholars, such as Erhard Blum and Martin Rose with whom I was in touch to offer my encouragement and support. After Oxford I connected again with the Canadian Society of Biblical Studies and scholars such as Paul Dion, my successor at Toronto, and any time I gave him an offprint or publication he would send me an extended evaluation and some critical comments and helpful suggestions.

In the spring of 1987 I received word that Professor William McKane had been awarded a fellowship to spend the academic year of 1987–88 at the National Humanities Center in the Research Triangle. When we had visited with William (Willie) and Agnes in St. Andrews, Scotland, in the fall of 1985, I had told both of them about the NHC and its resources for research with proximity to both UNC Chapel Hill and Duke, and Agnes McKane had taken very careful note of all this and urged her husband to consider it for his sabbatical and apply. When I heard the news about his fellowship I wrote to him immediately and told him how happy I was to hear about it. He wrote back that he was looking forward to this first trip to the USA, and they were both excited and nervous. He was a little worried about not having the books he needed for his research, the second volume of his great Jeremiah commentary. The great thing about NHC is that all you needed to do is give them a list of what you need and they will get the books and materials from Duke or Chapel Hill libraries or anywhere else if necessary. They arrange for all of the housing which is usually in Chapel Hill or Durham and they supply their own daily transportation from your residence to the NHC.

They had been assigned an attractive little apartment in Chapel Hill and shortly after they arrived we had a little dinner party for them. We knew that they were fond of hiking and the great outdoors, so we arranged to introduce them to the Blue Ridge Mountains. We picked them up on a Saturday morning in early autumn and with a big picnic basket headed for the Blue Ridge parkway. We drove a stretch of this beautiful road, gave them a sample of a couple of trails and had our picnic lunch on a beautiful autumn day. We picked up some guide booklets on the Blue Ridge and some of the great spots to see. The result of this trip was that they bought a second-hand car and used it to explore this region almost from one end to the other and most of the marked trails on it. We also got together for some social occasions, sometimes with others from NRC and sometimes just Elizabeth and I with Agnes and Willie in their apartment. We became good friends and it encouraged me to read more of McKane's work, even when it was not directly in my research interest, and the more I read, the more I grew to respect him as a very astute and learned scholar. My book, *The Edited Bible* (2006) was dedicated in memory of him and in it I make frequent reference to his work.

At the same time that McKane was at the National Research Center, the Israeli scholar Shemaryahu Talmon was also there. His primary field of expertise was textual criticism of the Hebrew Bible and he and Eric Myers of Duke University organized a two day symposium at NRC on the theme "The Hebrew Bible in the Making: From Literature to Canon" to be held in late April, 1988. At this gathering there was a wide representation of biblical scholars, Protestants, Catholics and Jews. The intent was to review the whole development of the making of the Bible from literature to Canon. But the predominant impression was that there is still much confusion and uncertainty about the whole subject. Brevard Childs and James Sanders, among others, had created a large movement in biblical studies that was focused on canonical criticism, canonical interpretation, and canonical theology, without establishing any real clarity on what the term "canon" entailed. One could not really escape a critical examination of this issue and I would have to spend some time on this subject to clear the fog. It was obviously one of the most abused terms in biblical studies.

For this symposium I was asked to respond to a paper by Kyle McCarter of Johns Hopkins, which was to be sent to me a month before the symposium so that I would have adequate time "to prepare a sound response." What actually happened is that he never sent me any paper at all. I did not even receive a text of his presentation when he arrived at the Center which I could have marked and underlined while he spoke. In fact he had only a few casual notes from which he spoke with little coherence, so my response was very brief indeed. The other respondent was Baruch Halpern and I remember it as the most hopeless pile of nonsense I believe that I have ever heard, his only excuse being that he also had not received any text from McCarter. McCarter made some empty excuses and apologies, but I lost all respect for him after that. The final insult of this episode was that eight months later Talmon and Myers asked the executive associate of NRC to contact me, requesting that I submit my response to McCarter's paper "as soon as possible" so they could proceed with publication. I responded by telling this official to remind Talmon and Myers that I had made it clear at the time of the conference that I would not be submitting any paper for publication because I had not received McCarter's paper as promised and would not now write something after the fact.

During this period of 1986–87 I was in frequent correspondence with the Israeli scholar, Alexander Rofé of the Hebrew University in Jerusalem, exchanging offprints and publications and expressing mutual appreciation for each other's work. Both of us were considered "mavericks" amongst many of our colleagues in the field of biblical studies and as I stated; "Some of us under siege in our own 'backyard' could use some mutual support." Rofé also indicated that he had a sabbatical coming up in 1988–89 and was exploring the possibility of coming to Chapel Hill for that period. One difficulty was that Israeli scholars on sabbatical needed some additional financial support from teaching a course or two in order to make it possible and, given our limited program in Hebrew Bible, to do that was not easy. The other option was to have him apply for a fellowship at the National Research Center, just as McKane and Talmon had done, and I supplied him with all of the particulars. As it turned out he was unable to follow through on any of these suggestions, but he was grateful for the effort and we remained good friends.

As Rofé had pointed out in one of his letters, we were both contributors to a collection of essays in honor of Brevard Childs. When I first heard about the project I discovered that I was not on the list, even though I was the earliest of all Childs's Yale students to have had him as a teacher. When I got in touch with Gene Tucker of Emory, who was in charge of organizing the volume and who had originally approached me about contributing, he immediately invited me to submit an essay. I had been working on Exodus and could work something up from my research fairly quickly. Childs had been the one to introduce me to the critical problems of the book in his Exodus seminar in 1959, so such an essay was quite appropriate. However, when I submitted the first draft to Tucker, he wanted a little more focus on biblical theology in keeping with the theme of the volume: "Canon, Theology and Old Testament Interpretation." I made some revisions to accommodate his wishes, but these had more to do with the implications of my research for the history of Israelite religion than they did for canon or theology. Among Childs's students, I was certainly an exception when it came to canonical interpretations of the biblical text. It was also slightly ironic that the essay that appeared first in the book was by James Barr, who had long been a "sparring partner" of Childs. Barr was critical of biblical theologies in general and of canonical theology and interpretation in particular, yet he also had been invited to contribute.

A Trip to My Brother in Vancouver

In the fall of 1987 I received a phone call from by brother Arthur, who at the time was the Principal of the Vancouver School of Theology on the edge of the UBC campus. He wanted me to come to VST the following summer for two weeks in July to teach in their summer school. In addition to the classes I would also give a public lecture. I told him immediately that I would do it and the very next day I sent out a description of the course on "Ancient Israel's National Tradition." The two weeks of lecture and discussion would focus on the biblical "history" from Genesis to 2 Kings and how the themes of this history were used to shape and reshape ethnic and corporate identity. For the public lecture I decided to focus on the topic of "Canon and Biblical Theology," especially after the symposium at NRC that I mentioned earlier.

The primary reason for wanting to take up this offer, however, was that it would give me an opportunity to connect with my brother Art and his family, at least those of his sons who were still at home in Vancouver. This fraternal contact had not happened for a long time. I would be staying with them in the Principal's residence and in spite of the busy schedule there would be lots of time to chat. We also made a weekend trip to visit my brother Fred's family in Penticton, BC. In addition to this trip I, of course, saw something of Vancouver and its surroundings and had a great time. It was my first trip to this region of the country. One of the students in my class, Robert Kugler, wrote to me afterwards a letter of appreciation. He later did graduate work and became a fine biblical scholar in his own right. After that summer Art and I stayed a little more in touch, especially when he moved to Knox College in Toronto, to become the principal there for the next ten years. And since Knox College is in the heart of the University of Toronto, Deborah, who was doing graduate studies now, also saw him quite frequently.

In Touch with Otto Kaiser and Hans Heinrich Schmid

After Oxford, in the fall of 1986, I sent off an article to Otto Kaiser for publication in *ZAW*, "The Primeval Histories of Greece and Israel Compared." When I was in his study in Marburg we had discussed the difficult text in Genesis 6:1–4 and its classical parallels and with his expert knowledge of classical literature he would help me avoid any mistakes. As soon as he got my letter with the article he wrote to me to tell me it had arrived and that he would publish it as soon as possible. He then confessed that he had not read it yet, "but I suppose you to be such a specialist in both the fields [of Bible and classics] that I have only to enjoy what you have written." He then expressed some regret that I had not been at the SOTS meeting in Manchester in July where he had given a paper on the so-called Succession Narrative of David because he knew that I held views different from his and he had hoped for some serious discussion on these matters. But I had told him that I could not take the time out of my research in

Oxford before I returned to America, and was also sorry that I had missed it. A year and a half later Kaiser sent me a published version his paper. This time I did respond with a critique in some detail and laid out briefly my own position. I concluded:

> So you see that I remain adamant, but I hope that you will not take my remarks amiss. Most have rejected my position without any response. You, at least, have paid me the compliment of taking my views seriously and have made me think about my arguments again. The discussion is far from over and I regret that I did not hear the paper when it was presented in Manchester in 1986.

Indeed, this debate over the David story would go on for some years, with neither side yielding much ground. At the same time, of course, I enclosed in the letter another manuscript for publication in *ZAW*, which again he did not hesitate to publish.

In the fall of 1986, after I returned to Chapel Hill from Oxford, Hans Heinrich Schmid was in touch with me again by mail to let me know that the two long papers that I did for the Swiss conference on the Yahwist and a lecture that I gave in Geneva on "Myth and History: The Problem of Origins," all of which Hans Heinrich had personally translated into German, had been accepted by the board of Theologische Studien and would appear under the title *Der Jahwist als Historiker*. It would appear in their monograph series in 1987. I was delighted at the news and very greatful to him because he had put a great deal of work into it when there was nothing personally in it for him and I wrote him quickly to tell him so. He also wrote to tell me that the American Academy of Religion, which meets together with SBL, had invited him in his capacity as chairman of the German Society for Theology to the annual meeting in Boston in 1987. This ment that we would have a chance to get together there, which of course we did.

Along with my Christmas greeting for 1986 I sent Hans Heinrich a copy of the aricle "The Primeval Histories of Greece and Israel Compared," which had been accepted by Otto Kaiser for *ZAW*. He responded to this with an unusually long letter. He heartily accepted my argument, based upon the Greek parallels and, against the prevailing German scholarship, that the primeval history in Genesis should be taken together with the patriarchal stories as a kind of heroic age, making the whole of the Yahwist's work a kind of archaic or antiquarian history—a very popular form in early Greek historiography. He saw this paper as complimenting the booklet *Der Jahwist als Historiker* and seemed very pleased and supportive of what I had done. It looked like I would have someone supporting me on the European scene against an entirely different approach to the Yahwistic material in the Pentateuch, spearheaded by Rendtorff and others.

But then came the other piece of news in the second half of the letter, which change all of that. I was like a fisherman reeling in a very big fish who had it almost in the net when the line broke and the prize was gone. Hans Heinrich informed me of his election by the University of Zurich to become its next full-time rector for four years, with a possible extension of re-election to a second term. As it turned out, it would be for a third term as well. This should not have come to me as a surprise, because we had talked a good deal prior to this about university politics. I was myself in my second term as chair of the Religious Studies Department and familiar with both the Canadian system at Toronto and the American state university system, such as at Chapel Hill. As he said: „You know that I have exercised some political activity within and without the university all along—now they caught me! I can imagine that hearing of this news you could a little shake your head. But on the other hand I am sure that there is no need to explain to a former or still active (?) head of department that there are things on earth that cannot easily be escaped." He went on to describe the election process in detail, which I had to agree made the choice rather inevitable. This was because he was so much involved in the whole reshaping of the office of rector and that explains why he was later so long in that position.

He went on to tell me that he would quit his chair in his department and move to the director's floor of the university in the spring of 1988. (I later had a tour of that executive suite.) He also expressed some optimism that he would be able to carry on with Old Testament studies, but I was sure that he would not be able to do both. As supportive as he had been of this North American maverick, I was well aware how much I had lost by this move of his to the office of rector and I quite selfishly regretted it. He ended with the statement: „I am hoping that you and Elizabeth will maintain your friendly relations towards me and Christa under these new circumstances as well." As we shall see below, we were able to get together from time to time when I was in Europe but there was no longer that lively academic engagement on subjects that had been our previous concern.

We did continue corresponding for a time and a few months later I told him about an invitation that I had received from the President of the IOSOT congress to be held in Leuven (Louvain), Belgium, in 1989 to give a major plenary address at the congress (more on this below). Hans Heinrich's response to this was that he would plan on being at the congress in Leuven in 1989 and that we were to plan a trip to Zurich for some holiday time together and I was to make sure that Elizabeth would accompany me. Since he was coming to the AAR/SBL meeting in Boston we could make all of our plans there. This was Hans Heinrich's way of insuring, despite his change in position, that we would stay in touch and spend some time together. Along with discussion of academic matters we always included some family news, and I continued to send him copies of my work from various publications.

In early 1989 Fred Winnett died, although I did not hear about it until sometime later.

As indicated earlier, I first encountered him as chairman of the Near Eastern Studies Department when I was an undergraduate student there and took some courses with him, including one on the modern Middle East about which he was very knowledgeable. He was largely responsible for my getting a scholarship that enabled me to go to Yale Graduate School, which resulted in my becoming a scholar with an academic career. I later encountered him again when I attended the Society of Biblical Literature while I was at Yale in the early 1960s and the meetings were then regularly held in New York. He was President of SBL in 1964 and gave the presidential address, published in *JBL* 1965, which became one of the most frequently cited *JBL* article. Later, when I joined the faculty in Near Eastern Studies at the University of Toronto, we were colleagues during his last year there and we remained close after he retired, and kept in touch even after I left Toronto for North Carolina. He was very supportive of my scholarship and publications.

The year 1989 was to be for me a busy and memorable one. It began with a trip to McGill in Montreal in February on invitation from my good friend Robert Culley and the Faculty of Religion, to give a public lecture and an informal seminar to students. In spite of the -22F weather this was a warm and friendly visit among old acquaintances, Robert and his wife Sasha and family, and Donna Runnals, Dean of the Religion Faculty, as well as their more recent faculty member Patricia Kirkpatrick. Patricia had been a doctoral student of Nicholson at Oxford and had produced a fine dissertation on folk tradition, which had just appeared in print in 1988 as *The Old Testament and Folklore Study*. Her interest in the subject had been partly inspired, as she told me, by my *Abraham* book, so it was good to have this chance to meet her and have a chat about her work.

The Second National Endowment for the Humanities Summer Seminar

In addition to all of the planning and preparation for the IOSOT congress, mentioned earlier, I had a busy summer ahead of me. I was again offering a National Endowment for the Humanities Summer Seminar in ancient historiography, which meant processing applications and selecting twelve participants for the seminar sessions. There were a number of good candidates, three from Harvard for which, somewhat ironically, Frank Cross was writing letters of recommendation, and all three, Steven McKenzie, Gary Knoppers, and Walter Bodine, became part of the final group. Since the appearance of my book, *In Search of History*, there had been a number of new publications which gave us lots to talk about. One of the recent works was by Baruch Halpern, *The First Historians: The Hebrew Bible and History* (1988), which was intended as Harvard's answer to my book. Needless to say, the book received rather harsh treatment in the group, not least by those of his contemporaries from Harvard. One glaring example can be seen in its title, "The First Historians," which makes no sense unless one understands it as an unacknowledged reference to the thesis of my book, *In Search of History*, that the Deuteronomist of the corpus from Deuteronomy to 2 Kings was the "first historian." Because Halpern argued that there were three historians within this corpus rather than one, belonging to three different periods, so that adding the plural designation made the title meaningless. Furthermore, it contradicted both his earlier and later publications, which identified yet earlier "historians." It was a very careless effort written to discredit my book.

I want to make special mention of two participants in that seminar group, Steven McKenzie and Gary Knoppers, both from Harvard, because I developed a long-lasting friendly and scholarly relationship with both of them. I know they were a little apprehensive when they first came, not knowing quite what to expect, but with an initial welcoming social for all and an attempt to treat them all as colleagues, not students, we soon broke down any barriers. One of my obligations as director of the group was to advise and assist them in their research projects. McKenzie had been working on a project prior to his arrival and had most of the manuscript in hand. He gave me a copy of his work on the books of Kings and asked me if I would look at it. As expected it represented the Harvard view of multiple "redactions." I read it through and made some notes at various places, most notably the very confusing variants, in the Septuagint, of the story of Jeroboam. Then we arranged for a coffee together and I told him that I was quite impressed with the work, but that I had one difficulty with it that I wanted him to consider before we discussed all of the other details. All of the arguments seemed to be constructed with only one viewpoint in mind, with no indication that he had seriously dealt with any alternative. I wanted him to go through the manuscript again and show me, and any future reader, that he knew and clearly understood the other point of view and could explain why his position was superior. He took the manuscript back and with this advice in hand he substantially made a major revision in the thesis and perspective of the book.

A couple of months after the seminar he wrote me a letter of thanks, stating: "I enjoyed the collegiality of the participants and found the discussions very stimulating. I have a great deal to think about." He went on to say: "I am particularly grateful to you for your close reading and insightful comments about my work on the book of Kings. You caused me to rethink the nature of the 'supplement,' which led to significant improvements in the MS." (The book finally appeared in 1991 as *The Trouble with Kings*.) Also in the same letter he spoke about submitting a proposal for a new program in SBL on the Deuteronomistic History. We had talked about this during the NEH seminar and I had encouraged him to move ahead with it. I was still quite involved with the Pentateuch group so I could not join another steering committee but I volunteered to write in support of the proposal. Steve also wanted me to offer a paper along with Baruch Halpern at a special session to debate the issues between us. I was willing to do so, but Halpern turned it down so it never came off. Once the group got going Halpern was also conspicuous by his absence. Steve McKenzie and I continued to keep in touch over the years.

The other Harvard graduate at the NEH summer seminar was Gary Knoppers, a young Canadian scholar who was teaching at Penn State University and who had come to Chapel Hill with his family. He also had come with a publication project in the book of Kings, although not as far along. Again I read part of the MS and made some suggestion which he later acknowledged in the final publication. A couple of months after the seminar he wrote to me, explaining to me that his position at Penn State was one on temporary contract and asking me if I would write a letter of recommendation in support of a tenure-track position there, as well as file a letter of recommendation with the Harvard Offices of Career Services. He also sent me some examples of his current research and future plans. I was more than willing to give him my strongest support and happy to hear from him later that he got the Penn State job which he has built into a very good department. Knoppers remained rather steadfast in the Cross/Harvard position. Nevertheless, we were very good friends and I participated in a number of his publication schemes. He later joined the Canadian Society of Biblical Studies and I saw him frequently at those meetings. Like myself, he was a Canadian, teaching in the USA. Much of his work was in the book of Chronicles where he attempted to apply what he had picked up through the NEH seminar regarding the application of Near Eastern historiography to the biblical text.

The third member of the Harvard group, Walter Bodine, was primarily in linguistics, but he seemed to enjoy the seminar and we became good friends. We occasionally roomed together at SBL because he no longer had his travel costs covered and I could help him a little this way. But he gradually moved further from the biblical field of study and I saw much less of him.

One member of my NEH seminar group was David Ladouceur, who was not in biblical studies at all but was Chair of Classical and Oriental Languages and Literature at Notre Dame. During the course of the seminar, to which he made frequent helpful contributions, he asked me if I would be interested in visiting Notre Dame to give a lecture to his department in the coming academic year. I told him I would be happy to do so. Once he returned to Notre Dame we worked out a date for the trip in the spring of the following year, and I suggested a topic that would compare the primeval histories of Greece, Mesopotamia and the book of Genesis. I also volunteered to offer a seminar to those in the Theology Department in which biblical studies was located. The lecture to the Classics and Oriental Languages Department was well received, but the response to my offer by the biblical people was a small group for an informal breakfast gathering. That was rather symptomatic of the contrast throughout my career between invitations to give lectures in North America and Europe. In Europe they were happy to have me come, in spite of the language barrier, whereas in North America they were leery that I might cause them some trouble with their students, I suppose.

The IOSOT Congress in Leuven

Let me return to the matter of the invitation from the organizing committee of the Leuven IOSOT congress in 1989 (Aug. 27—Sept. 1) mentioned earlier. Their plan was to invite papers for the first day concentrating "on the problems related to Deuteronomistic Historiography" with four major papers in the morning session. On the second day the major papers would deal with "questions related to the Pentateuch, its sources, and the history of redaction." My task would be to give a paper on the evening of the first day between these two groups of papers that "could function as a bridge between the two morning sessions" and they asked me for some suggested topics that would meet this criterion. This invitation was sent out from the President of IOSOT, Professor C. Brekelmans and the secretary of the congress, Professor Johan Lust, both belonging to the Catholic University of Leuven.

The invitation was a great honor, but it was also a most intriguing assignment and nothing like I had ever had before. It meant that those at Leuven were well aware of the full scope of my research and the fact that I worked very much in both the Deuteronomistic History and in the Pentateuch. It is entirely likely that Brekelmans was aware of this through the dissertation of van Steenis, who was probably a student of Brekelmans or Professor Marc Vervenne. For his project on my work I had supplied him with a complete and up-to-date bibliography. It was an ideal assignment and I quickly suggested the topic: "The so-called Deuteronomistic redaction of the Pentateuch," which they accepted.

I was also in touch with Albert de Pury because he and Thomas Römer had organized a major conference on the Pentateuch, which included a number of German and Swiss scholars, as well as Jean Louis Ska of Rome, and I was eager to get a report about it and when the publication of the collected papers would appear. In addition I sent him some of my offprints. He responded by reporting to me on the conference and indicating that he was busy translating all of those that had been submitted in German into French and when it was published he would send me a copy. In the meantime he sent me a copy of the long and useful introduction prepared by him and Thomas Römer. It was a real gem and I was eager to receive the rest, which I did in 1989.

I also got in touch with Römer in 1988 to tell him about my invitation to give a paper at the IOSOT congress in Leuven the following summer and the topic that I would address. As I told him: "I am particularly interested in looking at the land promise theme as a way of dealing with the so-called Deuteronomistic redaction of the Pentateuch. However, I am aware that this is the subject of your Heidelberg dissertation and so I am very interested to know the present status of your work. If I judge your views correctly they are largely compatible with my own." I received a reply from him confirming the fact that most of his results were compatible with my views and that "I got a lot of inspiration from your articles and books." He was at that time preparing for the final defense of his dissertation. The published version did not appear until 1990. I planned on meeting both Albert de Pury and Thomas Römer at IOSOT in Leuven.

I was also back in touch with Hans Heinrich Schmid about the IOSOT congress in Leuven at the end of August. The plan was to visit with the Schmids in Zurich for a few days before the congress. Hans Heinrich and Christa wanted Elizabeth and me to spend a much longer time, including a holiday in Vira opposite Lucarno on beautiful Lake Maggiore, but there was too little time for that. Classes at UNC had already started in late August. So the best we could do was to arrive in Zurich on August 23rd, leave for Leuven by train on the 26th and fly home from there on September 3rd. We had a wonderful time together with the Schmids. They had just finished making a beautiful guest room in the lower level of their house and we were the first to use it. We also took a sightseeing trip around northeastern Switzerland, including the art museums of Winterthur, the monastery of St Gall with its famous rare manuscripts library in St Gallen, and the picturesque cities of Appenzell and Stein am Rhein. Our time was short but very enjoyable. Then it was on to Leuven for Elizabeth and me.

The IOSOT congress, held every three years, was quite different from SBL. It was limited to the Old Testament, and was much smaller in size. It was dominated by European scholars and its setting moved from one location to another depending upon the person who was the president for that particular three year term. It was also much better organized, with plenary sessions in the mornings on the major areas of Pentateuch, historical books, Prophecy and Psalms and Wisdom, and smaller, more specialized groups in the afternoon. The evenings were reserved for special presentations or events. The whole atmosphere was much more congenial than SBL. One feature about the congress that discouraged American participation was that it was regularly held at the end of August and into September. This overlapped with the beginning of the fall semester in North America, but was only in the middle of the long break in Europe. This had kept me from participating in previous congresses, so that this was my first one.

There were many there that I had met on my previous trips to Europe and the UK and it was pleasant to renew acquaintances and through them to meet many more. There was always a large contingent from Israel as well and among them was Alexander Rofé, with whom I had been corresponding. Alex was very friendly and modest, but an outsider among his more "orthodox" colleagues at Hebrew University, so he valued the friendship of another outsider, and we got along very well. Among those from Leuven I met Brekelmans, Lust and Vervenne for the first time and reconnected with Anton Schoors, a friend of Jack Sasson, whom I met in Chapel Hill when he was there for a semester on sabbatical. Niels Peter Lemche from Denmark was also there and it was good to meet him in person after hearing so much about him from Fred Cryer. I had also recently submitted an article to the new journal, the Scandinavian Journal of the Old Testament, of which Lemche was the editor, and I had learned that it was always good to have a personal relationship with such editors. Lemche and I had much in common and this would only increase over the years.

For me the big moment was the evening of the first day when I had to give my paper on "The so-called Deuteronomistic redaction of the Pentateuch," which called into question what was very quickly becoming the accepted view in European Pentateuchal research. There was a full house and I could not have asked for a better opportunity to set out my views. After my lecture there was a lively question period and a lot of positive comments. Hans Heinrich and Christa had come up from Zurich that day and we went together afterwards for a late supper and fine wine to celebrate the occasion. I look back on this evening as one of the highlights of my career as a biblical scholar. Those who had invited me from Leuven seemed quite pleased with the outcome and I was now known by a far larger circle of European scholars than before, especially some of the younger scholars.

For each IOSOT congress there was a special congress volume published by *Vetus Testamentum*, and it consisted of all the major papers of the congress. The editor of *VT* was now John Emerton of Cambridge University, and he contacted me about the submission of my paper. Emerton had succeeded Piet de Boer as editor, and this was my first encounter with him.

There was also a young Swedish scholar, Erik Aurelius, a student of Mettinger from Lund, who introduced himself to me. He obviously enjoyed my lecture and gave me a copy of the printed version of his doctoral dissertation, *Der Fürbitter Israels* (Israel's Intercessor), which had just recently been published. It was a study of the figure of Moses in the Old Testament. I could see at a glance of the table of contents that it was going to be an important study for my current research and I thanked him for it. Needless to say, we hit it off very well. Shortly after we returned from Leuven to Chapel Hill I sent Aurelius a copy of my *In Search of History* in appreciation of his gift to me. He not only wrote to thank me for it but described how he started to read it but then could not quit until he had finished it. He went on to say: "It is for me as easy to read as the best American books and as clear, sound and thorough as the best German ones. Every page is an intellectual pleasure." He closed by thanking me again for "a really stimulating evening in Leuven." With such an enthusiastic response I could hardly resist sending him a number of comments and observations on his book and some recent offprints. His reply was a six-page hand written letter with comments on all the pieces that I had sent him, his present position as a pastor until he could get an academic position (he eventually did in Goettingen), his discussions with other young German scholars, and much more.

New European Contacts after IOSOT

One of the immediate consequences of my IOSOT lecture was that I was approached by Professor Martin Metzger, President of the *Wissenschaftliche Gesellschaft für Theologie* if I would be interested in giving one of the major papers at their society meeting at Hofgeismar, Germany, in mid-May of 1991. It would deal with the general theme of Exodus. As soon as I expressed my willingness to do so word got around so that there was talk among other scholars that while I was in Germany I might also visit some other places as well and give a talk to their students. Aurelius was also trying to work out some way with his professor, Mettinger in Lund, how I could make a visit for a lecture and then he could entertain me in Sweden. I heard from Mettinger soon after Erik's letter, and we explored the possibility, but May was not a good month for them for a visit so that one did not work out. My visit to Scandinavia would come much later.

Another young scholar whom I met in Leuven was Professor Hermann Spiekermann, a recent appointment to the position in Zurich vacated by Hans Heinrich. We had an interesting chat and among other things he was eager to get a copy of my *Abraham* book. It had been out of print for a while and I had urged Yale Press to do something about this. They decided at last to bring it out in a paperback version and I finally had a few copies at my disposal so I promised to send him a copy which I did. He sent me a letter of thanks, and describing the book as the "indispensable leaven in Pentateuchal research." He expressed the hope that this would be the beginning of an "intensive contact" and it was, but as in the case of so many other European scholars, it was difficult to maintain at such a distance.

Niels Peter Lemche was also back in touch with me in January of 1990 with the proofs of my article for SJOT, but also to inform me that he would be coming to SBL in November and that Diana Edelman, a former Chicago student of Ahlstrom was organizing for him a lecture tour around these dates. So, of course, I got in touch with Diana, whom I knew quite well, and we arranged for lectures at Duke and Chapel Hill. So in a short space of time I felt that I had gotten to know Lemche quite well. Lemche also heard, in due course, about my planned visit to the Hofgeismar conference in Germany and wanted me to make a trip up to Copenhagan as well. But that could not be worked out and would have to be put off a year until my Sabbatical in Cambridge (more on this later).

Another scholar with whom I had a lot of correspondence at this time was Paul Dion at the Department of Near Eastern Studies at the University of Toronto. I encountered him and his wife Michele Daviau almost annually at CSBS in Canada and this would lead to an exchange of offprints and inevitably a very careful scrutiny and critique by Paul of each piece. This would be followed by letters back and forth over the various points of disagreement, always in a most polite and respectful manner. We were and remain good friends. It was the kind of exercise that kept me on my toes, as if Paul was looking over my shoulder as I wrote. So I sent my friendly critic a copy of my IOSOT lecture to see what he would make of it. No one would give it closer scrutiny than he would. He wrote back: "It is superb. You deal satisfactorily with practically all the data. There is very little that I do not find convincing." After citing several more points of agreement, he came out with this honest confession: "At this point, however, perhaps it is only the fear of having to revise so much in my view of the historical and spiritual development of Israel that still prevents me from following you wholeheartedly and dating J after D. But would the consequences really be as far-reaching as I imagine?" I believe that he spoke openly and truthfully what so many others felt, but who refused to discuss or debate the issues openly with me. Paul always had my respect and I am glad to have had his, even when we agreed to disagree.

In the fall of 1990 I received a letter from a young Norwegian scholar, Käre Berge, who had received his doctorate at Oslo University five years earlier and was now teaching Bible in a Teacher's Academy in Norway. The purpose of his writing to me was first, to ask if I would help him to apply for a fellowship at the National Humanities Center in the Research Triangle for his sabbatical year of 1991–92, and second, if I would be available for consultation because he had a strong interest in the literary criticism of the Pentateuch and his new project was to work on a study of the call narratives of Moses in Exodus. In support of his claim to expertise in Pentateuchal studies he sent me a copy of his dissertation, *Die Zeit des Jahwisten* [The Dating of the Yahwists], which had recently been published as a supplementary volume to *ZAW* by Otto Kaiser. What Berge did not know was that I had recently written a review of his book so that I was already quite familiar with his work.

What I found even more remarkable is the fact that he wanted to come to Chapel Hill to consult with me when the essential point of his dissertation was to take issue with my late dating of the Yahwist in Genesis. By way of explanation, let me make a few remarks about his book. As he clearly states in his forward, his dissertation was written in response to the books of H. H. Schmid, R. Rendtorff and J. Van Seters and their attempt to re-date these texts to a much later period. While his work demonstrates a broad familiarity with the scholarly literature and a careful literary analysis of the texts, much of which I could approve, its weakness was that it rather blindly accepted the older notion that there was a Davidic-Solomonic kingdom that included both Israel and Judah, without any external critical appraisal from the more recent archaeological and historical data. By the time that his book appeared this view of a Solomonic Age as envisioned by von Rad and others had become obsolete for a large number of scholars. So my review could not be very positive on the main objective of his thesis, and this ultimately reflected on what he regarded as early tenth century texts and later additions.

In my response to him I volunteered to help him in any way I could with his application to NRC and other matters regarding his stay in the region. I also sent him a copy of my review and some recent offprints. He wrote back that he was already too late to apply for a spot at NRC in 1991–92, so he wanted to come as a visiting scholar to UNC in Chapel Hill and could I help him with visiting scholar status. It was now becoming clear that, in spite of my review of his book, he wanted to do his work at Chapel Hill in close association with me. So I had to tell him that I would also be on sabbatical for that same year and would be abroad in Cambridge while he was here. This meant a change in plans and fortunately he was able to team up with Douglas

Knight at Vanderbilt and spend his sabbatical year there. This was by no means the last that I heard from Berge because I ran into him again at a conference in Hofgeismar, Germany in the spring of 1991.

As I indicated earlier, I was invited by Professor Martin Metzger of the *Wissenschaftliche Gesellschaft für Theologie* to participate in their conference at Hofgeismar, Germany in May, 1991, and as the time for the Old Testament meeting of the society grew near the new president of the group, Jörg Jeremias was in touch with me about all of the details. I had given him the subject of my paper, "The Call of Moses," and provided an abstract. There would be only two papers a day, one in the morning and the other in the afternoon with lots of time for discussion, which meant lots of time in the hot seat. But I was prepared for that. This was the European style. I flew from the USA to Frankfurt and when I arrived I discovered that the airline had lost my luggage, but promised to send it on when they found it. From Frankfurt I took a train to Kessel and then changed for a train to Hofgeismar. While waiting for this train I noticed what looked like a number of other academics heading in the same direction. I soon discovered that one of them was none other than Käre Berge, who had come over from Norway to attend the conference because his new project was on the book of Exodus. This was a pleasant surprise and we chatted. He confessed that he was persuaded by my latest arguments to adopt a later dating for the Yahwist than the one advocated in his book.

By the time we arrived at Hofgeismar the group of academics on the train had all been introduced and we proceeded to the conference grounds together. When I arrived at the center I had no baggage so I had to find some basic supplies. The baggage did not get there until the day before I left the conference. But at least I had my paper with me. There were about thirty scholars there, all Protestant but one, Professor Erich Zenger, a Catholic, who was treated as a guest. The theological societies are strictly divided in Germany between Protestants and Catholics, which is most unfortunate for academic dialogue. I knew many of those there, and others I was happy to meet for the first time. Jeremias had written me ahead of time: "Knowing that you are coming I am sure the meeting won't be boring." And it certainly wasn't.

During the first day Zenger of Münster gave a paper on the socio-historical problem of the account of Israel's sojourn in Egypt in the book of Exodus. Like so many scholars before him he felt that the story of the sojourn must be based upon an early tradition because of the supposed reference in Exodus 1:11 to the two cities that the Israelites were said to have built as forced labor, Pithom and Rameses. This was the starting point for his reconstruction of the long history of this tradition in the text. In the discussion period I had to point out that in the course of the University of Toronto excavations at Tell el Maskhuta we discovered that Pithom was not built before ca. 600 BCE, which meant that the starting point for this biblical text had to be quite late. Furthermore, the results of our work had been published, although not in publications very accessible to most biblical scholars. Needless to say, those who supported a later date for the biblical story were delighted, while those who supported the early date were not, and I was next on the program on the following morning.

I gave my paper on the "Call of Moses" in Exodus 3–4, which had been used as the bedrock for the division of sources in the Documentary Hypothesis of Wellhausen, and tried to show that such a position could not stand up to close scrutiny. Many scholars jumped into the discussion that followed, most notably, the senior scholar Werner Schmidt of Bonn, whose massive commentary on Exodus depended upon that theory, and the younger Hans-Christoph Schmitt who agreed with me in my arguments against the Wellhausen view, but had his own solution to the perceived difficulties in the text. My difficulty was that they asked their questions in German and spoke rather quickly and some like Schmitt, asked five questions all at once. Nevertheless, I felt quite satisfied that I held my own and thoroughly enjoyed the whole exchange.

Mixed in with all of this were the social hours and the meals which were a great opportunity to become acquainted with some of the others. In particular, there were two younger scholars, Walter Dietrich from Germany and Timo Veijola from Helsinki. Both of them had studied under Rudolf Smend of Göttingen and created what became known as the Göttingen School in their literary criticism of the Deuteronomistic History, and something of a rival to the Cross/Harvard School, as reflected in the work of Knoppers and McKenzie. I told them about the recent efforts by McKenzie and others to develop a special group at SBL for the Dtr History and would they be interested in getting an invitation to such a meeting. They seemed keen on the idea. When the time came I talked to McKenzie about them and they came to SBL for a special commemorative session on Martin Noth, the forefather of the notion of the Dtr History. The whole Hofgeismar conference, conducted in this intensive European seminar fashion with no holds barred and mixed with pleasant social moments made for a very stimulating experience.

After the conference I went by car to Marburg with Professor Dietheim Conrad, a colleague of Otto Kaiser, who had not been at the conference. Prior to the conference I had arranged with Kaiser that I would come down to Marburg for a few days prior to my flight back to America. Since time was rather short, it was arranged that I would give a lecture on Monday morning and a seminar in the afternoon, and fly back on Tuesday. On the Sunday, Kaiser and I had dinner together and then chatted for a while but then he put me in the hands of some of his students for the rest of the day. I could tell that he was not quite full of his usual pep. The students were great fun and we had an enjoyable evening together. The next day when I came to the university from the little inn where I was staying, I met one of the students who told me that Kaiser had had a heart attack, and while it was not serious, he was in the hospital and would remain there for several days. My old friend from Yale days, Erhard Gerstenberger, took over and chaired the lecture and seminar. I also had a visit with Professor Würthwein for afternoon tea and cognac as I had five years earlier. In spite of Kaiser's illness, from which he made a complete recovery, it was a very enjoyable visit. After I returned to the US some of his students stayed in touch with me, especially Uwe Becker, who sent me a copy of his dissertation.

During the past school year I had also been working hard to finish my manuscript on *Prologue to History* and to get it in before I set off for my sabbatical in Cambridge, and I was able to do this, although dealing with the copy editing and proofs would have to be done in Cambridge. I was also keen about having a European edition and Hans Heinrich was working with his friend, the publisher of *Theologischer Verlag Zürich*, to have them do it. In addition he also explored the possibility of doing that edition in a German translation, but the cost of such a job and the time needed to get it out to compete with the English edition did not make this feasible. Nevertheless, Hans Heinrich did write up the book's description for the back cover of the European edition, although they did not include his name with it. He worked very hard on my behalf, for which I was very grateful.

7

Cambridge Sabbatical

The sabbatical leave in Cambridge, 1992–93, was much shorter (September to June) and the arrangements more simplified than the earlier sabbatical spent in Oxford. This time Elizabeth and I left and arrived together. I had arranged with my host, Professor Graham Davies, to assist me in finding accommodation and he put us in touch with a fine agent who found us a small two bedroom house on a side street (Hertford St.) and when we arrived we had no trouble meeting her at the house and making all of the rental arrangements. Davies also arranged for me to have an association with Fitzwilliam College as a visiting research fellow, which meant that I had lunch and senior common room privileges at the college during term, and was warmly welcomed as a member of college by its faculty. It was also within easy walking distance of my house. Within a short time we settled in, learning where to shop and how to get around. As in Oxford, we acquired bicycles and we used them a great deal to get around town. Soon after we moved it, we became acquainted with one of our neighbors, Mrs. Whitmore, an elderly widow, and became good friends, a friendship that lasted long after we left Cambridge. We often took afternoon tea with her, especially Elizabeth. We also registered with the local medical center for doctor's visits, when needed. This was covered by a modest resident's tax which we paid soon after our arrival.

Cambridge is a wonderful place to spend a sabbatical because the city itself offers so much to see and experience, quite apart from the academic side, whether traveling on foot or by bicycle. There is parkland all along the river Cam through the heart of the city and with bike paths that extend throughout the parks for great distances. We knew them well and used them frequently. In addition to Sainsbury supermarket for the basics there was also the central open-air market on market-day for fresh produce and flowers, and it was just a fun place. There were lots of concerts, such as the "Spanish Extravaganza," in the Corn Exchange concert hall, which we enjoyed greatly, and the Great St. Mary's Church Christmas candlelight service, in addition to a number of others events.

As was the case during the Oxford sabbatical, we used the opportunity to do a number of trips throughout the UK. There were, of course, frequent trips to London, many of which Elizabeth did on her own, with very convenient bus and train service from Cambridge. It was also easy to make day trips to many interesting places on the eastern side of England, such as Peterborough, Norwich, Saffron Walden, the Fens and Ely (once by boat along the Cam). We made a four-day bus excursion to Devon and Lorna Doon country with a larger group and a weekend bus and ferry trip to Paris, sightseeing, walking through the Louvre, and a side trip to Chartres Cathedral. We also had visits from family and friends, which meant a few outings with them.

Over the Christmas vacation period, when the University was largely shut down, we made a trip to Switzerland. This was a specially organized trip whose purpose was to do some hiking in the mountains above the town of Meiringen, and we had to purchase some special equipment for this activity. We flew out of Heathrow to Zurich, and took a bus from there to Meiringen and stayed in a very pleasant hotel. The town was made famous by its role in a Sherlock Holmes novel and the name of the detective was everywhere, including a special Sherlock Holmes museum. In the Morning we would take a gondola and cable car up the mountain and then from this great height work our way down the mountain to the town. Each day would be a different height with a different view. In between these hikes we would be on our own. Elizabeth and I set out one day to explore the famous Reichenbach Falls, which fell from the rocky hillside on the other side of the valley opposite Meiringen. We climbed to the top of this ridge and explored the falls, and a glacier further up the mountain. We also took the train to Brienz at the end of a beautiful lake. Because we were in Switzerland, we got in touch with Hans Heinrich Schmid and arranged to meet with him in Lucerne, a convenient midpoint between Meiringen and Zurich, and spent a pleasant lunch together. The whole Swiss trip was quite an exhilarating experience.

Another adventurous trip was a week in Scotland in mid-May. We rented a car and drove to the western Highlands, staying in a B&B in Fort William, which we used as a base to explore the region, by train, boat, mini-bus and even took a cable car to the top of Mount Ben Nevis. We took one train trip south along the coast down to Oben, and another train west to Mallaig, where we boarded a boat that took us across Loch Nevis to the village of Inverie, and went for a hike in the countryside. We also hired a driver with a mini-bus who took us on a scenic route to Kyle of Lochalsh, where we took a ferry across to the Isle of Skye, and then drove across it to Portree and back. The region around Fort William itself also offered a lot to see. The week was unforgettable.

I could go on at great length to describe the many joys and great experiences that we had while living in Cambridge during this year, and the fond memories that linger still. But the main purpose for my being in Cambridge and for which I was being paid was my academic work, and to this I must now turn.

Departmental Matters

First, let me say something about my relationship with my department in Chapel Hill during my sabbatical, because it was quite different from that of my time in Oxford. During that earlier sabbatical I was still the chair of the Department, which meant that I had to be in constant contact with my administrative secretary, as I have indicated earlier. In Cambridge that was no longer the case. However, one matter that still followed me to Cambridge was the future plans for the SBL Pentateuch Seminar. As chair of the seminar I had submitted a report with recommendations on how the format for the Pentateuch group/section should go forward. This was a significant departure from Knierim's seminar model and it was up to Thomas Dozeman to move it forward in the SBL executive committee, in spite of some resistance from Knierim. So Tom Dozeman kept me up-to-date on all that was happening on that front. He also wanted me to support him in applying for a fellowship that would permit him to study in Germany. In addition, he had a research grant for work on Exodus that would involve both Rolf Rendtorff and me acting as mentors in advising him on his research. So I had a rather steady flow of correspondence from Dozeman and there was a lot of contact between us in the years ahead. His leadership of the "Pentateuchal Group," as it later became known, was exemplary, and it flourished under him.

Before I left for Cambridge I had agreed to co-direct a Duke doctoral dissertation by William Whitt, together with Professor Orval Wintermute of Duke. Bill Whitt had taken some graduate courses with me and wanted to do a dissertation with me, but the only way he could do this was to have me as a supervisor together with someone on the Duke faculty, and that left few options. Wintermute, a language specialist, was quite agreeable and we got along well. In fact, the only time that I was invited to give a talk to Duke students during my twenty-three years at Chapel Hill was during a sabbatical of the Meyers, when Wintermute and Whitt conspired to have me give a presentation to a graduate students colloquium. Concerning his dissertation, Bill and I had talked about doing something on the whole problem of literacy in the Levant in the second and first millennium. He later wrote to me and said that the topic had become too cumbersome and he had changed it to deal with literacy at Ugarit as reflected in its administrative texts. He also sent me some of his work for comment. So I was doing some doctoral supervision for at least the latter part of my time in Cambridge, although most of it was completed in the year after I returned. His dissertation, "Archives and Administration in the Royal Palace of Ugarit," was, unfortunately, never published and he soon gave up looking for an academic position and left the field. He was a brilliant young scholar and a loss to the discipline.

Relationship with Fitzwilliam College

As indicated earlier, through the diligent work of Graham Davies I was given Visiting Research Fellow status at Fitzwilliam College, which was very convenient and enjoyable. I did not receive the official word on this until the beginning of term in mid-October, when I was sent a formal letter from the Master of Fitzwilliam College, Professor Cuthbert, informing me of my election as a Visiting Fellow for the coming academic year and outlining all of the privileges, which were significant. The Master was always very gracious and friendly, and the college included me in its major events. To this day, I still receive the college magazine as if I were an alumnus. This college had been the home college of Ronald Clements when he taught at Cambridge and he still lived in this city, and commuted to Kings College London. Graham Davies and I occasionally took lunch together at the college. We also shared a common interest in the study of the book of Exodus and in the geography and archaeology of the Egyptian delta region. Yet we never did establish the same kind of routine and relationship that I had with Nicholson, and our families never got together in the same way.

The Libraries

With visiting fellow status at Fitzwilliam I had no difficulty in gaining access to all of the necessary libraries, and above all, to the Main Library. Unlike the Bodleian at Oxford, I had direct access to the stacks in the Cambridge Main Library and could use a reading desk in the same area as the books that I was using, and this made working in this library very convenient and productive. I could get to the library on my bike when the doors opened in the morning and put in a good day's work. There were others from North America at the library, in particular, Walter Bruggeman, Patrick Miller and Jack Lundbom, and I would run into them there from time to time. I often had morning tea with Bruggeman in the library tea shop and we got to know each other a little better.

Another library that was often useful was that of the Oriental Studies Library, housed in the same building as the offices of the faculty, and this is where both John Emerton and Hugh Williamson had their offices. Emerton in particular enjoyed taking a coffee or tea break in the morning, and if I was working over there that day, we often had a cup and a chat together. He was a very gracious person and I enjoyed those times together. It was also helpful that he was now the editor of *Vetus Testamentum* and I was inclined to publish in the journal from time to time. Emerton was quite familiar with my work and was always happy to discuss it with me, even when he took a different point of view. The third library that I sometimes used was the Divinity School Library. Even though it was not a great collection and had little that could not be found in the Main Library, it was sometimes useful because I had borrowing privileges there and I could use some of the items while working at home. Davies office, as a member of this faculty, was also in this building.

Description of Research Project

The primary focus of my research in Cambridge was to continue my work on the Yahwist as an antiquarian historian, as reflected in the book of Genesis and published in my book, *Prologue to History*. The sequel to this earlier project was to examine the Yahwist as a historian in Exodus and Numbers, which was organized as a biography of Moses. This was later published as *The Life of Moses* (1994). It was my thesis that the Yahwist's historiographic work encompassed both the antiquarian history from creation to the patriarchs and the history of Israel from their rescue from Egypt to their encampment on the eastern side of the Jordan. This is the point at which the Deuteronomistic History takes up the story of Israel. The DtrH had used the earlier version of Deuteronomy as the prologue of his history, with some retrospective comments on the wilderness period, from Horeb to the edge of the Promised Land. The Yahwist incorporated this material, in a revised and expanded version, into his much larger history. It was my conviction that one could not understand the Yahwist's work without properly appreciating the work's genre within the context of just such historiography that was being produced in antiquity.

What greatly complicates this discussion, in my view, is the fact that the Priestly Writer has made extensive additions to this historiographic work. P's concern was not history but the mythical legitimization of the laws and customs of the Jews, and especially those that had to do with the Temple, priesthood and cult. A large part of my work in this study was to identify the P additions to the J corpus, as well as clarifying the relationship to Deuteronomy as a source for J. Scholars have long recognized the general distinction between J, D, and P. However, before the recent revisions in Pentateuchal studies, scholars had always thought of J as earlier than D, and had regarded P as an independent source that was later combined to J by a redactor. My new approach, namely, that J depended upon D and that P was composed as a supplement to J, led to quite different results in the literary criticism of the Pentateuch. This was the direction of my studies in Cambridge.

Lectures

Once the university semester was underway, the faculty and graduate students in the Old Testament Colloquium began to meet from mid-October onward, and these were regularly held in the Oriental Studies building. I gave a presentation at one of these on my current research on Exodus. In addition to Emerton, who ran the seminar, Graham Davies and Hugh Williamson were always there, and as I recall, Williamson was in charge of making tea. One regular visitor was the well-known Professor

Norman Whybray, now retired from Hull University and living in Ely, not far from Cambridge. He was quite familiar with my work and it was good to make his acquaintance. In his book, *The Making of the Pentateuch*, published in 1987, he produced a very useful survey of current scholarly views on the composition of the Pentateuch, including those of Rendtorff, Blum, Schmid and myself, and seemed kindly disposed to my position, which was gratifying. There was also a group of young students and scholars who regularly attended the colloquium who were from Tyndale House. This was an independent foundation run by Inter-Varsity Fellowship, which was theologically very conservative. I was familiar with this movement because I had been part of the Canadian version of this movement in my youth when I was in college at the University of Toronto. I am not sure what entitled the group from IVF to participate in the Colloquium, except that I know that Davies and Williamson had belonged to this organization at one time. I believe that there were quite a number of scholars in British biblical scholarship generally that came out of his IVF movement and gave to the discipline as a whole a rather conservative cast.

As mentioned earlier, Ronald Clements had been in touch with me shortly after I arrived, and his primary purpose was to invite me again to King's College, London to give a paper to their Seminar. This was arranged for a Tuesday afternoon in mid-November at which time I would speak on "The Tradition History of the Miracle at the Red Sea." This visit to Kings College was always a very enjoyable occasion and Clements along with Richard Coggins, Michael Knibb, and a few others took me out for dinner afterwards in a fine restaurant in the city of London. Not long after this, in mid-December it was time for the winter meeting of the Society for Old Testament Study, this time in Sheffield, and again I was invited to attend and to give a paper on my research, just as I had been when I was at Oxford. I was eager to go because this time around there were a lot of old friends there for me to see. When Ronald Clements heard that I was going he called me up and told me that he was taking the car to Sheffield and would be happy to give me a lift, which I readily accepted. This gave us a wonderful opportunity to chat and get to know each other better. He had had a rather conservative background, similar to mine, only as a Baptist, and this explained how he had a good relationship with American institutions, such as the Southern Baptist Seminary in Louisville and Baylor University in Texas. I had the highest regard for his scholarship and we got on very well. Sometime later, he and his wife Valerie invited Elizabeth and me, along with Norman Whybray and his wife, to dinner at their place in Cambridge. It was a most enjoyable evening.

A few months after the SOTS meeting, Paul Joyce, the "Home Secretary" of the society was in touch with me. He wanted to know if I was planning on attending the Summer Meeting in Dublin, and if so he would be delighted to list me as his guest. This was the procedure used for visitors to the meetings who were not members. The invitation was tempting, but it would not work out with the time-table of our return to the USA, so I had to decline. The other matter that he wrote about was whether

I would like to be nominated for associate membership of the Society. He stated: "I know this would please our members enormously." I could hardly turn it down, even though it would cost me £18 sterling, and I remained such a member for a number of years. As for Paul Joyce, who was now at Birmingham University, I had met him in Oxford, as I mentioned earlier, and by now we were good friends. He was also a friend of my brother Arthur, having taught for him in the Vancouver School of Theology Summer School.

A month or so before the winter SOTS meeting, a letter from a young scholar, Dr. Walter Moberly, of the University of Durham, invited me to give a lecture and seminar at Durham in the following semester. I had met Moberly at a prior SOTS meeting when I was at Oxford, and had read his study of Exodus 32–34, published in 1982, which was based upon his Cambridge dissertation done under Graham Davies. He had also been closely associated with Tyndale House, and was one of those religiously conservative scholars in British biblical studies. Davies had obviously spread the word around that I was at Cambridge. At SOTS in Sheffield we made the final arrangements, and in mid-February of 1992, I had a very enjoyable trip to the beautiful city of Durham. The presentations were well received and Moberly was a very gracious and hospitable person, putting me up over-night in his own home, and we subsequently exchanged some publications.

The next major speaking engagement was the Scandinavian tour that I made in late April and early May. I had been in contact with Niels Peter Lemche for quite some time previous about such a possible tour, and he had secured firm commitments from Professor Magnus Ottosson for Uppsala University and from Professor Timo Veijola for the University of Helsinki. Lemche was also in touch with Professor Mettinger in Lund, who had expressed to me earlier that I should visit Lund, but unfortunately that could not be worked out. Likewise, visits to Kiel and Hamburg were considered but these also could not be fitted into the schedule. I was also in touch with Ottosson and Veijola directly to decide on topics and final travel details. In the course of these communications I heard from Lemche that Gösta Ahlström, a good friend of his and a friend of mine, had died. Ahlström had been members of the Uppsala School under Ivan Engnell, although Ahlström was older than Ottosson and had been Ottosson's teacher as well. He spoke about his admiration for Gösta and how much he would miss him.

The three topics that I listed as subjects for either the lecture format or for a smaller advanced student-faculty seminar based upon my most recent research, were: "The Antiquities of Israel according to J," "Reconstructing the Past: The Yahwist's Historiographic Method in Exodus," and "The Call of Moses." The first of these was based upon the research for my book, *Prologue to History* that would appear in print in 1992. The other two were related directly to my current research at Cambridge. The value of lecturing on the first topic was to attract some interest in my forthcoming publication, whereas the other two topics would be to test my research and my arguments concerning the work in which I was now engaged.

The tour of three universities lasted ten days, from Sunday, April 26 to Tuesday, May 5, but the schedule was rather complicated because in the middle of it was the May 1st holiday, which amounted to four days in the middle of my visits in which no presentations could be made. I flew out on Sunday to Copenhagan and was taken to a hotel in the city center near the waterfront, from which I could do a little sightseeing. Monday was a busy day with both a lecture to students in the morning and a seminar in the afternoon, both of which were chaired by Lemche. Afterwards there was a reception with the faculty with Fred Cryer there and Thomas Thompson who had recently arrived to take up a position there. It also included the now recently retired scholar Eduard Nielsen, who gave me an inscribed copy of one of his books on the occasion. Nielsen had been on the faculty of the University of Copenhagan for thirty-five years. In the evening I was taken to meet Lemche's family who lived in the countryside some distance north of the city. The whole visit was a great experience and solidified the friendship between Niels Peter and myself.

The next morning I flew to Stockholm where I was met by Ottosson and some of his colleagues, and we drove to Uppsala, a short distance away, where we had lunch together. It was great to see Magnus Ottosson again after almost thirty years, but it was that same beaming face and infectious laugh. We had dug together with Pritchard in 1965, as I recounted earlier, and he was still preoccupied these days with archaeological excavations, now in northern Jordan. We had so much catching up to do. After lunch I was taken to my quarters in an old medieval building belonging to the earliest academy of Uppsala at the very center of the university. I was amazed to see that the walls of the building were about a meter thick! Its location was very convenient. Uppsala was a very old and prominent university with many historic buildings and a long tradition of scholarship in biblical studies in Scandinavia. My lecture was at 6:15 p.m., for about an hour, after which we would go to supper. This arrangement was fairly typical. At the lecture I was happy to meet another fine scholar of the biblical department, Professor Bertil Albrektson. Early in my career I had encountered his important book, *History and the Gods: An Essay on the idea of Historical Events as Divine Manifestations in the Ancient Near East and in Israel* (1967). This book had challenged a fundamental notion in biblical theology at that time, namely that the Bible was unique in interpreting historical events as the revelation of divine activity, and to this notion was attached the designation *Heilsgeschichte* (salvation history). Albrektson had clearly shown that such a notion was common throughout the ancient Near East of that time, and this critique had been picked up by Childs in his arguments against the biblical theology of the 60s. I also made considerable use of his work in my own discussion of Near Eastern historiography, so I was very pleased to meet him and we had an interesting exchange.

I was free the next morning so I asked Magnus if I could pay a visit to an old friend, the Egyptologist Professor Säve-Söderbergh, whom I knew was at Uppsala. I was taken to his suite of rooms in the basement of the Anthropology building. He was delighted to see me again after many years and I was happy to have this time with him. We shared our mutual interest in the history of the Hyksos, so he gave me a tour of his little personal museum of Egyptian artifacts, including some objects of the Hyksos period. We could gloat that we had been right about our views on the Hyksos all those years ago, against the views of so many prominent authorities. All the archaeological work of Manfred Bietak at Tell ed-Dab'a had confirmed our views. He was now retired but allowed to retain these quarters and to have an assistant to help him. We had a coffee together and then I left.

Ottosson and I had lunch with a colleague of his, R. A. Carlson, who had written a book on *David, the Chosen King* (1964), in the tradition of his teacher Engnell. It was a well-known and much discussed book in America and I was glad to make his acquaintance. I remember the lunch occasion particularly because I was persuaded to try the specialty of this restaurant, which was reindeer meat. Later in the afternoon, at 6 p.m. we had the seminar of grad students and faculty, in which I was to make a presentation on my current research. This lasted an hour, followed by another hour of discussion. It was an invigorating experience. After this there was a buffet reception put on by the students, which was most enjoyable. Ottosson was very much in his element with this crowd and I could understand why they were so fond of him, as I was.

The next day, April 30th, was the day of the annual student spring celebration. Magnus had warned me about this day before I had left for Scandinavia, so I asked the other visiting scholar at Fitzwilliam College, who was from Uppsala, about this day and he described the festivities to me. I had then informed Ottosson that I certainly did not want to miss this venerable tradition of spring celebration. In the morning of April 30th, the engineering students engaged in the "running of the rapids" on the river that flowed through the center of town. This they did by constructing ingenious floats, some quite obscene, and riding the rapids while trying to stay upright in the process. It reminded me of the engineering floats in the football homecoming parades of my college days at the University of Toronto, although this was somewhat more dramatic. In mid-afternoon all the thousands of students gathered on the slope of the hill in front of the university library (called Carolina Rediviva), with white caps in hand. Several floors up on the side of the library were a set of celebrity balconies. On the one were the leading officials of the university and on the other a few special guests, who could view the whole scene from this great vantage point. Magnus had managed to get me a spot on this balcony (what he told the university officials I do not know). At 3 p.m. sharp, the Vice-Chancellor made a signal by raising a white cap in the air, and a great roar went up from the crowd, throwing their caps in the air and then donning them for the first time, as a sign that spring had finally arrived, they then turned and swarmed down the hill to the town, many to the "student nations" houses, which were like the American frat houses. There they began their festivities in earnest, which included a lot of drinking and whatever else students do on these occasions. The celebration went on late into the night.

Magnus's wife, who had a teaching position in another town and stayed there during the week, was now at home for the holidays and weekend, and we all had supper together. The following day we had some spare time in the morning so we went for some sightseeing in the countryside and a lunch together before taking me to the Stockholm airport for my flight to Helsinki. The time with my old friend had been short but the Swedish hospitality had been wonderful.

I arrived in Helsinki in the early afternoon and was met by Martti Nissinen, Veijola's assistant, and I was taken to a guest house belonging to the university. It was spacious, well-equipped and convenient to the center of town and the university. Martti then took me on a tour of this region, beginning with Senate Square, a large open space flanked on four sides by the Cathedral, the University of Helsinki central campus, the National Library and the Government Palace. From here it was a short walk down to Market Square, a large open area by the seashore and close to the ferry docks. On this national holiday the square was covered with stalls, selling all kinds of goods and I could not resist buying a set of earrings for Elizabeth, with a little expert advice from Martti. Through the course of the afternoon I got to know this young scholar and new friend, and was very impressed. In addition to working with Veijola and others in the theology department, he studied Assyriology under Simo Parpola, and his expertise in this area was reflected in his later work. During my stay in Helsinki Martti gave me an inscribed copy of his recently published dissertation on Hosea.

The next day, Saturday, I spent with Timo Veijola. He took me on a tour of the university and the library, in which there happened to be on display his recently published book, *David* (1990), a copy of which he had given me when I first met him the previous year. He also took me to see a remarkable church, the Temppeliaukio Lutheran Church. It was built by carving out a massive rock so that from the outside one could see little more that the entrance doors in the front. Once inside one descended a set of steps into a large and very beautiful auditorium surrounded by the bare rock surface above and on all sides. There was some music being rehearsed for the next day's service and the acoustics were quite remarkable. We then went out to his home in a town several miles north of the city and I met his wife. He showed me around his church in which he and his family were very active. His home was located not far from a large wooded area and we went for a walk along a trail that was one where he was accustomed to go jogging every morning. There was also a large pond on this route where, at the end of his workout he would take a dip to cool off, except, as he told me, when the ice was too thick to make a hole in it. On the trail he also showed me an old wooden ski-jump, reflecting the long Finnish tradition in this sport, but this one was now no longer in use. After a pleasant evening meal together with his wife, he put me on the train back to Helsinki, and from the central station it was an easy stroll back to my guest-room.

Sunday was another free day and this time Professor Raija Sollamo, who was also the dean of the theological faculty, came with her husband to call for me and bring me to their place for Sunday dinner. I had met Raija very briefly at the IOSOT meeting in Leuven, probably through Albert Pietersma, because they were both in Septuagint studies, and she also knew John Wevers for the same reason. This gave me an opportunity to get to know her much better. After dinner she and her husband took me out to a historic site to see and walk through an old restored Finnish village. It was a very enjoyable day.

Monday was a work day again and in the afternoon I first gave a lecture to one group of students and then made a presentation to the Old Testament colloquium of the advanced students and scholars, much as I did on the previous occasions in Copenhagen and Uppsala. The discussion was lively and invigorating and always a pleasure. After this session Veijola and a group of his students took me to a Russian restaurant for the evening meal. The specialty of this place was "bear meat"! This time I declined, although some in the group actually ordered it. It was clear to me that these students held Veijola in great respect and admiration, as did I. This would not be my last encounter with Veijola. The next day I returned to Cambridge.

My final speaking engagement during my time in Cambridge was a visit to Oxford for a talk to their Old Testament colloquium. So in mid-May I took a bus ride over to Oxford and once again met with the Oxford Colloquium as I had done so many times on my previous say in this city. John Barton, who had succeeded Nicholson in the Old Testament chair at Oriel, was now in charge of the colloquium and we had agreed that I would give a presentation on the plague stories in the Priestly source of the book of Exodus. We had a good time discussing these texts. In the evening I was invited out to the Barton home in Abingdon together with a number of other faculty friends and a great dinner by Mary Barton. It was a wonderful evening together. The next day I was on the bus back to Cambridge.

During the time that I was in Cambridge I had been corresponding with a number of scholars on various issues. First of all, I finally heard from Otto Kaiser about his health. I had written to him about it and had been kept informed by some of his students, and he finally wrote most apologetically that it had taken him so long to reply. However, this was quite understandable since he had taken quite a while to get back on his feet and there was a considerable backlog of work that had piled up in the meantime. He had also just retired and there was a search on for his replacement, which was eventually filled by Jörg Jeremias. He also wrote about the progress of Christoph Levin's manuscript on the Yahwist, which he was reworking for publication. It would not appear until 1993, appearing between the first and second of my volumes on the Yahwist. Kaiser was most interested in comparing our two studies. He also brought me up-to-date on the progress of his own students, two of which sent me their works when they were finished.

The IOSOT Congress in Paris

About a month after I returned from Cambridge to the USA I was off again to Paris for the IOSOT Congress (July 19–24), to catch up with so many of my European and British friends and to make new acquaintances. Few Americans attended in those days. The plenary sessions were held in the Sorbonne, whereas the group sessions with shorter papers took place in the Collège de France. Having done my major paper in the previous congress, I would be giving a shorter communication on my studies in Exodus, along with others in the Pentateuch group. Another scholar who was also working on Exodus was Professor William Johnstone of the University of Aberdeen. We had briefly met before at SOTS, but now we had a chance to discuss our research interests in detail, and we later corresponded and exchanged off-prints of our articles.

Another scholar who was in the Pentateuch group with a strong interest in the study of Exodus was Hans-Christoph Schmitt, now of Erlangen University. We discussed these issues together and afterwards I sent him an article on the plagues narrative that I was currently preparing for publication. He not only wrote to thank me for it but set down at length the areas on which we were agreed, and a few in which we still had some difference of opinion. Just as in the exchange we had at the Hofgeismar conference, he was a keen debater and we exchanged a lot of correspondence. He also wanted me to come and visit him in Erlangen, but that would have to wait until my next sabbatical. We remained very good friends.

With the congress being in France, the organizers wanted some French speakers, and the secretary of the congress, André Lamaire, was a specialist in Aramaic studies. So it was not surprising that he invited my good friend Paul Dion, of the University of Toronto, to give a major paper on this subject. Paul had established his reputation in this field. It was good to see him there, and although he rarely went to the IOSOT congresses, he could hardly turn this one down.

In addition to meeting old friends, I also made some new ones. One was Johann Cook, a South African from the University of Stellenbosch, a few miles north of Cape Town. His field in Old Testament studies was textual criticism of the Greek Septuagint, and of course he knew Al Pietersma and John Wevers well. However, he was also familiar with my books on *Abraham* and *In Search of History*, and he took the liberty to introduce himself and we had some lively conversations. Johann was also a lot of fun. There were a number of Dutch persons at the congress, Al and Margaret Pietersma, Johan Lust from Leiden, as well as Cook and myself and we all got together one evening and went to an open air café down by the Seine River. In the course of drinking a little beer someone started to sing an old Dutch lyric and everybody in the group joined in. Pretty soon it was one Dutch folk song after another. I had learned a number of them when I was young so I had no trouble doing my part. We had a great time although I am sure the Parisians did not quite view it in the same way. In fact, this singing group became something of a tradition at subsequent IOSOT congresses. After the Paris congress, Johann wrote to me to thank me for my friendship in Paris. He wrote, "I enjoyed all those social and more serious academic moments with the 'great John van Seters'. Who would ever have thought I would meet you." We would continue to meet at a lot of conferences and correspond frequently. The South African scholars were rather isolated by virtue of geography so such congresses were their lifeline to the larger world of biblical scholarship. Johann Cook and I would be close friends from that time onwards.

In Paris I also met, for the first time, three other young scholars who were very much interested in Pentateuchal studies, Jean Louis Ska, from the French speaking region of Belgium and teaching in Rome, Christoph Levin, about whom Kaiser had spoken so much, and Rainer Albertz, a former student of Claus Westermann at Heidelberg. Rainer's father had been the former mayor of Berlin. We spent a good deal of time together discussing my published views over a pint of brew, and I established a connection and a rapport that we enjoyed for years afterwards. While I had few advanced students of my own I was able to attract the attention and interest of a large number of other teachers' young scholars and through them to have some impact on the field of biblical studies.

During the congress I was also involved in the production of a documentary film on the Bible and the Abraham story in particular. Prior to the congress I had a letter from Abraham Segal, a young French film producer, asking me if I would be willing to be interviewed for a documentary film, called the "the Abraham File." In the script, a copy of which he sent me, he makes mention of a number of scholars whom he intended to interview, covering a wide range of opinion about the Abraham tradition and its supposed connection to history. Among these scholars he mentioned me and my book, *Abraham in History and Tradition*. From André Lamaire at the Collège de France he had heard that I would be attending the congress. He expressed the desire to interview me about my work and even to arrange to get some of the interview on film. He wanted to see me as soon as I got to Paris in order to make plans for such a session. So I made plans to arrive at the congress a day early, and we took some time over lunch going over the material that he had sent and discussing the whole project.

Segal had also arranged with Lamaire for the use of his very spacious office in the Collège de France, for a filming of the interview. I had some time free on one of the afternoons, and they did a lot of filming. The sequence was to be fitted into a narrative context in which a young man is trying to come to terms with the traditional view of the biblical story of Abraham and the bewildering array of scholarly opinion about the Abraham tradition. The selection of scholars to be interviewed was intended to reflect this range and how the young man comes to terms with them. I thought the whole conception of the documentary was quite ingenious and helpful and I supported it strongly. In addition to the film Segal was also writing a book, *Figures of Abraham*, using much of the same material. A couple of months later, he sent me a letter from Tel Aviv, telling me that he was happy about the way in which the interview sequence turned out and sent me some pictures. He also discussed my views with a number of Israeli scholars, among them, Professor Nadav Na'aman, Chair of the Department of History of the Jewish People at Tel Aviv University. He stated that Na'aman held my work in high regard and that he was trying to persuade some conservative scholars to extend an invitation to me for the World Jewish Congress in Jerusalem in the coming year. (More about this trip later).

I never did see the documentary film, but he eventually published the book under the title *Abraham: Enquête sur un Patriarche* in 1995 and sent me a copy. In it he presents a rather full version of the interview conducted in Paris and its results in a rather clear and understandable presentation of my views. I put this down to his very careful questions and a skillful editing and I could not be happier with the presentation. He also puts this in the context of the views of many other scholars in the field. My copy of the book is inscribed with the statement: "To John Van Seters, the best detective on Abraham's file," alluding to the original title of his project. One could hardly ask for a better compliment.

The SBL Group on the Deuteronomistic History

Another project in the fall of 1992 that occupied my attention was my participation in the new SBL group on the Deuteronomistic History at the San Francisco meeting in November. Steve McKenzie, who now chaired this meeting, had been in touch with me while I was still in Cambridge, with the proposal that they headline an opening session of the group with presentations by Baruch Halpern and me on the nature of historiography in the Deuteronomistic History. Since these would be radically different presentations on this issue, as our books indicate, we would also respond to each other's paper before opening up the discussion to the floor. This was obviously intended to attract a crowd, to kick off the activity of this group. Halpern would have none of it and would not even attend SBL, which did not surprise me because Steve had tried this proposal two years earlier and it had not worked. Nevertheless, Steve McKenzie and the co-chair Richard Nelson wanted me to give a forty-five-minute presentation on "Historiography in the Deuteronomistic History" with Burke Long and Richard Nelson as respondents, to which I would also be allowed to respond to them. This was fine with me since I knew both scholars very well.

The plan was that I would submit my paper at least a month before the meeting in order to send it to Richard Nelson and Burke Long, and they, in turn, would send me a copy of their comments. As usually happens in these cases, my paper was sent in good time, but I never heard from either Nelson or Long before the meeting. I was not greatly perturbed because I thought I knew what they would say, and Nelson did not disappoint me. But Long, with whom I had worked hard to assist him in his two-volume work on the Books of Kings, made a presentation that had little to do with the subject and completely mystified me and everyone else. Consequently, my own response to them focused almost entirely on Nelson's views, which were in the Frank Cross tradition of multiple Deuteronomistic editors. There was a good crowd at the session and I was fairly happy with the way it went in spite of Long's remarks.

Steve sent me a letter of thanks after the session. His comments on my presentation were that it was "absolutely perfect for the purposes of our session. It was well written, thoughtful, and provocative. I heard nothing but compliments on the session in the subsequent days." I was very pleased for Steve because it was clear that this group was going to be a real success. He worked very hard at it and it became one of the strongest groups in the SBL program. They already had ambitious plans for the coming year. It also helped to cement that relationship between us that had started in the NEH summer seminar in 1989. Also, at a session of shorter papers in the Dtr History group, Graeme Auld from Edinburgh gave a rather controversial paper on an aspect of the David–Solomon story, which produced a lot of discussion from McKenzie and me, to whose works he had made particular reference. Afterwards I gave Auld a copy of my paper and he promised to send me a copy of his, which was part of a forthcoming book, and this he did. Auld continued to be a regular at SBL and in this section of the program in particular.

When my book *Prologue to History* finally appeared in mid-1992, I sent out copies to a number of friends. One went to John Wevers, to whom I had dedicated the book, because I owed him more for my career development than he could imagine. He wrote me a touching personal letter as soon as he received it, about how pleased he was that I had done this. He of course brought me up to date on his Göttingen Septuagint project. Whenever I was in Toronto to visit family or for other reasons I would drop in to see him. He was already retired for some years but maintained an office in the department. He regularly sent a Christmas letter to Elizabeth and me every year so we kept in touch. I also sent a copy of my new book to Kaiser for which he thanked me and said that he had not yet had time to read it except for the conclusion. This alone was enough to get him started on how his view of these matters differed from mine. Then he promised to read the rest and continue the discussion after that. Like some others he was always ready to take me on, but in a most friendly manner. I was also asked by a couple of Kaiser's students, one of whom I knew from my trips to Marburg, to write a piece for Kaiser's Festschrift, which I was happy to oblige. In recognition of the friendship that I had established with Walter Brueggeman in Cambridge I sent him a copy of *Prologue* for which he thanked and congratulated me. He also commented that he missed the "quiet time in Cambridge library, and the times to sip tea with you." I also sent a copy of my book to Dr. Diana Edelman, a former student of Ahlstrom, for which she thanked me. She was about to take up a position at James Madison University in Virginia, which meant that she would be in the SBL Southeast regional meetings and would be an interesting person to chat with about subjects of mutual concern, as was her mentor, Ahlstrom.

In the fall of 1992 I had a letter from my brother Arthur indicating that at the end of that term he was going to end his ten and a half years at Vancouver School of Theology and move to a new position as Principal of Knox College, the Presbyterian Seminary on the campus of the University of Toronto. Between the two appointments he would take a half year sabbatical in Edinburgh. Ever since I had been at his summer school in 1988 we had been more closely in touch, and now he laid out his plans for 5 months in Scotland. Of course, by this time I knew some of those at the divinity school there, so I was sure he would get a warm reception. He regretted that our sabbaticals had not coincided. But it was an important break for him. Art was always so active, visiting seminaries around the world, in Japan, Korea, Africa, Latin America and also his work for the Presbyterian World Service and Development program. It was very rare for him to have such a complete break for a few months to get some writing done, perhaps the only such stint he ever had until he retired. His whole life was focused on service to his church, his students, his theological school, his foreign aid projects, and much more. The move to Toronto meant that he would also be in contact from time to time with Deborah, who was by that time in graduate school.

Late in 1992 I received a letter from Kare Berge concerning his sabbatical year (1991–92) in Nashville at Vanderbilt. As I related earlier, he had intended to come to Chapel Hill to work on a Pentateuchal project in order to be able to consult with me, but because I was on sabbatical the same year he chose to go to Vanderbilt, and according to his letter, that had been a very good choice. His study was focused on the book of Exodus, and specifically on the Call of Moses in Exodus 3–4 as a way of testing the methodology of classical literary criticism. He told me how this American environment, with people such as Douglas Knight and James Barr, had proved most helpful in giving him some distance from his training in the Germanic tradition. He ended up with a book that radically questioned "the methodological assumptions of source criticism," which "rests on foundations which seem to break down when confronted by new literary and text linguistic perspectives on H.B. texts." This transformation in his thinking and dynamic change of approach was gratifying to me and reflected a quite remarkable shift from his earlier book on Genesis. A few years later when his book was finally published, *Reading Sources in a Text. Coherence and Literary Criticism in the Call of Moses* (1997), he sent me a copy. It proved to be a very creative and stimulating work, which, because it was out of the mainstream of European scholarship, did not get the attention that it deserved.

The Search for a Chair of Near Eastern Studies at the University of Michigan

Towards the end of my sabbatical and on into the fall term I received information first from Brian Schmidt and then from the Department of Near Eastern Studies at the University of Michigan that they were looking for a departmental chairman, combined with expertise in one of the areas covered by the department. The attraction for me was to be once again in a Near Eastern Studies Department with very good colleagues in supporting fields and have a complete focus on my own specialty and the prospect of some good graduate students. I was not particularly eager to chair a department, but it looked like I would be doing more of that at Chapel Hill anyway, so I could put up with it and I had lots of experience. Ann Arbor was also much closer to Toronto than was Chapel Hill. So, in spite of the prospect of another long move, I decided to explore this opening. I submitted my application in September and was invited to Ann Arbor in the fall of 1992 to meet with the faculty and graduate students over several meals and meetings. I met with the university administration, and also separately with the chair of the Search Committee, Professor Ludwig Koenen who was a senior professor and chair of the Department of Classics. We got on very well together and discussed some issues in classical studies in which we had a mutual interest. I gave a public lecture and conducted a graduate seminar. Brian Schmidt was, of course, my host and constant companion through all of this and he did his best to support my candidacy. But he was just a junior faculty member and could hardly compete with Piotr Michalowski, professor and former chair of the department, who had his own candidate in the running, a close friend in the same field of Assyriology. Michalowski also had a close rapport with the administration so there was really no contest among the three finalists. Although the visit had been pleasant enough in its own way, it was a waste of time from the start. Early in the new year (1993) I heard from Brian that Michalowski had persuaded the search committee to choose in favor of Norman Yoffee and they were in negotiation with him, while keeping me in reserve. I then sent in a letter withdrawing my name from further consideration.

After the decision on Yoffee's appointment was finalized, Professor Koenen wrote to me on behalf of the Search Committee and the Department to express their "thanks for your remarkable lecture, your exciting seminar paper, and your very useful advice in our public and private discussions of the future direction of the Department." He went on to add, "As before, I add the personal note that I indeed enjoyed your lecture and seminar. I found your arguments about the possible influence of the Greeks on the composition and development of the Pentateuch very intriguing . . . . In any case, this is a research area of great importance for a classicist and to which I know I shall return in research and lectures." He also expressed the hope that we would stay in touch, but unfortunately this did not happen. However, the fact of the matter is that my work on biblical historiography was often appreciated more by classicists than biblical scholars.

It was also remarkable how quickly word got around between September and January that I was up for consideration for the Michigan position, although for good reasons I had not mentioned it to anyone. Like the Johns Hopkins affair, there was no way that I could compete to get a major chair in any Near Eastern Studies Department in North America. My decision to leave Toronto in 1977 meant that I had effectively closed that possibility for the rest of my career.

At the same time that I was involved in the search for a departmental chair at Michigan, there was a similar internal search for a chair in the Religious Studies Department at Chapel Hill for the year beginning in 1993–94. Sasson was in the final year of his term and was not interested in serving a second term. This appointment was entirely in the hands of the dean's office and, as previously, it was the dean's practice to canvas privately the members of the department as to their preferences. I sent him a detailed assessment of all those eligible for the post and it was not very optimistic. After this poling process Stephen Birdsall, Dean of the College of Arts and Sciences, informed me that I was the overwhelming choice, which was not unexpected although it did not exactly thrill me. Once I made my decision to withdraw from the Michigan search I entered into some negotiation about the position. I knew that this was the one time that a prospective chair had the best chance to get commitments on behalf of the Department, and one had to extort as much as possible. In addition to my shopping list, which included very little increase in monetary compensation personally, I made it clear that I only intended to hold the position for a couple of years until a recent senior appointment, Professor Carl Ernst, could get some familiarity with the Department and its operations and then take over the job.

In April of 1993 I received my letter of appointment from Dean Birdsall for a five-year term from 1993–98, with the understanding that "depending on developments within the Department, you may wish to step down before the end of your term and ask only that you give me as much notice as possible." The only significant personal benefit was that I received additional travel funds. The rest of the letter had to do with the various items that we had negotiated. Birdsall was the third dean with whom I had worked, and I was quite familiar to him when he served earlier as Associate Dean. The staff in the dean's office, including the financial officer, Faye Gray, all knew me well. So for the next two years I spent time in two offices, the chairman's office with all the departmental files, and my own study office down the hall. This meant that a large percentage of my time was taken up with administration, which for me was not exactly an exciting prospect.

Publications and Papers

In early 1992, while I was still in Cambridge I was asked by some of Otto Kaiser's former students if I would write an article for inclusion in a *Festschrift* for Kaiser on the occasion of his 70th birthday in 1994. I agreed to do so and in May of 1993 I submitted my manuscript, "The Theology of the Yahwist: a Preliminary Sketch," a subject that I was sure he would enjoy. About the same time I also received a request to contribute an article for a *Festschrift* for Jacob Milgrom. Since we had worked together in the Pentateuchal Seminar in SBL, I agreed to do a piece for it also. Then in the spring of 1993 I had another request to contribute an article for a *Festschrift* for my old friend from graduate school days, George Coats. George was no older than I was, but he had a neurological injury dating back to high-school football days, and it was beginning to affect his memory so that he had to take early retirement. Hence the move was made to honor him at this time. George and I had shared a strong interest in Pentateuchal questions and it was sad to see that we would not be able to discuss these issues and enjoy our friendship at SBL and other meetings anymore. While one felt obliged to contribute such articles in recognition of such scholars and personal friends, the price for doing so was often to have such a piece lost from view, because many such *Festschriften* had quite limited sales and circulation, in comparison with articles published in leading journals of the field. As a consequence, many of my articles in journals were frequently sited, but those in *Festschriften* rarely so. Nevertheless, I continued to write them when asked.

From time to time I was asked to do short pieces for dictionaries, encyclopedias, and other study collections and to some I contributed, but many others I turned down. There seemed to me to be a glut of such works whose primary purpose was to make some money from a lucrative publication genre. However, one quite useful collection was a four-volume work, *Civilizations of the Ancient Near East*, edited by my colleague Jack Sasson, who asked me to do a chapter on "The Historiography of the Ancient Near East." This I wrote up after my return from Cambridge.

Among those to whom I sent a copy of my book, *Prologue to History*, soon after it was published was Steve McKenzie. Through the NEH seminar of biblical historiography I had gotten him interested in my comparative method and I was particularly interested to see how he would react to my interpretation of the Yahwist as a historian in comparison with Greek antiquarian history. He had sent me a copy of his book, *The Trouble with Kings*, which he had worked on during his participation in that seminar and I had commented extensively on it and he did the same with my book. It was an entirely different approach from that of his Harvard training. His reaction to my book was very positive and he went to considerable length in his comments and appreciation of the work. We continued this close contact and sharing of our publications and plans. A case in point was my application to NEH to conduct a summer seminar for college teachers in the summer of 1994. NEH had asked me, as a former director of such a seminar to consider applying again. One of the letters of recommendation was from McKenzie and he gave a rather glowing statement on my behalf. Nevertheless, I did not get it. In the review that they sent me, the primary reason for not giving it to me this time was that I did not have enough applicants in my previous seminar. Consequently the pro forma process of urging all previous directors to apply again is quite deceptive and unnecessarily results in a huge waste of time. At the same time that they turned me down they sent me a form letter asking me to apply again in the following year. I also went to Washington on a few occasions to serve on one of the panels judging proposals, and I discovered that the mix of disciplines on such panels does not always produce the best results.

Steve McKenzie and the Martin Noth Symposium

As I have mentioned earlier, Steve McKenzie was very much involved in developing the Deuteronomistic History group within the SBL program, and in 1992 I had assisted in this group with my major presentation on this theme. For the 1993 program Steve had organized an international symposium in celebration of Martin Noth's publication of his most acclaimed work on the subject of the Deuteronomistic History fifty years earlier, *Überlieferungsgeschichtlicke Studien* (1943). I had given him enthusiastic support for the idea and suggested some names of European scholars, among them Walter Dietrich and Timo Veijola, and both of them had agreed to come. McKenzie also wanted to have Frank Cross there to represent his position on the Deuteronomistic History, but he declined, as did Rudolf Smend, the teacher of Dietrich and Veijola. I wrote to Veijola to tell him I was happy to see him on the program and he responded by indicating that he had been a little hesitant in participating, but since this was his first trip to America and the meeting was in Washington, his wife would join him on the trip for some sightseeing and we could get together for a meal. He obviously did not care much for such big conferences, nor did Dietrich who was a little lost in the crowd. Nevertheless, Steve was a great host and he and Dietrich became very good friends.

Steve had also invited another young European scholar, my friend Thomas Römer, to give a paper. Römer thrived on the SBL environment and became a regular at the meetings and in the Dtr History group. I saw a lot of him and we met together regularly at the SBL, along with McKenzie and some others. The Dtr History group, along with the Pentateuch group, attracted a lot of European scholars and became the backbone of that connection in the Old Testament part of the SBL program. The symposium also produced an impressive collection of the papers given at the 1993 session and was the first of a number of such collections produced by the Dtr History group.

I also stayed active in the South-East regional SBL, and coming off my sabbatical with all of my recent research on the Moses tradition in Exodus–Numbers, it was easy to give a paper on some aspect of that subject, which I did in 1993. As a consequence Professor Marvin Sweeney, who was the incoming President of SBL-SE and whom I knew quite well from his participation in the Pentateuch Seminar, invited me to give a plenary address at the 1994 meeting in Atlanta, on the subject, "Methodologies of Comparison in Biblical Studies." Both the American Academy of Religion and the American Schools of Oriental Research regional meeting also met with SBL and the plenary presentation was open to all, so it was an enjoyable and well-attended occasion.

As I indicated earlier, I had been involved with the Classics Department at Chapel Hill in helping to persuade the History Department and the Dean of the College to fill a vacancy created by a recent retirement in the position of ancient history, and to do so with a major appointment. This appeal was successful with the fine appointment of Professor Richard Talbert. As it happened, like me he was moving to Carolina from Canada, which meant that he had to go through all the red tape that I had endured, so he sought out my advice on these matters and we became good friends. Talbert was involved in a massive project of producing a huge atlas of the Greek and Roman world, to include over a 100 large and small scale maps. This was to be done using the latest digital technology and a large number of submissions from a team of compilers. I was on his mailing list, along with all his friends and financial supporters, as well as in personal contact from time to time. I was happy to maintain these connections with the classical world. It also happened that from time to time a classical scholar would get in touch with me about my work. In May of 1993, a classicist Professor Stanley M. Burstein, whose work on Berossus I had used, wrote to me to ask for an offprint of my article, "The Primeval Histories of Greece and Israel Compared," which of course I was happy to send him.

In the fall of 1993 I received a request from the office of the University of Toronto, to represent the university as an alumnus at the inauguration of the new President of Duke University, Dr. Nannerl O. Keohane., and I agreed to do so. All it meant was attending a big buffet luncheon and being greeted personally by the President, and then lining up for the procession with the oldest institutions (Harvard and Yale) in front and the rest marching in order to the special seating in the front rows. I think I was about number nineteen, with McGill a little ahead of me, and this put me in the second row, not bad for the show that followed, if you like long boring speeches. There was a reception afterwards and that was about it. President Prichard of the University of Toronto thanked me for my services in a letter: "Your role ensured that the University was ably represented." There were a lot of other alumni doing the same thing for their institutions. My gown colors were Yale, but who knew the difference. I had no further contact with Duke's President after that event.

In May of 1993 I had a letter from the famous, some would say notorious, Professor Jacob Neusner. At any rate he was quite remarkable and produced an enormous number of books, mostly on Rabbinic Judaism. In the letter he states: "I have spent several days with your *In Search of History* and have had a good bit of pleasure from this fine work of yours. I was on the AAR book prize committee that awarded its prize to you, so I was not surprised and in fact, I was prejudiced in your favor. But I still found the work marvelous, even having read it before it was fresh and interesting." In fact he had told me about his role on that committee more than once before, almost every time I encountered him at the AAR/SBL meetings. However, the reason why he was writing me, he said, was to find out whether I spelled the Van in my name with upper or lower case v, because it was not evident from the title page. Yet at the end of the preface and elsewhere it is clearly spelt as Van, and I wrote to give him the correct spelling. Apparently he was writing a book on *The Concept of History in Rabbinic Judaism*, and he informed me that he was using my work as the basic structure for his chapter on Hebrew Scripture and the requirements of historical thinking, because out of a huge bibliography on the subject he found mine to be still the best. Well, no matter what other people thought about Neusner, after those flattering remarks, Jake was OK.

During the two-year period from the fall of 1991 to the spring of 1993 the Department had a postdoctoral fellow, using funds from the James A. Gray endowment fund, and the person appointed was Dr. Hector Avalos, a graduate of Harvard. Avalos suffered from a breathing disability, which severely limited his physical activity, but he had a wonderful spirit and did everything expected of him and more. I was away on sabbatical for his first year, but I saw a lot of him during the second year of his fellowship. He was not a doctrinaire Harvard product, but very open in all of our discussions. At the end of his stay he wrote me a letter of thanks for this opportunity the department had given him, not only in teaching in his field of biblical studies but also in Latin American religious movements, the region from which he had come. He also concluded his letter with these remarks: "As a bonus, I had the opportunity to converse with you on a variety of issues, even if only for my last year of the fellowship. I hope that another young scholar receives a similar opportunity under your chairmanship. Thanks a bunch!!!" Hector Avalos and I kept in touch and I tried to help him in his future quest for academic positions, in spite of his obvious handicap.

8

Third Term as Department Chair, 1993–1995

Departmental Matters (1993–1994)

A recitation of all the activities involved in the routine business of being a department chair makes for rather dull reading, primarily because it is rather dull in its execution, so I will skip over what took up a very large portion of my time. It inevitably reduced both my teaching time, with fewer classes, and less time for research during the term. There was, however, one major issue and its resolution that defines the role of chairman more than anything else, and that has to do with making a new appointment. This is especially the case when it comes of having first to arrive at a departmental decision as to the area or field within the department where such an appointment is to be made. Usually when a vacancy arises within a certain field, then an agreement is quickly reached to fill that particular spot whose need and student popularity has already been demonstrated. Occasionally, however, that is not so obvious, especially when the fields of study become re-defined and the instructional needs shift over the course of time. That was the case with such fields as comparative religions or philosophy of religion, areas of study that had at one time been prominent in the Department but that were no longer treated as such under these rubrics. The hold-over from that earlier period was Professor William Peck, who was now associated with the field of Religion and Culture, even though what he actually taught had little to do with the courses taught my either Ruel Tyson or Tomoko Matsuzawa. Peck's research specialty was the German theologian Dietrich Bonhoffer. There was no possibility that we were going to fill Peck's place with anyone remotely like him.

This meant that the departmental faculty had to reevaluate that position in terms of what was most needed in the Department as a whole. This was going to be a very sticky situation because the field of Religion and Culture took the attitude that they had proprietary rights to the position, but that was never ever the case with any field.

Only the endowed chair, the James A. Gray Chair, had to be in biblical studies. So I invited my colleagues to suggest those areas in our current program that were most in need of this position and to discuss these options in terms of detailed justifications, i.e. specific areas of need within the field to be covered by the appointment, courses and students that would be serviced, a faculty balance in the fields, etc. In the end, the choice narrowed down to two fields, Religion and Culture (represented by Ruel and Tomoko) and Western Religious Tradition (represented by Peter Kaufman alone). The presentation by R&C was very slim and merely presented the need for someone else to do largely what Tomoko was already doing, whereas Kaufman's presentation for his field was very carefully laid out with the choices of various areas of study that a new position would complement, rather than duplicate what he was already doing. In terms of student demand, there was really no comparison. Kaufman already taught far more students than Tyson and Matsuzawa put together, both on the undergrad and graduate level, and he had strong support outside of the Department as well. Of course, Ruel and Tomoko also had their friends outside the Department and they were prepared to cause trouble.

Because I had not been particularly close to either Ruel or Tomoko, I had a lot of conversations with and memos from John Dixon, a former member of the Religion and Culture field, to get his inside take on that field. Dixon was now a retired member of the Department who was also an art historian with a joint appointment in the Art Department. The picture he painted of R&C was pretty bleak and he personally supported the proposal by Kaufman, even though he did not have a vote and had not always gotten along with Kaufman on a personal level. Nevertheless, his arguments for his choice between the two were very persuasive and agreed with my own assessment of the situation, and I was willing to put my chairmanship on the line on this decision. I proceeded to canvass everyone in the Department by secret ballot at a Department Meeting as well as those who had not been able to come to the meeting and I did not reveal the results until all of the votes were in. The result was a clear 7–2 in favor of Kaufman's field of Western Religious Traditions. That should have settled the matter, but as far as Ruel and Tomoko were concerned, it did not.

It was now towards the end of the school year and the search for the position would not begin until the new school year in the fall. Ruel and Tomoko attempted to rally their support outside of the Department, since they obviously lacked it among their colleagues. So I received letters from Professor James Peacock of Anthropology, whom I knew very well and who was a close friend of Ruel, and from Professor Craig Calhoun of Sociology and Director of the University Center for International Studies, the new hotbed of culture studies and a close friend of Tomoko. There was the clear insinuation that the "intention of the Department [had not been] arrived at through appropriate collective discussion," and that the Department must be out of its collective mind by not supporting "a strong concentration in religion and culture," which had national recognition. Calhoun had obviously hoped for another cross-appointment to his newly emerging empire. I made it quite clear to them that I did not approve of this meddling in the affairs of our Department and that the decision had indeed had much deliberation and the procedures had been very fair.

Ruel, however, was not finished. He could not take the matter to the dean, because he knew very well that I had the complete confidence of Dean Birdsall, so he tried to go one better. He was in charge of a university program that was directly under the office of the provost, so he went to the provost with his case. I received a call from the provost's office wanting to know if I could arrange a meeting with him. I suggested that we could perhaps meet over lunch at the Carolina Inn (on his tab, of course), since both of us were very busy. It was arranged and we had a pleasant lunch together. He was a reasonable person and wanted to hear my side of this dispute. I simply took him through the various stages of the departmental deliberation and the way in which the vote was taken and its results. When he heard that the vote was overwhelmingly in the favor of Kaufman's proposal, he was quite shocked, because he had been informed quite differently. We ended the meeting on quite cordial terms, and as it worked out we got to know each other much better. He soon became aware of my scholarly and administrative reputation, and I had no more difficulties from that direction and no more interference from Calhoun, whose center was also under the provost's office. This would not be the last of such contests of power.

The Publication of The Life of Moses *and Its Response*

The second volume of my study of the Yahwist entitled, *The Life of Moses: The Yahwist as Historian in Exodus–Numbers,* appeared in the summer of 1994, and I sent a number of copies to friends and scholars, particularly those in the field of Pentateuchal studies. The book was dedicated to Professor Brevard Childs of Yale Divinity School, because, as I indicated in the preface, "my indebtedness to his scholarship and past friendship is more than can be adequately acknowledged here." Even though my book had made extensive use of his commentary on Exodus, there were strong differences in its whole purpose and perspective, and I was not at all certain how it would be received. He responded as soon as he found the book in his mail after several months abroad, and thanked me for it and the dedication to him which he said was "a great honor and greatly appreciated." However, the initial rush of classes starting the new school year meant that he had to postpone reading it for a few weeks. He was also suffering from a long bout with Meniere's Disease, which held him back.

Two weeks later I received another letter from him that was altogether different in tone and in the intensity of his remarks. He began his remarks with the statement: "I confess that I am at a loss just how to respond." He was not going to quibble about particular details of agreement or disagreement, but on the overall impression of my treatment of the particular author—the Yahwist. To him there was nothing exciting about my exegesis, no emotional ups and downs, no surprises, only a rather dull and all too systematic analysis and predictable conclusion. Even my final treatment of the "Elements of the Yahwist's Theology" did not please him. He concluded his analysis with the remarks: "I fear deeply for the future of the church, if this is all that we can say about this glorious book." At the end of this letter he added: "Please recognize the pain and sorrow which the writing of these harsh words has worked in me. They do not come easy and continue to cast a dark shadow."

To say that I was taken aback when I received this letter was putting it mildly. I was not writing for the church and the approach to which he objected was exactly what I considered a virtue. I had not produced a homiletical or theological commentary. I had not been teaching in a seminary for many years. I did not dispute that some of the stories within the Yahwist's work could be presented in a moving way, but it would take a von Rad or a Martin Buber to do it, not me. I am sure that in his Introduction to the Old Testament classes in Yale Divinity School this is exactly what Childs himself did. He had a great reputation as a teacher. But he should not impose those kinds of expectations on me. I could assure him that the church will not even see the book, much less be affected by it. In any event I wrote him that I understood the concerns from which his remarks were written, and they did not in any way affect my great admiration for him. I also regretted that I did not see him more, but he had not come out to SBL for many years or to the congresses in Europe, and we no longer had occasion to visit New Haven. And I mentioned my recent sabbatical in Cambridge because I had heard that he spent some time there as well.

In his reply, Childs thanked me "for your gracious letter of Sept 26th. I have worried much after sending you such a harsh response, and I greatly appreciate your receiving the criticism in the spirit in which it was intended. I am greatly relieved that it will not affect our long and treasured friendship over many years." He explained to me why he did not get involved in SBL and other big conferences—he disliked large crowds. He spoke about his sabbaticals in Germany and his lecturing at German Universities, much as I had done, and his stay in Cambridge where he met with the crowd of Clements, Emerton, Davies, and Williamson, much as I had done. He then proceeded to criticize the work of some who attempted to do theological or homiletical criticism, such as Terry Fretheim and Walter Bruggemann, whom he regarded as being "more injurious to the life of the church than that posed by traditional historical criticism." I suppose that remark was intended to make me feel better. But then I had some difficulty trying to imagine which works of our contemporaries would have satisfied him. We had another round of letters but this was followed by no further contact.

Brevard S. Childs was one of the most notable figures of biblical scholarship of the twentieth century. His primary field of expertise was Old Testament but he believed so strongly in the unity of the Bible that he tried to develop a standing in New Testament studies and theology as well, but complained to me that the New Testament scholars did not read his works. He developed an approach to biblical studies known as Canonical Criticism that had quite a following except that he did not like the term and there were few who did it like him. He was made a Sterling Professor by Yale University, a mark of recognition by the university reserved for only a select few. His teaching career extended until 1999 at the age of 76, forty years after I had had him as professor of a seminar on Exodus. Yet in spite of the fact that he had a large number of graduate students over the years, he was very much a loner and there is very little continuation of his particular style of biblical studies. I believe that it was that frustration that came out in his letters to me, not only about my own approach but also in the work of others.

In addition to Childs, I sent copies of my book on Moses to my long-time Canadian friends, Robert Culley of McGill and Paul Dion of Toronto, with whom I kept in touch, largely through the Canadian Society of Biblical Studies and also ASOR/SBL. Culley and I regularly exchanged publications with each other. Dion's response was always gracious and self-effacing, but his comments revealed that he had read the work carefully and had some important observations on particular texts for me to consider. He wrote a little about recent departmental politics and the University's plans to merge Near Eastern Studies with Middle East and Islamic, but he preferred to avoid getting involved.

I also sent copies of *The Life of Moses* to my European friends, Martin Rose of the University of Neuchatel, Thomas Römer in Lausanne, Horst Seebass in Bonn, Rainer Albertz in Siegen, and Timo Veijola in Helsinki. The usual response, in addition to expressions of thanks and appreciation, was to send me copies of their recent publications. With some, such as Albertz, Veijola, Römer, and Seebass it often led to further correspondence on various points of interest and plans to meet at some upcoming conference. Since a European edition of my book had been published by Kok Pharos press in the Netherlands, it was very convenient and much quicker to have that press sent out copies to those in Europe and the UK, rather than from the USA.

In the UK, Graham Davies, John Barton, and Ronald Clements had written favorable comments for the book's dustjacket, so they had their own copies from the press, but I also sent a copy to Ernest Nicholson, now Provost of Oriel College. I had not been in touch with him for some time. When it came to matters of Pentateuchal study we did not always agree, but he was very gracious and genuine in his response. Concerning this book, together with my earlier one on Genesis, he states: "yours represents the most comprehensive study of the problem of the Pentateuch." In spite of our differences he acknowledged, "You must know, however, how greatly I admire your scholarship and envy your knowledge of the ever extending literature. I always have admired your vigorous independence of mind." He promised me a copy of a book on the Pentateuch on which he had been working at least for the last ten years. It did finally appear in 1998, but I never did receive a copy from him.

At the same time that Nicholson had written this letter to me he had just published an article on "Story and History in the Old Testament," (1994) in which he challenged my understanding of biblical historiography in general and the Deuteronomic Historian in particular. Yet he had not mentioned this to me in his letter, nor did he send me an off-print. I had missed seeing it because it was buried in a *Festschrift* to James Barr and I was preoccupied at that time with my new project on Hebrew Law. However, later in his 1998 book on the Pentateuch he also disputed my understanding of the Yahwist as a historian. This time I took him up on the challenge and wrote a response to both the article and the book. For the Greek evidence Nicholson had focused almost exclusively on Herodotus to the exclusion of other forms of Greek historiography, most notably the antiquarian tradition to which I had called attention in my earlier publications. He likewise limited his support from classical scholars to only a few whose work could be used to support his position and avoided others who would make his comparisons quite problematic. It was also the case that at the time that Nicholson was writing his first article a very important study by a noted classical scholar, E. Gabba on *Dionysius and the History of Archaic Rome* (1991) had just been published. This work spelled out in considerable detail the characteristics of antiquarian historiography in the history of Dionysius, viewed as the culmination in the early Roman period of a long and venerable tradition of many centuries within Greek historiography. What was most remarkable was the fact that so many of these same characteristics were also present, albeit in rudimentary form, in the work of the Yahwist, which I felt confirmed my thesis very well, as I tried to point out in my article: "Is there any Historiography in the Hebrew Bible? A Hebrew—Greek Comparison" (2002). Nicholson did not respond to my challenge and I have not heard from him since then.

In the USA, I sent a copy of *The Life of Moses* to Steve McKenzie, with whom I regularly exchanged publications and discussed matters of historical criticism. While his specialty was in the Dtr History, about which he kept me informed on the latest development, he was very appreciative of receiving copies of my works in Pentateuch. After reading the work he wrote to me a long complimentary letter on his impression of it and its persuasive impact on him as one coming from a quite different orientation from the Harvard school. He also sent me a major paper that he would be giving the following year in Switzerland and he wanted my comments and suggestion, which I gave him and for which he was grateful. That was typical of our relationship.

I also had some correspondence about my *Life of Moses* from Tom Dozeman. He had received a copy of the book for review and he sent me a copy of the manuscript. At the same time I received a manuscript of Dozeman's latest work from Oxford Press as an expert reader for their consideration. This ended up being a difficult task for me, because I was intended to be a consultant on this project, along with Rolf Rendtorff, but my input was rather limited and reading through the manuscript I was troubled by a lot of unfounded statements that he was making. I gave the Press the go-ahead on it but I sent many of my remarks to Dozeman for his consideration. The end product, *God at War: Power in the Exodus Tradition* (1996) was not greatly modified. Dozeman represented the new generation of Pentateuchal scholars, who were less burdened by older views and open to new considerations and it was important to pay attention to them. However, sometimes it was frustrating to see these young scholars making grand statements without more careful attention to the details of the text.

Another young scholar who appeared on the scene in Pentateuchal studies was David Carr of the Methodist Theological School in Ohio. We had met at SBL in the Pentateuch Seminar after my return from Cambridge in 1992 and, with the recent publication of my book on *Prologue to History* and his growing interest in doing research on Genesis, he was keen on entering into a dialogue with me on the issues surrounding this biblical book. His plan was to be on sabbatical leave in Heidelberg in 1993–94, which meant that he would play off the views of Rendtorff and especially Blum with those reflected in my resent book on Genesis. So we began a correspondence during this period between Heidelberg and Chapel Hill. To begin with, he asked me to comment on a recently published article on the creation narrative of Genesis 2–3, which I did, and from an exchange on this we moved on to a more detailed exchange on my book, *Prologue to History*. He then sent me large parts of the manuscript of his forthcoming book *Reading the Fractures of Genesis* for similar scrutiny.

After he returned from his sabbatical abroad we met in Chapel Hill to go over my reading of his manuscript and my notes on it. In this process it became clear to me that David Carr was a very promising and gifted scholar who would read my work with great care, and any time spent in this exchange was very worthwhile. On many important points I was able to convince him of my position; on others he inclined more in the direction of the work of Erhard Blum, so that his book was something of a compromise between the two approaches, although he would consider it the best of both worlds. He was a very careful and knowledgeable scholar and later was given the well-deserved senior position in the biblical field at Union Seminary in New York.

Papers and Publications

During the year 1994 I was particularly busy giving papers at various conferences and then revising some of them for subsequent publication. As indicated above, in the spring I gave the plenary address at the Southeast Regional meeting of the SBL. Then in early June I attended the Canadian Society of Biblical Studies meeting in Calgary and gave a talk there on the Balaam story, which was later published in the George Coats *Festschrift*. This trip out west was an excellent chance to combine a little business with pleasure and so Elizabeth came along. For about a week before the conference we arranged a marvelous tour of the Rockies, in which we rented a car and toured through the Rockies from Banff to Jasper, staying in first class accommodations at each place: Banff Lodge, Lake Louise Chateau and Jasper Mountain Lodge, while visiting so many great sites and views on the way. We also did a fair bit of hiking on forest and mountain trails to scenic waterfalls. We even tried one of the hot springs bathing spots north of Jasper. It was an unforgettable trip. I remember waking up at dawn in our hotel room on the fifth floor of the Lake Louise Hotel, which overlooked the lake, and seeing Elizabeth sitting by the window. The view of the sun coming up over the mountains and the light on the mountains and lake was quite spectacular.

The World Jewish Congress in Jerusalem (June 21–29, 1994)

In the summer of 1994 I attended the World Jewish Congress in Jerusalem, where I had been asked to give a paper at one of the plenary sessions. I was not all that keen on going to Jerusalem under the current political regime, but I was persuaded to attend by Nadav Na'aman, who had worked hard to get me invited. I stayed in a small modest hotel in west Jerusalem, along with Jim Crenshaw of Duke University in the same hotel, so I saw quite a bit of him and we shared some meals together. On the first full day of the Congress I attended a few sessions, held at the Hebrew University on Mount Scopus, and had lunch with some of the faculty and students of Tel Aviv, including Na'aman and Moshe Anbar, which was very pleasant. The rest of the day I spent walking in the Arabic neighborhood of East Jerusalem, the familiar district north of the Old City. It was all under Israeli guards and checkpoints, though they did not bother with me. But it was very distasteful to me. I stopped at a shop to speak with an older shop-keeper about the good old days of the mid-sixties. I also spent some time exploring the suq of the Old City. On the next day there was little on the program of interest to me so I went for a visit to the Israel Museum with Crenshaw. In the evening Jim and I found a pleasant local restaurant with an open garden where we had supper.

The next day, Friday, the Congress went for only half a day and then closed for Shabbat until Sunday. On this day I gave my paper at the plenary session in the auditorium, along with William Hallo of Yale and some other well-known scholars. Needless to say, my paper upset some of the conservative Israelis, which was to be expected. After the session I was invited to Professor Baruch Levine's grand apartment near the Knesset. There was a big buffet with lots of guests, including Hallo and Crenshaw. There was one couple from Toronto and I learned in conversation with them that the woman went to high school with my sister at Harbord Collegiate in Toronto. Afterwards I went for a walk along the side of the valley overlooking the western side of the Old City and then I had a snack at a little Palestinian restaurant inside the Jaffa Gate.

On Saturday, because of Shabbat, there was no Congress and West Jerusalem was dead with no busses or transportation running. So I set off on foot to East Jerusalem and as soon as I "crossed the line" on the road along the north side of the Old City everything was alive and bustling. I passed the Damascus Gate, the old and still familiar bus station, up Salah ad-Din St., and dropped in to see St. George's Cathedral, where I met the dean of the cathedral. He showed me about the place and gave me some lemonade. He knew our good friends Ted and Margie Campbell, among others. I also called in at the American School (Albright Institute) and ran into Omar, the major domo, who was the chef when we were there in the 60's and we had some tea together. I then hiked back through the Old City to the south side, down to the pool of Siloam, and then returned to the Armenian Quarter and had a little lunch at a small café inside the Jaffa Gate. I returned to the hotel, quite tired, so I took a nap. Later I showered and then set out for supper at the home of Professor Alex Rofé, a good scholar and friend. It was a very pleasant gathering.

On Sunday I had a nice private lunch with Na'aman at the Congress where we became personally acquainted with each other for the first time, and he talked quite candidly about the recent developments in biblical studies in Israel, including the quite different perspectives of the more liberal Tel Aviv University as compared with the Hebrew University and some of the other institutions. The Tel Aviv scholars are a group with which I found a lot in common, and I have benefited a great deal from my association with them. In the evening I went to the home of Moshe Greenberg, a rather conservative scholar who had moved to Israel from University of Pennsylvania, many years earlier. It was a very fine buffet and much the same pleasant group as at the other buffets. On Monday I was asked, on rather short notice, if I would chair a morning session on the book of Chronicles. It went fairly well, in spite of the fact that the presentations were rather conservative when discussing the nature of the Chronicler's historiography. After this session I ran into Abraham Segal, the French journalist who had interviewed me in Paris at the IOSOT Congress. He suggested that we go to the École Biblique and he made arrangements by phone. We took a cab from the Hebrew University to the École Biblique (not far from the Albright Inst.) and were warmly received by Professor Langlemet and invited to lunch. Others there included Professor Gonzolvas and Burton McDonald (with whom I had dug at Tell el-Maskhuta, and who was in residence at EB). It was a great lunch with a good red wine. Langlemet gave us a tour of the place; so much had changed since I had worked in the library here in 1964–65. Those at the École Biblique were all very cordial and treated me like a celebrity, which was almost embarrassing. I had an open invitation to visit and use the wonderful facilities of the school whenever I wanted, but I did not take it up. Segal and I took a cab back to the Congress and I went to hear Rofé's paper. He was followed by Meir Sternberg, and I knew that he would be insufferable, so I left. Jim Crenshaw told me later that Sternberg had simply decided to take 1½ hours, giving two separate papers and refused to quit, leaving the rest of the program for that session in shambles. He is a very arrogant person.

In the evening I went to yet another reception at Ed Greenstein's place: I knew him through SBL. His place was crowded and served lots of goodies. The next morning I took Jim Crenshaw for a tour through the Old City and the Damascus Gate and up Salah ad-Din to the Albright Inst. Crenshaw had stayed at the St. George's Hotel near the Old City previously, but had never been in East Jerusalem. He seemed a little nervous about going there. The Israelis completely avoided it. In the afternoon I took a cab to the airport and began my journey home. I returned from the trip with very mixed emotions. Establishing a closer association with the Tel Aviv group and a few other Israelis was a great boon, but the biblical part of the program at the World Jewish Congress was very weak and mostly a waste of time. It was also disheartening to see the great decline in east Jerusalem and in the suq of the Old City since the mid-60s. On this trip I could not travel outside of Jerusalem, but that would happen a few years later with Max Miller.

Later in the summer I attended the SBL International Meeting in Leuven, where I gave a paper on "Solomon's Temple: Fact and Ideology in Biblical and Near Eastern Historiography." Leuven was becoming a familiar place for conferences and later the location of my last sabbatical. A few weeks after the Leuven meeting I saw, in the ASOR/SBL program for the fall meetings, that Na'aman was also speaking on the subject of Solomon's temple-building in his paper to ASOR. I told him that I had just given a paper on the same subject that summer and suggested that we exchange copies of our papers. I took the liberty of sending him a copy of mine. He wrote back promptly and gave me a lot of comments on details of my paper. On the whole we were in agreement that the description in the book of Kings should be dated to the time of the author in the late seventh or early sixth century BCE and not to the time of Solomon, but on matters of detail there were some differences of opinion. Nevertheless, it was a friendly exchange and the beginning of many more over the years. He sent me some of his recent off-prints. As it turned out he had to cancel his trip to the USA but sent me a copy of his paper for my comments. My contact with the "Tel Aviv School" of biblical scholars grew considerably over the years.

My paper on Solomon's Temple was later submitted to the *Catholic Biblical Quarterly*, and during 1995 I had considerable correspondence with the editor Aelred Cody, whose work I knew but I had never met personally. At the same time I also made application to Joseph Jensen, the Executive Secretary of the Catholic Biblical Association for associate (non-Catholic) membership and Cody acted as my sponsor. I knew a number of members in this organization and occasionally attended their summer meetings, which were usually quite enjoyable. My article on Solomon's Temple was published in *CBQ*, 1997.

I also attended the national SBL meeting in Chicago where I gave two papers. The one was in the Deuteronomistic History section, dealing with "Compositional Techniques in Near Eastern and Greek Historiography and in DtrH," and the other in a special session of the "Chronicles Group" on the theme of the Chronicler as Historian. My specific topic was "The Chronicler's Account of Solomon's Temple-Building: A Continuity Theme." I argued that the Chronicler deliberately modified the description of the temple that he took over from the book of Kings to make it conform more closely to that of the Mosaic Tabernacle in the book of Exodus. This last piece was later published in a collection of the special session papers as *The Chronicler as Historian* (1997).

Also during that same month of November, 1994, I was involved in a special bicentennial celebration of the birth of Edward Robinson, at Hamilton College in Clinton, NY. Robinson had made a name for himself as the pioneer of biblical archaeology in the mid-nineteenth century in the area of biblical geography, traveling about Palestine and attempting to identify the location of ancient cities. I was invited to take part in this bicentennial as one of a series of speakers invited to make a presentation during the fall semester of 1994, and I was happy to do so. In mid-November I made a trip to Hamilton College and spent an enjoyable time lecturing and meeting with the faculty of Religious Studies there.

While at the college I also spent some time in their library because they had a collection of Robinson's works. I was particularly interested in Robinson's great respect for German biblical scholarship of that period in the early nineteenth century and his attempts to introduce it to American biblical studies. Although Robinson would be viewed as quite conservative today, he was open to the best of theological scholarship and spent a lot of time in Germany. While at Andover Theological Seminary in Massachusetts, Robinson, in 1831, founded and edited a journal *The Biblical Repository*, in which he published a series of four articles (143 pages) on the theme of Theological Education in Germany. He had spent four years there (1826–30), studying in German universities. In his articles he explains the whole system of higher education in Germany in general and theological education in particular and his experiences in visiting a large number of different German institutions, attending lectures and making interesting comments on various scholars and theologians of that day. I found the articles quite fascinating and could not get through them all in the short time I had to examine them so I had the college library make me a copy of them and I still have them on file. I have often thought that it would be worthwhile having such a collection of pieces reproduced in print as an important document on the history of the discipline of biblical studies.

While at the summer meeting of the British Society of Old Testament Studies in the UK in 1995 I spoke with Professor John Rogerson about these materials on Edward Robinson that I had come across in Hamilton College. Rogerson was an authority on the history of biblical scholarship in the nineteenth century and was very interested in these documents that he never knew existed. So when I returned home from the UK I sent him information about contacts at Hamilton from whom he could gain information and copies of documents. He was grateful for this and also passed on the information to Professor Rudolph Smend of the University of Göttingen, who also worked on the history of biblical scholarship. That is what happens at these conferences, the constant interchange of ideas and information in the most direct and personal way. It is also the case that when you take another person's work seriously, they are inclined to do so with yours and you both gain.

Also in the summer of 1994 I received an interesting request from the University of Dublin, asking me whether I would be willing to evaluate John R. Bartlett for the degree of Doctor in Letters (Litt.D.), based upon the scholarly quality of his publications. In Ireland, and perhaps also in the UK, it was the custom of someone who did not have an earned doctoral degree to be evaluated for this honorary doctorate of Litt.D. if the candidate had "assembled a substantial corpus of work," which in North America would have merited the status of full Professor. I wrote back that since I was already familiar with a number of Bartlett's publications I would be glad to do so and to write up my appraisal. They sent me a packet of his writings that was really quite substantial. I wrote back to tell them that going through the publications had been a very enjoyable and rewarding task and I had found the total output of this mature scholar very impressive. I then gave a detailed assessment of his publications and his remarkable range of competence and suggested that John Bartlett fully deserved to be a full professor in the best academic institutions in America, if he were a member of their faculties. I therefore hoped that their institution would see fit to honor him with the degree of Litt.D. My report, along with one other, went to the University Council and the degree was granted. After John Bartlett received the degree he learned of my involvement and thanked me very much for it. I also sent him a copy of my *Life of Moses*, since I now owned so many of his books, and for this he also thanked me and suggested that I plan to make a trip to Ireland. We discussed the possibility but I regret that it never came off.

Departmental Affairs 1995

The spring semester of 1995 was my last as chairman and I informed Dean Birdsall in good time of my intentions not to continue. He accepted it but stated that he had hoped I would be in the post a little longer. Nevertheless, he expressed his gratitude for all the work that I had put into the Department over the years and for my last two years as Chair. Elizabeth and I were also invited by him and his wife, along with the other retiring Chairs, to a dinner of appreciation for "the time, energy and attention that you have devoted to the leadership of your department." It was a very pleasant time. Another pleasant departmental task was to team up with Peter Kaufman to draft a letter in support of a junior colleague, Assistant Professor Laurie Maffly-Kipp for a scholarly achievement prize. Laurie had recently joined the Department in the field of American Religion as a replacement for Grant Wacker, who had gone to a post in Duke Divinity School. Maffley-Kipp had published a beautifully written book, *Religion and Society in Frontier California*, with a wonderful treatment of the role of women in the days of the gold rush, within the context of American religious history. Most of the letter of support was written by Kaufman in his most elegant style and I was only too happy to sign my name to it. Needless to say she won the prize, but it also gave to Kaufman's colleagues the sense that he was not as much an outsider as he was generally made out to be.

Within the university I continued to be involved in the lectures within the Humanities and Human Values Program. It was always great fun. In the fall of 1995 they dreamed up a seminar on *Heroes and Heroines* and asked four faculty members to participate: Professors Julia O'Brien from an all-women's college in Raleigh to do a talk on Ruth, Jack Sasson, my colleague, to talk on Gilgamesh, Peter Smith from Classics on the heroes of Homer, and I would talk on Moses. Once these talks got going it was very easy to get into the spirit of the seminar—three of us had lots of experience at it, and Julia, who was new to the group, caught the spirit and did a superb job. The audience reviews were great, which always made the effort worthwhile.

Contact with Foreign Young Scholars: Cynthia Edenburg and Jan Wagenaar

Early in 1995 I received a letter from Cynthia Edenburg, a doctoral student of Professor Nadav Na'aman at Tel Aviv University; we had met briefly earlier at the World Jewish Congress in Jerusalem. She wanted to consult me on the topic of her dissertation: "The Story of the 'Outrage at Gibea' (Judg 19–21)—its Composition, Sources and Historical Background." Under the tutelage of Na'aman she had become familiar with my work on biblical historiography. It was clear from her letter that she had absorbed a good deal of my methodology and views, and it was quite apparent that her study was going to be a very interesting one. She was planning a trip to the Washington D.C. area in May and wanted to make a trip to Chapel Hill to see me. I wrote back and told her that she was most welcome to visit me, that I was in agreement with her late dating of this unit, but at this point she probably knew more about it than I did. I made some suggestions about recent bibliography and had her also send on my greetings and some information to Na'aman about my recent publication on a topic of mutual interest.

In her further reply to my letter, she informed me that she was no longer able to make the trip to the US in May. She was indeed already familiar with the works I cited and pushed the discussion still further to some of my own work on the Yahwist. This was a young scholar who demonstrated very fine literary sensitivity in the study of the Hebrew Bible, especially having to do with the Deuteronomistic History.

Sometime later she gave a paper at SBL, based upon her dissertation, and it was very impressive indeed, and I told her so at the meeting. She also sent me copies of some other papers she did. Over the course of time I wrote letters of recommendation for her for positions and grants. Her views, however, were strongly resisted by a large majority of quite conservative Israeli scholars, and apart from her position at the Open University of Israel, she could not get the first rate level of appointment that she deserved.

Another young scholar with whom I made contact through my publications was a Dutchman, Jan Wagenaar. My first contact with him was when in 1989 he sent me a copy of his master's these, in Dutch, which was done at Utrecht University under K.A.D. Smelik (with whom I was also acquainted). Jan's thesis was on the relationship between the story of the crossing of the Red Sea in Exodus 13–14 and the crossing of the Jordan in Josh 3–4. This work was strongly influenced by my work on these texts and for a master's thesis was certainly a very impressive piece of work. (The 140 pages in Dutch took me a little longer than usual to read.) A short time after I received it, I met the young man at the IOSOT congress in Leuven.

For the next few years Wagenaar worked on his doctoral thesis on the book of Micah under Professor Bob Becking at Utrecht, and while we saw each other at European conferences from time to time, there was not much discussion about his research, which was out of my field. When the thesis was completed in 1995 he sent me a copy and then announced to me that he was returning to "the problems of the Jahwist and the Deuteronomist." In connection with this he was going to read one of the short papers at the Colloquium Biblicum Lovaniense in August of that year, which I would also be attending (more about that later) and we would meet up again. He also wanted me to write on his behalf in support of a research grant to the Dutch Foundation for Scientific Research, for a project on the book of Joshua under the supervision of Bob Becking, which of course I did. I was to be a co-supervisor of the project. He did not get the grant, but it was the beginning of numerous subsequent letters of recommendation and a succession of temporary appointments for him.

Conferences (1995): SOTS in Wales, IOSOT in Cambridge, Colloquium in Leuven, SBL in Philadelphia

In 1994 I was made an honorary member of the Society for Old Testament Studies in the UK and subsequently received information about their plans for a summer meeting in Bangor Wales in 1995. I offered to present a short paper and Paul Joyce, the Home Secretary of SOTS, asked me if I would consider doing a long paper of forty minutes instead, followed by discussion. I agreed, and since I was working on an article on the Chronicler's view of the Solomonic Temple I offered to do that. Since I had planned to be at IOSOT meeting in Cambridge a few days later I could easily combine both conferences. I knew that Timo Veijola would also be giving a major paper at SOTS on a subject that interested me, and it would be a good chance to see him again. It was a very pleasant conference with lots of old friends there. We also did a bus tour around northwestern Wales, including the fascinating place, Porthmadog, which was built as an outdoor museum resembling an Italian village and like nothing else in Wales. Since Kristin De Troyer of Kok Pharos Press, was at the SOTS meeting and was also going by car to Cambridge to the IOSOT meeting she offered to give me a lift over to Cambridge, which I gladly accepted.

The International Organization for the Study of the Old Testament Congress in Cambridge was like homecoming week. I even stayed in a room in Fitzwilliam

College. Graham Davies was the congress secretary and John Emerton was the president. Most of the meetings and activities were centered in St. John's College, which was Emerton's home base and a beautiful setting. There was such a wonderful gathering of old friends, it was unbelievable and impossible to properly visit with all of them. From the old Toronto gang there was John Wevers and Albert Pietersma, Ernie Clark, John Revell. Johann Cook of South Africa and Johan Lust of Leuven were also there, which together with Pietersma meant that we had our Dutch folksong singing group, which we tried out in a British pub. Of course the Brits were there at the congress in full number, including William and Agnes McKane, Ernest Nicholson, John Barton, Ronald Clements and David Clines, and many more. The Americans were also out in greater strength than usual, many for the first time, such as Brian Schmidt, Steven McKenzie, David Carr, and of course Walter Bruggemann, for whom Cambridge was very familiar territory. Naturally, the Europeans were also out in full force, even Kaiser and his former students, Hans-Christoph Schmitt and Uwe Becker as well as Eric Aurelius, and the young graduate student from Zurich, Konrad Schmid (Hans Heinrich's son). I did spend some time with Marc Vervenne of Leuven. I would be attending a symposium in Leuven later in the summer that he was organizing, but I also wanted to speak with him about the possibility of spending a sabbatical in Leuven a couple of years down the road. Most of the value in these conferences is not merely in the papers, but in the meeting and exchanges with individuals on a one to one basis. A highlight of the congress was a banquet at St. John's College, which was one of the traditions of the congresses.

There was a young graduate student from the University of Oslo, Marit Skjeggestad, whom I met at the congress during a coffee break, and we got onto the subject of Professor William Dever. Apparently she had written an article for the *Scandinavian Journal of the Old Testament*, edited by Niels-Peter Lemche, in which she criticized the work of Dever, and he had retaliated by labeling her as a "minimalist" and dismissing her work as unscientific. So she wanted me to tell her what I thought of him. I assured her that she was in good company because he was equally critical of me, but it was really his problem and not ours. After the congress she sent me some of her off-prints, including a review of Dever and wanted me to comment on it. She was also working on her doctoral study: *Methodologies of History in the field "Ancient Israelite History" in the Twentieth Century*, and stated "your books and articles will of course be among my primary sources in the project." So she wanted to keep in touch.

About five weeks after the IOSOT Congress I was off to Leuven Belgium to participate in a much smaller, more focused *Colloquium Biblicum Lovaniense* dealing with the book of Exodus, organized and run by Marc Vervenne. He asked me to give one of the main papers at this colloquium. By this time I was beginning to get involved in the study of Hebrew Law and specifically the Covenant Code of the book of Exodus (Exodus 21–23). My earlier study of the Moses Story in Exodus had deliberately set aside the investigation of this unit in Exodus for further study as a separate project, and this paper was a preliminary foray into that issue. I knew this would be a problem for Eckart Otto, who was also attending this colloquium and who regarded himself as the great authority on Hebrew Law, but it did not deter me in the least. In fact, I was looking forward to the exchange.

As expected, Otto and I did have a lively discussion over my treatment of the Covenant Code and its relationship to the other codes of the Pentateuch. His own paper arguing for a Deuteronomistic Redactor of the Pentateuch in Exodus, an idea that he took from another German scholar, was strongly disputed by both Erhard Blum and me. And there was lively discussion of many of the other papers. This was the opening salvo between Otto and me over the matter of Hebrew Law in general and the Covenant Code in particular. It would go on for several years. I also met some of the other scholars for the first time, notably Cees Houtman, a Dutch scholar, who was working on a massive commentary on Exodus, including a volume on the laws, and we later exchanged publications and correspondence. He was somewhat conservative in outlook, but very open and pleasant to talk to. I quite enjoyed his company and respected his scholarship. It was not surprising to also find Johann Cook in Leuven. South Africans loved to come to Leuven to do their research and Cook was there frequently. It was an enjoyable and productive time.

Jean Louis Ska, a Belgian and a good friend, who taught at the Pontifical Biblical Institute in Rome was also there. We had already begun some serious discussion earlier in the year following my sending him a copy of my book *The Life of Moses*, and at that time he had sent me the manuscript copies of two reviews that he had done of the book in major journals, the *Catholic Biblical Quarterly* and *Biblica* (both in French). So I sent him my response to some of the issues that he had raised in these reviews. We not only continued this dialogue in Leuven but have continued to do so for many years up to the present.

The last major conference of the year for me was the SBL annual meeting in Philadelphia in November. Earlier in the year, in February, David Carr, who was the incoming president of the Pentateuch group, informed me about plans to have a special session on the Yahwist and the planning committee was asking three other scholars, in addition to myself, Erhard Blum, Richard Friedman of U of California, San Diego, and Anthony Campbell of Australia, to make presentations on their various positions and then enter into a moderated dialogue with each other. Friedman and Campbell were there to defend the classical documentary hypothesis while Blum and I would advocate the new and quite different approaches to this non-Priestly corpus in the Pentateuch. It was clear that this was going to be a lively and controversial session. David tried to control the presentations by posing a number of questions which each speaker was to address and we would be given a rough draft of each other's treatment of these questions well before the meeting in order to be prepared for an intelligent debate. As so often happens in such cases, I got all of my materials in early and stuck to the questions David had suggested, but the others, particularly Friedman and Campbell were more interested in attacking my views and those of Blum than in explaining their own. David encouraged them to stick to the agenda, after he saw their outline, but they paid little attention.

The session was in late afternoon in one of the large meeting rooms in the hotel and it was packed out. It was quite lively, as I expected and I was given the last spot of the four presentations. Of course I was fully prepared for Friedman and Campbell; that was the easy part. Blum and I had a good debate, as usual in our frequent encounters. And many heard my views on the Yahwist first hand. David wrote to me a few days after the meeting, thanking me for my participation, which was an obvious success. He added: "Although more should read your work, I think sessions like this are sometimes required to get people preoccupied with their own work to take recent research seriously. Many people approached me afterwards to express appreciation for the session, and your presence on it was a crucial element of its success." This would not be the last of such special sessions in which I was involved.

At just about this time David Carr had also put a bid in for an opening in Old Testament at Duke Divinity School and I had strongly supported him in this endeavor. As it turned out, he did not get it, primarily because they did not offer him tenure, which he had in his current position. It would have been very good for me to have him just down the road. I am sure that it would have opened up a lot more cooperation between the two schools in the OT field. But it was not to be. Nevertheless, we stayed in close contact for some time.

I would also like to mention some correspondence with Richard Friedman earlier in the year that will put the Pentateuch session at the SBL meeting in some context. As early as 1993 Richard Friedman had written a review of my book, *Prologue to History*, for the popular journal, *Biblical Archaeology Review*. I usually do not pay much attention to this journal, but I knew Friedman and I thought that his treatment of my book was quite unfair, so I wrote to the editor, Hershel Shanks, whom I knew and sent him some remarks as a reply. Hershel suggested that I expand it into an article, which I did and then they sent that to Friedman for a one page response, and this was published in mid-1994. All of this became something of a battle between the two of us. So, about a year later, in anticipation of this up-coming session at SBL Friedman wrote to me to acknowledge that the whole affair was somewhat embarrassing to him and he wanted to clear the air. He had never intended it to devolve into a Friedman vs Van Seters contest. As often happens with Shank's publications, they are developed to create the maximum sense of confrontation. Friedman emphasized that whatever disagreements we had he did not want me to take it personal. He also invited me to come out to their department in San Diego at their expense to conduct a seminar with his colleagues to discuss these matters. It was a tempting proposition, a kind of Daniel in the lion's den, but I did not take him up on it. At least during the SBL meeting he was quite civil and conciliatory.

Publications

Since 1992 Yale Press had been keeping me informed about the fact that my hard cover and paperback editions of *Abraham in History and Tradition* and *In Search of History* had been going out of print, and by 1994 my good friend the executive editor, Charles Grench, informed me that they were not going to do another printing of these volumes. In mid-1995 a number of presses approached me about reissuing one or both of these books, so I asked Yale Press to send me the certificates of Copyright Registration, reverting the rights of these books to me, which they did. After conversations with various publishers, I decided to go with Eisenbrauns, who was interested in doing both volumes. He began with a new edition of *In Search of History*, which appeared in 1997 and he never did do a reprint of *Abraham*, which later appeared by another publisher. In the new digital age such works are now accessed directly online.

During the year 1995 I was also approached by Brian Schmidt and Diana Edelman if I would be interested in participating in a new commentary series called *A Social Scientific Commentary*, in which I would author one of the introductory volumes, the one on *The Pentateuch*. After considerable discussion about what they meant by the "social production of the Pentateuch," which seemed to be the equivalent to the historical-critical approach of viewing the various strata of the Pentateuch as the products of particular socio-historical environments, I accepted the assignment and signed an agreement with Sheffield Academic Press in early 1996, with the final manuscript sent in the following year. It was finally published in 1999. At the same time that Diana Edelman and Brian Schmidt were talking to me about this project they were also trying to get Thomas Römer committed to do the introductory volume on the Deuteronomistic History of Joshua to Kings. His volume finally appeared in 2005, but now under a new press, T&T Clark. There never was a commentary series as such. Just recently Bloomsbury Press, which took over T&T Clark proposed that I do an update of *The Pentateuch* for a second edition. This appeared in 2015 under Bloomsbury T&T Clark.

9

The Last Five Years in Chapel Hill, 1995–2000

Departmental Matters

With my second tenure as department chair ending in mid-1995, I returned to full-time teaching in the fall of 1995, and this seems like an appropriate place to reflect on my teaching career, up to this point. My appointment to the department was as the James A. Gray chair in biblical studies, and this chair had been endowed specifically for the teaching of undergraduates in this field. My predecessor had taught introductory courses in both Old and New Testament, but since the department already had a very good scholar in New Testament I was chosen for my expertise in Hebrew Bible/Old Testament and I taught a large introductory course every year on that subject, even in those years when I was chair of the department. The department, over the years that I was there, had a reputation for undergraduate teaching, especially among the younger scholars, and it regularly won teaching awards. I had rather mixed feelings about these awards. On the one hand, I invested particular effort in writing in support of the younger faculty, not just because they were good teachers and carried a large share of the load that justified our existence in the eyes of the dean's office, but also because it was a way of augmenting their low salaries. I never won such an award and would have been embarrassed if I had as the highest salary in the department. On the other hand, teaching and grading students while at the same time being evaluated by these students through annual end of term student course surveys encourages a strong tendency towards grade inflation and making the classes a form of entertainment. This was especially the case with the large introduction courses. In spite of all this, one could still learn a lot from visiting the large introduction classes of the younger scholars, as I did prior to any recommendations that I submitted on their behalf. I built a close relationship with almost all of my younger colleagues.

There was a practice at UNC that one could sit in on a class for non-credit as an auditor, with the permission of the lecturer. It was usually in the larger classes that a number of older retired alumni did this. I often had one or two of them in my big introduction class. A few of them became friends and occasionally we would take lunch together at the alumni-faculty club, always on their bill. Sometimes they would offer a suggestion, not on the content of the course, but on the mode of presentation, which was always helpful. Occasionally, an individual who had audited some of our lectures would send a note to the Chancellor in praise of the quality of teaching that he had witnessed in these classes, and I would get a copy of the letter and some acknowledgement from the Chancellor, which was always gratifying.

One such individual was Albert Sawyer, who identified himself as retired and in his 70s, who wrote to the chancellor in response to complaints made about undergraduates who never see a real professor, only graduate students, as their teachers. In his reply to this he describes his pleasure of sitting in on the undergraduate courses of Jack Sasson's "Civilizations of the Ancient Near East," my course on "Prophets of the Old Testament" and Bart Ehrman's "Introduction to the New Testament" with very favorable comments about each one. He then concluded with this comment: "So you see, Chancellor Hooker, in response to any complaints of graduate students teaching courses, you can offer the Department of Religious Studies as an example of nationally famous, perhaps world famous, professors teaching undergraduates. And I must say that I have never enjoyed anything more, or learned more, than from these courses in that department." I had learned early on that it pays to encourage the presence of such non-credit auditors in these larger classes.

On the graduate level, the program was rather small, especially in the field of Hebrew Bible and Ancient Near East, because it was only covered by Jack Sasson, David Halperin and me, with little cooperation from our counterparts at Duke. This was in sharp contrast to New Testament in which Bart Ehrman had strong support from his counterparts at Duke, resulting in a joint program. Given our limitations in Hebrew Bible, I was reluctant to accept graduate students, especially since most of the applicants were rather weak, with poor background in the field. But Jack Sasson was eager to have students and encouraged admission. However, once admitted I ended up with most of the teaching responsibility for them, and directing all of the MA theses and the two doctoral dissertations. In addition to these chores, the department had an initial required course, for all incoming grad students, surveying the history of the academic study of religion. I was one of only three or so of the faculty who took this on, but I ended up enjoying it and became acquainted with more of our graduate students than would otherwise be the case. It meant a lot of reading for the students, and some expanding of my own horizons, although I already had a fair collection of works in this field. It also served my students well to view their own studies of Bible within this context.

I want to make some particular remarks about my two doctoral students, Kenton Sparks and Mark McCormick. They both entered the program about the same time in the late 80s, and both were from quite conservative backgrounds, Kent from a fundamentalist Bible College and Mark from Southeastern Baptist Seminary (a Southern Baptist school). I knew Mark's professor of Old Testament well, Samuel Balentine, and while Sam was conservative he was not a fundamentalist and so Mark's training in the basics and Balentine's recommendation could be trusted. After a short time in the program, Mark soon became employed by us as a teacher of undergraduates in basic Hebrew. The admission of Kenton was far more doubtful, but as usual Sasson argued for it and Halperin followed his lead, so he was admitted and as usual he fell into my lap. Yet he proved to be a diamond in the rough, and since I had so few advanced students, especially beyond the MA level, both of these two received a lot of close scrutiny and personal supervision, and both chose to do their thesis work with me, in spite of the fact that I clearly posed a greater threat to their conservative beliefs and orientation. Mark, as student of Balentine, took much of this in stride, but if Kenton was to survive, he needed a little more mentoring, and I could do this because I had survived the same kind of experience and was aware of what it was like. In his personal remarks about my teaching, published in my *Festschrift* in 2000, Kenton makes some comments about these mentoring sessions and what they meant to him.

Unlike some doctoral programs where the supervisor virtually dictates the topic of the dissertation in support of his own work, I was concerned to let both of my students find their own area of special interest, just as I was permitted to do at Yale. Both of them chose topics that were interdisciplinary and novel for the field of biblical studies. Kenton chose the topic of "Ethnicity and Identity in Ancient Israel," which interested me very much. He had approached Sasson first, because he was still a little nervous about working under me, but Sasson showed no interest in the topic and wanted him to do something else. When Kent realized that I was keen on his doing it, we got on very well. During the dissertation oral in 1996, Sasson's final critique of the dissertation was a little severe, but that was probably a good thing in the end in terms of revisions that were made before its final publication in 1998, when it was quite well received.

Mark took a little longer before he found his topic, which had to do with the structural and artistic iconography of Sennacherib's Palace in comparison with the verbal iconography in the biblical description of Solomon's Temple. Again, as with Kent, he made use of expertise outside of the biblical studies field, and indeed outside of the Department, to great advantage. His use of Assyriological material might have suggested Sasson as his advisor, and he certainly consulted him closely on those matters in his research. But my own prior work on the biblical account of the Solomonic Temple and my enthusiasm for the topic made him eager to work with me. His dissertation, "Palace and Temple: A Study of Architectural and Verbal Icons," was accepted in 1999 and it was later published in a leading German monograph series (Beihefte zur Zeitschrift für die alttestamentlicheWissenschaft 313) in 2002, edited by my good friend Otto Kaiser. I had written to Kaiser in support of its publication and about the particular merits of the work, and he respected my opinion on this matter. It was remarkable and gratifying how far these two young scholars had come in such a short time.

After graduation, Mark received an appointment at Stillman College in Tuscaloosa, Alabama, with a heavy work load and soon he was absorbed with teaching and administration with little chance to develop his research—something that happens too often for promising young scholars. He would come to the annual meetings of the Society of Biblical Literature and, together with Kenton, this would give us a chance to get together periodically. Kenton, on the other hand, remained for some time employed by a church in Raleigh that allowed him generous time and some funds for his research, and we got together frequently to talk about his next big project, which was a handbook covering all of the various literary genres that would be relevant and useful for the study of the Old Testament. This was a massive undertaking that would take some years to complete. It was the sort of work that one might only expect of a senior scholar, let alone one so early in his career. On the other hand, coming from his conservative background, it was precisely this determination to come to grips with the whole spectrum of literary texts and their *Sitze im Leben* that would help him understand the true nature of biblical literature. And there was nothing available that could be so easily consulted by a student of biblical literature. We had several sessions together in the early stages of this project, but after he got going on it, and especially after he settled into his appointment at Eastern University in Pennsylvania, he was largely on his own. The work came out in 2005 as *Ancient Texts for the Study of the Hebrew Bible: A Guide to the Background Literature*, a marvelous achievement to great praise. I was doubly delighted that it was dedicated to me. Kenton has published other books since his dissertation and there will be more, but his name will likely be associated with this one more than with any of the others.

Scholarly Contacts and Correspondence

As should be obvious at this point in the narrative, a large part of my career was dependent upon, and stimulated by, my correspondence with scholars, primarily from Europe and Great Britain, and this became increasingly the case, the more I became introduced to them through such conferences as the IOSOT. One such scholar that I met through a session on the Pentateuch at the 1992 meeting was Professor Horst Seebass of the University of Bonn, a lively person about my age. After my book, *The Life of Moses* appeared in 1994 he got in touch with me in May of 1995, having carefully read through it, particularly the part that related to his current publication project, a commentary of the book of Numbers. It was to be published in fascicles, of which the second would appear shortly and he would send me a copy, which he did. He admitted that being a student of Martin Noth, he did not agree with all that I had written, particularly on my late dating of the text. Nevertheless, there was much in it that he found stimulating and wanted to continue in a dialogue on these matters. I responded by thanking him for his kind remarks and affirmed my intention to keep in touch with him, and he would continue to send me fascicles on his Numbers commentary. Thus, in 1996 when I sent an article I had published in 1996 in the German journal *ZAW* on "The Law of the Hebrew Slave," I received a letter from Seebass expressing his approval for much that was in it. This new discussion of biblical law had become a hot topic so it was most appropriate that I work on this subject during my coming sabbatical.

In order to give some idea of the extent of some of the scholarly correspondence that I received and the contacts with whom I was in touch during the period (1995–96), let me list a fair sample of these. The young Dutch scholar, Jan Wagenaar of Urtecht, whom I had mentioned earlier, was constantly in touch with me during this period, both for my support of research grants as co-supervisor of his proposal and with letters of recommendation to two different foundations. He also sent me his recently published PhD dissertation on the book of Micah (in Dutch). He was also looking for employment, which resulted in letters of recommendation to a number of different schools for this purpose. It was hard to see a gifted young scholar, who also had much part-time teaching experience at University of Utrecht and a good publication record, unable to find permanent employment.

Another younger scholar, whom I had mentioned earlier, was Stuart Lasine at Wichita State University. I had helped him make the transition from the field of comparative literature into biblical studies and find a position in his present employment, and he was in touch with me again. He wanted me to look over some of his recent conference papers to see if they would be appropriate to combine with some earlier published articles into book form. In his typical self-effacing way, he stated: "I realize you may not have the time to read through these long quirky papers. Please don't read them if you don't have time to spare." He then ended by saying: "Thanks again for all the help you've given me over the years." Well of course I would make time and answered his request within a week.

In late 1995 I receive a letter from John Bartlett, now professor and principal of The Church of Ireland Theological College in response to my sending him a copy of *The Life of Moses*. John, with that typical Irish hyperbole, praised the book as "a most splendid book, a most generous gift from one of the most distinguished biblical scholars of today. I am really very touched by your generosity; you have already done so much for me (as I discovered this summer!) and it is I who should be sending gifts to you." Of course he did not need to send me any of his works because I already had them as a result of my review for his Litt.D and promotion. He then invited me to come to Ireland and would try to find a way to do this. I wrote back and told him, "I see that you have discovered the reason for my generosity. I would love to visit Ireland." I went on to mention that Elizabeth and I had often talked about the possibility and that with a sabbatical coming up in 1997–8 we might be about to discover a way to do it. As it turned out, however, we did not get there.

In response to a letter I sent him on the critical study of the book of Kings, Nadav Na'aman gave me his own views on the matter and sent me some of his offprints. This exchange became a regular practice that still continues and I have accumulated a large file of his offprints. While we did not always agree, the dialogue was very useful for both of us, and through him my association with the Tell Aviv School of Historical and Archaeological Studies greatly expanded.

In late 1996 I received a request from Joseph Blenkinsopp, a senior professor in biblical studies at Notre Dame University, to write on his behalf in support of a grant proposal, so he could get an academic year's leave. His research topic had to do with the narrative context of biblical law, and since my own research was moving into the study of biblical law, our interests were complimentary, and I was happy to read through his proposal and write in support of it. I knew Joe fairly well through the SBL meetings, but helping out a colleague in this way invariably drew us closer and stimulated more conversation in areas of our common research.

About this time I received an email notice of a change of address from a younger German Old Testament scholar, Rainer Albertz, whom I had met at a conference in Paris. I could see that he now had a position at Münster University and I sent him a quick reply congratulating him on this new appointment. He sent me a message back, pleased with my good wishes and expanded on some of the opportunities this new position offered him and his plans to participate in a special session with me at an international conference in Lausanne, organized by my good friend Thomas Römer. He said that he was eager to stay in touch and we have done so over the years, to mutual benefit (more on my visit to Münster later).

In early 1996 I sent a manuscript to the German journal, *ZAW*, and its editor Hans-Christoph Schmitt, who succeeded Otto Kaiser in that post. Since Schmitt and I shared common interests in Pentateuchal studies, I was sure that my article, "The Law of the Hebrew Slave" would be of interest to him and facilitate its speedy publication. His response assured me that I was not mistaken. He also took the opportunity to share some of his own views on Pentateuchal issues, and I responded with my own, and this we did over a number of years. I also told him, in subsequent correspondence, of my plans to spend some time during my upcoming sabbatical in Leuven, Belgium, and we made plans for a trip to Erlangen at that time. (more later). Schmitt, as newly appointed editor of the *ZAW,* also continued the policy of his predecessor Kaiser of quickly reviewing and publishing articles that I sent to him. In 1998 I was made a member of the editorial board of the journal, which was primarily an honorary position.

While at Chapel Hill, I did attempt to stay in touch with Canadian colleagues in the biblical field through the Canadian Society of Biblical Studies, which met together with the Conferences of the Learned Societies, and to offer papers there. In 1996 the meeting was to take place in late May at Brock University in St. Catharines, Ontario. The highlight of this conference for me was not in CSBS but in a session of the Canadian Historical Association where my daughter Deborah, who was then a graduate student in History at the University of Toronto, was giving a paper. It was, of course, superb and very well received. Elizabeth and I had driven up from North Carolina so that we had the car to get around. While at the meetings, we made a side-trip to Hamilton to visit with Malcolm Horsnell, an old friend from my time teaching in the Near Eastern Studies Department at the University of Toronto. He was a student then but was now on the faculty of McMaster University. We had corresponded earlier and had been invited to dinner with his wife Janet at his home. We had a wonderful visit there. Our primary reason for visiting Hamilton and McMaster was to consider retiring to this location in 2000 and to look over the housing in the region and other such matters, and I had been in touch with other members of the faculty as well. In the end, however, we chose to retire in Waterloo, Ontario.

In mid-1996 I received a request from the chair of the Department of Modern Languages and Comparative Studies of the University of Alberta, Richard Young, concerning the promotion of Ehud Ben Zvi to Full Professor. This might seem like an odd request in two respects, the relationship of biblical studies to this department, and the fact that Ben Zvi had received his doctorate only six years earlier. However, this department apparently contains a number of divisions, one of which includes Religion. Also Ben Zvi came to University of Alberta from Emory University, where he did his PhD with a prior MA from Tel Aviv University, and Max Miller told me at that time that he was a very exceptional student. At any rate, he had in six years produced quite an impressive list of publications, so that I and two other external assessments were able to persuade the University Faculty of Arts to promote him to Professor. I saw a lot of Ben Zvi through the meetings of academic societies to which we belonged, particularly the Canadian Society of Biblical Studies, and our friendship has continued up to the present day.

It is often the case that a scholar who has gained some notoriety in the field of biblical studies, is asked by young scholars, and not necessarily one's own students, for assistance in the form of writing a recommendation for an initial or improved academic position. I had a flood of such requests and after a while I had a file of earlier requests that I could use and update for the next time. Sometimes an institution, such as Southern Methodist University, would asked you for your advice on providing a number of possible candidates for a particular position, such as the William Power chair in biblical Hebrew. (I had known Bill Power for many years, since he was a graduate student at the University of Toronto when I was an undergraduate there.) So for Bill Power's sake, I took this on and gave them an extended list of the best eligible scholars I knew with an extended statement of their strength's. As it turned out, it was a waste of time because they simply gave it to the person that was already there. The other names were just window dressing for the university administration.

The Syrian Trip with Max Miller (1996)

One of the highlights of 1996 was the trip to Syria and Jordan with Max Miller and a group of faculty and doctoral students from Emory University. In early March of 1996 I received some email correspondence from Max about this trip, indicating that he had received a considerable amount of funding support, so that the cost to faculty would be $1500 each and for students $1000 each, which would cover only a fraction of the total cost of this 20 day tour. Julene Miller, Max's wife, who ran the travel agency, Academy International Travel Service Inc., would arrange for all of the details of the trip. Max was very familiar with the whole region of Syria, Jordan and Israel in which he had traveled often over many years and we had talked about making a trip together through Syria, where I had never been (except for that overland taxi ride from Beirut to Damascus and then to Jordan in 1964). My academic research and travel fund would cover the $1500 part of my expenses, so it was a wonderful opportunity for me. While the Emory travel fund, which would cover most of the expenses, was designed to be exclusively for the Emory Hebrew Bible Department, Max was able to swing including me in the group. When he asked if I was interested in the trip, I jumped at the chance. The group would consist of four Emory faculty members (Max Miller, John Hayes, Carol Newsom, and Neal Walls) and myself, along with 11 students. In addition to Max I also had known John Hayes for many years. I had met Carol before, but did not know her well before the trip, and Walls was a young scholar who had just joined their faculty. The students were, of course, quite unknown to me, but all of that would change over the course of three weeks.

In preparation for our trip, we all had certain assignments which included preparing presentations at various archaeological sites to help us interpret the ruins and understand the significance of the places that we were visiting. This included site plans and other materials that would be helpful in the presentation and inspection of the site. We all met at the Atlanta airport on the afternoon of July 21 and took off for Frankfurt, Germany, where we arrived in the morning the next day and then had a seven hour wait until we boarded our flight to Damascus, which arrived in Damascus at 7 p.m. in the evening. We stayed in a beautiful five-star hotel near the airport, the Cham Palace, a chain of hotels that we used throughout Syria. We had the hotel almost to ourselves and it was very comfortable after our long flight. I shared a room with a grad student, Armin Siedlecki, who was a Canadian from Saskatchewan, and we got on very well.

The next day we explored the city by tour bus, stopping at the great mosque and other important Muslim sites, and the great Damascus Suq (market place). We also drove up the side of the mountain to an Aramaic speaking village with an ancient church, still in use. On the following day we headed north by bus to the site of ancient Kadesh (Tell Nebi Mend) made famous by a battle between the Hittites and Ramesses II (who claimed a great victory, even though he was forced to retreat). Kadesh lies at the headwaters of the Orontes River. From there we moved north along the Orontes Valley to the great medieval Crusader fortress of Krak des Chevaliers, then on to the huge mound of Qatna, so long neglected but now being excavated by Syrians and Italians. From there we went to Hama (biblical Hamath) where we spent the night in the heart of the city. I also gave a talk on this site, which had been excavated many years earlier by my archaeology professor, Harald Ingholt, but the mound was now covered by vegetation and gardens, so that it was hard to find the contours of the old excavation.

The next day we set out from Hama following the Orontes and visited the great Roman city of Apamaea, then Tell Qarqar, the site of another famous battle between the Assyrians and a coalition of forces that included the rulers of Hamath, Damascus and Israel, the latter being none other than King Ahab. The Assyrians in their inscriptions claimed a great victory, but it was more like a draw. Heading across the Orontes Valley we climbed the western mountain range and visited the great fortress of Saladin at Qal'at Saladin. From there we descended to the Mediterranean coast and the resort city of Latakia. Our resort-hotel was right on the beach and we had time enough for a nice cool swim before our evening meal. This city was much more relaxed and western than those of the interior. The next morning we were off again heading north to Ras Shamra, ancient Ugarit, where, some years earlier, an interesting cache of literary texts in an alphabetic script of the fourteenth–thirteenth century BCE had been found among the impressive ruins of the Late Bronze Age, a find that had a great impact on biblical and Near Eastern Studies. This was Neal Walls's specialty and he made his presentation at this site. We then set off for Tell Mardikh (Ebla), another major site with a remarkable library of texts from the late third millennium BCE. This site was the discovery of Italian archaeologists. From there it was on to Aleppo for two nights and a day.

There was much to see in Aleppo itself, including its large market place (suq) and the citadel at the top of a very large ancient mound that was only beginning to be explored. Since our visit to Aleppo, much more has been done at this site. From Aleppo we made an excursion north to the Christian ruins of Qal'at Samaan near the border with Turkey. This overlooks the Orontes Valley and ancient Antioch, and beyond to the point where the Orontes River empties into the Mediterranean Sea. The whole valley is covered with the ancient ruins of churches of the mid- to late first millennium CE. On our way back to Aleppo we stopped at an Iron Age city of Ain Dara, where the archaeologists have uncovered the remarkable ruins of a temple of that era. There was also the statue of a huge Lion, lying on its side. It undoubtedly stood as one of a pair at the entrance to the city. Max took a picture of me standing beside it. We then returned to Aleppo for the night. I was struck, on the way back, at how many ancient tells (mounds) one could see as one traveled along the road through the countryside.

From Aleppo, the next day, we set out across the northern part of the Syrian desert until we came to the Euphrates at the point where it exits a large lake created by a modern dam and flows south towards the Iraq border. We followed it south, exploring the ruins of the Christian site of Resafa (Sergiopolis) in the desert and the historic Muslim site of Raqqa on the eastern side of the Euphrates, a slight detour along the main route. The road on the western side of the Euphrates brought us to our next stop at Deir ez-Zor. Our hotel had a large pool and although the water was not exactly cool, it was refreshing. The next day we made an excursion out of Deir ez-Zor to Dura Europos, a major Roman period city on the Euphrates, made famous by the ruins of a synagogue and early church found on the site. Large parts of the interior painted murals of these structures had been preserved and were removed and taken to the museum in Damascus (more on this later). Much of the city wall remained standing to a considerable height. Because the Synagogue and the church were built close to the city wall, when the city wall was being fortified against attach, these buildings were partly buried and thus much of their inner walls were preserved.

From Dura we headed south to Tell Hariri, close to the Iraq border. This was the site of ancient Mari, which was at its height in the time of Hammurabi, king of Babylon (ca. 1700 BCE). The rulers of these two cities were rivals and eventually Hammurabi destroyed the city of Mari. The great palace that was excavated by the French with its many cuneiform tablets was one of the great discoveries of the early twentieth century. My colleague Jack Sasson was an authority on these Mari texts that were so important for biblical studies in the Albright era. Much of the excavated ruin is under a canopy to protect it from the weather. From this site we returned to Deir ez-Zor to spend the night at our hotel.

From Deir ez-Zor the next morning we headed west across the Syrian dessert to the great oasis of Palmyra. The ride in the buss was very hot, even with some air-conditioning. The ruins of this great Roman city with its many temples and public buildings, its paved streets, its amphitheatre, its tower tombs and more, are very impressive. My Yale teacher, Harald Ingholt, did a lot of archaeological work here many years earlier, excavating tombs and publishing inscriptions. There were professional guides to help interpret the various structures on the site. (It is the monuments of this great city that have been so badly destroyer by Isis). We stayed the night in Palmyra and then headed west again to Damascus. We spent the afternoon in Damascus visiting the Museum with its many treasures. The most remarkable display, however, was the reconstruction of the interior of the Dura Europa synagogue with its amazing painted murals. One had to descend a set of stairs into a lower level of the museum and then enter a room with subdued light and take in the marvelous paintings covering the walls and ceiling. I had studied these paintings many years earlier with Professor Goodenough at Yale and was familiar with the fine replicas that the Yale expedition had made of these paintings for their own art museum, but this sight of the original murals was quite overwhelming. We also took a trip to the Suq in Damascus for any final souvenir purchases. I remember some of the meals that we had in the restaurants in Aleppo and Damascus and they were absolutely superb. Max knew all of the right places to visit.

From Damascus, the next day, we headed south towards the Jordanian border. Just north of the border were the ruins of the great Roman city of Bostra (Bosra). Here the ancient buildings were made from the black volcanic rock of the region. The finest structure was the very-well preserved Roman theatre with quite marvelous acoustics, so that in the top row of seats, still preserved, one could hear quite clearly the person speaking on the stage below. There was also a large Roman bath, and a reservoir. This remarkable site, like so many in Syria, was badly in need of major archaeological excavation and investigation. We stayed in the fine 5 star hotel in Bostra, which was almost empty. I also noted large parking areas that looked as if they had scarcely been used. Apparently, these had all been built in anticipation of some general peace accord with Israel that was to bring in a great influx of tourists, as it did in Jordan, but this was something that never happened. It should be noted that in the Roman period the city of Bostra was one of a number of major cities of the region then known as Arabia, which stretched from Bostra in the north, running east of the Jordan valley, to Palmira in the south.

The next morning we set out from Bostra and just beyond the Syrian city of Dara we crossed the Yarmuk River, which is the border with Jordan. Our first stop was the Roman city of Jerash, which I had visited a few times so many years before. I was amazed to see so many changes in the unearthing and reconstruction of the ancient ruins. There had been much more archaeological work, uncovering many more ruins of buildings along the main north-south street and so much more work on the major temples, theaters, and other public buildings. There is now also a charge for admission along with many souvenir shops, so that the whole place is commercialized. Nevertheless it is quite an impressive Roman city, and it gives some indication of what could happen with exploration and reconstruction of Bostra, Apamea and other such sites in Syria. From there we visited Aijlun to the west on the edge of the high plateau that overlooks the Jordan Valley. This site contained a castle fortification from the time of Saladin. After this visit we drove to Amman where we would stay for two nights. On the first full day in Amman we explored some of the sites in the city. It had grown quite dramatically from the place that I knew in the mid-60s. We also explored some of the sites in the region, such as Arak el-Amir in the Wadi Sir, which is a dramatic canyon that leads down from Amman to the Jordan River. Then we moved on to the town of Madaba with its famous ancient map mosaic on the floor of one of the churches, and to Mount Nebo, the traditional site from which Moses is thought to have viewed the promised land. On the day of our visit, the visibility was too poor to see very far. We also visited the archaeological site of Heshbon and some others in the region. We spent the night back in Amman.

We set out from Amman the next morning on a long journey south through biblical Moab and Edom. On the way we passed by the ruins of Dibon, capital of the

Moabites, then descended into the deep gorge of the Wadi Mojib (the Arnon River) and up again to the high Moabite plateau and south to Kerak, the great crusader fortress guarding this southern route. This time under the expert guidance of Max Miller we saw much more than I had on my previous visit in '65. Proceeding south we crossed another impressive valley, the Wadi Hasa (Zered River), and into Edom proper, passing various sites, including Buseira (Bosrah), the ancient capital of the Edomites. After a long day of travel we arrived at Petra and settled in at one of the new hotels outside the ancient city, with a grand view from which one can see Jebel Arun (Mt. Hor, the traditional site of the burial place of Aaron). What a dramatic change there was at Petra from that earlier visit thirty years before, from one small Department of Antiquities hostel at the entrance to the wadi that leads into the ancient site, to this great array of tourist hotels and all of the business activity that goes with it. The city of Petra inside the siq was also transformed with all of the archaeological activity that had taken place, to say nothing of the large number of vendors selling their trinkets and services. One place that I had not visited the first time was the famous "high place" (an ancient place of worship), which meant a long trek up the side of the mountain. We also climbed another mountain to the temple of ed-Deir. It was a busy and exhausting day.

After an overnight in Petra we headed south towards Aqabah. On the way, in Wadi Rum, we ran into mechanical problems with the coach, including a loss of air conditioning and then power, so that we had to disembark and wait in this desert region with no shade anywhere, until another coach was sent up from Aqabah. We finally got to the Israeli border, which was not busy but it still took a long time before our party was processed and permitted to proceed. Now we had a new coach and a Palestinian driver. We headed north up the Wadi Arabah that extends all the way from the Red Sea to the Dead Sea, much of it descending a long way down below sea level. From the Dead Sea we climbed up the Judean highlands to the ancient city of Arad. The plan had been to arrive there before the gates to the ancient city were closed, but with all of the delays, we were too late, and we could only view it from a distance behind a large perimeter fence. We stayed overnight in Arad.

Early the next morning, we left for Masada and climbed up to this ancient fortress built by Herod the Great and used later by the Jewish Zelots in their last stand against the Romans in their war of 66–70 AD. We visited the ruins on top, especially the remains of the synagogue, and then took an aerial car down to the bottom. From there we went to Ein Gedi, where we had lunch and some went for a dip in the Dead Sea. From there we went up to Qumran. Even though it is in the West Bank, it is completely controlled by the Israelis now, including the tourist trade and book shop there. I personally found this visit very depressing, by comparison with my earlier visit. However, the visit to Jericho was even more depressing than that of Qumran. The modern city of Jericho is a Palestinian enclave surrounded by Israeli control and is in a sad decline from the city I had known, which then had a constant connection by bus and cab with Jerusalem. That is no longer possible. Needless to say, the site of ancient Jericho was in sad shape with no funds to keep it up. From Jericho we went up to Jerusalem and booked into the Notre Dame Hotel, within a short walk from the old city.

The next day we headed north from Jerusalem to visit various archaeological sites. On our way we stopped at Birzeit University, to be joined by Dr. Khaled Neshef, professor of archaeology, and a group of his students. Because of the severe restrictions on their movement, these students were not able to visit the sites of Shechem and Samaria, so we took them there in our coach, which had such permission. There were military check-points on the way (we held our breath at each one), and made it to these places. Again, Samaria is also suffering from few tourists because of the Israeli restrictions. We travelled on some of the new highways build for the convenience of the Israeli settlers, on which the Palestinians are not permitted to travel, at very great inconvenience to them. This is because the old road that formerly crossed the path of the new highways were simply cut and blocked. We had great difficulty finding a route to ancient Bethel and Ai. One of the students who was from Gaza told us he could not return home for a visit the whole time he was in university because if he did he would not be able to return to school. Foreign tourists and visitors to Israel never see this side of the picture. The next day we made a visit to Bethlehem (through checkpoints) and had an informal lunch with the mayor. It was very pleasant and informative. In the wee hours of the morning of the next day the bus came for us and took us to the airport for the flight home. It is these personal experiences, both from my time in Israel, Palestine and Jordan in 1964–65 and these more recent visits that have shaped my perspective on the Israeli-Palestinian problem and made me impervious to the popular pro-Israel jargon that saturates the western media.

The Academic Year 1996–1997

The fall semester of 1996 was rather uneventful for the most part, with one exception. There was a hurricane that came through Chapel Hill during the night of September 5–6, which caused a lot of damage and power outage for two days in our area. Elizabeth and I were up in the middle of the night, aroused by the noise of the wind as it tore through the trees that surrounded our place on three sides. Some of these were huge oaks that we could see through a large window at the back of the house, and they were swaying back and forth as if they were mere saplings. It was terrifying and above the roar of the wind one could hear the breaking of tree limbs and the uprooting of trees down the slope behind our house. Fortunately, none of the trees fell on our place. The experience of that night was quite unforgettable. Surveying the damage in the neighborhood and along the trail in Bolinwood Park the next day, the number of large trees that littered the landscape was quite astounding. All of this happened over a weekend so that by Monday morning life was getting back to normal.

In contrast to the fall of '96, the spring semester of '97was quite busy. Because I was planning a sabbatical leave for the fall of '97 and the spring of '98, this meant that I had a lot of work to do in advance. The university would support me for half a year but it was up to me to find support for the other half, which I have regularly done in the past with considerable success. Even the university leave was given on a competitive basis so I had to submit my request along with my research plans for the period of the leave, and I was successful in obtaining a promise of support for the fall of 1997. For the spring of '98 I had for some time been in touch with Professor Marc Vervenna of the Catholic University of Leuven, Belgium, about spending this period of time at the Theological Faculty, doing my research there. It had a wonderful library that was very well equipped in biblical studies and other facilities that made it a great place to work. While I supplied all of the necessary documentation and a copy of my research proposal, Marc did all of the local ground work in ferrying the application through the necessary channels and by July of 1997 I was assured of an appointment as a visiting professor for the spring on '98.

Invited Lectures

During the spring semester of 1997 before my sabbatical, I was kept busy with three invited lectures. The first of these was an invitation to give a special presentation to the Swiss Society for the study of the Ancient Near East for its one-day seminar, to be held at Bern University on Feb 15th. The theme of the "So-called Succession Narrative" had to do with the literary history of the story of David. The plan was that both Otto Kaiser and I would present major papers on this theme and that we would exchange copies of our papers at least a month before the meeting. As has so often happened with me in the past, I had my paper in his hands in very good time while he did not give me a copy of his paper until he arrived at the meeting itself. In addition to Kaiser and me, Steve McKenzie was also there to give a paper, which was to be a response to the papers of Kaiser and me. However, as it turned out, his paper was largely in response to my paper, since he had it ahead of time, and he did not of course have Kaiser's paper. The final paper of the session was by Thomas Naumann of Bern University, a junior colleague of Walter Dietrich, which focused on the story of David's adultery and murder of Uriah, as set forth in 2 Samuel 11–12.

There was, as usual, some lively discussion and an opportunity to get to know some people a little better, including Walter Dietrich, whom I had met before, and Thomas Naumann, his assistant, whom I met for the first time. As a result of discussions with the latter I sent him a copy of by book on Abraham, which he did not have and for which he thanked me. He was later in touch with me about his appointment to the Old Testament professorship in Siegen as successor to Rainer Albertz who had moved on to the more important chair in Münster. Professor Ina Willi-Plein of Hamburg (successor to Klaus Koch's chair in Old Testament) was also at the Bern meeting and pressed me with a number of questions about my presentation, which I attempted to answer. Unfortunately, she and her husband Thomas Willi had to leave early, so I could not follow up immediately that discussion, but I wrote to her afterwards and sent her some recent articles. I told her that I felt badly that we did not have a chance to follow up the issues that were raised. She responded in due time with a very friendly letter, saying that she was "very sorry" that I felt badly and made clear that there was much more agreement with me about the need to treat the text as literature and was as critical as I was about the dangers of the current German approach. She expressed the hope that we would meet again at future meetings and we did, becoming good friends until the present day.

Another person I was glad to see at the Seminar was Hans-Heinrich Schmid. He had come down for the day, and even though he was no longer an active member, his son Konrad was now a young scholar in the field, and he was there, as well as many old friends of Hans-Heinrich. During the society's business meeting, which Hans Heinrich, Otto Kaiser and I did not attend, the three of us spent time drinking coffee and chatting together as old friends. At the end of the day I took the train from Bern back to Zurich with Hans Heinrich and stayed over at his place, giving me a chance to catch up with the family, and then flew out of Zurich the next day.

The next engagement I had in the spring semester was in mid-March of 1997. I had previously received an invitation from Christopher Matthews, secretary of the New England SBL to give the plenary address at their spring meeting at Wheaton College in Norton, Mass., which I accepted. Arrangements were then made over the course of several months from November to March, including the choice of a topic and the selection of two responders, who would receive copies of the paper a month before the meeting. The topic I proposed was "Methodologies of Comparison in the Study of Israelite Religion," which was agreed upon and the responses would be made by Kent Richards, the "CEO" of SBL, and Richard Clifford of Weston Jesuit School of Theology, which was closely associated with Harvard Divinity School, in Cambridge Mass. I knew both of these scholars. Clifford got in touch with me about these arrangements, but Richards did not bother to do so.

My interest in this topic stemmed from the fact that our department had a required course in the history of methodology in the study of religion for all first year graduate students and I had taken my turn on a few occasions to conduct this seminar. This forced me to become familiar with a wide range of methods, a number of which had been used rather indiscriminately in biblical studies. The paper would attempt to identify a number of major "schools" of biblical studies from the nineteenth and twentieth centuries and a few important examples of their application of a particular method to their understanding of Israelite religion. This is the kind of topic that would invite some lively exchange. As it turned out, this worked quite well with Clifford, who was well prepared, while Richards was completely unprepared and his remarks were largely ignored. In an email to me a few days later Chris Matthews wrote: "I am pleased that you enjoyed your stay with us in New England. You did us a great service with a superb and stimulating presentation. Comments in the wake of the session were positive to the degree of wanting a further session to begin working right away on some of the issues you highlighted."

The one-day conference ended with a wonderful dinner together. The next day I was taken back to Boston where I had an informal session with Harvard graduate students, but no faculty showed up for that. I later received a letter of apology from Peter Machinist with an excuse for not being able to attend. I sent him a copy of my address and we continued to be on good terms. There was among the group, however, a graduate from Harvard, Marsha White, who had recently completed her dissertation under Machinist and had it published with Scholars Press: *The Elijah Legends and Jehu's Coup*. We got into conversation at the meeting and she told me that she wanted to send me a copy of her thesis for some feedback on it. A few days later I received a copy. It was less than 100 pages of text, excluding end material, which is rather characteristic of Harvard dissertations, so it was a rather quick read, and after going through it, I sent her some remarks on it. It took her several months to answer my letter and my comments. In spite of our differences, she became one of my Harvard friends.

At about the same time that I received the invitation to the New England SBL, I also had an invitation from the Eastern Great Lakes SBL to be the "guest speaker" at their meeting in April of 1997. This request came from its president, John Barclay Burns of George Mason University in Fairfax,Virginia, with whom I was acquainted from previous SBL meetings. He was a former student of William McKane of St. Andrews in Scotland, for whom we shared a mutual admiration. Burns had a great sense of humor. The meeting would be held in Erie, Pennsylvania, not the easiest place to get to from Chapel Hill. The paper that was chosen out of the list of options I had submitted was "The Quest for Origins: Historical Criticism in the Late 19th and Early 20th Centuries." This topic, like the former one, looks at the obsession with "origins" in religious studies in this period and its impact on Old Testament studies as reflected in the figures of Wellhausen, Gunkel, Albright and others. As in the case of the previous topic, this one also received a good response. Most Old Testament scholars are trained in theology and their biblical interpretation is oriented to the latest movement in biblical interpretation. A few become obsessed with a current method in the study of religion without a wider historical context of the discipline. Ever since working with Goodenough, I became sensitive to the importance of understanding my discipline within this wider context and of encouraging this awareness among my students and colleagues in biblical studies.

At the same time that I was involved in the preparation and presentation of these guest lectures for the regional SBL conferences, I was engaged in correspondence with distant academic friends. One of these was Nadav Na'aman of Tel Aviv University, who sent me some recent off-prints of his publications in early 1997, and of course they required some response to make this dialogue worthwhile. I wrote at length to him about them, and he replied in kind. Na'aman is such a careful scholar of the period of the monarchies of Judah and Israel and so well informed of all the relevant data that he became a valuable source of information. I told him about the Syrian trip the summer before and especially about the Ain Dara temple. He of course could not travel to Syria but he had read all the published reports and had lots to say about it. Our correspondence was a very fruitful interaction and led to my close association with others at Tel Aviv as well. One of Na'aman's former students was Cynthia Edenburg who was now teaching at the Open University of Israel and whom I had met earlier. In the summer of '97, she sent me a copy of the paper that she had given during the World Congress for Judaic Studies and was preparing for publication, with the request: "If you have the time and the subject matter interests you, I would greatly appreciate any comments you might have." I found the time and I did reply. The piece was published the following year in the *Scandinavian Journal of the Old Testament*.

Another regular interlocutor was Steve McKenzie, mentioned earlier, whose primary focus was the Deuteronomistic History, and who wrote to me about his latest research and publication on this topic in order to solicit my views, as he did in the spring of 97. He also asked me to write a chapter on "The Pentateuch," the opening piece of about 50 pages for a text book, *The Hebrew Bible Today*, which he was editing for Westminster/John Knox Press. That was also done during this period. He sent me his revisions in July of 97, and the book appeared the following year. I was no sooner finished with that project when I had a request from John Barton of Oxford, asking me to do an article on "Moses" for a reference volume *The Biblical World*, following a very precise format, and covering about 14 pages in print. This was done during the summer of 97, although it did not appear until about 5 years later. I was also asked in April to do an article for a *Festschrift* for my good friend Robert Culley of McGill, being put together by his students. This I also wrote up that summer.

In July of 1997 the SBL International Meeting was held in Lausanne, Switzerland, and Thomas Römer played a major role in organizing it, although he was given little credit for his efforts. He also was responsible for bringing together a number of prominent scholars for three sessions on the topic of "The Future of the Deuteronomistic History," most of them close friends of mine. I contributed a paper: "The Deuteronomistic History: Can it Avoid Death by Redaction." Römer also laid out a memorable reception for participants and friends at his home. Subsequent to the meeting the manuscripts of the special sessions on the Deuteronomist were submitted and published in 2000 under the same program title and edited by Römer.

The Sabbatical Leave of 1997–1998

As indicated above, I was on sabbatical leave for the whole academic year of 1997–98, but during the fall semester I stayed in Chapel Hill. I tried to avoid my office in the Department as much as possible and did much of my work on my research project in the

UNC and Duke Divinity School libraries. The latter has a very fine collection in biblical and ancient Near Eastern studies. I also worked in my study at home. Nevertheless, I could not avoid some of the responsibilities as a senior member in the Department. During the fall semester I nominated Bart Ehrman for a Bowman and Gordon Gray Professorship. It is an award designed for particularly promising younger faculty and has a three-year term with an annual salary supplement of $5,000. Its special emphasis is on teaching and Bart was very strong in this area, in addition to his scholarship. He was awarded the fellowship in 1998. It was a big bounce up the ladder to what has become for him a very successful career.

The topic of my sabbatical research was the so-called Covenant Code of Exodus 21–23, and I had already anticipated this project with a paper in Marc Vervenna's Leuven conference in 1995, which was entitled "Cultic Laws in the Covenant Code (Ex 20:22–23:33) and their Relationship to Deuteronomy and the Holiness Code." This was published in a collection of the conference papers in 1996, and in the fall of 1997 I received a request from Bernard (Bernie) Levinson for a copy of the paper. He also sent me an invitation to join and participate in the newly formed Biblical Law section of SBL. Since I was already committed to the sections on Pentateuch and on the Deuteonomistic History I could hardly commit to the one on Law, but he assured me that I would be welcomed to participate whenever possible. Eckard Otto, with whom I had a strong difference of viewpoint on biblical law, was also prominent in that group and Levinson was a kind of mediating force between the two of us. Bernie had also just published his book on *Deuteronomy and the Hermaneutics of Legal Innovation*, a work that would get serious attention in my own work on the Covenant Code and its relationship to Deuteronomic law. So for the next few years Bernie and I would engage in much lively discourse over biblical law.

In late fall of 1997 at the SBL meeting in San Francisco I gave a paper on "The Geography of the Exodus," in which I argued that the only period of time in which the account of the route out of Egypt and the place names given in the story made any sense was the early to mid-sixth century BCE, and that this was important to dating the Exodus story and this particular author. I sent a copy to my old friend Don Redford, the Egyptologist, at the University of Toronto, and he wrote back expressing his strong support: "I was absolutely delighted by your paper. I see eye-to-eye with you on 95% of it," and then proceeded to discuss his point of disagreement (which I could not accept). However, getting this much agreement with Don was a rarity for anyone and I highly respected his opinion on matters Egyptian. He has done so much travel and excavation in various parts of Egypt and is recognized as a world class scholar in Egyptology, but unfortunately our paths do not often cross as they did when we were colleagues so many years earlier.

As indicated above, the preparations for my sabbatical and writing of applications for support are extensive and began a year or more earlier. After getting approval and promise of adequate funds for my fall leave and for my spring stay in Leuven,

Belgium, I then was involved in the process of gaining all of the necessary documentation (far more than for the UK), in order to get the required residency permissions, funds, and housing in Leuven. This process did not even end until after we arrived and were settled in Leuven, which demands special permission to live within the city boundary. Even though I was recognized by the Catholic University of Leuven as a Senior Fellow, the documentation provided by the university to the local authorities used the status of "student" for housing. There was, of course, little point in trying to understand these matters.

Study Leave in Leuven, Belgium, January to June, 1998

The last few days before departure were hectic, with all the packing for the six months from winter to summer and all the equipment and research materials. My son Peter and his partner Kris would be taking care of our place in our absence. We left on New Year's Day. The flight over the Atlantic was about the roughest we have even had, dealing with a large storm, which would follow us and arrive in Belgium a day or so after our arrival. We were met by Marc Vervenna at the airport with a small car so that getting all of our belongings into it, in addition to ourselves was a challenge, but we made it. We stayed in an apartment in the Begijnhof. We had stayed in this place previously in the summer of 1989 during the IOSOT congress, when it was mostly empty of students and it was quiet and pleasant. But it was not so suitable now, and was very noisy and rather cold in the winter, so we were disappointed with these accommodations. But we made do. It was at least convenient with easy access to the university and other facilities. It took a few days to get settled in with all of the registration as aliens, my status with the university, banking and change of currency, shopping, etc. At the theological school of the university I was set up with an office in the library, equipped with a computer and email access, all of which was very convenient for my work. I also had easy access to other parts of the seminary and to the senior lunch and coffee room, where I could get my morning coffee and occasionally meet with other faculty there. I was very cordially received by those in the seminary, especially Marc Vervenna, who was also dean of the theological faculty, and his two students, Hans Ausloos and Benedicte Lemmelijn (husband and wife) who had both just completed their doctoral degrees. In addition I had a close association with Professors Johan Lust in Old Testament at the seminary and Anton Schoors, who was in the university faculty in the Department of Near Eastern Studies. I had a lot of contact with all of these persons and they were very helpful. In addition to these, there was Professor Erik Eynikel, who was a frequent visitor to the theological faculty where he did his research. He was a member of the faculty at the Catholic University of Nijmegen in the Netherlands, but was also involved with Lust in a research project in the theological library in Leuven. As it turned out, Vervenna was becoming so involved with administration (he later became President of the University) that I saw much more of Lust,

Schoors and Eynikel. In fact, Elizabeth and I met and were entertained by Eynikel's family in their home and became good friends.

Leuven is a wonderful place to spend a sabbatical, quite apart from all the academic reasons. The city, better known by its historic French name as Louvain, is a wonderful place to explore, with its many historic buildings, gardens, and shops. It also has easy access by train and busses, to other great cities and towns, such as Brussels, Antwerp, Ghent, Brugge, Mons, and many smaller places, with so many great art galleries and museums and fine architecture and parks. Right next door to Belgium is the Netherlands, which is equally accessible, and while we had been there before, we took in many new sites and places during this sabbatical. And to the east of Belgium was Cologne in Germany, with its magnificent cathedral and many other places beyond, including Luxembourg. We often took advantage of Saturday, Sunday or weekend railway specials. When members of Elizabeth's family—her brother John, his wife Nancy and daughter Barbara and Elizabeth's sister Eunice and her daughter—came for a visit, we took them on a tour of some of the places with which we were now familiar.

With Leuven so convenient by train to both the Netherlands and Germany I was frequently invited to participate in conferences or serve as a guest lecturer. When the Dutch society for Old Testament studies had its winter meeting in late January I was a guest speaker at which I gave a paper on my current studies in biblical law, with particular focus on the Covenant Code of Exodus 21–23. While the meeting was conducted in Dutch, I gave my paper in English, which everybody there understood, although I had no trouble with Dutch, the language that was spoken at home in my childhood. The subject of my paper was also of special concern to a leading Dutch scholar, Cornelis Houtman, who had published a commentary on the Covenant Code (in German) at just about that time and he was called upon to respond to my paper. I had met him earlier at a conference in Leuven and had a high regard for his work. He was more conservative than I but a very learned scholar. We had a good exchange of views about my paper and remained on good terms, and I wrote a piece for his *Festschrift* a few years later.

Some months after this conference, I made another trip to the Netherlands. A special symposium was organized in early April by Bob Becking of Utrecht University, which consisted of a couple dozen scholars from the Netherlands, Germany, Switzerland, Scandinavia, UK, and Israel. I was invited to join the group as the lone representative from America, because I was conveniently close by in Leuven. The theme of the symposium was *The Crisis of Israelite Religion* with a special focus on the exilic and post-exilic periods, and it took place at a conference center in Soesterberg near Utrecht in April, 1998. My own contribution, entitled "In the Babylonian Exile with J," was an attempt to show how the Pentateuchal author, the Yahwist, understood and transformed the traditions about Israelite's origins to make them meaningful for the Babylonian exiles in the mid-sixth century BCE. Such occasions as this, spending a few days together with a small group of scholars from different regions, allowed one to renew old relationships and make new ones, in a stimulating atmosphere. In particular, I became better acquainted with Bob Becking and later I made a separate trip to Utrecht to give a guest lecture at the University of Utrecht.

Sometimes when I was invited to a conference or a separate speaking engagement, Elizabeth would join me and we would build a trip around the event. Thus, the symposium in Soesterberg gave us an occasion to visit some of my father's family before the meeting, one cousin and her husband (Nel and Dick) who lived in a suburb of Utrecht, another cousin and his wife (Jaap and Adri), who lived in Ermelo, as well as an old Aunt who live in Apeldoorn. Then after the symposium we visited two of my cousins in Arnhem on my mother's side of the family, and took in some sites, such as the "bridge too far" over the Rhine, with its memorial to the Canadians who had fought there in the Second World War. This was the first time that I had met all these cousins and we kept in touch with at least some of them for a while afterwards.

On another occasion in late May, when I went to Erlangen as a guest of Hans-Christoph Schmitt to give a lecture there, Elizabeth came with me, and Schmitt and his wife were very gracious hosts. They took us to see Nurnberg and Bamberg and a drive around the region of Franconia. That evening we had a wonderful celebration dinner at the home of Hans-Christoph Schmitt and his wife, along with a few of his grad students and spouses, which was most enjoyable. We stayed in a pleasant country inn overnight, and the next day we went into Erlangen to the university where I gave a guest lecture while Elizabeth did some sightseeing in town. We had a fine lunch with faculty and grad students, one of whom gave me a copy of his dissertation. I was quite close to Schmitt, who was also the editor of *ZAW*, and he was always after me to publish in that journal, which I was happy to do.

From Erlangen we went to Munich, which was not intended as an academic stop, but the chance for Elizabeth to see some of the city, which I had toured on a previous trip. The next day we did a tour of the city center on foot and walked out as far as the University. While at the hotel that evening I received a phone call from Christoph Levin, which was a great surprise, because I do not know how he knew I was in the city and at this particular hotel. He was now a professor at the University of Munich and wanted us to get together. It was arranged that we would meet for a coffee or beer at a place outside of the city's main art galleries while Elizabeth spent her time looking at works of art. I had first met Levin earlier in Paris in 1992 and we were good friends. He brought along a few companions from the university and we had an enjoyable visit. After another day of touring Munich and enjoying some good meals we returned to Leuven.

At other times I made the trip alone. I went to Muenster in Germany to give a lecture to the Protestant faculty of theology at the invitation of Rainer Albertz, and was also a guest in his home. No one from the Catholic faculty was present at the lecture, which I considered odd, even though I knew some in Old Testament studies on that faculty. This division between Protestant and Catholic was typical of Germany in general. At the University of Toronto shared activities between Catholic and none Catholic institutions was very frequent. On another occasion I was invited by Eric Eynikel to give a lecture on the David story at the University of Nijmegen, this time to a Catholic faculty. For Eric, who lived in Belgium, this trip was just a daily commute and we traveled together. For me these simple occasions of giving quest lectures and meeting new colleagues were always stimulating and enjoyable. In fact I have been a guest lecturer at far more institutions in Europe and the UK than I ever have in North America, and as a consequence I am far better known there, and am acquainted with far more scholars there than on this side of the Atlantic.

Leuven (Louvain) is an old city of great historical interest. Founded in 1425, and with a university and town center over 450 years old, it was celebrating its anniversary with parades and open houses of the university, the Cathedral, and the town hall on the last day of May and the beginning of June. We took the tours, watched a "medieval" parade and had a very enjoyable time. During the rest of the month of June, with the end of our time in Leuven in site, we tried to take every chance we could to see places that we had not yet visited. While I was still working in the libraries, Elizabeth took a train trip to Ieper (Ypres) with its memorials to WWI and was most impressed by the whole experience. Then on Saturday we went down to Ghent to view the famous "Mystic Lamb" in one of the churches, and visit the Folklore Museum. The following Saturday we took a train up to The Hague and toured the city center with a guide book. The next day we did Antwerp's art museum and a wonderful zoo and gardens in the center of the city. The following Saturday we were off to Luxenburg and walked around the center. A day later we toured Mons with its World War I Canadian Museum and memorials. Our final trip on the last Saturday was to Maastricht, that southern-most extension of the Netherlands just north of Liege. It was a very pleasant finale to our sightseeing trips. A few days later and after much final packing and other last minute matters we there off on our return flight to the US and home.

Last Two Years in Chapel Hill

Returning to Chapel Hill on the first of July hardly meant the beginning of a holiday, but rather the need to get everything ready for the new school year, which started about mid-August. In addition there was always a flood of other academic matters, once it was clear that I was back in town. While I had been away I had been made vice-president of the Canadian Society of Biblical Studies, which meant that I would be on the executive committee with certain responsibilities for the next two years, with the second year, 1999–2000 as president. One of my tasks as v-p was extending an invitation for the Peter Craigie guest lecture for the meeting in 1999. In this case it was to be Professor James Kugel of Harvard University (which he accepted) and then working out the necessary travel arrangements. It also meant chairing the business meeting at the conference, as well as the session that featured the presidential address. One of the members of that executive was William (Bill) Morrow, whose specialty was in biblical law, and I got to know him very well. The annual meeting of my presidential year was held in Edmonton in late May, 2000 on the University campus. My presidential address was "Creative Imitation in the Hebrew Bible," which was later published in the Canadian journal *Studies in Religion*, 29 (2000) 395–409. The reason for this choice of publication was that it was a longstanding commitment by the society to support the journal in this way, but the obvious drawback is that few biblical scholars abroad would ever see it.

Honors Received for Service and Scholarship

In the spring of 1999 Thomas Römer, as Professor of Old Testament and Dean of the theological faculty of the University of Lausanne put my name forward to the counsel of deans of the university as a candidate for an honorary doctorate of the university. I was notified in a letter from the rector of the university, dated June 11th, that I was accepted for this honor, which would take place on Saturday, 30 October 1999, and they would also cover the expenses for transportation and hotel for two days. I replied on June 22 that I accepted their invitation to their convocation to receive this honorary degree and to be their guest for that weekend. I stated: "This will be one of the great highlights of my academic career and I am deeply moved by this recognition of my work from a major European university."

On the Thursday of October 28 I took the overnight flight to Geneva, arriving the next morning, where I was met at the airport by Thomas and took a train from there to Lausanne. I was booked into the hotel which was down by the lakeshore. After relaxing for the afternoon, Thomas again picked me up and took me to meet the theological faculty at a special dinner for the occasion, after which I returned to my hotel. The next morning, after a breakfast at the hotel Thomas met me and took me to the appropriate building in the university. All of those involved in the ceremony, those receiving honorary degrees, their academic sponsors and university academic officials and rector gathered to don their gowns. From there we proceeded in orderly procession to the auditorium for the ceremony, which consisted of a learned presentation by one of the degree recipients, followed by each of the honorees receiving their degree along with a statement of their special accomplishments. This ceremony was followed by a fancy lunch put on by the rector for all of the honorees and their sponsors.

It was apparently the practice at this time of the academic year for the theological faculty to have a gathering of the department, chaired by the dean, in this case Thomas, in which an invited guest would give a lecture, and the afternoon was taken up by this event. Among those at this meeting I was surprised to see Albert de Pury, who had come up from Geneva. He told me that he had come because he and others, such as Hans Heinrich had expressed their strong support for this honor and he wished to congratulate me personally. After a quiet supper with just Thomas and myself I returned to my hotel and the next day took a flight by way of New York back to Chapel Hill.

Less than a month after I returned from Lausanne, another pleasant surprise awaited me at the annual SBL meeting, which takes place the last weekend in November before American Thanksgiving. It is customary in this great mob of scholars for a group of friends whom you only see once a year to get together for a lunch or dinner on an informal basis, and some of my associates suggested that we get together for a dinner on the last day, which suited me just fine. So after some afternoon sessions we met at an agreed place to walk to the restaurant. I was a little surprised that there was a rather large number and someone had already decided on a place to go that could handle this group. When we got there I discovered that a place had been reserved for our large group, just for us. This was too much and I asked how all this happened. Only then was I informed that this was a special get together in my honor, and after the wonderful meal there was the surprising revelation that a book had been put together—a *Festschrift*—which was then given to me. It was put together by Thomas Römer, Steve McKenzie and my former student Kenton Sparks, who had gotten in touch with a broad spectrum of old friends. There were 22 contributors in all, and they all reflected so many memories of good times and pleasant relationships that are mentioned in these narratives.

The title of the book I was given, *Rethinking the Foundations: Historiography in the Ancient World and in the Bible* (Essays in Honour of John Van Seters), picks up on the 1965 *JBL* article of Fred Winnett: "Reexamining the Foundations," and the contributions by the authors strongly represent this spirit of "reexamining" by all these scholars. In addition to all of these articles there are two sets of opening remarks that are deeply personal. The one is an opening tribute by my very dear friend, Hans Heinrich Schmid, entitled "John Van Seters: Freund und Kollege," which radiates the wonderful friendship that we had. He will always be someone very special in my memory. A second piece was done by Kenton Sparks, "A Tribute to John Van Seters" which contains a biographical sketch, my role as "mentor" and "academic advisor" and as "a friend." That friendship has continued to the present day. Likewise in Steve McKenzie's remarks in the book's introduction, he recalls the time of our first encounter, which I have outlined earlier in these memoirs, and they are worth repeating here. Steve states:

> I first met John as a participant in his NEH summer seminar on historiography at Chapel Hill a decade ago. Since then I have come to think of him as a good friend. We have traveled together at conferences and remained in close contact through email. I frequently solicit his scholarly opinion and have found him unfailingly generous in sharing his insights. I greatly admire the unique combination of literary sensitivity and critical acumen that is the hallmark of his work and that has resulted in *rethinking the foundations* of biblical scholarship. Cheers, John.

One could scarcely ask for a greater reward for a scholarly career than such tributes as these.

The spring semester, in addition to my teaching and departmental responsibilities, was taken up with preparations for our move back to Canada and to the new house that we had purchased in Waterloo, Ontario. While I was preoccupied with my responsibilities at the university, Elizabeth travelled to Waterloo to take care of the final settlement of the purchase and possession of the newly built house. In the course of packing up my academic library, I gave some of it to my two doctoral students, Kent and Mark. Regarding the department, the academic year ended on a somewhat sour note, due to a split among my departmental colleagues over the granting of tenure to a recent junior appointment. I supported the giving of tenure against the view of some of my colleagues, but the granting of tenure prevailed. However, it left those who had opposed that outcome unhappy. As a result the department sendoff that Elizabeth and I received at the home of one of my colleagues was a very modest one with the conspicuous absence of a few of the sore losers. The young scholar who had been awarded tenure had a Bar Mitsvah for his son, to which I was invited, to express his appreciation for my support for his career, and it was a very happy occasion. At the end of the school year I was no longer the James A. Gray Professor of Biblical Studies. Instead, the University made me Distinguished University Professor Emeritus by the Faculty of Arts and Sciences. This honor was made in recognition of both my lengthy tenure as chairman of the department and my scholarly publication record.

A few years later the University honored me again. A wealthy contributor to the Faculty of Arts and Sciences had financed the creation of a number of 5 year "professorships" to serve as supplements to salaries and research expenses for promising young tenured scholars in Arts and Sciences. However, instead of the donor's name being attached to these awards, each 5-year award would be named after a particular distinguished retired professor in the Arts and Sciences, but the recipient could not be someone in the same department as the named scholar. Now it so happened that after having been retired for a few years I received a notice from the Faculty of Arts and Sciences that a young scholar in the History Department had been awarded the John Van Seters Professorship for the next 5 years. After those 5 years were up I was again informed that the John Van Seters Professorship was awarded to a young scholar in Psychology. And if I live long enough it could happen again. In each case I was given the name of the recipient and the information in how I could get in touch with him, which I did, and I enjoyed my extended email dialogues with both of them.

At the end of the spring semester and the school year of 2000, which corresponded with the end of my teaching career, we had been heavily preoccupied with all of the tasks that were involved in our move back to Canada. The house was sold in Chapel Hill and a new one purchased in Waterloo, Ontario. All of my books and other possessions were removed from my departmental office and packed for the movers. My son Peter and his partner Kris would stay in their home in Durham, NC, which would mean that in the future visiting them, or their visiting us, would entail a long trip of about 800 miles by car. In addition to this, the move back to Canada entailed a major break with so many family friends and university colleagues, in spite of all the promises to keep in touch, which usually meant an extended note on a Christmas card. In the end, the major factor in the decision to move back to Canada was that we were Canadians and that sense of identity had never really left us the whole time that we were in the US.

10

The Move Back to Canada and Life in Retirement

The move back to Canada went quite well, with the moving van arriving at the US-Canadian border at the same time as we did, and after going through the repatriation process and customs clearance, we all set out for our new home in Waterloo. All of our furnishing were unpacked and put in their appropriate place, including a spacious study where I would begin my new career of research and writing in retirement. Of course, with a newly built house in which the property had received minimal landscaping, there was a lot of gardening work to make it the way we wanted it, but that still left me a lot more time than I had had in the past, for research and writing. I had access to the use of two libraries, one at Wilfrid Laurier University (the institution in which I had taught with Norm Wagner the first two years of my career) and the other at the University of Waterloo, both of which were easy to get to by bus or bicycle. If the books were not in either library, I could order then from interuniversity library loan. There was also a group of biblical scholars, most of them retired, who met on a regular basis for a "Biblical Colloquium." While it was a pleasant social gathering, its primary purpose was to discuss a paper by one of the members of the group that had been distributed in advance. Needless to say, I presented a number of my articles, which I had previously written, for discussion on these occasions. While the facilities for research in Waterloo could not compare with those at the University of Toronto and at Duke Seminary in North Carolina, the arrangement worked out fairly well.

At the time that we moved from Chapel Hill to Waterloo my daughter Deborah was finishing up her doctoral studies at the University of Toronto and living in a nearby apartment in the city. She received her doctorate in history along with her boyfriend, Adam Crerar in the same field of study, and within a short period of time they were married. The search was then on for Adam to find an academic position, which was no easy task. It just so happened that a position in the History Department opened up at Wilfrid Laurier University and after being interviewed, Adam was given the job. This was good fortune in many respects for all of us, and we set about to help them find a house, which we succeeded in doing, not far from the university. Not very long after that our grandson, Hugh Crerar was born. Of course, in all of these events, the graduations, the marriage and the birth of Hugh, the joy was shared my Adam's parents, Tom and Dory Crerar, who lived in London, Ontario, about an hour and a half's drive from Waterloo. Our good fortune of having the family of Deborah, Adam and our only grandson, Hugh living nearby cannot be emphasized too much.

After five years of living in a large house in Waterloo we decided that it was too much for us to continue there and so we sold the house and moved into a townhouse that was part of Luther Village, a retirement community near the center of town, across the street from the large Waterloo Park. It was also much closer, within easy walking distance, to the two universities and the home of Deb and Adam. Luther Village consisted of two main components. The central component was the main building which contained all of the offices and activities components, including a chapel and a restaurant, as well as five floors of apartments. The second component was made up of several streets with semi-detached townhouses, of which ours was one of them. All of this was contained within the large grounds owned by Luther Village. One could engage in the many activities or not as one wished. The facilities of Luther Village was owned and operated by a Lutheran organization that was located in northern Waterloo at Lutherwood on Benjamin Road, and revenue made from this retirement community was used to finance their charitable projects. The residents at Luther Village had a Residence Advisory Board, whose task it was to communicate with the management their various concerns about how the place was being run and maintained. About a year after we moved in I was approached by some of the residents to become a member of the Resident Advisory Board (RAB), and after frequently rejecting the appeals I was eventually persuaded to become a member, and two years later I ended up as Chairman of the Board. There were a number of major issues that had arisen between the residence and the Lutherwood board over a long list of repairs and who was to be responsible for the expenses they entailed, and the timetable for their being done. This involved three of us from RAB in particular, myself as chairman, the vise-chairman, and the chair of the budget committee. While we were reasonably successful in our efforts, it was very time consuming and not quite what I expected to do in my retirement. Consequently, after my time as chair ended I left RAB and could not be persuaded to get involved again.

A word must be said about my relationship with the academic community, while living in Waterloo. While I missed very much my association with all of my former colleagues in Chapel Hill, Durham and the surrounding region, I did for a time try to renew and maintain some relationship with my former department at the University of Toronto. Some of my old colleagues, such as Jack Holladay and John Wevers, were still there, and new connections were made with the current faculty. However, as time passed, some, such as John Wevers, passed away and my trips became less frequent. A few remarks, however, should be made about one couple, Paul Dion and Michele

Daviau, who live in Waterloo and who still have strong connections with the Near and Middle East Studies Department in Toronto. I had known Paul since my time at WLU in the 1960s through the Canadian Society of Biblical Studies, when he taught at a Catholic university in Ottawa. Later he came to the Department of Near Eastern Studies in the mid-1970s, at the time when I was teaching there, to do some advanced work in Aramaic for a doctoral degree. When I left Toronto for Chapel Hill, Paul was given my position in the department and he remained at the University of Toronto until he retired in 1999. While at Toronto Michele Daviau came to the department to do some graduate work in Near Eastern Archaeology under Jack Holladay and received her doctorate in that field. During this period Paul and Michele fell in love and married. After Michele graduated she was given a position in the field of archaeology at WLU in Waterloo, while she continued to maintain a connection with the department in Toronto. Paul, however, kept his place of residence in Toronto until his retirement. Both Paul and Michael were active in the Canadian Society of Biblical Studies so that when I went to the CSBS meetings rather frequently while in Chapel Hill, we became good friends. When Paul retired from Toronto he moved to Michele's residence in Waterloo, where I saw a lot of them. Michele established an international reputation with her archaeological work in Jordan. They are both retired now and recently moved into the Luther Village where Elizabeth and I live, so we see a lot of them.

Some Notable Trips and Conferences

The Von Rad Centennial—October 2001

Early in 2000 I was informed that there would be a Centennial Conference in honor of Gerhard von Rad on the 100th anniversary of his birth (1901) in the form of a grand four-day symposium (October 18–21, 2001) to take place in Heidelberg, Germany. To this event I was invited, along with a large number of other scholars (at least 100), all travel and accommodation expenses paid for by the University of Heidelberg. In addition to the opening ceremonies on the first day, the following two days were taken up with scholarly papers presented in 8 parallel groups with assigned responses made to each major paper. The group that I was in was concerned with the Old Testament and history and the particular issue assigned to me was to discuss whether the Pentateuch was primarily a law book (Torah) or historiography. For me the issue was not either/or but both/and, with the title of my paper, "The Pentateuch as Torah and History: In Defence of von Rad." My contribution was intended as a criticism of Professor Rendtorff of Heidelberg and a number of scholars who had recently chosen to follow him. This session was chaired by Erhard Blum, a student of Rendtorff, who had little to say about my paper at that time, but kept his comments for the publication of the session papers when they later appeared. This, of course, deprived me of responding to his criticisms at the time of the conference itself.

The person who was actually assigned to respond to my paper was the Israeli scholar, Alexander Rofé. I had sent him a copy of my paper well ahead of time, but he had decided to do something quite different and wrote up a short paper of his own. I was quite surprised by this and not too happy about it, because my paper did not get the attention it deserved, until much later when Blum produced a response for the conference publication. Now Alex Rofé was a good friend of mine and he sensed that this move of his had not been such a good idea, so after the session he apologized and invited me to lunch at an Italian hotel where he had stayed for a while before the symposium started. He also gave me a copy of his paper at that time. What was remarkable about this copy was that it had been hand written and made on the stationary of this same hotel a few days earlier.

A collection of the papers given in this section of the symposium did not appear until four years later with Erhard Blum serving as the editor responsible for its production. What is significant is that Blum rearranged the order of the papers, placing Rofé's paper (which was supposed to be a response to my paper) ahead of mine and then adding a long paper of his own right after mine, which was clearly intended as a response to my paper. Furthermore, Blum's paper was written well after the symposium because it made reference to an article of mine that was published a year *after* the symposium. The result was that he had the last word on the subject with no chance for me to respond to his paper. In fact, there was nothing new in what he had to say.

During the symposium Erhard Blum invited the group in our section, along with a few others to an evening of festivities at his place in Mannheim. Since it was several kilometers west of Heidelberg, transportation was arranged for us. Blum was a very gracious host and it was an enjoyable evening together. Whatever our differences on the academic level may be, I continue to have great respect for him, and it took far too long for him to receive the respect and the academic appointment that as a scholar he so richly deserved.

In addition to the symposium there was a certain amount of sightseeing of the city, most notably the great castle high up on the slope of the mountain that overlooks Heidelberg. The castle, with its high defensive walls, was almost a city in itself with many great buildings constructed by different rulers and enclosed within the castle walls. There were guides at various locations to explain the buildings and palaces and their histories. In Old Town there were many other attractions, such as the large Gothic University Church, and other buildings of the old University. On the day after the symposium, three of us, Bernard Levinson, Bill Morrow, and I, who were all staying an extra day, decided to take the old bridge across to the north side of the Neckar River and climb up the high hill to get a great view of the Old City. The map we were using had a number of viewing spots marked, depending how high you wanted to go, the higher up, the better the view. Much of the mountain was all woodland, and the highest lookout spot on the tourist map had a great view of the city. However, the road and trails seemed to go up higher to something beyond so we climbed up further.

Eventually we came into a clearing in the middle of the woods in which there was an open-air theater looking down on a stage. On a sign there was an explanation that this place was built and used during the period of Nazi domination for the indoctrination of the youth. It presently does not receive much notice in tourist brochures and we all agreed that looking down on it now was a very chilling experience.

For me personally the high point of the conference came at the end of the opening day (the 19th) in which there was a banquet at the Prinz Carl building in the Kornmarket. When I arrived at the entrance I was met by Konrad Schmid, who told me that a place had been reserved for me and took me to a table near the front of the hall, where, to my surprise, were seated his father and mother, Hans Heinrich and Christa. For us this was a wonderful reunion. They had come up to Heidelberg from Zurich just for this occasion and would be returning the next day. Also at the table was another friend of both Hans Heinrich and me, Professor Klaus Koch of Hamburg University. Needless to say it was a very enjoyable evening. Little did I realize at the time that this would be the last time that I would see Hans Heinrich and Christa, so the memories of that evening are especially dear to me.

South Africa: August 24—September 23, 2002

One of the highlights of 2002 was my trip to South Africa for a month of travel and lectures. For some time prior to this event, Johann Cook of the University of Stellenbosch, and a close friend for many years, had been speaking to me about the possibility of making such a trip and it was finally arranged that I would do so in the late summer of 2002, which was early spring in South Africa. The one problem that had to be overcome was the fact that Johann specialized in textual criticism and Septuagint studies, whereas my work was in historical and literary criticism of the Hebrew Bible. To overcome this barrier Johann negotiated the cooperation of Professor Andries Breytenbach of the University of Pretoria to act as my sponsor and solicit a request for funds from the National Research Foundation. All of the arrangements for making the application were worked out at the IOSOT meeting the previous summer in Basel, Switzerland. It was arranged that I would spend the first half of my time in Pretoria and the surrounding region under Breytenbach's supervision, making 7 presentations to various groups. Then I would go south to Stellenbosch and join Johann Cook, who would be in charge of my lectures in this region. There was, however, one flaw in this whole arrangement, of which I was not entirely aware at that time, since I had never met Breytenbach and his colleagues prior to meeting them at IOSOT in Basel. This group of South African scholars were great admirers of Eckart Otto, who was quite a regular visitor to the region, which was bound to affect their attitude towards me. Nevertheless, Breytenbach was always most hospitable towards me and did everything to secure the funding and make the arrangements for all of the talks in the northern region.

Thus it was that on August 24, 2002 I took a flight from Toronto to Atlanta and from there to Pretoria, a 17 hour flight. I was met at the airport by Breytenbach, who took me to his place to meet his family, feed me and then take me to a very nice bed and breakfast near the University. Even though it was clearly an upscale neighborhood, I was warned that I should be very careful about walking on the street after dark. The B&B where I stayed was surrounded by a high wall and high iron gates, and all the properties on the street had high fences and many with guard dogs. Nevertheless, I did venture forth for some short walks, especially to the large shopping mall on the main street that ran beside the B&B. The day after I arrived I went with Andries Breytenbach to pick up my expense money, and this in itself was a new experience. I was to receive all of the funds for my expenses in cash for the whole time that I was to be in South Africa. To get into the bank one entered through a specially controlled door, one at a time, admitted by a guard. It was quite a pile of bills that I received from the teller and Andries and I split the amount that each of us would carry and then hurried through a busy intersection to the car and took off for the university grounds. Most of it was then put into a safe at the residence where I was staying. Another curious feature of this arrangement was that I paid for all the expenses related to my trip so that whenever I went with some of the faculty to dinner in a restaurant, I footed the bill with the research money! This also included a trip on a weekend to the Pilanesberg National Park to see some wild animals.

The individual talks that I gave to the various academic institutions, three seminars at the University of Pretoria, one talk at the Rand Afrikaans University and one at the University of South Africa were all very small groups and very poorly organized. The seminars in particular were ignored by some of the OT faculty at Pretoria U, as if deliberately boycotted. At the other institutions they were at least polite and friendly. I also was asked to give a presentation at a theological training college, which I found rather awkward. The main event of this part of the trip, however, was my participation in a three-day Pro-Pentateuch conference at the retreat center in Hammenskraal and it is to this conference that we will now turn.

The "Pro-Pent" was instituted by Eckart Otto of Munich in cooperation with Andries Breytenbach and a number of other scholars of the region who were sympathetic to Otto's views on the Pentateuch, and it was held annually at this retreat center in Hammanskraal. I was invited to make two presentations for discussion, which would represent positions that were alternatives to Otto's views. The first one, "Deuteronomy and the Covenant Code: a Revolution in the Study of Biblical Law," (based upon my then forthcoming book, *A Law Book for the Diaspora*, 2003), which suggested that the Covenant Code of Exodus 21–23 was later that the Deuteronomic law code in Deuteronomy 12–28. This was fundamentally different from Otto's own extensive study of biblical law, which regarded the Covenant Code as the oldest law code of the Pentateuch. The second paper, "Deuteronomy between Pentateuch and the Deuteronomistic History," was a direct challenge to Otto's views about the non-legal portions of the Pentateuch, with a detailed critique of his treatment of a number of biblical texts, as well as similar views by some other scholars. Needless to say, Otto was not very happy about this challenge to his views on what he regarded as his own turf. In the evening of the last day there was a celebration with a big barbeque dinner and when I sat down with my share of food and a beer to drink, Otto chose to take his place opposite me. His intention was to set me straight and it was not very long before he started to attack me. The basic point of his whole invective was that I was a North American scholar who did not understand the fine points and complexities of German biblical scholarship. That, of course, was nonsense, because, to the contrary, my competence in the German scholarly tradition had long been recognized by Otto Kaiser, Hans Heinrich Schmid, and many other leading scholars. Long after others had left for their beds, he was still going at it, until I finally decided it was enough and turned in for the night. Ironically, after we returned to Pretoria the next day, Otto and I were invited to dinner at Andries Breytenbach's home and it was all smiles and pleasantries between us. However, whenever Otto had a chance to review anything I wrote, he always attacked me in a quite openly hostile manner. Otto was the one European scholar with whom I did not get along. Other European scholars, regardless of any differences of opinion on biblical matters that we may have had, always treated me most cordially.

Let me turn now to the second half of my South African adventure, which was entirely different from that of the first half, primarily because it was organized and arranged under the supervision of my good friend Johann Cook. The original plan was to drive down to Stellenbosch with Andries to attend a conference at Stellenbosch University, but some domestic problems in the Andries household made a change of plans necessary and instead I was taken to the airport in Johannesburg in good time, passed quickly through the boarding process, and had a window seat in the small plane with a good view and lots of leg room. The flight was very enjoyable and I entered into conversation with a native South African business man who was very pleasant and helpful in understanding the present political and social situation in the country. When approaching Cape Town he spoke with the steward who then took me to the cockpit of the plane and I sat in the third seat behind the pilot and co-pilot while we were making the long descent over the coastal mountains to the north of Stellenbosch and into the Cape Town airport. It was a wonderful view and a great experience. I got my bags and met Johann Cook who was waiting for me but also for another friend of his who was flying in from Spain a short time later. When the flight arrived I met Natalio Fernandez Marcos, who was also in South Africa on the same type of government lectureship grant that I was on but with Johann as host, so for the next several days we were a threesome. We were taken to our rooms in the same university housing at Stellenbosch U. This was the beginning of a new friendship with Natalio and a very significant scholarly relationship. His specialty was in textual criticism, and specifically that of the Septuagint in which he had an international reputation, having just published a very important reference work, *The Septuagint in Context: Introduction to the Greek Versions of the Bible* (2001), and hence his close connection to Johann, but also to others such as John Wevers and Albert Pietersma of the University of Toronto. With all of these mutual friendships we were in store for a great time together.

Natalio and I had arrived in Cape Town the weekend prior to the beginning of the conference and Johann had planned on a little excursion to fill in this gap. So the next day we left at 10 a.m. for the region of the Cederberg Mountains and the town of Clanwilliam. This was springtime in South Africa and the season of beautiful wild flowers, which covered the landscape of this region. We drove through the broad valleys until we came to Citrusdal, pausing on the way to take pictures. In Citrusdal we stopped at a wine-tasting shop of one of the vineyards. The atmosphere was very informal and great fun. We sat at a table and sampled some whites and reds and then selected a red wine to go with our lunch. We also bought four bottles and the total bill for everything was 149 rand (ca. $15 US)! Natalio and I covered all of the expenses for these outings with our grant funds. From here we went north on more back roads through beautiful mountain valleys with flowing streams and wildflowers in abundance, until we finally came to Clanwilliam. We booked into a very Victorian style Strasburg Hotel and before supper we visited the local wild flower reserve with numerous varieties in bloom, a beautiful display. The evening meal in the hotel was a fine buffet and very inexpensive. We turned in early and the next morning, after a big breakfast we had an early start and headed down the mountains for the west coast of South Africa. After passing through a number of pretty little towns (Piketberg, Velddrift, Vredenburg) we came to Saldanha on Saldanha Bay. A few years earlier a new harbor for large ocean ships was built by my cousin Jan (a son of my aunt Jo, my mother's sister). We followed the shoreline south to Langsbaan. This place has a beautiful beach where Johann goes for his summer holidays. It has a number of pretty Greek style summer places. Here we stopped at a special fish-fry place under tents on the shore and had a ten-course meal, along with one of our own wines from Citrusdal. After this we went to the West Coast National Park, which was quite close-by, with its beautiful flowers and wild animals and the sea on both sides of the park, all very different from Pilanesberg. We then took the road south through Malmesbury (basically the same name as Malmberg, Elizabeth's maiden name) to Stellenbosch. This was a great weekend and by now we were close friends.

Monday morning was the start of the conference of the South African Society for Near Eastern Studies; it was held at the Theological Faculty Building of Stellenbosch University. This was the week of spring-break vacation for the university. Natalio opened the conference with his paper on the Septuagint, which was excellent. The gathering was not a large group but the quality of the papers was quite good. Piet Venter, whom I had met earlier in Pretoria, showed me a good place for lunch, and Natalio and I made a habit of going there in the days that followed. Monday night the conference had its lamb barbeque (braai) in the sports complex and the three of us consumed some more of the Citrusdal wine. The following evening, after another day of conference papers, I was called upon to give the Van Selms Memorial Lecture at the Conservatorium—the main university lecture hall—a beautiful place. (Professor Van Selms was former professor of biblical studies who was internationally known and respected.) The title of my talk was "The Covenant Code and the Babylonian Legal Tradition: What's the Connection?" There was a respectable size audience for the size of the place and a great reception afterwards. The lecture even made the local Stellenbosch newspaper with a photo of Johann and me.

The following day was the start of the Old Testament Society of South Africa conference. The opening session was a good one, with quite a good audience, and I attended a session on law in early Judaism. In the evening we had a fish-fry at the athletic "Stal" again, which was very enjoyable. The next day two old friends, Zefira and Yehoshua Gitai, whom I have known from my first years at Chapel Hill, came up from Cape Town to give two papers on Job, with Zefira presenting a slide show on the artistic portrayal of Job and Yehoshua on the literary character of Job, both well done. Natalio gave another very good paper on rhetorical expansions of biblical traditions and I did my paper on "The Rhetoric of Imitation as a Means to the 'Truth' in the Story of David," which received a good response. That evening we had a great banquet dinner and wine-tasting. The next day in the evening, after the last day of the conference, the three of us went to Johann's place for a very pleasant dinner with his family. His son played a piece for us on his guitar.

The weekend was now free again for some sightseeing, so on the Saturday we made a trip down to Cape Town and went up Table Mountain by cable car to the top, which, as the name suggests, is remarkably flat for such a height. It was very windy and clouds were moving in from the sea, but the top was clear and still gave spectacular views of the neighboring mountains, the city and the sea. The top of Table Mountain is very beautiful, covered with flowering shrubs, plants and hiking paths, and look-outs to both the Atlantic and Indian Oceans. After we descended we drove through the city and along the shoreline south to Hout Bay, a very wooded region on the shore, where we had a fish lunch. We went along the shore road which was very beautiful, but had to stop because the road ahead was closed and make a detour over the coastal mountains to the other side of the peninsula and head south along the Indian Ocean side and then cut back to the Atlantic side again at Scarborough and into the Cape Peninsula National Park and the Cape of Good Hope. This region is all very beautiful. We arrived at Cape Point, the southern tip and ascended to the lookout by funicular cable car for a great view where the two oceans meet. When we came down to the parking lot to get our car there was a baboon on top of our car. We waited until it left, along with other members of the baboon family, and as we drove north again we saw some Antelopes. We now drove up the Indian Ocean side through the beautiful towns of Simon's Town, Fish Hoek, and Muizenberg, and eventually headed inland to Stellenbosch. It was a great outing. That evening I was invited by Hendrick Bosman, the professor of Old Testament, to his home, along with several others from the OTSSA conference. The Bosmans were very fine hosts, although I did not fit in too well with what was clearly a group from the conference that knew each other from previous visits. Hendrik, however, went out of his way to include me in the conversation of the evening.

On Sunday morning Johann picked up Natalio and me about 10 a.m. and we headed to the wine country just east of Stellenbosh over the mountain range. Here two beautiful valleys meet between the mountains on either side. To the south east is Franschhoek, named after the Huguenots who founded the region, and in the town we visited the memorial in their honor. We then took the car up the side of the mountain to get a wonderful view of the whole valley. From there we drove north to Paarl at the other end of the valley on the Berg River. Here is a remarkable monument built on the side of the mountain and dedicated to the Afrikaans language, and from this height we had another grand view of the valley. The region is, of course, very well known for its wines and so on the other side of the city of Paarl we visited a great winery for tasting and Sunday brunch: Rheboksklоof. The setting in the gardens, parkland and little lakes was beautiful and the brunch was a feast. We first tasted 7 wines to select the one we wanted and then we had a great table on the veranda overlooking the garden with a delicious Sunday brunch and all of it very reasonable. By mid-afternoon we returned to Stellenbosch.

The next day Natalio and I went to the university in the morning to have coffee or tea at the Classics and Near Eastern Studies Department with Johann and to meet his colleagues. After this we made a tour of the university library, which is on two levels, but all of it is underground below the main campus square in the center of the university. It was quite impressive. Then we went to have a chat with the vice-rector for research, Professor Classen (a former member of Near Eastern Studies), who kept us an hour. This left just enough time for brunch before Natalio went to make a presentation to Johann's class and I returned to my rooms to make further preparations for the evening session. At 7 p.m. Natalio and I went back to the department for a faculty seminar which I conducted on "The Redactor in Biblical Studies: A 19th Century Anachronism," which was quite well received as it was appropriate for both classics and biblical studies. A very pleasant reception followed, and then Natalio and I went back to our apartments. As Natalio was leaving early next morning we bid farewell, but it was clear to both of us that this was just the beginning of a warm friendship.

After Natalio left, the pace of activity for the rest of the week was much more leisurely. On Tuesday morning I prepared for my seminar session to be given later in the afternoon at the Theological Seminary for Hendrick Bosman's class in the afternoon. At about 1 p.m. I walked from my apartment rooms to the seminary through a beautiful part of town all in bloom in the mild spring weather, and then spent some time in the seminary's library until tea from 2:45–3:15, when the session started with Bosman. The students continued to arrive for another fifteen minutes after the session had begun. My topic for discussion was: "From Child Sacrifice to Pascal Lamb: A Remarkable Transformation in Israelite Religion," which argued that the biblical author in Exodus 13:11–16 had intended to replace the practice of child sacrifice, which had been common in Judah during the late monarchy period and was strongly condemned by the prophets, especially Jeremiah, by instituting the redemption of the first-born son by the sacrifice of the pascal lamb. Although I had given instructions and materials by which they could be prepared for discussion, they were poorly prepared. Nevertheless they seemed to enjoy the session. It was also a rather small group. This presentation was later published in a South African Journal, *Old Testament Essays* (2003).

On the next day (Wednesday) I went with Yehoshua Gitay down to the University of Cape Town, which is located, quite literally, on the side of the mountain. There we had lunch together. Then we visited the Rhodes monument which gives a grand view over the city. Back at the university I gave my paper to the scholars and students in the Jewish Studies program: "Is There any Historiography in the Hebrew Bible? A Hebrew-Greek Comparison." Gitay had strong interests in the Greek/Hebrew comparisons, which he had advocated his entire academic career since I first met him in Chapel Hill. This was a very cordial and friendly group.

Thursday and Friday were rather quiet days that allowed me to do some shopping for souvenirs and drinking tea, and going for lunch with Johann to a lovely wine-tasting place on the edge of town. On Friday I also gave a class lecture for Johann on "King David and the Current Debate on Hebrew Historiography," a study of the David narrative that became part of a much larger work some years later. During these last few days I also became acquainted with a colleague in Johann's department, Paul Kruger and we spent some time together drinking coffee with his wife at a café. Paul also took me for a pleasant hike one afternoon up the side of the mountain behind the sports complex. He is a very kind and thoughtful person.

My last day of activity, Saturday, Sept. 21, I spent participating in a one-day meeting of Classical scholars in Stellenbosch, and giving an invited paper on the subject: "Is there any Historiography in the Hebrew Bible? A Hebrew-Greek Comparison," which appeared later that year in the South African *Journal of Northwest Semitic Languages* (2002), edited by Johann Cook. This was a response to Ernest Nicholson's earlier study of mine in *Prologue to History*, so I was very interested to see what the response would be by this group. I was pleased to find that it was very positive. The conference had a big luncheon after the morning session to which I was invited and I remember sitting opposite a gentleman who was a member of the South African Supreme Court, as well as an amateur classicist. He informed me that he had been working on the revised law code for the new constitution and had closely examined the Canadian constitution, and about this we had a very interesting conversation. He deeply impressed me with his learning and perspective on the current situation in South Africa. The next day I flew back to Johannesburg and from there to Canada.

The whole of my South African trip was a wonderful experience, quite different in many ways from my many trips to the UK and Europe, which were also rewarding for my earlier scholarly development, and I am indebted to both of my South African hosts, Andries Breytenbach and Johann Cook. Both did much to make the experience an enjoyable and memorable one. This was especially the case for the second half of the trip in Stellenbosch and vicinity, which cemented a close friendship with both Johann Cook, whom I had known for some time, and with Natalio Fernandes Marcos, whom I had met there for the first time. Both would give me strong support and encouragement in my subsequent research and publication project, *The Edited Bible.* I was also given an honorary life long membership in the Old Testament Society of South Africa and receive the society's journal, *Old Testament Essays*, three times yearly. Two of the talks I gave during my trip I published as articles in this journal. My presentation at the Pro-Pent conference was likewise published in the *Theological Studies*, the journal of the Faculty of Theology of the University of Pretoria, of which Andries Breytenbach was the chair. Two of the papers that I gave while in Stellenbosch, the one on "The Redactor in Biblical Studies" and "Is there Historiography in the Hebrew Bible?" were published in the *Journal of Northwest Semitic Studies*, another journal published in South Africa by the Department of Ancient Studies at the University of Stellenbosch, with both Johann Cook and Paul Kruger on the editorial board.

Cultural Memory in Biblical Exegesis

In the fall of 2008 I was asked by my good friend Niels-Peter Lemche of Copenhagen University if I would be interested in participating in an all day session on the theme of *Cultural Memory in Biblical Exegesis* at the summer meeting of the European Association of Biblical Studies (EABS) at the University of Lincoln in England in the summer of 2009. A number of European scholars known to me would be there participating in the program and the topic interested me so I agreed to go and present a paper. The location and size of the conference (about 150–200 participants) was ideal with broad representation from Europe and the UK, but also some from the USA and other countries. It was held on the grounds of the university, which was largely empty of students so that it could easily accommodate those attending the conference, with lots of space for all the meetings. The main tourist feature of the place was Lincoln Cathedral, which one could reach by a long trip up the steep road to the cathedral at the top of the hill. The conference meals were also served in a large cafateria in the main building so that it was easy to make arrangements to have a meal with one's old friends.

In preparation for this meeting I did some reading of the classic work by Maurice Halbwachs (*The Collective Memory*, 1980) and the very useful studies of Joyce Appleby, Lynn Hunt and Magaret Jacob, *Telling the Truth about History* (1994). In the morning session of the first day, I was asked to present the leadoff paper for the Cultural

Memory program. The first part of the paper was intended to define cultural memory as the collective memory of a particular group or population, beyond the personal memory of the individual, and its history, which helps to define who they are. This is not objective impersonal history but the reconstruction of the past in such a way that it identifies who we are within that history. Changing times and circumstances of the group require a certain transformation of that collective past. To the extent that one can identify the various layer of the biblical history, one can identify and relate those changes in the cultural or collective history to the times and group for which it was written. This is what the paper attempted to demonstrate in its examination of the Dtr history, the Yahwist, the Priestly writer, and the David Saga. Following my paper there were eleven more papers in the rest of the morning and afternoon, all on the same general theme of Cultural Memory and History, ending with a panal discussion of seven scholars, in which I also took part. Five of the other six I knew very well and were good friends of mine so it was a lively and enjoyable time.

For the following two days I was free of obligations and could pick and choose the papers that I wanted to hear or just go for a stroll. There were also some special evening presentations. One of them featured Nadav Naaman from Tel Aviv, Israel, and a good friend of mine, speaking on the subject: "Does Archaeology Really Deserve the Status of a 'High Court' in Biblical Historical Research?" He was a very fine historian who worked closely with Israel Finkelstein and other first rate archaeologists at Tel Aviv University. There were so many of my academic friends at one place, most of which I would probably never see again.

Two Unusual Symposia in Europe in 2010

In the spring and fall of 2010 I was invited to participate in two quite different scholarly symposia dealing with themes and subjects that were not part of my regular areas of expertise or publications, but both of them turned out to be very enjoyable and stimulating experiences. The first of these was *The Göttingen Symposium on Dating Egyptian Literary Texts*. Early in 2010 I received an email inviting me to a symposium in Göttingen to be conducted in the university by Egyptologists on the theme of dating the literary texts of the Middle to Late Kingdom periods. It would include a number of scholars from Europe and Great Britain, and they would be pleased if I would join them, all expenses paid. My first response was to suggest that this invitation must be a misunderstanding, that I was not an Egyptologist and had done no serious work in the field since my dissertation, and that was a long time ago. It was true that I did publish an article in 1964, attempting to date the Admonitions of Ipuwer to the Second Intermediate Period of Egypt, but I had done nothing comparable to it since. Their response was that it was precisely because of this "pioneering" work that they would like me to be part of this symposium and make a presentation. All my expenses would be paid for. So I agreed to go and I prepared a paper for the occasion. Besides, I had never been to Göttingen before and so I added a couple of extra days.

The Egyptology group informed Professor Hermann Spieckermann, an Old Testament scholar in the University's Theology Faculty (and a good friend of mine), and he also invited me to arrive early and give a paper in Hebrew Bible to his seminar. As it turned out, he met me at the train, and gave me a tour of the old city, including the cemetery where Julius Wellhausen was buried. In addition, it was pointed out to me that the old center of the city is surrounded by the ancient city wall which is now largely covered by trees and vegetation. One can easily find a path up to the top and then follow this path at the top all the way around the old city wall, with I did. I also gave a paper to the biblical studies group organized by Spiekermann on the David story, which went off very well.

When the day arrived for registration and the beginning of the Egyptology symposium, I went to the University's Egyptian Department and joined those registering, all strangers to me. I gave the person in charge of registration my name, and suddenly all these young scholars present wanted to meet me and welcome me to the symposium. I was speechless and had not prepared for such a reception. The sessions were held in an old historic building in the center of town, an easy walk from my hotel. In addition to those directly involved in giving papers and in the following discussions, there were a substantial number of others sitting outside this circle as observers. It was clear from the presentations that the majority of the group were in favor of dating many of the literary texts to periods later that those previously suggested, but some were more conservative and argued for the more traditional dating and more historical in their content, much as one finds in biblical studies.

In addition to the symposium sessions, there was time for socializing, and being a stranger to the group they made sure that I was not left alone. So at the lunch beak I was invited out to join a group of them for lunch with lots of lively conversation. The same applied to the evening meal. There were also special events. The one was a picnic supper at an outdoor restaurant at the top of a high hill that overlooked the city of Göttingen and much of the country side and beyond. It was a great occasion. I remember sitting with an older member of the group who told me that when she was a much younger scholar she and some others began to take my method of dating a literary text seriously and develop a methodology that was quite new to their discipline, leading up to the sophistication in dating texts that they have today. "So," she said, "you see that you were a pioneer in this field, whether you knew it or not." On another evening all the participants were invited to the beautiful concert hall featuring a very gifted cellist. As I returned home I reflected on how fortunate I was to have been invited by these scholars. My dissertation on the Hyksos, of which this element of dating a text had been a vital part, had turned out to have had a far greater impact than I could ever have imagined. As indicated earlier (chapter 3), the excavations at Tell el-Maskhuta, with its discovery of Hyksos period graves, completely confirmed my dating of the *Admonitions of Ipuwer* to this period. It suggested that these foreigners had migrated into this region from southern Palestine in a manner described in this piece of Egyptian literature, just as I had indicated in my doctoral thesis of 1965.

The second scholarly symposium to which I was invited that year was *The Madrid Symposium on the Standardization and Transmission of the Hebrew Bible.* Early in 2010 I was informed by my good friend Natalio Fernandes Marcos that plans were being made to hold an international symposium in Madrid at the Centre for Human and Social Sciences, CSIC. The theme of the symposium was "Fixing, Transmitting and Preserving: Early Jewish and Rabbinic Literature in the History of the Hebrew Bible." This had to do with the debate about the standardization or fixing of the Hebrew Text by the *sopherim* (scribes), the transmission process by the Rabbis and the preservation of the Masoretic text. Natalio was himself a scholar at this centre, but his specialty was the Greek Septuagint and not the Hebrew Bible, which was under the direction of Elvira Martin-Contreras, who would get in touch with me about the details. Of course I immediately accepted this invitation to be a part of the symposium, because it would be a great opportunity to test my work on the issue of whether or not the *sopherim* were responsible for fixing the "standard edition of the Hebrew text." Since Emanuel Tov was also invited to be part of this symposium, this would certainly result in a lively discussion of this issue. In his textbook, *Textual Criticism of the Hebrew Bible*, 2nd ed. (2001), Tov strongly advocated the standardization of the Hebrew Bible, against which I had written. The trip would also mean seeing my friend Natalio again, whom I had not seen for some time.

After my acceptance I received all of the particulars about the symposium and deadlines for the title of the paper and a draft of its contents, so that the program could be drawn up. The date of the symposium would be September 20–21, which meant arriving the day before and leaving the day after. All the foreign participants would stay in a hotel within easy walking distance from the CSIC building where the meetings were held. Before the symposium I was in contact with Emanuel Tov, who was aware of the fact that I would be attending the symposium along with him. He also had recently acquired a copy of my book, *The Edited Bible*, and was just becoming aware of its content, especially the section pp. 314–331, where our views differed concerning the *sopherim* and the editing of the Hebrew Bible. He was very cordial and generous with me and gave me access to his website with its collections of his publications. So we both looked forward to this encounter.

When the time came for the conference, I took the long flight to Madrid and booked into the hotel being used by the symposium participants the day before it started. Most of those attending this symposium were unknown to me at the outset, because my primary field of research was not in text criticism and the participants were from so many different countries. The morning of the start of the symposium we all met on the ground floor of the hotel as instructed and then we were escorted to the building where the meeting was taking place. We had all been issued passports that were shown to the guards at the entrance and then we were taken to the conference room. Natalio opened the session with greetings on behalf of the CSIC, although he was not otherwise involved. Then we proceeded to the program proper. The way in which the program was set up, the first three papers on the first morning dealt with the question of the stabilization or standardization of the text in the Hebrew Bible. Emanuel Tov's paper led off with the theme: "The Myth of the Stabilization of the Text of Hebrew Scriptures," which argued that the standardization of the text was not something created consciously by the Rabbis but was a particular text tradition, used by the Rabbis, that survived the war of 70 CE, while those diverse texts used by the Essenes of Qumran were lost from public view. My paper, which was next, "Did the *Sopherim* Create a Standard Edition of the Hebrew Scriptures?" argued against the popular view that it was a special class of Jewish scribes who consciously created a standard biblical text out of great diversity. I was followed by Arie van der Kooij who gave a paper titled: "Standardization or Preservation? Some Comments on the Textual History of the Hebrew Bible in the Light of Josephus and Rabbinic Literature." This presentation was built upon the assumption that what later became the Masoretic text was based upon the text preserved by the priests in the Temple from earliest times, and which was then reproduced by scribes to become the standard text.

While both Tov and van der Kooij have given up the older view that the *sopherim* were responsible for creating a standard edition of the Bible, their alternative proposals are not without problems, which make them unacceptable. If, as Tov suggests, the rabbis were responsible for the preservation of the Masoretic text tradition, that finally became the standard by 100 CE, then how is it that Rabbi Meir, a notable rabbi, was producing quality Bibles for synagogues which did not reflect the Masoretic text tradition? According to Elias Bickerman, the rabbis were not scholars concerned with the biblical text but were sages, and as such were not concerned with the preservation of a particular form of the text. Rabbi Meir, however, was also a scholar (*sopher*) and as such created copies of the biblical text. In the case of van der Kooij, he has more justification in associating the form of the biblical text with the priesthood, but he overplays the notion of the priests being custodians of the correct version of the text, the so-called Temple scroll, and that this special scroll in the Temple could be used as the standard for the reproduction of new texts. As I argued in *The Edited Bible*, this is based on a very dubious text, dating to a time several centuries after the Temple's destruction. Furthermore, an elegant copy of the Hebrew Bible, which was taken from the Temple by the Romans before its destruction, was restored to the Jews by the Roman emperor, Severus, and its remains clearly indicate that it was not a text of the MT type. In the case of Homer's *Iliad* and *Odyssey*, it was not a group of scholars that were responsible for the final form of the texts of Homer, as classical scholars once claimed, but the gradual movement by the book sellers towards a standard form of the text. The same thing happened with the biblical text over an extended period of time. The rest of the papers, while all very interesting and informative, were outside of my area of expertise and needs no further comment here.

There were six papers each day, with a coffee break after the first two and lunch after the next two, from 2 to 4 p.m., with the final two papers from 4–6 p.m. This allowed for lots of general discussion during the sessions and more one on one dialogue between sessions. Lunch was in a cafeteria in another building, which involved a couple of blocks walk. This was a time when we also had a chance to become better acquainted with some of the rest of the group. It was over lunch that I was able to chat with Elvira and she told me how much help my book, *The Edited Bible*, had been to her when she had to prepare for her doctoral defense a few years earlier. It was clearly the reason why I was invited to join this group. After the last session of the day we were on our own for the evening. So a few of us formed a little group and went to a local restaurant that evening where we got to know each other a little better.

The routine of the second day was much the same as the first. Most of these papers dealt with the later period of issues related to the study of the Masorah, which was beyond my range of studies and area of interest. The afternoon session ended with all of us gathering outside to have our group picture taken. Also fitted into the afternoon schedule was a tour of some of the research facilities, including the library. This was led by Natalio, who took the occasion to point out a recent acquisition, my book, *The Edited Bible*. More important was the display of some very fine ancient Bibles. We were also informed that in the evening some taxis would call at the hotel to pick us up and take us to a location in the center of town where we would have our evening meal. It was quite a spread that they put on and Natalio was there also, the last time that I would see him. He also arranged for me to sit beside Julio Trebolle and I enjoyed his company very much. Since he was from Madrid and did not stay in the hotel with the rest of us, it was the first chance I had to meet him personally. Steve McKenzie knew him and always spoke very highly of him. Steve speaks Spanish very well and has spent time in Spain and got to know him there.

The next morning at breakfast we expressed our thoughts about the symposium and the strong approval about its very profitable outcome, with assurances from various persons that they would keep in touch. Then we set off in taxis to make our various flight connections. During the symposium Natalio had given me a copy of his wonderful book on the Septuagint, a large part of which I read on the long flight home, and within a few days after I returned I sent an email to thank him for it and for all he did in getting me to the symposium and the chance to see him again. I also thanked him for the opportunity to meet his Spanish colleague Julio Trebolle Barrera and to enjoy his company at the dinner on the final evening of the conference. I was also in touch with Emanuel Tov, as before, and Giuseppe Veltri of the University of Halle in Germany, who sent me some of his articles and continued by email to discuss some of the issues raised at the symposium. It is ironic that I have had more serious dialogue and appreciation of my book, *The Edited Bible*, with scholars in text criticism than in my own specialty of literary criticism of the Hebrew Bible. The collection of the symposium papers was published as *The Text of the Hebrew Bible: From the Rabbis to the Masoretes*, edited by Elvira Martin-Contreras and Lorena Miralles-Macia (Göttingen, 2014). These two trips in 2010, to Göttingen and Madrid, were the last of such foreign trips abroad for the purpose of presenting learned papers. Even though I received a number of requests inviting me to do so, my memory problems made such presentations increasingly difficult.

Publications: 2000–2015

I will conclude this presentation of my retirement years by making some comments on my publications during this period. This will focus on the major topic of research and the books produced, together with the scholarly reactions to them and some article reflecting my response. In addition I will mention a few articles on subjects of special interest that were not directly related to any of the above.

My first major publication during my retirement was *A Law Book for the Diaspora: Revision in the Study of the Covenant Code*, in 2003. The date for this work is misleading because it was a sequel to my earlier books on the Yahwist even though it appeared nine years after *The Life of Moses* (1994). It was always my understanding that the so-called Covenant Code in Exod. 21–23 was the work of the Yahwist and an integral part of the Moses Story. There was a very large body of studies on the Covenant Code, many of them in German, with little agreement as to its unity, dating of historical and social context, and the relationship of the legal corpus to the non-P narrative in Exodus. I argued in this work and in subsequent articles that the Covenant Code was the work of the Yahwist, produced within, and strongly influenced by, the Babylonian environment. The work is an integral part of J's treatment of the Sinai theophany, directly dependent upon the earlier model of this even in Deuteronomy, telling of the giving of the law, but with significant modifications reflecting the new environment and circumstances of the Babylonian captivity.

The next major project had to do with my response to the great proliferation of editors or redactors as a means of explaining what many scholars believed was the complex nature of the non-P (J) composition of the Pentateuch. For a long time, since my initial criticism of Rendtorff's studies of the Pentateuch and the Heidelberg school that followed him, I called into question the use and abuse of redactors in Pentateuchal studies. This concern finally resulted in the production of *The Edited Bible: The Curious History of the "Editor" in Biblical Criticism*, 2006. It is not appropriate, within the context of these memoirs, to give a detailed summary of my book. Instead I will make a few comments on matters that lie at the heart of the current dispute, which are examined in great detail in the book. First, all the evidence shows that editors or redactors were none existent until the sixteenth century, at which time they were clearly identified as such, and some such as Erasmus were quite famous for their editorial work. By contrast, authors were well known in antiquity and often identified as such, especially in Greece and Rome, but not in Judea until a much later period. In the early stages of the modern classical studies it was suggested that Homer's *Iliad* and *Odyssey* actually consisted of a collection of stories put together in their present form by "editors" in the sixth century BCE, and when they became corrupted by later additions, Alexandrian scholars of the third and second centuries BCE, "edited" them. This single model from classical studies became the standard example of evidence for the existence of editors for many years in both classical and biblical studies, until it was proven to be erroneous. By the mid-twentieth century, classical studies gave up any association of editors with early Greek and Roman literature, while biblical studies continued its love affair with the editor without any further evidence for its existence. Within Jewish and Christian biblical studies the notion of editors was related to the supposed standardization of the biblical text. However, neither the *sopherim* nor the church fathers ever functioned as editors or created standard editions of the biblical text. Consequently, there is no clear evidence in antiquity for the existence of editors or redactors. By contrast, the origin of the editor came about with the rise of the printing press and the earliest editing of the Christian and Jewish Bibles in the sixteenth century.

It was only with the rise of the prestige of editors of the Bible in the sixteenth century that scholars began to read the role of editors, quite anachronistically, back into antiquity. Hence, there arose the "editing" of Homer in the late eighteenth century and the rise of classical criticism throughout the nineteenth and early twentieth centuries until its demise in the mid- twentieth century. By this time the notion of ancient editors was abandoned by classicists when the lack of evidence for their existence was clearly demonstrated. In contrast to this, the "editor" in biblical criticism from Richard Simon in the seventeenth century to the present day, including such important figures as Wellhausen, von Rad, and Noth, and many other important figures, has persisted down to the present day. This was the case not only in literary criticism but also in textual criticism. There was also an effort to establish a relationship between the role of the "editors" and the creation of the canon, which was undertaken by a number of scholars but particularly that of Brevard Childs, a former teacher of mine. As indicated earlier, the conference in Madrid called into question any possibility of the *sopherim* of antiquity had anything to do with creating an edited version of the biblical text. The same can be said for the conference held at the University of Toronto in 2007 under the direction of John S. Kloppenborg and Judith H. Newman, to which I contributed the opening paper, "The Genealogy of the Biblical Editor." The papers were later published by John and Judith as *Editing the Bible: Assessing the Task, Past and Present* (2012).

The primary purpose of my book, *The Edited Bible*, was to encourage a dialogue with my fellow scholars in Pentateuchal studies, and apart from those in textual criticism, this was a complete failure. They simply refused to take the challenge seriously and there was nothing that I could do about it. In contrast to this I decided to get in touch with a scholar outside of biblical studies whose work I had used within the book and whom I greatly respected, Professor Anthony Grafton of Princeton University. He sent me this response:

> Dear Professor Van Seters,
>
> Thank you so much for your letter. I am delighted to be in contact with you. Your own work—especially *In Search of History*—has been very important to me, and I'm most grateful to you for your insights and for keeping up the tradition of connecting the study of the ancient Near East with that of Greece and Rome (this was, of course, the method of the early modern scholars about whom I know the most). I have read and enjoyed your *Edited Bible.* And while we differ on some technical points, about which I do not propose to pick any bones, I liked being read closely and taken seriously by a scholar whom I respect so much.
>
> It would be a great pleasure to have a copy of the book, and if you could spare one . . . I would be extremely grateful. It is a shame, of course, that Momigliano is no longer alive to read it. He would have done so with a deep appreciation, as I know he read your earlier work, which we once discussed.
>
> All the very best.
>
> Yours, Tony Grafton

To have a someone of the scholarly stature of Anthony Grafton say such positive things about the book, on the one hand, and to have those in my own field so easily dismiss it or else completely ignore it, is beyond my comprehension.

The Biblical Saga of King David

In 2009 I put into practice what I had laid out in the *Edited Bible* when I wrote *The Biblical Saga of King David* (2009). As I indicated in the preface, this book had been many years in the making. I first became fascinated with the David story and what scholars called the Succession Narrative when, as a student, I heard Gerhard von Rad lecture on it at Princeton Theological Seminary, where he was a visiting professor in 1961. His remarks on the Succession Narrative were part of a larger discussion of the rise of historiography in ancient Israel, and it gave me a lasting interest in this subject. A number of years later, in 1974, when I was on the faculty at the University of Toronto, John Wevers, as chairman, organized a faculty seminar on ancient historiography, as I mentioned earlier. I will not repeat all the retails of this conference, except to say that my own study in this series, on "History and Historians of the Ancient Near East: The Israelites," became the basis of my later work, *In Search of History* (1983), one chapter of which gave special attention to the story of Saul and David.

At the same time in the mid-70s, at a meeting of the Society of Biblical Literature David Gunn, a British scholar and I were engaged in a lively exchange of views about the literary nature of the David story and this resulted in a number of articles by both of us, as well as his stimulating book, *The Story of King David* (1978). Our dialogue was also reflected in my treatment of the David story in *In Search of History*. While my primary research in the 80s and 90s focused on the historiography of the Pentateuch, as reflected in my studies on the Yahwist, I did return from time to time to questions relating to the Deuteronomistic History and to the story of David, in particular. In a symposium held in Bern in February, 1997, I was asked to offer my views on the Succession Narrative (or Court History as I then called it) in dialogue with Otto Kaiser and others, and this debate was published in *Die sogenannte Thronfolgegeschichte Davids*, edited by Albert de Pury and Thomas Römer (2000). My own contribution, "The Court History and DtrH," centered on the debate concerning the relationship of the Court History to DtrH, and I argued, as in *In Search of History* but in greater detail, that the Court History was a later addition to DtrH. This late dating of the Court History became a major issue in understanding what the Court History was all about.

My study of the Court History was taken up again in a greatly expanded form in *The Biblical Saga of King David* but it now extended to include the account of David's rise to power as well, as part of the same literary work, so that it was more than just a "court history." Consequently, I can safely assert that over the last four decades I have consistently maintained the view—against the consensus reflected in the works of Leonhard Rost, Gerhard von Rad, Martin Noth, and many who have followed them—that a large part of the David story, including the so-called Succession Narrative, is a late addition to DtrH, and that it was a product of the Persian period. I have also attempted to follow the archaeological discussion as it has to do with appraising and reconstructing the period of David's reign and the development of the Judean state, and as both of these relate to the socio-historical context of the David story. What I could not have known in the 70s and early 80s when I first began to develop this thesis was that the archaeological evidence would so overwhelmingly confirm my position about the development of the David story. We now know with a high degree of probability that the archaeological evidence from the tenth century cannot support the advanced socio-historical context reflected in the *David Saga*. This account of David's life is therefore not historical but a work of fiction that must belong to a much later age. What Rost, von Rad, and Noth could not have known, namely the great advances in archaeological evidence, we can now use to understand and interpret the David narrative as it has come down to us.

Once one has accepted the notion that the story of David is not the product or inspiration of a period contemporary with a ruler of Jerusalem in the tenth century, but is the work of two or more authors of times far removed from that period, then the form of the story and its interpretation must be radically different from those proposed by earlier scholars. The accounts of David's rise to power in place of Saul and the eventual succession to the throne by Solomon, usually construed as two documents, were understood as apologies written by members of the court in defense of the Davidic dynasty. Such an understanding of the David story's genre and interpretation is no longer tenable. Already at the beginning of my study of the David story in the mid-70s I raised questions about this mode of interpretation, but it still persists against all evidence to the contrary, so that I argued at some length in this work why the old view must be set aside and a different approach taken to understanding this literary masterpiece.

One other approach that has arisen, as a steady piecemeal retreat from the older position, is to relegate everything that might possibly be construed as later in time than the "original documents" to the work of a series of "redactors." As a consequence, not only was Noth's Deuteronomistic historian, who was thought by Noth to have used these earlier "sources" for his history, now construed as one of these "editors," but the whole of what was thought by earlier scholars as the finest example of classical Hebrew prose is now fragmented into a myriad of small pieces and understood as endless additions to the original. And this literary process is stretched over a very long period of time. This makes it all too easy for some to despair of the historical-critical effort altogether and to opt for a holistic or final form approach to the David story. While I sympathized with the frustration that many have with critical scholarship, I nevertheless remained committed to the historical-critical method of literary analysis on the one hand, and, on the other hand, to an appreciation of the literary quality of a large part of the David story, as recognized by Rost, von Rad and others. My book was an attempt to present a balance between these two goals.

This is not the place to go into any great detail about the content of my study in *The Biblical Saga of King David*, except to say that the biblical story of David is primarily the combination of two quite extensive and conflicting presentations, the first being that of the Deuteronomist, which presents David in the most positive light and which was a fully self-contained narrative. The second is the *David Saga*, which was a large addition made to the earlier version many years later, with the object of discrediting David and the institution of the monarchy in general. It is clear from the book of 1 Chronicles that this presentation of David in the *David Saga* was quite unacceptable to many, so the Chronicler eliminated most of it from his own version and replaced it with a version that was much more positive. What I have also tried to make clear is that there were no editors/redactors involved in this major addition to the David story. It is true that some later additions were made to the David story in 2 Samuel 21–24, which interrupt the continuity of the *David Saga* between 2 Samuel 20 and 1 Kings 1, but these all seem to be quite late and of little consequence to the rest of the *David Saga*.

What I find most depressing is the obsession with creating as large a number of editors as possible by breaking up the text into many little pieces and producing a text in the end that has no particular purpose or meaning. This is why so many scholars end up dismissing the whole point of literary criticism and shifting their interest to dealing only with the final form of the text. To me that is not the answer to understanding the text and it is much more rewarding to find this second author of the *David Saga* and understand what he is trying to say about the monarchy over against any desire to restore it in the late Persian period, based on Dtr's earlier idealization of David.

What is it that the author of the *David Saga* is trying to say? He is not just trying to entertain his audience. The artistry of the *David Saga* is serious and it is playing to a sophisticated audience of the late Persian period that is familiar both with the national tradition as reflected in the Deuteronomistic History and with the power politics of the Persian Empire. The whole cast of players in the *David Saga* are clothed in this period garb, and each particular act and scene is set in this time and place. With all the grand dreams about the revival of a Davidic empire from the Euphrates to the border of Egypt, the reader is confronted by the question: Is this what you want? This question is implied by the author's consistent and unrelenting attack upon the Deuteronomist's central theme of the divine promise to David, which became the basis of messianism in the later period. For the author, the *messiah* or "anointed one" is nothing more than the product of a political action taken by those in authority, the elders of the people, or the result of a military coup, a status that can just as quickly be withdrawn or rescinded. And religious officials in the form of prophets and priests are just as likely to be involved in power politics as anyone else. The same applies to the use of religious pronouncements, such as the divine promises to David that are cited as justification for immoral actions, such as murder and assassination (1 Kings 1–2).

Included within the vision of a future messianic age are the Deuteronomic notions of a pure state that involves racial cleansing and the exclusion of foreigners and infidels. The author of the *David Saga* undermines such ideas by populating David's state with all kinds of foreigners. There is the Philistine Obededom who has an estate on the outskirts of Jerusalem, whose household is blessed by Yahweh, because of the presence of the ark. This is in stark contrast to Dtr's portrayal of the ark in Philistine territory, where it causes so much trouble. And then there is Uriah the Hittite, who is far more devout than David in his obedience to the Law of Yahweh, but who pays for it with his life. One can find many other foreigners throughout the whole saga, not least of which are the numerous foreign mercenaries who are at the very center of power. For the author of the *David Saga* it is totally unrealistic to think of an ethnically pure state. Given also the fact that David freely intermarried with foreign wives without any divine expression of disapproval, it would appear that the author was not in agreement with the policy of Ezra 9–10 to annul mixed marriages.

Furthermore, the author does not seem to subscribe to the ideology of a greater Israel as a single entity inclusive of both northern Israel and southern Judah. He consciously goes against Dtr by recognizing Judah and Israel as distinct polities throughout David's reign, and he even suggests the same for Benjamin and for other regions of the country. His view of the make-up of David's state (by which the author means the ethnicity of his own state) is a very cosmopolitan one, in which people are judged for who they are, regardless of such ethnic or tribal affiliations. His outlook may well reflect a kind of "secular" wisdom perspective that is competing with the more "doctrinaire" views of his time. What is remarkable is that it found a firm response which resulted in its uncontested place within the corpus of Samuel-Kings and it took a quite distinct work, namely, that of the Chronicler, to excise the *David Saga* from his own historical record and restore the pious image of David and Solomon and the unity of Greater Israel.

This gives us a different picture of competing ideologies and radically different understandings of social identities during the late Persian and early Hellenistic periods within the province of Jehud and the surrounding region and among those who were part of the same intellectual and religious tradition, broadly speaking. With the appropriate placement of the *David Saga* as a competing narrative by a highly gifted writer within this time-frame and one who was willing to take such surprising liberties with the "historical" tradition that he had received, there are some interesting new possibilities for understanding the history of the biblical tradition in this and later periods.

Since the publication of this book in 2009 I have not been able to engage in a serious dialogue regarding the thesis of this book with any of my colleagues in biblical studies. This is partly due to the fact that for the last few years I have been unable to attend conferences to engage directly with my colleagues in biblical studies. Publications dealing with the biblical stories of David, with a few exceptions, have simply chosen to ignore what I have had to say on the subject in the *David Saga* and in my critical reviews of such studies on David.

The Yahwist: A Historian of Israelite Origins

After my publication of the *David Saga*, I turned to my final book project on the subject that had been my primary focus in biblical studies for over forty-five years, namely, the Pentateuch in general and the Yahwist in particular. My earlier publications on this subject in book form, *Prologue to History* (dealing with the Yahwist in Genesis) in 1992, *The Life of Moses* (the Yahwist in Exodus–Numbers), in 1994 and *A Law Book for the Diaspora* (the Yahwist's Covenant Code in Exodus 21–23), 2003, covered over 1000 pages and one could hardly expect that many readers would take the time to work through them all. For the most part they have been largely ignored in contemporary Pentateuchal studies. Consequently, I have written a new book on the Yahwist that is much shorter, *The Yahwist: A Historian of Israelite Origins*, as my swan-song. It is divided into two parts: part 1 is an outline of the Yahwist's history, beginning with his story of creation and early prehistory, continuing with the Patriarchs, the sojourn of their offspring in Egypt and their exodus under Moses, and the wilderness wanderings up to their arrival at the Jordan River. All of this is covered by my book in about 140 pages and presents the basic argument for why I regard this non-P corpus as evidence that the Yahwist was a historian, in much the same way that the Greeks in antiquity understood this term for their histories. This goes directly against the common approach in European biblical scholarship, which regards this same non-P corpus as the work of multiple "redactors," against which I have argued so adamantly. In fact, this appeal to redactors is completely arbitrary and inconsistent. How is it that the P material in Genesis is recognized as "priestly" when there is not a priest in sight in the whole book, nor any temple or sacrifices, and the connection made back to Genesis in the book of Exodus by P is limited to one isolated passage in Exodus 6:2–9, which could just as easily be attributed to a "redactor," if they existed? In contrast to P, the non-P source in Genesis makes very strong and frequent connections between the deity of the patriarchs and the deliverance of the Israelites in Exodus–Numbers. Yet these connections are all viewed as secondary additions by mysterious "redactors." Furthermore, as I have shone in this brief survey of the J corpus, this history from beginning to end is a clear and consistent composition, whereas the P material is made up of many smaller or larger additions that by themselves do not form an independent composition. Much of the time they are intended to deliberately contradict the earlier J presentation.

What does all of this mean for early Judaism, in which the place of worship in the diaspora is controlled entirely by the laity and their elders as reflected in the institution of the synagogue, with no priests, temple or sacrificial cult. This is in contrast to Jerusalem with its temple, priests and sacrifices, while the laity are merely spectators? A close reading of the text makes it clear that the J source represents the only approach to a completely lay form of religion with no priesthood in sight. Even Aaron, the Levite, never functions as a priest, whereas the additions of the P source make every effort to present the institution of the Temple form of worship as having originated in the wilderness with all of its elaborate regalia. This was a deliberate attempt to replace the lay meeting place by identifying the priestly tabernacle as a "tent of meeting" and repeating this connection 150 times! The current practice of splitting this Pentateuchal corpus into so many pieces, for no particular reason has had the effect of making the Pentateuch rather meaningless. To be sure, there have been some late additions made to the text, besides those of P, but these can be clearly identified and are hardly an excuse for splitting up J in the way that has been done.

Furthermore, contemporary scholars who are inclined to date the Yahwistic Tent of Meeting and all of the texts related to it later than the Priestly references to the Tabernacle completely ignore the fact that in DtrH's references to places of worship before the time of Solomon, none of them reflect any Temple such as that described in P. Indeed it is clear that J's Tent of Meeting is directly dependent upon the Deuteronomist's description of just such a tent in the time of David (2 Samuel 6:17–18; 7:1–17) and therefore P has deliberately contradicted both DtrH and J on this matter. It is very disturbing to see authors so deliberately ignoring clear evidence of this kind in their obsession with redactors and the total fragmentation of the historical narrative.

In part 2 of my book I have included twelve "studies in defense of the Yahwist," six of which have been published previously but the rest appear in this volume for the first time. The first three studies deal with whether the Yahwist may be viewed as a historian comparable to those in ancient Greece, whether the non-P corpus should be considered as a literary work by an author or merely a collection of pieces by editors, and whether the kind of study that I have produced in part 1 is now simply obsolete. The rest of the studies deal with various parts of the Yahwistic corpus from the flood story to the end of the desert journey and their relationship with Deuteronomy. The intention is to examine in greater detail questions regarding these units in the light of the broader discussion about them and how my understanding of the Yahwist answers these issues.

There are two studies that I made after writing my book on the Yahwist that I will mention here. The first of these, "Dating the Yahwist's History: Principles and Perspectives" (*Biblica*, 2015), is a detailed presentation of the rather substantial evidence for placing the Yahwist in the Babylonian exile as contemporary with Second Isaiah in the reign of Nabonidus. The close familial association of this king with Ur of the Chaldeans in southern Babylonian and with Harran in the north, and his famous migration from Babylonia by way of this northern region through Syria-Palestine the Trans-Jordon to his new dessert residence at Teima in the Arabian desert, seems to have been the inspiration for J to use much the same route for Abraham's migration from Ur by way of Harran to southern Judea. There are so many additional direct associations with this period that are not appropriate to any other period either before or after, and this, to my mind, make this date beyond dispute. This matter of dating a text is very important for understanding the message of this writer and why it is specifically directed to the Jews in exile at this time. This particular corpus in the Pentateuch was clearly the inspiration for the message of Second-Isaiah, who alone of all the prophets makes specific references to the content and language of the Yahwist. To understand the Yahwist's history, it must be read within the context of this time and place in the Babylonian exile.

The second study, "The Tent of Meeting in the Yahwist and the Origin of the Synagogue" (*SJOT* 29, 2015), is an attempt to date the origin of the synagogue ("meeting place") in the Babylonian exile and to see the Yahwist's "tent of meeting" as providing a legitimation by putting its origin in the time of Moses. The Yahwist based his reference to such a meeting place in this period on Dtr's references to such a structure in 2 Samuel 7:6–7, which also dates its origin to the time of the wilderness journey. This "tent of meeting" in J gives theological legitimacy to a completely lay institution for prayer and worship controlled by a body of elders, i.e. a synagogue, and makes the need for a temple and priesthood quite irrelevant.

Epilogue

Looking back on my life and my career as a scholar of the Ancient Near East and Biblical Studies, I can only say how very fortunate I was to have enjoyed such a life of learning and to have had so many wonderful mentors, colleagues, and friends in the process. The depression and war years of my youth, together with a rigid Calvinistic upbringing taught me discipline, albeit within the context of strong religious beliefs, and this was what led me into a career in biblical studies. Of course much credit also goes to primary and secondary school teachers such Mr. Gilbert and Vera Vanderlip for my early development as a student. The remarkable training in Ancient Near Eastern history and Biblical Hebrew, together with Classical history and Greek at one of the best universities in North America, allowed me to be accepted at Yale Graduate School with a good scholarship, and the program at Yale did wonders for me. The faculty of Albrecht Goetze, Marvin Pope, Brevard Childs, Harald Ingholt, W. Kelly Simpson, and Erwin Goodenough were always very helpful and opened my eyes to this great field of study without forcing me to adopt any particular school of thought. That was the pattern that I followed in my own career of teaching. The topic of my thesis on the Hyksos was entirely my own choice, which covered areas of expertise of both Ingholt and Simpson, and they gave me lots of help, but never tried to dominate how I was to treat it. They helped me to get it accepted by Yale Press and it became a great success, as I have shone above. Pope, Ingholt, and Simpson assisted me in getting support for my marvelous travels and eight months in Jerusalem, Egypt, and the Near East. All of this laid a wonderful foundation for the rest of my career.

From this memoir it should be obvious that I had contact and a close association with a very large and widely scattered number of other scholars in my field of study. These scholars reflected a wide variety of different methods and approaches to the biblical text and I had opportunity to enter into extended dialogue and discussion with many of them without my ever becoming committed to any particular "school." My memoir reveals how frequently I was invited to give a guest lecture, or present a paper at a society meeting, or contribute an article for publication, always with the expectation that I would produce something new, and I tried not to disappoint. This was much more the case in Europe and Great Britain, were I spent three sabbaticals, than it was in North America, where contact was largely restricted to attendance at learned societies, and fraternization in such a large crowd was very limited. I also had the wonderful opportunity to be invited to so many different universities as a guest lecturer throughout Europe, Scandinavia, Britain, Scotland, Israel, and South Africa, where there was always time spent to become more acquainted with my host and establish new friendships.

I think it is true to say that scholars in biblical studies specialize two narrowly in a particular field, whether in archaeology, biblical criticism, text criticism, the history of interpretation, etc. and this may lead to a distortion of their perspective. While I had my own specialty in Pentateuchal studies, and to a lesser extent, in the historical books of Joshua to 2 Kings, I also did a lot of work in ancient Near Eastern history, in archaeology, in textual criticism, even in Babylonian, Assyrian, and Egyptian history, which was all very important in developing a proper understanding of Israel's and Judea's place within this world. Even a solid basis in Greek history and culture was fundamental in drawing any comparisons with comparable parts of the biblical tradition and I regularly received the support of classical scholars when I made such comparisons. As I have pointed out in my memoir, I am greatly indebted to my undergraduate training at the University of Toronto and graduate studies at Yale for such a broad outlook in my discipline.

There are two fundamentally different approaches to the study of the Hebrew Bible, the strictly historical and non-sectarian approach to the biblical content as the work of various writers living primarily in the mid-first millennium BC, and secondly the study and literary analysis of the Bible within the context of theological studies and the preparation of students for the ministry. My training at both the University of Toronto and Yale was strictly non-religious, with the one exception being Brevard Childs in the seminary at Yale, and although his course on Exodus was strictly academic, his personal approach to the Bible was theological, and for this reason he did not want me to do my dissertation with him. Throughout my career I worked within the context of non-sectarian institutions, with the exception of three years at Andover-Newton where I tried to combine the two approaches within a quite liberal environment, but it did not work very well. So the rest of my teaching of Hebrew Bible, while it had much to do with the religion of ancient Israel, it had nothing to say about its relevance for contemporary theology. This makes a huge difference between classical scholarship and that of biblical studies for most scholars in the field because classical studies is not considered relevant for the present theological world of study; and I have been constantly criticized by biblical scholars for making any such comparisons between classical works and the Bible, whereas classical scholars readily accepted such comparisons as significant and helpful.

Finally, something must be said about the history of my approach to the competing documentary and supplementary hypotheses. These two approaches have existed side by side for a long time, going back to the early nineteenth century. The supplementary approach, which viewed the Pentateuch as the result of growth by additions made over time by various authors to the earlier text that was handed down from the past. The number of layers in the Pentateuch (J, E, D, P, etc.) was a matter of endless debate. The documentary hypothesis arose as a refinement and modification of the supplementary approach, which argued that the various layers were actually separate documents that were pasted together by editors, who attempted to fit the pieces together by retaining as much of the original pieces as possible, together with only minimal connecting links added by the editors. Since the work of Wellhausen this became the dominant view in scholarship, although the supplementary hypothesis was still used by many scholars. As I indicated in my memoir, in my *Abraham* book (1975) I followed the lead of Fred Winnett ("Reexamining the Foundations," 1965), who worked with the supplementary hypothesis. By contrast, Rolf Rendtorff, in his book (1977) created a documentary approach, which virtually did away with authors altogether, replaced by editors (redactors), who put together a myriad of bits and pieces of popular tradition. In the revolutionary years of 1975–77, along with myself, Hans Heinrich Schmid and his students followed the supplementary approach while Rendtorff and his many students of the "Heidelberg school" followed the documentary approach. With Hans Heinrich's departure from biblical studies, his exit from the European field left me without his support and I could not compete. The old system of the authors, J, E, D, P, was considered dead and was replaced in the "Heidelberg school" by innumerable editors, and dialogue between the two approaches largely ended. Nevertheless, the problematic nature of these ancient editors cannot be ignored if useful dialogue about the compositional nature of the biblical text is to be understood.

My career in ancient Near Eastern and biblical studies has come to an end, and as I have tried to indicate in this memoir, it has been a wonderful life such that I could never have imagined in my youth. It gave me the opportunity to meet and become friends with such a large number and a wide range of scholars in so many different countries and institutions, to say nothing of the hospitality that I enjoyed from so many of them. And even if I can no longer participate in such scholarly activities, I still have these memories to enjoy.

Major Publications

1966 *The Hyksos: A New Investigation*. New Haven: Yale University Press. Reprint, Eugene, OR: Wipf & Stock, 2010.

1975 *Abraham in History and Tradition*. New Haven: Yale University Press.

1983 *In Search of History: Historiography in the Ancient World and the Origins of Biblical History*. New Haven: Yale University Press. Reprint, Winona Lake, IN: Eisenbrauns, 1997.

1992 *Prologue to History: The Yahwist as Historian in Genesis*. Louisville: Westminster John Knox.

1994 *The Life of Moses: The Yahwist as Historian in Exodus–Numbers*. Louisville: Westminster John Knox.

2003 *A Law Book for the Diaspora: Revision in the Study of the Covenant Code*. Oxford: Oxford University Press.

2006 *The Edited Bible: The Curious History of the "Editor" in Biblical Criticism*. Winona Lake, IN: Eisenbrauns.

2009 *The Biblical Saga of King David*. Winona Lake, IN: Eisenbrauns.

2013 *The Yahwist: A Historian of Israelite Origins*. Winona Lake, IN: Eisenbrauns.

2014 *Changing Perspectives 1: Studies in the History, Literature and Religion of Biblical Israel*. London: Taylor & Francis.

2015 *The Pentateuch: A Social-Science Commentary*. 2nd ed. Cornerstones Series. London: Bloomsbury T. & T. Clark.

www.ingramcontent.com/pod-product-compliance
Lightning Source LLC
LaVergne TN
LVHW081602100826
845153LV00004B/436

* 9 7 8 1 4 9 8 2 9 9 5 6 5 *